Learning about Learning

an A–Z of training and
development tools and techniques

About the author

Samuel A. Malone is a training consultant and learning expert, and an accomplished author. A part-time lecturer with the Dublin Institute of Technology, he runs a variety of training programmes and workshops on management and supervisory development and lifelong learning.

The Chartered Institute of Personnel and Development is the leading publisher of books and reports for personnel and training professionals, students, and for all those concerned with the effective mangement and development of people at work. For details of all titles, please contact the Publishing Department:

tel. 020–8263 3387
fax 020–8263 3850
e-mail publish@cipd.co.uk
The catalogue of all CIPD titles can be viewed on the CIPD website:
www.cipd.co.uk/bookstore

Learning about Learning

an A–Z of training and development tools and techniques

Samuel A. Malone

Chartered Institute of Personnel and Development

Design by Pumpkin House
Phototypeset by Intype Libra
Printed in Great Britain by The Cromwell Press, Trowbridge, Wiltshire

ISBN 0-85292-989-7

Charted Institute of Personnel and Development, CIPD House,
Camp Road, London SW19 4UX
Tel: 020–8971 9000   Fax: 020–8263 3333
E-mail: cipd@cipd.co.uk   Website: www.cipd.co.uk
Incorporated by Royal Charter.   Registered Charity No. 1079797

CONTENTS

A

Ability – Accelerated learning – Accidental learning – Accreditation – Acronyms – Acrostic – Acting as if – Action learning – Action plans – Activist – Activity-based learning (ABL) – Adult learners – Advance organisers – Affirmations – Age – Alcohol and learning – Alphabet system – Alzheimer's disease – Analogies – Analytical intelligence – Andragogy – Aptitude test – Artificial intelligence (AI) – ASPIRE model – Assessment centres – Association – Asynchronous learning – Attention – Attention span – Attitude – Audiovisual methods of learning.

B

Barriers to learning – Barriers to memory – Behavioural objectives – Behaviourist theory of learning – Beliefs – Benchmarking – Biofeedback – Biography work – Biorhythms – Blended learning – Bloom's learning model – Brain – Brain and learning – Brain hemispheres – Brain LION model – Brainstorming – Brain waves – Breaks as an aid to memory – Briefing and debriefing – Business games – Buzz group.

C

CAP model of learning types – Career anchors – Career counselling – Career development – Case studies – Categorisation – Cerebellum – Cerebrum – Certification – Chunking – CIRO model of evaluation – Coaching – Cognitivist theory of learning – Comfort zones – Commitment – Community of practice – Competencies – Comprehension – Computer-based training (CBT) – Concentration – Conference –

Confidence – Constructivist theory of learning – Continuous assessment – Continuous improvement and learning – Continuous professional development (CPD) – Co-operative learning – Corporate university – Corpus callosum – CRAMP model of on-the-job learning skills – Creativity – Credit Accumulation Transfer Scheme (CATS) – Criterion-referenced instruction (CRI) – Critical incident technique – Crystallised intelligence – Cues – Curiosity – Cybernetic model of learning.

D

Deep learning – Déjà vu – Demonstrations – De-roling – Development – Development centres – Diagnostic instruments – Discovery learning – Distance learning – Double-loop learning.

E

Educational psychologist – E-learning – Emotional intelligence – Emotions and learning – Empowerment – Empty-chair technique – Encoding – Energisers – Enthusiasm for learning – Environments for learning – Episodic memory – Evaluation – Expert – Expert systems – Experiential learning – Experimental psychologist – Explicit knowledge – Extrovert learners.

F

Facilitation – False memory syndrome – Feedback – FIBRES model of memory – Fishbowl – Flexible learning – Flow – Fluid intelligence – Force field analysis – Forgetting curve – Formal learning.

G

Games – Gender differences – Genius – Gestalt – Goals – Graveyard slot – Group dynamics – Grouping – Group learning – Group norms.

H

Habits – Handouts – Happiness sheets – Hawthorne effect – Herrmann's model of learning styles – Herzberg's motivation-hygiene theory – Hippocampus – Holistic –

U

Understanding – Unlearning – Using your brain.

V

VAK model of learning – Values – Verbalise – Vicious learning cycle – Video conferencing – Virtual learning centre – Virtual reality (VR) – Virtual teams – Virtuous learning cycle – Visits to other organisations – Visualisation – Vitamins and learning – Voluntary organisations – Von Restorff effect.

W

Whole-brain learning – Whole method – WIIFM – Wisdom – WISE model of memory types – Workshop – Workplace learning – Write it down – Writer's block.

Y

Youth

Z

Zeigarnik effect

PREFACE

This is an A to Z guide to the most widely-used terms, themes, theories, models, and concepts in learning, whether in an academic or a training and development context. The book is a judicious mixture of the theory and practice of learning in all its contexts. In fact, everything you ever wanted to know about learning but were afraid to ask is contained within the covers of this guide.

The book is aimed at trainers, educators, learners, self-developers, students, and all who want to learn about learning. As well as a jargon-buster and source of information, they will find it a great source of ideas, many of which can be immediately put into practice to improve their learning skills. In recent years responsibility for training and development has moved away from centralised training and development departments to line managers. In addition to human resource development managers, therefore, line managers and others such as facilitators, mentors, and coaches will find this book a very useful reference and resource.

Students pursuing certificate, diploma, degree and post-graduate qualifications in education, and training and development including CIPD qualifications, such as the Certificate in Training Practice, will find the book a comprehensive reference. The topics are categorised in alphabetical order and a list of headwords is provided for ease of reference. Mnemonics in the form of acronyms are used throughout the text as useful memory aids.

This book is intended as a reference and resource on learning and training and development, and the entries are for that reason discussed in more depth than would be found in a conventional dictionary. In addition to learning, the text covers such relevant and associated topics as educational psychology, personal development, accelerated learning, study skills, memory, the brain, nutrition, and training and development. Those interested in personal development will find many ideas they can put into action. Similarly, trainers will find the content extremely useful.

In total more than 400 terms are explained in the text. The entries are written in a user-friendly style to make the process of learning about learning as accessible and easy as possible. In addition to a detailed bibliography, useful website addresses pertinent to learning and associated subjects have been included for those who want to pursue topics in further depth.

A

Ability   Ability denotes competence in a job, profession or activity. It is a product of inherited and acquired characteristics. To say a person has the ability to do something means that he or she is able to do it right now without further training. Basic or general abilities are important for a wide range of tasks. Measures of basic intellectual abilities almost always include verbal, comprehension, and quantitative reasoning. Aptitude tests and psychometric tests are used in business to measure ability. The core abilities needed for the workplace might include: working productively, learning effectively, communicating clearly, working co-operatively, acting responsibly, having positive self-esteem and thinking logically and creatively. Several people's ability test results can be compared so that conclusions can be drawn about their probable ability to do a particular job.

See also **Aptitude test**.

References
Armstrong, Michael (2000) *A Handbook of Human Resource Management Practice*. London, Kogan Page.
Stewart, Andrew (1994) 'Diagnosing needs' in the *Handbook of Management Development*, edited by Alan Mumford, Aldershot, Gower.
http://www.hcc.hawaii.edu/intranet/committees/FacDevCom/guid.../cor-abil.ht

Accelerated learning   The term 'accelerated learning' was coined by the followers of Dr Georgi Lozanov, a Bulgarian educator who developed a teaching method known as 'suggestology'. Children are naturally accelerated learners – they are not experts, but they are expert learners, naturally attentive and inquisitive, and if properly nurtured may continue to learn everything at an accelerated rate. It is well known that very young children find it no problem to learn languages (in the right environment) whereas adults may do so only with difficulty. However, when adults really want to learn something they often experience feelings of childlike wonder and enthusiasm which accelerate their learning.

Accelerated learning is about acquiring, understanding, and retaining information quickly, as if returning to that childlike state. It is based on the premise that words when combined with music (especially baroque music) and delivered with emotion are easier to learn. The method involves techniques to relax students and create a stress-free environment, attractive wall posters, music to encourage a suitably receptive mood and state, and varied tone and intonation while speaking. Dr Lozanov's methods have been used successfully in many areas of training and learning including language and memory training. Accelerated learning has been broadened to include developments in techniques of memorisation, visualisation, speed-reading, and the use of learning maps.

One way to remember *the principles of accelerated learning* is through the mnemonic MACHINE, which stands for Multi-level learning, Action-oriented learning, Collaborative learning, Holistic learning, Imagery in learning, New meanings in learning, and Emotive learning.

- multi-level learning – Learning takes place simultaneously at many levels including the conscious, subconscious, intellectual, emotional and physical. The brain is a parallel processor rather than a sequential one and thus is designed to do many things at once. The brain can grow new cells as a result of learning. Some experts maintain that the brain can actually 'rewire' itself to compensate for loss of brain cells.

- action-oriented learning – Learning is through experience, by doing rather than by passive listening. We learn to drive by driving a car, we learn to swim by swimming, we learn computer skills by using a computer, and we learn to manage by managing. Practice is a better teacher than theory, provided that there is time for feedback, reflection and reinforcement. Games, role-play and activities can make learning a fun and stress-free event.

- collaborative learning – We learn best in a social context by interacting and relating to other people. Collaboration energises learning whereas competition slows it down.

- holistic learning – Learning is a whole-mind-and-body affair. Learning is left-brained and right-brained and through all the senses like sight, hearing, touch, taste and smell. Training should therefore be designed to engage the whole person, and involve whole-brain learning styles, and multiple intelligences and methods of reception (visual, auditory and kinesthetic).

- imagery in learning – Active imagination and visualisation enhances learning. The brain is an image processor rather than a word processor: it does not differentiate between a mental rehearsal and actually doing it. This is why mental rehearsal is nearly as effective as doing the real thing. Concrete images are easier to learn than abstract ones.

- new meanings in learning – To make new learning meaningful we must make it our own by reinterpreting and integrating it with our prior knowledge and experience. Using associations can help people learn sequences, and using stories can aid memory.

- emotive learning – The mind has a significant effect on learning. Positive feelings enhance learning whereas negative feelings inhibit learning. Learning should be fun, flexible, focused, and friendly. Severe stress is a barrier to learning. Trainers must act as role models for learners: they must believe that people have a vast capacity for learning, and therefore have high expectations of their learners.

One way to remember *the core elements of accelerated learning* is through the mnemonic FIREARM, which stands for Framework, Instructor, Reinforcement, Environment, Atmosphere, Role-play, and Music.

- framework – The framework gives the content structure. Trainers should suggest to learners that it is easy to learn the material. Give an overview of the topic and connect with learners' prior knowledge, experience and expectations. Build in periods for reflection and review. Celebrate success.

- instructor – Trainers should be proficient in accelerated learning and win the confidence of learners. Each trainer should use the intonation in his or her voice as an instrument for emphasisis and to capture the attention of learners.

- reinforcement – Peripherals such as posters and other visuals are used to reinforce key learning points. The learning is absorbed by the subconscious mind while listening to the trainer.

- environment – Lighting, temperature, colour, plants, posters, and décor are used to enhance the learning environment. Seating arrangements are open and flexible to encourage interaction and participation.

- atmosphere – From the start the atmosphere has to be friendly, relaxing and non-threatening. Positive language is used to allay fears and build up self-esteem. The trainer builds rapport with the learners from the start.

- role-play – The trainer uses activity-based training techniques to involve all the senses of each learner. Role-play, simulations, case studies, problems, discussions, teamwork and storytelling should be used to illustrate key learning points.

- music – Baroque and other classical music has been found to enhance learning. Before the course programme starts music may be used to create a relaxed and welcoming atmosphere for learners. Upbeat music may be used at appropriate stages of the course programme to energise learners. A cautionary note – some learners may find music distracting.

See also **Relaxation**.

References
De Porter, Bobbi and Hernacki, Mike (1993), *Quantum Learning: Unleash the genius within you.* London, Piatkus.
Meier, Dave (2000) *The Accelerated Learning Handbook.* New York, McGraw Hill.
Pattison, Sherry A. (2001) 'Staff meetings: an opportunity for accelerated training of employees', *Journal of Workplace Learning*, Volume 13, Number 4, pp172–179.
Rose, Colin (1988) *Accelerated Learning.* Missenden, Accelerated Learning Systems Ltd.
Rose, Colin and Nicholl, Malcolm J. (1997) *Accelerated Learning for the 21st Century.* London, Piatkus.
Ostrander, Sheila, and Schroeder, Lynn (1999) *Super-Learning 2000.* London, Souvenir Press.
http://www.newhorizons.org/trm_deporter.htm

Accidental learning   Accidental learning is learning from or through experience, without formal training. Also called incidental learning, it happens by chance but is recognised by the individual and followed by reflection. Accidental learning occurs in such activities as job rotation, observation, coaching, mentoring, learning from mistakes, or learning from new job challenges. But learning from experience is a normal everyday event for most people. Mishaps and frustrations often provide the spur. People often like to conduct their post-mortems by talking it through with other people. Mumford (1997) maintains that managers can learn more from such experiences than from formal management development programmes.

Most of us do not reflect on our experiences enough, and so miss out on a great opportunity for learning.

References
Mumford, Alan (1997) *Management Development Strategies for Action*, 3rd edition. London, IPD.

Accreditation   Accreditation is the official recognition of learning or training by a statutory awarding body, and the appropriate credits given. Many people prefer to do training programmes with bodies that are recognised by employers. The National Council for Vocational Qualifications (NCVQs) was set up by the Government to grant accreditation to qualifications-awarding bodies that meet specified criteria. Many universities give credits for appropriate work-based experience. This is recognition of the value of informal learning. The accreditation of prior learning (APL) is based on evidence of the successful completion of formal programmes. The accreditation of prior experiential learning (APEL) is based on a portfolio of work experience.

See also **Certification; National Vocational Qualifications (NVQs)**.

References
Reid, Margaret Anne, Barrington, Harry and Kenney, John (1992) *Training Interventions.* London, IPM.

Accreditation of prior learning (APL) See **Credit Accumulation Transfer Scheme (CATS)**.

Accreditation of prior experiential learning (APEL) See **Credit Accumulation Transfer Scheme (CATS)**.

Acronyms   Acronyms are 'words' made up of the first letters of a name, title or list consisting of several parts. Used to assist memory, and sometimes pronounced arbitrarily, acronyms are also called 'the first-letter association technique'. Examples include:

- NATO, which stands for the 'North Atlantic Treaty Organisation'

- FARM-B, which stands for the five classes of vertebrate animals: fish, amphibian, reptile, mammal and bird

- HOMES, which stands for the five great lakes of North America: Huron, Ontario, Michigan, Erie, and Superior

- SCUBA, which stands for 'self-contained underwater breathing apparatus'

- PEST, which stands for 'political, economic, social and technological'.

The main advantage of an acronym is the use of one 'word' to recall a whole name, title or list. The main disadvantage in creating acronyms is the difficulty in putting together (and pronouncing) a word from the letters involved, especially if the name or list that the acronym summarises involves a specific sequence. Once created, moreover, the acronym must be mentally rehearsed and repeated until recall becomes automatic. An acronym is nonetheless a very useful memory jogger.

See also **Acrostic; Mnemonics**.

References
DePorter, Bobbi and Hernacki, Mike (1993) *Quantum Learning: Unleash the genius within you.* London, Piatkus.
Higbee, Kenneth L. (1990) *Your Memory: How it works and how to improve it.* London, Piatkus.

Acrostic   An acrostic is an arbitrarily invented sentence or phrase that uses for the first letters of each word the first letters in a list of words you want to remember. For example,

- To remember the names of the planets in their order from the Sun, take the first letters of the names of the planets – M-V-E-M-J-S-U-N-P. These letters do not by themselves form a pronounceable word (acronym). However, an acrostic can be created in which those first letters are used as the initial letters of words to make up a sentence. Such a sentence might, for instance, be 'My very educated mother just showed us nine planets'. There remains the difficulty of repeated letters. In this case it is necessary to be sufficiently familiar with the solar system to know the first M stands for Mercury and not Mars.

- The acrostic 'Every good boy does fine' (or similar) has been used for generations to teach students of music the notes that correspond to the lines of the treble clef on a musical stave (E-G-B-D-F).

- Many a medical student has memorised the acrostic 'On old Olympus' towering top, a Finn and German viewed some hops' (or similar). This has helped them to recall the 12 cranial nerves (olfactory, optic, oculomotor, trochlear, trigeminal, abducens, facial, auditory, glossopharyngeal, vagus, spinal accessory, and hypoglossal).

The acrostic is more versatile than the acronym, is easy to create and is extremely useful as a learning technique. Almost any type of information can be remembered using an acrostic. However, in respect of both acrostics and acronyms some familiarity is essential with the subject matter to be recalled because in each case there is only one letter per item to jog the memory.

See also **Acronyms**; **Mnemonics**.

References
Hermann, Douglas (1995) *Super Memory: A quick-action programme for memory improvement.* London, Blandford.
Higbee, Kenneth L. (1990) *Your Memory: How it works and how to improve it.* London, Piatkus.

Acting as if Pretending to do or to be, or pretending to be capable of doing something. Such behaviour can be reinforced by positive affirmations and visualisation, because the subconscious does not know the difference between a real and an imagined event. Mental rehearsal of actions 'lights up' many of the same brain areas as does actual performance of the movements. Some personal development experts believe that you can acquire competence in an area quicker if you adopt the 'acting as if' approach. So the next time you are giving a presentation, why not *act as if* you were a competent public speaker? You may find that the audience will respond in a positive way which, in turn, will reinforce your new-found behaviour and boost your confidence. The 'can do' approach has contributed significantly to the overall economic success of the USA.

References
Malone, Samuel A. (1999) *Success Skills for Managers.* Dublin, Oak Tree Press.
O'Connor, Joseph and Seymour, John (1995) *Introducing NLP: Psychological skills for understanding and influencing people.* London, Thorsons.
Tracy, Brian (1993) *Maximum Achievement.* New York, Simon & Shuster.

Action learning   Action learning is learning from work-based experience through group discussion and reflection, trial and error, and personal discovery. Developed by Reg Revans, taken on board in Belgium, and now getting the recognition it deserves elsewhere, its main precept is learning from one another in the workplace.

The action learning process is based on the critical cycle of plan, act, observe, and reflect. The process involves an individual, a set consisting of about six people, and a set adviser; it confronts a work-related problem, and relies on the interaction of individuals to address issues.

- The set of six action learners is required to co-operate to solve the problem. Each set member acts as a consultant, adviser, and devil's advocate for every other set member. The set members need not be specialists but must be competent and committed to the process. The set should be composed of people from different disciplines who will each bring a fresh outlook to the problems.

- The role of the set adviser is to act as facilitator. The set adviser may be an academic, a consultant or a trainer. He or she acts as a resource by prompting with relevant questions and suggesting useful reference sources. He or she ensures that a certain amount of time is set aside to review learning in addition to the normal ongoing work reviews.

- The process involves identification of the problem, collection of information, examination of data, developing alternatives, selecting an appropriate course of action, implementation, and feedback on whether the proposed solution worked. Set meetings typically last about 30 minutes and usually take place on a regular basis over six to nine months. Each participant is given an opportunity to speak. Open-ended questions may lead to new insights about the nature of the problem. Meetings conclude with action plans for accomplishment by the next meeting.

The advantages of action learning are:

- The action learning set may solve important problems and real-life issues and develop leadership skills.

- Members of the set are empowered by being encouraged to take responsibility for solving their own problems.

- Transfer of learning is facilitated since set members can take immediate action.

- Opportunities are created to make organisations more efficient and effective while at the same time providing for personal development. Learners become internal consultants for their organisations.

- It develops hard skills like finance and marketing and soft skills like interpersonal relationships and communications. Learning is primarily with and through others in the set rather than from a professional trainer.

■ It is probably more cost-effective than traditional learning. This is so because participants solve real organisational problems, the benefits of which are readily apparent.

■ It develops learning-to-learn skills. Participants develop the capacity to become lifelong learners.

Action learning is learning by doing through the study and resolution of real-life work problems in the working environment. Because of its context, it provides maximum motivation for managers to turn problems into learning opportunities. Action learning is based on the premise that real work can provide excellent learning opportunities. It subjects formal and informal knowledge to critical questioning and reflection. You learn by doing things and reflecting on how you performed – reflection is at the heart of the action learning process.

Various universities now offer diplomas and degrees right up to doctoral level through the action learning approach.

See also **Activity-based learning (ABL)**; **Experiential learning**.

References

Dotlich, David L. and Noel, James L. (1998) *Action Learning: How the world's top companies are re-creating their leaders and themselves*. San Francisco, Jossey-Bass Publications.

Koo, L. (1999) 'Learning action learning', *Journal of Workplace Learning*, Volume 11, Number 3, pp89–94.

Mumford, Alan (1997) *Management Development Strategies for Action*, 3rd edition. London, IPD.

Revans, Reg (1998) *An ABC of Action Learning*. London, Lemos & Crane.

Zuber-Skerritt, Ortrun (2002) 'The concept of action learning', *The Learning Organisation*, Volume 9, Number 3, pp114–124.

http://www.free-press.com/journals/gajal/articles/publish/gajal-article-082.htm

http://www.btinternet.com/~m100/call/definition.html

http://www.btinternet.com/~m100/call/interpretation.html

http://www.btinternet.com/~m100/call/river.html

http://www.pelion.com.au/pelion/actlearn.htm

http://idt.net/~tjell/actlrng8.html

http://www.free-press.com/journals/gajal/articles/publish/gajal-article-050,htm

http://www.bhtafe.edu.au/scitech/acthtm.HTM

http://www.linkageinc.com/newsletter8/research.htm

http://www.free-press.com/journals/gajal/articles/publish/gajal-article-081.htm

http://www.world.std.com/~lo96.10/0064.html

http://www.free-press.com/journals/gabal/articles/gabal-article-002.htm

http://www.free-press.com/journals/gajal/articles/gajal-article-056.htm

http://www.free-press.com/journals/gajal/articles/gajal-article-034.htm

http://ericacve.org/docs/pab00009.htm

http://www.findarticles.com/cf_0/g2602/0002/2602000219/print.jhtml

Action plans   An action plan sets out exactly what your learning objectives are; it includes deadlines by which to benchmark progress on the way to achieving the objectives, pointers on how they may be achieved and notes on the resources required. Having a vision and objectives is one thing, but without an action plan, doing something about it is quite another matter.

The more specific your stated objectives are, the better. For example, you decide to work towards a degree in training and development. The degree takes four years of part-time study. Your overall objective is to achieve your degree in four years. Sub-objectives are that in each year you will have to sit and pass an examination. In addition, you will have to write an assignment each year for the first three years on some aspect of training and development. In the final year you will have to complete a thesis of 15,000 words. The content of the degree programme will be in line with the syllabus provided and the reading lists. Classes will be provided over two nights each week during the academic year. The lecturers, tutors and fellow students provide support which will be supplemented by handouts, class discussion, and so on. The criteria for success are passing the exams and successfully completing the assignments each year to the standard required and in the time specified, and finishing the thesis in the final year. Part of your action plan will be the class timetable supported by your personal study timetable. Learning logs and learning contracts may be used to support the planning and review process. Time management is an important part of action plans.

See also **Learning contract**; **Learning log**; **Time management**.

References
Turner, David (1996) *Managing Personal Development*. London, The Industrial Society.
Reid, Margaret Anne, Barrington, Harry and Kenney, John (1992) *Training Interventions*. London, IPM.

Activist   In the learning context, 'activist' is one of the four learning styles: activist, reflector, theorist and pragmatist. Activists enjoy getting things done. They enjoy learning new experiences even if they have little practical application. They like variety, excitement and action. They are very much involved in the here and now. They tend to be reactive rather than proactive. They tend not to reflect on what they are about to do. This may be a weakness if they rush too often into unconsidered action. They thrive on crisis management. They enjoy brainstorming and lateral thinking. They love being involved in teamwork activities. They are gregarious and attention-seeking, and like to be the life and soul of the party. They are more at home in operational management roles than in strategic roles. They do not learn well from passive situations such as reading a book or listening to a lecture. They may react negatively to lectures they consider to be too theoretical. Activists make good line managers because they put a huge emphasis on getting the job done. Active learners say 'Let's try it out first and see how it works.'

In practice, people are a combination of the four learning styles with a preference for one or two.

To summarise, activists like:

■ novel experiences

■ business games

■ outdoor experiential training.

■ role-play

■ competitive teamwork

■ problem-solving.

■ to be thrown in at the deep end.

To develop an activist style, do something new – initiate conversations, switch from your routine, volunteer, and practise thinking on your feet.

See also **Pragmatist; Reflector; Theorist**.

References
Honey, Peter (1994) 'Styles of learning' in the *Handbook of Management Development*, edited by Alan Mumford, Aldershot, Gower.
Honey, Peter and Mumford, Alan (1986) *Using Your Learning Styles*. Berkshire, Peter Honey.
Mumford, Alan (1997) *Management Development Strategies for Action*, 3rd edition. London, IPD.
Mumford, Alan (1995) 'Putting learning styles to work: an integrated approach', *Industrial and Commercial Training*, Volume 27, Number 8, pp28–35.

Activity-based learning (ABL) This is an accelerated learning approach which encourages learners to be physically active while learning in order to engage both the body and mind in the learning process. People generally learn more from activities and real-life experiences than from presentations or lectures. The belief is that periodically getting course participants up and moving awakens the body and improves circulation to the brain, and thus has a positive effect on the learning process. Every trainer knows that 'the mind can't absorb what the backside can't endure'. Most of us find it very difficult to concentrate for long periods of time without doing something physical.

See also **Action learning**.

References
Fee, Kenneth (2001) *A Guide To Management Development Techniques*. London, Kogan Page.

Adult learners Adult learners are different from learners who are children or young students because they learn in a different way and have far more complex backgrounds in terms of accumulated life experiences and responsibilities.

Points to remember about adult learners include:

■ They see themselves as independent and self-directed; they like to have control over and be responsible for their own learning.

- They have a lot of experience that they like to share with others.

- They are motivated by the prospect of achieving goals and they like to know the reason why they are doing something. They like training programmes to be well organised and to have clearly defined course objectives.

- They are practical and like to solve problems. They like to learn things that will be useful in their career or to their self-development. They are committed to making sense of a learning experience and working out the implications once the course is over.

- They are sometimes intimidated by formal learning situations and do not like to lose face.

- Because of their life responsibilities they have things other than learning that may occupy their minds.

- They may have set habits which they find hard to change – but which they can change.

- In a formal learning situation, they prefer the trainers to adopt a facilitator style rather than a lecturing style. They like trainers to relate theories and concepts to practical issues and to the learner's experience. Trainers when teaching should focus more on the process and less on the content. Learning strategies such as case studies, role-playing, discussion, simulations, reflection, and self-evaluations are most useful.

- They like feedback at appropriate intervals. Learning from feedback gives them a sense of achievement and personal growth.

- They like a feeling of belonging, recognition and respect. They appreciate the value of giving or receiving support. Remember: the sweetest sound to many people is the sound of their own name. They like to be treated as equals and should be given freedom to express their views.

- They expect the tutor or trainer to act as a role model, to be an expert in the topic, to be well prepared and to practise good presentation skills.

- They have different priorities depending on what stage of the life cycle they're at.

- They like a supportive learning climate in which there are few blocks to learning, creativity, and risk-taking.

- Their past experience may act as an obstacle to new learning. They may have to unlearn negative attitudes towards learning, old ways of doing things, long-held prejudices and stereotypical thinking.

- They like to be challenged just beyond their present level of ability. If challenged too much, however, they become stressed and demotivated and give up. If challenged too little, they become bored and switch off.

It would be wrong to think that adults are a homogeneous group. They differ in 'class', gender, culture, race, personality, attitudes, beliefs, learning styles and life experiences. Every trainer should also be aware of these factors when dealing with adults.

See also **Andragogy**.

References

Meizirow, J. (1991) *Transformative Dimensions of Adult Learning.* San Francisco, Jossey-Bass Publishers.
Merriam, Sharon B. and Caffarella, Rosemary S. (1999) *Learning in Adulthood: A comprehensive guide*, 2nd edition. San Francisco, Jossey-Bass Publishers.
http://www.learnativity.com/adultlearning.html
http://www.ed.gov/pubs/HowAdultsLearn/Greeno.html
http://www.hcc.hawaii.edu/intranet/committees/FacDevCom/guid.../adults-2.ht
http://www.hcc.hawaii.edu/intranet/committees/FacDevCom/guid.../adults-3.ht

Advance organisers   Advance organisers are like road maps – when you are striving to reach learning objectives they show you where you are and indicate the journey you must take to get to your final destination. For example, training in stages helps learners plan their work and evaluate progress. A way of assisting learners to absorb information by creating a context, advance organisers thus serve as a conceptual framework.

Trainers can use advance organisers by giving an overview of the topic at the start and continually previewing material during the programme to alert learners to new topics or concepts coming up. Learning maps can be used as advance organisers giving learners a bird's-eye-view of the subject.

See also **Learning map**.

References

Davies, Ivor K. (1971) *The Management of Learning.* London, McGraw-Hill Book Company Ltd.
Huczynski, Andrzej (2001) *Encyclopedia of Development Methods.* Aldershot, Gower.

Affirmations   Affirmations are reinforcements of positive ideas and feelings. The subconscious mind believes what you constantly feed it. Feed it with positive messages about your ability to learn, memorise and concentrate. Positive self-talk conditions the mind for success. Affirmations should be personal and made in the present tense – for example: 'I am a confident learner,' 'Every day in every way my memory gets better and better,' 'I am an intelligent, talented person,' 'I'm learning more each day.'

See also **Positive thinking**.

References

Blakeslee, Thomas R. (1997) *The Attitude Factor: Extend your life by changing the way you think.* London, Thorsons.

Davies, Philippa (1996) *Total Confidence: The complete guide to self-assurance and personal success.* London, Piatkus.

Tracy, Brian (1993) *Maximum Achievement.* New York, Simon & Schuster.

Age   To discriminate against anybody on the grounds of age is known as ageism – and is illegal in many European countries and in the USA. Ageism is rife in workplaces and very often leads to a waste of a potential valuable resource. It is a long-standing myth that intelligence peaks in adolescence and then deteriorates. Eyesight, hearing and reaction time do deteriorate with age, but cognitive skills such as decision-making, reasoning, the use and extension of vocabulary, and general wisdom tend to improve. The relation of conventional IQ tests to time of response is biased against older adults because the reaction time of many older adults is slower and the tests do not make allowances for it.

In fact, the brain does not reach its maximum weight until an individual is about 30 years of age. Better news still is that the integration of the right side with the left side is not fully developed until the age of around 40. Because connections between brain cells increase as you age, you are probably smarter at 50 than you were at 20. Although there is some evidence that the brain does deteriorate after 60, this deterioration is very gradual and, for all practical purposes in the healthy brain, is minuscule. Research shows that the memory of older people for general knowledge is just as good or even better than that of younger adults. As we age, we tend to take longer to learn new information – but this is often compensated for by our accumulated experience. Most adults tend to peak and experience significant personal growth at midlife.

Many well-known creative people have seemed to peak as they reached senior citizenship. Frank Lloyd Wright, the famous architect, designed one of his most innovative buildings, the Guggenheim Museum in New York at the age of 88. Giuseppe Verdi at 81 composed *Falstaff*, one of his best operas. Pablo Picasso produced some of his best work when over 90. Senator John Glenn, the first American to orbit the Earth in space, made history when at the age of 77 he returned to space aboard the Shuttle *Discovery*. Some scientists believe you can improve brain function and reverse decline by challenging yourself with active learning or by living in an enriched learning environment.

Research has also found that exercised brain cells have more dendrites – the connections between brain cells. Intelligence is thought to be determined by the complexity of the dendritic connections rather than by the number of brain cells. However, older adults participate less in higher education programmes than others, and they also receive less training in the workplace than younger workers do. Research into 700 elderly nuns in a convent in Manikota, Minnesota, who donated their brains for a scientific study, showed that the more educated nuns had a thicker cortex, more densely-packed brain cells, and more synapses and dendrites which are known to facilitate communication between the brain cells. These nuns continued to learn, read, write and intellectually challenge themselves throughout life. During old age sensory and perceptual skills, reaction times, muscular strength, and memory tend to diminish, although intelligence does not. With the trend towards early retirement it is likely that more older adults will take part in adult learning than heretofore.

References
Buzan, Tony and Keene, Raymond (1996) *The Age Heresy*. London, Ebury Press.
Malone, Samuel A. (2000) *Learning Skills for Managers*. Dublin, Oak Tree Press.
Whalley, Lawrence (2001) *The Ageing Brain*. London, Weidenfeld & Nicolson.
http://tip.psychology.org/cross.html
http://www.newhorizons.org/blab_diamond1.html
http://www.newhorizons.org/blab_diamond2.html
http://www.newhorizons.org/blab_diamond4.htm
http://mindpub.com/art325.htm
file://C:\Program Files\Britannica\BCD\Cache_31_PreviewRil.htm
http://www.happychild.org.uk/acc/tpr/gtm/1199boty.htm
http://www.library.utoronto.ca/bulletin/oct25_99/artl3.htm

Alcohol and learning

Although alcohol is socially acceptable, many people do not realise that consuming alcohol in excessive quantity can cause memory and learning problems. Even moderate drinking may interfere in the short term with memory and the ability to concentrate. So it is not a good idea to drink alcohol when preparing for formal examinations. However, moderate drinkers do enjoy some health benefits, such as a reduced risk of coronary heart attack.

Heavy drinking over a long period may damage the liver, which together with the commonly associated dietary deficiency may lead to a serious shortfall in the required uptake of vitamin B1 (thiamine). As a result, nerve cells are damaged and memory problems ensue. The brain uses up 20 per cent of the oxygen needed by the entire body when at rest. Chronic heavy drinking causes permanent damage to the brain because it constricts blood vessels. This in turn reduces blood flow and restricts available oxygen to the brain. Worse still, the need for oxygen increases as we age.

Long-term alcohol abuse can lead to Wernicke-Korsakoff syndrome, which is the medical term for a rare combination of alcohol-induced symptoms that include severe and irretrievable memory loss.

See also **Korsakoff's psychosis**.

References
Noll, Richard and Turkington, Carol (1994) *The Encyclopedia of Memory and Memory Disorders*. New York, Facts on File Inc.
Ratey, John (2001) A *User's Guide To The Brain*. London, Little, Brown.

Alphabet system   In the learning context the 'alphabet system' corresponds to a mnemonic memory technique based on the 26 letters of the alphabet – which may be regarded as 26 hooks on which to hang things you want to remember. The idea is to invent words to represent each letter of the alphabet and commit these to long-term memory. For example, let's say that A is ace; B is bee; C is sea; D is deed; E is easel; F is effigy, G is g-string; H is H-bomb; I is eye; J is jay; K is cake; L is elbow; M is ember; N is entrance; O is oboe, P is pea; Q is queue; R is artist; S is Eskimo; T is teapot; U is U-boat; V is vehicle; W is wc; X is X-ray; Y is wire; Z is zebra. Some of these may not stick in your mind so you should change them for images more meaningful or memorable to you. The words chosen may have a similar sound with the letter of the alphabet for easier recall, but that is not essential – best to select the word with the strongest image that comes most readily to mind, and stick with it. So if you want to remember 26 items, you link or associate them with these ready-made hooks.

The alphabet system is a good technique for memorising long lists of items in a specific order. It enables you to detect missing items very quickly. It is an effective memory technique, easy to learn and fairly easy to use. It does, however, take some time and effort to commit the system to memory.

See also **PLAN model of memorising systems**.

References
Hermann, Douglas J. (1995) *Super Memory: A quick-action programme for memory improvement.* London, Blandford.
Higbee, Kenneth (1990) *Your Memory: How it works and how to improve it.* London, Piatkus.
Rupp, Rebecca (1998) *Committed to Memory: How we remember and why we forget.* London, Aurum Press.
http://www.mindtools.com/alphabet.html

Alzheimer's disease   A progressive degenerative condition of the brain that affects an estimated one in ten people over 65 years of age. As a result there is impaired memory and thought function. Several studies show that *Ginkgo biloba* helps slow down memory loss associated with normal ageing or due to degenerative brain diseases such as Alzheimer's. Aluminium poisoning is thought to be one possible cause of Alzheimer's disease. Researchers believe that a commitment to lifelong learning may help to prevent Alzheimer's disease. A study into a group of nuns revealed that a positive emotional outlook at an early age increased longevity and intellectual acuity and may ward off degenerative disease.

See also **Age**; **Using your brain**.

References
Noll, Richard and Turkington, Carol (1994) *The Encyclopedia of Memory and Memory Disorders.* New York, Facts on File Inc.
Ratey, John (2001) *A User's Guide To The Brain.* London, Little, Brown.
http://brain.com/about/article.cfm?id=21005&cat_id=16

Analogies   Analogies are functional comparisons. A good way of understanding something you don't know much about is to make a working comparison between it and something that you do know a lot about.

For example, you might compare human memory with computer memory. Short-term memory could be compared with random access memory (RAM), which is the computer's temporary memory: RAM chips lose their content every time the computer is turned off. Long-term memory could be compared with read-only memory (ROM): ROM chips provide permanent storage – their information is retained even when the computer is switched off. The ROM chip contains the information the central processing unit (CPU) needs to function.

A discipline that makes special use of analogies is *synectics*, which is a method for defining problems that makes the strange familiar and the familiar strange. It uses emotion and non-rationality to generate ideas, and it does it through the use of analogies or finding new ways to look at a problem. It uses four types of analogy:

- the personal analogy, which is where you imagine yourself to be the object you are working on. For example, you might ask yourself: 'What would it feel like to be a chair?'

- the direct analogy, which is used to find a similarity between two different objects or processes. For example: 'What do a football team and a business have in common?'

- the symbolic analogy, which uses symbols, stories or myths to describe a problem. For example, the story of Beauty and the Beast makes the point that beauty is only skin deep – so you might conclude that one should not confuse business relationships with true friendship

- the fantasy analogy, which suspends logic and reality to come up with wild ideas. Albert Einstein's fantasy in which he saw himself riding a beam of sunlight played an important part in developing the theory of Relativity.

References

Gamez, George (1996) *Creativity: How to catch lightning in a bottle.* Los Angeles, Peak Publications.

Williams, Scott (2001) 'Increasing employees' creativity by training their managers', *Industrial and Commercial Training*, Volume 33, Number 2, pp63–68.

Analytical intelligence   Analytical intelligence is one of the seven styles of intelligence described by Howard Gardner in his book *Frames of Mind* (1984): it refers to the intelligence of the logical or mathematical learner. People with this intelligence are good at reasoning, logic, problem-solving and mathematics. They like to do experiments, solve puzzles, work with numbers and explore patterns and relationships. Accountants, actuaries, engineers, scientists, mathematicians, computer programmers, and lawyers are the types of people who value this ability.

In everyday life, people good at household budgeting, organising and time management have this style of intelligence. It is usually noticed early in life and peaks at between 30 and 40 years of age. Like linguistic ability, it is highly valued in the academic and business world. We all have this ability to one extent or another. People with this style of intelligence learn best by categorising, classifying and working with abstract information. Logical intelligence is fundamental to business acumen and scientific thinking. Scientists when doing research establish a hypothesis, test it, and then modify it in the light of the results.

Get learners to exercise their logical intelligence by comparing and contrasting situations, doing cause-and-effect analysis and creating Gantt charts. Watch science, court, and business programmes on television and visit museums.

See also **SIMILAR model of intelligences**.

References

Armstrong, Thomas (1993) *Seven Kinds of Smart: Identifying and developing your many intelligences.* London, Plume.

Gardner, Howard (1993). *Frames of Mind: The theory of multiple intelligences.* London, Fontana.

Stine, Jean Marie (2000) *Super Brain Power: Six keys to unlocking your hidden genius.* New York, Prentice Hall.

Vincent, Annette; and Ross, Dianne (2001) 'Personalise training: determine learning styles, personality types and multiple intelligences online', *The Learning Organisation*, Volume 6, Number 1, pp36–43.

http://www.famu.edu/sjmga/ggrow/7ln/Logical.html

Andragogy   Andragogy is the art and science of helping adults to learn. The term was invented by Malcolm Knowles as an intentional contrast with the term *pedagogy*, which refers to the art and science of helping children learn.

Andragogy is based on five assumptions about the adult learner:

- As people mature they move from being dependent learners to self-directed learners. Trainers should allow learners to discover things for themselves, giving guidance and helping as mistakes are made. Trainers should take on the role of facilitators rather than that of teachers.

- Adults possess accumulated experience that is a rich source of learning. Trainers should therefore take into account the widely differing backgrounds of learners.

- Adults are more ready to learn if the learning experience is relevant to their jobs.

- Adults are more future oriented and more problem centred than subject centred in learning.

- Adults are motivated more intrinsically than extrinsically.

Progressive educationalists now believe that the principles of andragogy can equally be applied to teaching children. Andragogy means that trainers should focus more on the process and less on the content when delivering training. Strategies such as business games, case studies, role-play, simulations, discussion tasks, project work, and self-evaluation are most useful. Trainers must become facilitators rather than lecturers.

See also **Adult learners**.

References

Cheetham, Graham; and Chivers, Geoff (2001) 'How professionals learn in practice: an investigation of informal learning amongst people working in professions', *Journal of Industrial Training*, Volume 25, Number 5, pp247–292.

Knowles, M. S. (1974) *The Adult Learner: A neglected species*. Houston, Gulf.

Knowles, M. S. (1980) *The Modern Practice of Adult Education: From pedagogy to andragogy*. Chicago, Follett.

http://tip.psychology.org/knowles.html

http://www.learnativity.com/andragogy.html

http://www.ed.gov/databases/ERIC_Digests/ed305495.html

http://www.infed.org/lifelonglearning/b-andra.htm

Aptitude test Aptitude is the measurable ability of a person to acquire a desired skill after appropriate training. An aptitude test is any test designed to measure potential for achievement and learning. It assumes little in terms of prior knowledge and experience. Various types of aptitude tests are available, classified as special, general and multiple.

- Special aptitude tests are those designed to measure potential for a restricted, single capacity – eg mechanical, clerical or musical aptitude.

- General aptitude tests are broad-based tests designed to determine potential in relatively non-specialised areas – eg intelligence tests.

- Multiple aptitude tests are test batteries in which a number of factors are assessed.

In organisations, aptitude tests can be used to find out a person's suitability for a particular occupation or job. Such tests may be designed to ascertain verbal, numerical, spatial, diagrammatical or mechanical aptitudes. For example, in accountancy work an aptitude for figures and logical thought is probably essential. On the other hand, interpersonal skills might be a requirement for a job in marketing or human resource management. Some mechanical aptitude might be required in a job as an airline pilot.

See also **Ability**.

References

McKenna, Eugene (2000) *Business Psychology and Organisational Behaviour*, 3rd edition. Hove, Psychology Press Taylor and Francis Group.

Stewart, Andrew (1994) 'Diagnosing needs' in the *Handbook of Management Development*, edited by Alan Mumford, Aldershot, Gower.

Artificial intelligence (AI) Artificial intelligence is the capacity of a computer to do what human brains can do. It has also been defined as giving to a computer the means of solving any problem a human can solve, but faster. Developments include pattern recognition, voice recognition, machine learning, simulations, diagnostics, and forecasting. Robotic systems and expert systems have been modelled on the human brain. Conversely, the computer has sometimes been used as a model to understand some of the complexities of the brain.

In practice, scientists have found it very difficult to mimic human creativity, human intuitive processes, human ability to learn from experience, the subtlety of human movements, the human senses (seeing, hearing, tasting, smelling, touching), the richness of human memory, and the uniqueness of common sense. Particular challenges include computer vision (building a system that can understand images as well as a human) and natural language-processing (building a system that can understand and speak language as well as a human). However, progress has been made and is expected to go on being made in the future. Artificial intelligence is an enhancement of and an extension to human brainpower rather than a replacement.

References
Blakemore, Colin (1988) *The Mind Machine*. London, BBC Books.
Greenfield, Susan (1999) *Brain Power*. Shaftesbury, Element Books.
Malone, Samuel A. (2000). *Learning Skills for Managers*. Dublin, Oak Tree Press.

ASPIRE model   The ASPIRE model is an acronymic guide to self-development: following the model should help you to realise your goals in life. It is based on and adapted from a mnemonic by Dr Michael Waters (1996).

ASPIRE stands for:

- Assess your current position – clarify your vision, values and goals.

- SWOT – do a Strengths, Weaknesses, Opportunities and Threats analysis on yourself.

- Plan – draw up an action plan to achieve your short-term and long-term goals.

- Implement your plan.

- Review – compare your progress against your goals.

- Evaluate – work out how successful you have been in achieving your personal development vision, and take corrective action as appropriate.

See also **Self-assessment**; **Self-development**.

References
Malone, Samuel A. (2000) *Learning Skills for Managers*. Dublin, Oak Tree Press.
Waters, Michael (1996) *The Element Dictionary of Personal Development*. Shaftesbury, Element Books.

Assessment centres   An assessment centre is an event rather than a location, and is designed to provide a range of techniques and instruments that:

- measure individual skills, knowledge, abilities and attitudes relevant to success in the work situation

- help in the selection of new recruits for the workplace

- assess the potential of people for management positions and for the future requirements of the company

- identify training needs

- reduce the risk of expensive mistakes – eg the cost of a mistaken promotion.

Assessment centres combine in-tray exercises, role-play, case studies, diagnostic analysis, business games, simulations, group discussions, group tasks, presentations, questionnaires, report-writing and interviews. Psychometric tests may be used to help managers identify strengths and weaknesses in behavioural areas. All exercises must be realistic and credible to participants.

Assessment centres may be used for selection, placement, the identification of potential, promotion, and management development and training. Competency frameworks that measure high and low performance in behavioural terms should be employed so that evaluations can be benchmarked. Assessors are usually drawn from senior functional and line management. Although sometimes used for judging potential, an assessment centre may be more productive when used to identify the development needs of managers, in which case it may alternatively be called a development centre.

It is important that an assessment centre fits the strategy, structure and style of the company on whose behalf it is organised.

See also **Development centres**; **Learning centre**.

References

Garavan, Thomas, Costine, Pat and Heraty, Noreen (1997) *Training and Development in Ireland.* Dublin, Oak Tree Press.

Mumford, Alan (1997) *Management Development, Strategies for Action.* London, IPD.

Stewart, Andrew (1994) 'Performance appraisal' in the *Handbook of Management Development*, edited by Alan Mumford, Aldershot, Gower.

Winter, Barry (1995) 'Assessment centres keeping up with and getting ahead of changing organisations', *Journal of European Industrial Training*, Volume 19, Number 2, pp15–19.

Association   In a learning context, association is the purposeful linking of one concept or thought with another. We remember things if we associate them with previous experience or with something we know already. Make the information personally meaningful by relating it to your life, experience, prior knowledge or goals. If you need to remember two or more different things, see if you can find some mental connection between them.

Things can be associated by imagining them:

- being placed on top of each other

- crashing into each other

- dancing with each other

- fighting with each other

- orbiting around each other

- penetrating each other

- connected in any other bizarre or amusing way.

Apply the questioning technique to build up the necessary links and to engrave the subject on your memory. Why is this so? How is this so? When is it so? Where is it so? Who said it? How reliable is the source of information? What else can be deduced?

The more the brain is used, the more memory associations are formed. The more triggers and links that are formed, the easier it is to remember previously acquired information, and also to form new associations. For example, an easy way to tell the difference between 'stationary' and 'stationery' is that you use stationery to write a letter and envelope starts with an 'e'. To remember how to spell 'believe', never believe a lie.

There are three laws of association:

- *the law of similarity* – This states that two ideas may be associated if they resemble each other – for example, people with the same name. Also, you are more likely to associate a bus with a car than with an aeroplane. In examinations, students are often asked to show the similarities and differences between various theories.

- *the law of contrast* – This states that two ideas may be associated if they contrast with each other – for example, tall and short, day and night, black and white. It is easier to learn the differences between 'hot' and 'cold' than between 'hot' and 'warm'. The laws of similarity and contrast suggest that comparing and contrasting ideas is a very effective way of learning information.

- *the law of contiguity* – This states that two ideas may be associated if they have occurred together – for example, if two important events happened on similar dates, one may be recalled by reference to the other. We all know that World War I started in 1914. Frederick Winslow Taylor, 'the Father of scientific management', died the following year in 1915.

See also **Laws of learning**; **Link system of memorising**.

References

Hermann, Douglas J. (1995) *Super Memory: A quick-action programme for memory improvement.* London, Blandford.

Higbee, Kenneth L (1990) *Your Memory: How it works and how to improve it.* London, Piatkus.

Rupp, Rebecca (1998) *Committed to Memory: How we remember and why we forget.* London, Aurum Press.

http://www.web-us.com/memory/improving_memory.htm

http://www.premiumhealth.com/memory/htiym2.htm

http://www.mindtools.com/assimloc.html

Asynchronous learning

Asynchronous learning   Asynchronous learning is learning that does not rely on teacher and student working simultaneously. The term is thus used most commonly in reference to e-learning, by which learning materials are put on the Internet by the teacher or trainer, and accessed at a different time by the learner. The learner may access the material at a time that suits him or her. A correspondence course is another example of asynchronous learning.

See also **Synchronous learning**.

References

Sloman, Martyn (2001) *The E-learning Revolution: From propositions to action.* London, CIPD.

Attention   Attention may be defined as a directed focus of awareness, in which the individual is switched on to a specific kind of signal or sensory input. All learning requires initial curiosity and attention. There is more information around you than you can possibly process at any one time. When we pay attention we single out some specific information that matters to us from the world about us while allowing the remainder that doesn't interest us to be ignored or at most to recede into the background.

Lack of attention or concentration is a major reason for mistakes and accidents in the workplace. Without adequate powers of attention it is impossible to learn effectively. It is amazing how focused our attention is when our curiosity has been aroused. For example, at a cocktail party, the mention of our name in another group, will often focus our complete attention on the conversation and we are able to tune in despite the noise and chatter all around the room.

Temporary moods and attitudes can affect attention. When we are feeling rather inadequate or sorry for ourselves we can be quick to notice any slight or fancied insults. Also, it is hard to pay attention if we are distracted, interrupted, tired, rushed or under stress. We attend, in fact, to anything that happens to fit in with our interests or attitudes of the moment, and we can remain quite blind to information we find uninteresting.

Educational psychologists have noted various factors that influence attention:

- The intensity of a stimulus can attract attention – eg loud noises or bright colours.

- Novel stimuli or unusual shapes attract attention – hence the use of italics in a textbook to highlight key learning points.

- A variable or changing stimulus attracts attention – trainers should use pitch, intonation, tone and inflexion to vary the sound of their voices and maintain the interest of learners.

- Certain colours are more attractive than others – adults may pay more attention to red and white designs than black and white ones; orange may create a warm feeling.

- Trainers may give clues or hints as to what is important, and so attract attention – for example, verbal cues such as 'Look at this carefully' or physical cues such as pointing. Similarly, advance organisers such as overviews may be used by trainers at the start of a training session to help learners structure and organise the learning material.

- Interest, or lack of it, determines the degree to which we pay attention.

- Fatigue and illness affect the ability to pay attention. We shall not remember information if our attention wanders.

- Activities and ideas that we are not expecting attract our attention.

- Characteristics of personality can affect the ability to pay attention – in general, extroverts are more likely than introverts to become distracted during long training sessions.

See also **Attention span**; **Concentration**.

References
Hermann, Douglas J. (1995) *Super Memory: A quick-action programme for memory improvement.* London, Blandford.
Higbee, Kenneth L. (1990) *Your Memory: How it works and how to improve it.* London, Piatkus.
Rupp, Rebecca (1998) *Committed to Memory: How we remember and why we forget.* London, Aurum Press.
http://onhealth.com/ch1/briefs/reuters/item,76452.asp
file://C:\Program Files\Britannica\BCD\Cache_9_PreviewRil.htm
file://C:\Program Files\Britannica\BCD\Cache_7_PreviewRil.htm
file://C:\Program Files\Britannica\BCD\Cache_5_PreviewRil.htm

Attention span   The attention span is governed by interest and our powers of concentration. The reason we forget something is that we didn't pay sufficient attention to it in the first place. Without sufficient attention, information is unlikely to be encoded strongly enough for retention in the long-term memory. Your attention span is unlikely to be more than a continuous 20 minutes. In a learning session of one hour, this would suggest that mini-breaks every 20 minutes or so are essential.

The attention span is also influenced by factors of personality. Extroverts are generally unable to concentrate for as long as introverts. One of the easiest ways to help your attention span is to drink sufficient water throughout the day. Dehydration can cause attention difficulties. So take a drink of water during your mini-breaks. Short attention spans seem now to be part of our way of life. For example, the frequency of commercial breaks on American TV is supposedly dictated by the short attention span of many Americans. In contrast, the genius of Newton relied partly on his ability to concentrate on particular problems for very long periods of time.

See also **Attention**; **Concentration**.

References
Malone, Samuel A.(2000) *Learning Skills for Managers.* Dublin, Oak Tree Press.
Ukens, Lorraine L. (2001) *What Smart Trainers Know.* San Francisco, Jossey-Bass Pfeiffer.

Attitude   Attitudes have been defined as mental predispositions to act in a certain way in a particular situation. Experience, opinions, values and beliefs influence attitudes. Attitude has much to do with whether you remember something or not. In learning and memory, as in other areas of life, a positive mental attitude is all-important. If you think you can, you will. If you think you can't you won't. It is now well established that a person's mental and emotional states have a powerful impact on his or her health. Research links negative thoughts and emotions to the secretion of hormones that accelerate the ageing process, attack the immune system and ultimately cause disease. Another study has shown that negative reaction to stress is more destructive to health than is cigarette smoking.

It was William James who said that 'The greatest discovery of my generation is that a human being can alter his life by altering his attitude of mind.' You are more likely to remember something if you find it interesting and expect to remember it. Say to yourself, 'I will remember everything I study today.' If you find a topic boring, however, or believe that you have a bad memory, you are unlikely to remember much of it. Stereotypes concerning memory and age are prevalent. Note that judges and medical specialists tend to be older people who are more likely to have the required experience, judgement and wisdom.

Many older people are programmed to believe that the memory declines with age. Because of this their memory performance is likely to suffer in comparison with that of people of a similar age who believe their memory is good. The fact is that stereotypes about memory are generally inaccurate. Provided you are in good health there is no significant decline in memory with age. In fact, when it comes to specialist knowledge, younger people are at a disadvantage compared with older people who are experienced in the field. On the other hand, attitudes tend to become less flexible with age: older people with negative attitudes about their ability to learn may therefore have great difficulty changing them.

Attitude surveys, by means of interviews or questionnaires, can be used to get information about the attitude of employees to learning and training and development. The repertory grid technique may be used to assess a change in attitude. Sometimes it may be more helpful just to see if an actual change in behaviour has occurred.

See also **Beliefs**; **CAP model of learning types**; **Knowledge**; **Positive thinking**; **Repertory grid technique**; **Skills**; **Values**.

References

Blakeslee, Thomas R. (1997) *The Attitude Factor: Extend your life by changing the way you think*. London, Thorsons.

Bland, Glenn (1996) *The Power of Thought: Ageless secrets of great achievement*. Rocklin, Md, Prima.

Bramley, Peter (1994) 'Evaluation', in the *Handbook of Management Development*, edited by Alan Mumford, Aldershot, Gower.

Clements, Phil (1995) *Be Positive*. London, Kogan Page.

Malone, Samuel A. (1999) *Success Skills for Managers*. Dublin, Oak Tree Press.

Waters, Michael (1996) *The Element Dictionary of Personal Development*. Shaftesbury, Element Books.

File://C:\Program Files\Britannica\BCD\Cache_18_PreviewRil.htm

http://www.cba.uri.edu/Scholl/Notes/Attitudes.htm

Audiovisual methods of learning

Audiovisual methods of learning consist of video and film recordings with sound (including CD-ROM and DVD), slideshows with commentary, and resources on the Internet that display in sound and vision. Audiovisual methods that rely on a teacher's personal instruction often involve the use of flipcharts, whiteboards, blackboards, posters and/or display boards. Such display boards may be covered with material to which Velcro will adhere. Alternatively, display boards may be made of metal for magnetised objects.

When learners are allowed to watch training videos in a passive manner, the training is often ineffective. The trainer should stop the video at appropriate points to allow questions and discussion. This will create active participation and feedback. Slides may be used to support points made in a lecture. Graphics help simplify the presentation and capture the interest of learners – because more of the senses are involved, a lecture with graphics is likely to be more effective.

See also **Video conferencing**.

References

Reid, Charles W. and Kleiner, Brian W. (1996) 'Which training methods are effective?', *Management Development Review*, Volume 9, Number 2, pp24–29.

B

Barriers to learning Barriers to learning include all kinds of distractions and inhibiting factors. Many of them can be recalled as a list by means of the acronym RESTATE, which stands for Resources deficiency, Environmental difficulties, Style of learning or training complication, Time restrictions, Attitude problems, Training mismatch, and Experience inadequacy.

- *resources deficiency* – Resources that may be deficient include personal resources such as self-esteem, self-confidence, self-belief and intelligence; and organisational resources such as a culture for learning and such facilities as a corporate learning centre or an educational support scheme. One of the most valuable resources that managers may allocate to foster learning is time. Lack of money, of childcare facilities and/or of transport may also be a problem. Information about learning opportunities may also be inadequate or unavailable altogether.

- *environmental difficulties* – The environment may not support learning. According to Argyris (1995), individuals react to threatening situations by using defensive routines which inhibit learning. People may be tired of classroom situations. The environment should allow for social interaction – people learn from each other in a social context. A bureaucratic culture inhibits rather than supports learning. Workplace practices and processes may inhibit learning. Teamworking encourages collaborative learning. Modern ways of life are not good for learning: for example, poor lifestyle and diet, ongoing emotional stress, and environmental pollutants all damage fragile brain cells.

- *style of learning or training complication* – Adopting an inappropriate style hinders learning. If you are a visual learner, feed your visual senses using videos, CD-ROMs, DVDs and other visual media. There may be a mismatch between the trainer's style and the learner's style. In the work situation a participative style of management is more conducive to learning than an autocratic one. Supportive supervision and active encouragement is positively related to employee learning.

- *time restrictions* – Learning can be hard work and any worthwhile learning takes time. You may have insufficient time because of responsibilities such as family, career and social commitments. Insufficient time will create tension and frustrate learning. You must allocate an appropriate amount of time to learning. Also, you must be in a relaxed and receptive state to learn effectively. Institutions that offer learning may have inconvenient schedules or locations for programmes. In addition, the programmes offered may be irrelevant or inappropriate to your needs.

- *attitude problems* – Negative attitudes evoke negative outcomes. Some people may have had an unpleasant learning experience in school and thus have a fear of learning. Other people may feel they are too old to learn. Most people have a fear of the unknown, and prefer to stick to the tried and familiar. They feel uneasy moving away from their comfort zones to learn new things. Confidence, self-esteem and self-belief are needed for successful learning. Some people may not recognise that they need to learn – they are at the 'unconscious incompetence' stage of learning. In other words, they don't know that they don't know. Ignorance is bliss. To learn, they need to progress to and through the next stages of learning: conscious incompetence, conscious competence, and finally unconscious competence.

- *training mismatch* – The training may be presented without the needs of the adult learner in mind, or the training may be irrelevant. Learning should be designed in relation to specific needs. The trainer should show the relationship between training, greater productivity and improved promotion prospects. Many people are sent on courses because it is 'their turn' or because budgetary resources ought to be used up before the year's end. Rewards and reinforcements should be in place for learning.

- *experience inadequacy* – The learner may have insufficient experience or knowledge to make the links and associations necessary for effective learning. Good trainers present a series of novel challenges to keep learners motivated that are neither too easy nor too hard for each person's stage of development.

See also **Barriers to memory**.

References

Argyris, C. (1995) 'Action science and organisational learning', *Journal of Management Psychology*, 10(6), pp20–26.
Beaver, Diana (1994) *Lazy Learning: Making the most of the brain you were born with*. Shaftesbury, Element Books.

DePorter, Bobbi and Hernacki, Mike (1993) *Quantum Learning: Unleash the genius within you.* London, Piatkus.
Malone, Samuel A. (2000) *Learning Skills for Managers.* Dublin, Oak Tree Press.
http://granite.cyg.net/~jblackmo/diglib/style-c.html
http://www.campaign-for-learning.org.uk/aboutlearning/abtlearn.htm

Barriers to memory

Barriers to remembering include all kinds of distractions and inhibiting factors, including:

- memory overload – The memory span is only seven plus or minus two items

- lack of social, physical, or mental cues, such as mnemonics

- failure to process information properly in the first place, possibly due to lack of motivation or overconfidence

- anxiety – If your mind is occupied with negative thoughts, there is no room for anything else. For example, test anxiety can cause a student to forget factual information irrespective of how well it has been learned. Management of test anxiety has helped many students pass exams

- damage to brain structures such as the hippocampus, hypothalamus, thalamus and temporal lobes, causing memory problems.

- certain medications – Some medications may hamper memory: consult your doctor when medications have been prescribed for you

- failure to write down what is to be remembered – Taking appropriate notes and keeping a diary is often the best memory aid

- lack of physical exercise – Exercise gets more blood to the brain and improves alertness and memory performance

- smoking, which lowers the amount of oxygen reaching the brain – Studies relating to a test of verbal and visual memory have shown that smokers who smoke one or more packs of cigarettes a day had difficulties in remembering people's names and faces, compared to non-smokers

- sensory overload – If you are trying to do too many things at the same time, your brain may become overloaded and fail to process short-term memories. For example, if you are trying to remember a lot of information at once, you may forget where you put your car keys, where you parked your car, or when you are meant to attend an essential appointment.

See also **Barriers to learning**; **Forgetting curve**.

References
Hermann, Douglas (1995) *Super Memory: A quick-action programme for memory improvement.* London, Blandford.

Higbee, Kenneth L (1990) *Your Memory: How it works and how to improve it*. London, Piatkus.
Rupp, Rebecca (1998) *Committed To Memory: How we remember and why we forget*. London, Aurum Press.

Behavioural objectives   Behavioural objectives are learning objectives that specify what behaviour a learner must demonstrate to show that learning has taken place. The learning outcomes should be observable and measurable. Without a behavioural objective it is difficult to determine what a particular training session is supposed to achieve.

It is important to translate session learning objectives into behavioural terms – generally expressed as what you will be able to do as a result of the learning, and especially as what you are able to do that you were not able to do before the learning. Other behavioural objectives may specify levels of expected performance in terms of speed, accuracy, and quality.

The statement of a behavioural objective normally includes:

■ *conditions* – the conditions or circumstances under which the newly learned behaviour is to be performed (which might certainly include the work context)

■ *a verb expressing the required behaviour* – that is, a word that describes observable learner behaviour, such as 'identify', 'name', and 'describe', which are behavioural because it is feasible to observe the act of identifying, naming or describing; verbs such as 'understand' or 'appreciate' are not behavioural because 'understanding' and 'appreciating' are not visible activities

■ *criteria* – a measure of how well the learner must perform the newly learned behaviour (perhaps relating to existing performance standards).

See also **Goals**.

References
Garavan, Thomas N., Costine, Pat and Heraty, Noreen (1997) *Training and Development in Ireland*. Dublin, Oak Tree Press.
Truelove, Steve (1992) *A Handbook of Training and Development*. Oxford, Blackwell Business.
http://members.spree.com/teach2prime/objectives.htm

Behaviourist theory of learning   The leading theorists in this field include John B. Watson, C. L. Hull, E. R. Guthrie, Edward L. Thorndike, B. F. Skinner, and Ivan P. Pavlov. Three basic assumptions underlie the behaviourist theory of learning:

■ Learning is manifested by a change in behaviour. The focus of study should therefore be observable behaviour rather than internal thought processes, and the learner's perceptions and motivation are not considered.

■ The environment shapes behaviour.

■ The principle of contiguity and reinforcement are central to the learning process.

The principle of contiguity is that two things are easily remembered if they occur together. If behaviour is reinforced or rewarded, it is more likely to occur again in similar conditions. Reinforcement can thus be used to shape behaviour.

The behaviourist theory has four key principles for learning. These can be recalled by means of the acronym ROAR, which stands for Repetition, Objectives, Activity, and Reinforcement.

- *repetition* – Practice makes perfect, and practice makes permanent. If you want to learn a skill, you must practise frequently. Repetition is also needed to memorise key learning points.

- *objectives* – As trainers we are taught to formulate our objectives in behavioural terms – eg 'By the end of this training session participants will be able to . . .'

- *activity* – Learning is more effective when the learner is active rather than passive: learning by doing is best.

- *reinforcement* – Positive reinforcers like praise, rewards, and success are better than negative ones like punishments and failure. Feedback is an important part of the process.

Systematic training design, training objectives, programmed learning, computer-based training, and competencies are grounded in behaviourist learning theory. This approach is suitable where objectives are unambiguous, where performance criteria can be clearly defined, and where the learner has little knowledge. Examples include computer programming, studying accountancy procedures or learning to operate a sophisticated machine. Behaviourist principles have thus been applied extensively to the development of low-level psychomotor skills. In addition, neuro-linguistic programming practitioners have applied the principles to their technique of visualisation and modelling. In business the concept of modelling has been used in role-play exercises.

Today the environment is constantly changing so that we must be very flexible and adaptable. In such cases different approaches to learning are more appropriate. In addition, behaviourist theories of learning do not allow for the relevance of thoughts, feelings or motives in the learning process, regarding learning as merely a series of conditioned responses with an emphasis on inputs and outputs.

See also **Cognitivist theory of learning**; **Constructivist theory of learning**; **Humanist theory of learning**; **Social theory of learning**.

References
Merriam, Sharon B. and Caffarella, Rosemary S. (1999). *Learning in Adulthood: A comprehensive guide*. San Francisco, Jossey-Bass.
Knowles, M. S. (1974) *The Adult Learner: A neglected species*. Houston, Gulf.

Knowles, M. S. (1980) *The Modern Practice of Adult Education: From pedagogy to andragogy.* Chicago, Follett.
Cheetham, Graham and Chivers, Geoff (2001) 'How professionals learn in practice: an investigation of informal learning amongst people working in professions', *Journal of European Industrial Training*, Volume 25, Number 5, pp247–292.
http://www.learnativity.com/edpsych.html

Beliefs

Beliefs   Whatever you believe with feeling becomes your reality. Beliefs shape attitudes and so create tendencies for people to behave in certain ways. Beliefs can be empowering or disempowering. Sometimes barriers to learning are traditional and psychological rather than real – your limitations are all in your head. The problem with disempowering beliefs is that they tend to become self-fulfilling prophecies. The theory of multiple intelligences suggests that we have the ability to do almost anything we want provided we have the self-belief and make the commitment.

See also **Attitude**; **Confidence**; **Values**.

References

Denny, Richard (1997) *Succeed for Yourself: Unlock your potential for success and happiness.* London, Kogan Page.
Tracy, Brian (1993) *Maximum Achievement.* New York, Simon & Schuster.

Benchmarking

Benchmarking   Benchmarking, also known as intercompany learning, is the continuous process of measuring company products, services and practices against those of the toughest competitors, or of other companies renowned as industry leaders, in order to achieve superior performance. In other words, it is a method of learning from the best practices of excellent companies. At the product level, reverse engineering may be used to benchmark and learn from competitors. It is during visits to other organisations that ideas for external benchmarking may arise. In addition to suppliers, competitors and non-competitors, customers are also a good source of ideas for external benchmarking.

In practice it is easier to get information from non-competitors than from competitors, who may not be willing to share commercially sensitive information. Some organisations are, however, willing to share information. For example, benchmarking co-operatives are groups of organisations who get together to learn from each other.

Internal benchmarking can be used so that the best practices elsewhere in the organisation can be adopted throughout.

References

Forrest, Andrew (1995) *Fifty Ways To Personal Development.* London, The Industrial Society.
Kouzmin, Alexander, Loffler, Elke, Klages, Helmut and Korac-Kakabadse, Nadia (1999) 'Benchmarking and performance measurement in the public sector', *The International Journal of Public Sector Management*, Volume 12, Number 2, pp121–144.
Lock, Dennis (1998) *A Handbook of Management.* Aldershot, Gower.

Biofeedback   Biofeedback is a method of regulating a normally involuntary body function by monitoring internal information such as brainwaves, blood pressure, the respiration rate and the activity of certain muscles. Biofeedback machines and equipment provide individuals with feedback about physiological information that they would otherwise be unaware of. The fact that it works – that with such information an individual can regulate certain body functions – proves how the mind can affect the body. With this technique a person can exercise control over such metabolic conditions as nervous tension, the pulse rate, body temperature, blood pressure or breathing patterns.

Types of biofeedback machines are available to help a person develop control over one or more of these normally unconscious body functions. Once learned, control can be exercised without the equipment. That the mind evidently can affect the body means that our mental attitude may have a bearing on the effectiveness of our learning and, indeed, our overall well-being. Couture *et al* (1999) report that one study found the accuracy of police firearm shooting improved significantly through a combination of biofeedback and meditation. A good self-image and self-belief as a learner can enhance your ability to learn.

See also **Stress and learning**.

References
Couture, Roger T., Singh, Mohan, Wayne, Lee, Chahal, Paul. Wankel, Leonard. Oseen, Margaret and Wheeler, Gary (1999) 'Can mental training help to improve shooting accuracy?', *Policing: An international journal of police strategies and management*, Volume 22, Number 4, pp696–711.
Davis, Keith and Newstrom, John W. (1985) *Human Behaviour At Work: Organisational behaviour*. New York, McGraw-Hill.

Biography work   Working on one's own biography – actually better described as 'autobiographical work' – can be a useful and fulfilling exercise. It certainly represents a unique learning opportunity in which to reflect on the whole of your life, past, present and future, featuring everything you have done, are doing and are likely or want to do in times ahead. A simple time-chart is a good starting exercise for working on your biography.

We tend to spend more time planning our holidays than we do our lives. But as important as our activities to our biography work are our motivations, which should also be recorded. What are the motives that drove you in the past, and what are the motives that will drive you in the future? You should be clear in your mind why you want to succeed in your career. The motives are called 'career anchors' or 'career drivers', and may include (for example) income, power, achievement, recognition, and security.

References
Megginson, David and Whitaker, Vivien (1996). *Cultivating Self-Development*. London, IPD.

Biorhythms Biorhthyms correspond with your biological clock, which is generally attuned to the 24-hour day. The clock's most obvious manifestation is the regular cycle of sleeping and waking. Body temperature and the concentration of hormones that influence mood and behaviour also regularly vary over the day. Alteration of habit, such as shift work and air travel, may put your biorhythms out of phase, causing malaise until it has had time to adjust. It is easy to monitor biorhythms: electronic and mechanical biorhythm calculators are available. There are also software packages available for use with a home computer.

An unproven theory suggests that humans are governed by three biorhythms, all of which follow a predictable rise-and-fall wave pattern over specific durations:

- *an intellectual cycle* (lasting 33 days) – This rhythm is believed to originate in the brain. In the first half of the cycle a person is able to think more quickly and clearly, the memory operating more efficiently. In the second half, the individual finds learning more difficult, and thinking is less clear and precise.

- *an emotional cycle* (lasting 28 days) – This appears to originate in the nervous system and shows itself in emotional changes and degrees of sensitivity. During the rising part of the cycle creativity is greatest and the person is optimistic and cheerful. On the downswing there is a tendency towards negativity and irritation.

- *a physical cycle* (lasting 23 days) – This rhythm is believed to be rooted in the action of muscle fibres. It influences physical strength, endurance, energy levels, resistance to infection and self-confidence.

Certain days in each cycle are regarded as 'critical', and even more so if one such day coincides with that in another cycle.

Research has shown that for some reason memory ability tends to be at its best on Friday and Saturday – probably because the anticipation of the weekend improves a person's outlook and mood. People who go to bed early and wake up early learn more readily in the morning when their attention is best, whereas those who have a later schedule experience the opposite. Are you an owl or a lark? What are your best times for physical activity, mental concentration, dealing with others, study and relaxation? Most people experience a period of peak efficiency somewhere between 11am and 4pm. Every person's internal body clock is different, however. Some people find that an hour spent studying early in the morning is worth more than two hours at night. Others find they do not wake up fully until about 11am. Many people tend to become drowsy in the afternoon and to pick up again after 7pm.

Whatever your biorhythms, you need to build your learning, studying, and personal development activities around times when you are most alert. The daily biological cycles inevitably influence your powers of concentration and, therefore, of retention and learning.

References
Greenfield, Susan (1996) *The Human Mind Explained: The control centre of the living machine.* London, Cassell.
Guinness, Alma E. (1992) *Marvels And Mysteries Of The Human Mind.* London, Reader's Digest

Blended learning   Blended learning – a term used in e-learning – is an approach that blends, mixes, or combines on-line learning with classroom instruction, coaching or mentoring. The number of blends or combinations is limited only by human creativity. Blended learning offers the best of live experience with the flexibility of on-line learning. Many of the 'soft' skills need face-to-face experience which can be supplemented by on-line instruction. Other skills, such as accounting and finance, can be acquired through on-line learning and conventional correspondence courses.

References
Rossett, Allison (2002) *The ASTD E-Learning Handbook.* New York, McGraw-Hill.

Bloom's learning model   Benjamin Bloom's model, developed in 1956, presents six levels or stages of adult learning:

- Knowledge – which means simple knowledge of facts, terms, theories, etc: the ability to recall previously learned information. Examiners use words like 'list', 'define', 'describe', 'identify', 'show', 'label', 'tabulate', and so on to test learning at this level.

- Comprehension – which means understanding the meaning of this knowledge. This might involve demonstrating knowledge in the form of interpreting facts or showing comparisons or contrasts between theories or information. Examiners use words like 'interpret', 'compare', 'contrast', 'distinguish', 'differentiate', 'estimate', 'discuss', and so on to test learning at this level.

- Application, or the ability to apply this knowledge in new and concrete situations to solve problems. This might involve using methods, techniques, concepts, theories and models in new situations. Examiners use words like 'apply', 'demonstrate', 'calculate', 'illustrate', 'solve', 'examine', 'classify', and so on to test learning at this level.

- Analysis, or the ability to break material down into its constituent parts and to see the relationships between them. This might involve examining the information to draw conclusions or find evidence to support recommendations. Examiners use words like 'analyse', 'order', 'explain', 'connect', 'classify', 'arrange', 'select', and so on to test learning at this level.

- Synthesis, or the ability to reassemble these parts into a new and meaningful relationship, thus forming a new whole. This may require divergent or creative thinking. Examiners use words like 'combine', 'integrate', 'modify', 'rearrange', 'design', 'compose', 'formulate', and so on to test learning at this level.

■ Evaluation, or the ability to judge the value of learning material using clear criteria, either of one's own devising or derived from the work of others. This might involve assessing the value of theories or models and making choices based on reasoned argument. Examiners use words like 'assess', 'decide', 'rank', 'measure', 'recommend', 'judge', 'conclude', and so on to test learning at this level.

Trainers should be aware that adult learners need to participate in small group activities to help them move beyond understanding to application, analysis, synthesis and evaluation. Adults like an opportunity to share, reflect, and generalise their learning experiences.

See also **Learning by objectives**.

References
Bloom, B. S. (1956) *The Taxonomy of Educational Objectives. Handbook One: Cognitive Domain.* New York, McKay.

Brain   Some facts about the human brain:

■ It weighs only about 1.4 kilograms (3 pounds).

■ It accounts for only 2 per cent of the body weight.

■ It burns 25 per cent of the calories we consume, enough to light up a 15- to 25-watt bulb.

■ It uses up 20 per cent of the oxygen used by the entire body when at rest.

■ Our cerebral cortex is 3 millimetres (an eighth of an inch) thick and covers an area of 2,360 square centimetres (354 square inches).

■ Two-thirds of the brain mass consists of the two hemispheres, which are wrapped around all the other parts.

■ Research has found that the left hemisphere is anatomically larger than the right. It is also more active than the right in most adults.

■ We have up to 100 billion brain cells.

■ Each brain cell is connected to other brain cells by between 10,000 and 50,000 dendrites.

■ Each impulse received by a brain cell is passed on as a pulse of electric charge.

■ A cell's filament-like axon ends at a synapse (a gap-like junction with the extremities of other brain cells) and releases a chemical neurotransmitter, which jumps across to the next cell.

- Nerve impulses travel quickly and may reach speeds of 160 metres (525 feet) per second.

- Short-term memories and some long-term memories are located in the hippocampus and other parts of the temporal lobe.

- Many long-term memories reside in the frontal lobe.

- Loss of nerve cells in the temporal lobe, and in parts of the frontal lobe, results in memory loss.

- About 90 per cent of the brain's mass is water – hence the need to drink sufficient water so that our brains do not become dehydrated.

- The cerebrum is the largest part of the human brain, making up about 80 per cent of its weight.

- The human brain has a visual cortex that is five times larger than the auditory cortex: this is probably why visual learning is so effective.

- Physical movement is regulated by the cerebellum, which stores skill memory. This type of memory is particularly long-lasting – it is how an individual never really forgets how to ride a bicycle or swim.

See also **Brain LION model**.

References

Carper, Jean (200) *Your Miracle Brain*. London, Thorsons.
Greenfield, Susan (1999) *Brain Power: Working out the human mind*. Shaftesbury, Element Books.
Greenfield, Susan (1996) *The Human Mind Explained: The control centre of the living machine*. London, Cassell.
Ratey, John (2001) *A User's Guide To The Brain*. London, Little, Brown.
http://www.newhorizons.org/arts_research.html
http://faculty.washington.edu/chudler/facts.html
http://brain.web-us.com/brain/aboutthebrain.htm
http://suhep.phy.syr.edu/courses/modules/MM/Biology/biology.html

Brain and learning　　During the past few years there has been an explosion in the information available about the brain and its implications for learning. Such implications are of great importance to trainers and educators, and can be recalled by the acronym ECCLESIASTIC, which stands for Emotions, Conscious/unconscious learning, Challenge, Learners pattern meanings, Engaging the entire person, Simultaneous whole/part processing, Innate meaning, Attention and peripheral perception, Spatial memory, Two types of memory, Imagination, and Complexity.

- *emotions* – Learning is influenced by our emotions. Confidence, self-esteem, expectancy, our need for social approval, biases and prejudices, attitudes and beliefs, all influence our capacity to learn. Trainers should design course programmes that meet the emotional as well as the intellectual and social needs of learners.

- *conscious/unconscious learning* – We learn at both conscious and unconscious levels simultaneously. Suggestology, on which accelerated learning is built, is based on the theory that suggestions can and do affect the outcome of learning. Everything in a learning environment such as a training room should suggest success. Music, colour, posters and the words and body language of the trainer should be combined to create a relaxed, non-threatening learning environment. During a course, programme learners should be given adequate time to actively process their experience through discussion, review and reflection.

- *challenge enhances learning* – Learning is enhanced by challenge and inhibited by threat. The course material should be difficult enough to challenge and capture the imagination of learners. Course material that is too difficult may frustrate learners and create a sense of helplessness. Course material that is too easy will not retain their interest. Trainers must create a state of relaxed alertness in learners, low in threat and high in challenge.

- *learners pattern meanings* – The brain is designed to perceive and generate patterns. Learning is an active dynamic process of constructing meaning through the formulation of patterns. The brain loves to complete jigsaw puzzles but must be provided with meaningful pieces to do so – it resists meaningless patterns imposed upon it. Trainers must connect course material to learners' past knowledge and experience and show how it can be used in a job context. Learning maps are a technique for showing patterns of connected information. Learning maps are thought to mimic the brain's own structure of interconnected brain cells. Neuroscientists believe that learning occurs through a change in the strength of certain synaptic connections. A frequently used synapse becomes stronger, whereas an infrequently used one may grow weaker over time.

- *engaging the entire person* – Learning is a mind/body phenomenon. The mind affects the body and the body affects the mind. Trainers must be aware of the necessity for stress management, psychological support, nutrition, ventilation, exercise and relaxation as important ingredients in the whole learning process.

- *simultaneous whole/part processing* – The brain has two halves, called hemispheres. The right side is the artistic side and the left side is the scientific side. The two sides work together and interact all the time, whether a person is dealing with words, maths, music, or art. Learning is cumulative and developmental. Trainers should demonstrate how the parts of the course programme or course session relate to the whole, and how the whole is made up of contributing sessions or parts. Learning requires context for meaning.

- *innate meaning* – The search for meaning and purpose in our lives is a fundamental requirement in humans. We all need to make sense of our experiences. Just as the body needs nutritious food, the brain needs challenging information. Trainers must present interesting and challenging course programmes in a stimulating and supportive learning environment. Course work should provide realistic worklike opportunities to learn so that they are as meaningful as possible.

- *attention and peripheral perception* – Learning involves concentration and peripheral perception. Our concentration is engaged by the total package presented. In addition to the course material, visuals and illustrations, the learning environment and the demeanour of the trainer also influence learners. The trainer is the role model. A trainer's enthusiasm is infectious. The way the trainer facilitates, coaches and manages the learning process sends out important non-verbal signals as to the value of what is being learned.

- *spatial memory* – Activity-based learning is remembered better and longer than any other type of learning. Experiential learning is best. Hence the importance of on-the-job training because it is active, practical, and meaningful. In formal training programmes, trainers must make activities as realistic as possible. Demonstrations, simulations, projects, case studies, role-play, real-life examples, metaphor and group discussions are all good ways of doing this.

- *two types of memory* – We have at least two different types of memory. One is spatial and naturally engaged by experience. The other is dependent on rote learning and repetition. Course material that is very theoretical and unconnected to a learner's prior knowledge and experience and work-related issues can be learned only through rote learning. Because the learning is not meaningful it will be soon forgotten. Some memorisation may be useful in certain circumstances. However, trainers should facilitate learning by connecting with the prior knowledge and experience of the learner and the work situations to which the learners will return.

- *imagination* – The brain is a parallel processor. Existing imagination, thoughts, emotions, and predispositions operate simultaneously and interact with new knowledge and experience to provide unique interpretation and meanings for the learner. The trainer should try to engage all the multifaceted aspects of the learner's brain.

- *complex and unique* – Our brains may be similar in many ways but they are moulded uniquely by different genetic, cultural and life experiences. Learning changes the structure of our brain. The more we learn, the more developed and complex our brain becomes. In Wernicke's area of the brain, which deals with word understanding, the nerve cells have more dendrites in university-educated people than in people with only a secondary school education. Trainers should take the unique learning styles of course participants into account when designing training programmes. They should engage the visual, auditory, kinesthetic and emotional senses of learners.

See also **Brain hemispheres**.

References

DePorter, Bobbi (1998) *Quantum Learning for Business*. London, Piatkus.

DePorter, Bobbi and Hernacki, Mike (1993). *Quantum Learning: Unleash the genius within you*. London, Piatkus.

Meier, Dave (2000) *The Accelerated Learning Handbook*. New York, McGraw-Hill.

Rose, Colin and Nicholl, Malcolm J. (1997) *Accelerated Learning for the 21st Century*. London, Piatkus.

http://www.21learn.org/arch/articles/caine_interview.html

http://www.newhorizons.org/blab_diamond2.html

http://www.newhorizons.org/ofc_21clicaine.html

http://www.newhorizons.org/restr_bamburg1.html

http://www.newhorizons.org/ofc_21cliusebrain.html

http://www.sciam.com/explorations/020397brain/020397explorations.html

Brain hemispheres   The cerebral cortex of the brain is made up of two halves or hemispheres. The left hemisphere controls the right-hand side of the body and the right hemisphere controls the left-hand side of the body. Similarly, the visual field is split down the middle and crossed. The left visual field travels to the right side of the brain. The right visual field travels to the left side of the brain.

Much of what is known about brain function has been found by studying people with brain damage or split-brain patients after lobotomy operations. Damage in one side of the brain may result in malfunction or paralysis of the opposite side of the body.

It would be wrong to think that the two hemispheres are independent of one another. They are interconnected by the corpus callosum, the communication link between the two. The functions of the two hemispheres are not as specialised as was once thought. Most activities are processed by both sides of the brain. In fact about 40 per cent of left-handers process speech in both hemispheres. The verbal aspect of writing is logical, but the actual process of writing uses motor and visual skills.

Parts of the brain do, however, seem to specialise in specific skills. For example, Broca's area is devoted to the grammar and syntax of speech, whereas Wernicke's area is devoted to comprehension of the spoken and written word. In fact, Wernicke advanced the first evidence for the idea of distributed processing, which is the modern view of mental functions. He suggested that only the most primary mental functions –

those concerned with simple perceptual and motor activities – are localised to a single area of the brain. More complex intellectual functions result from interconnections among several functional sites. Broca's and Wernicke's areas are in different parts of the left hemisphere. Damage to these areas of the brain may adversely affect language skills, although other faculties such as intelligence and memory may remain intact.

Long-term memory and intelligence is spread over the entire cerebral hemisphere on both sides of the brain. Although writing is considered a left-brain skill, it is now known to require the co-operation of both sides. Using brain-scanning techniques, we now know that learning new information involves activity in the right hemisphere. On the other hand, recalling past memories involves the left hemisphere. Different activities stimulate different parts of the brain.

To stimulate the left brain, try doing the crossword puzzle in your daily newspaper. To stimulate the right brain, try doing jigsaw puzzles. Crossword puzzles help with speech and writing. Jigsaw puzzles can help with spatial skills such as map-reading. If you have good verbal skills, try drawing, painting or pottery. If you are more artistic, keep a diary or take up writing short stories. To get the most from your brain you need consciously to use both sides.

See also **Brain and learning**; **Cerebellum**; **Cerebrum**; **Left-brained**; **Right-brained**; **Triune brain**.

References
Beaumont, J. Graham (1994) *Brain Power: Unlock the power of your mind.* London, Grange Books.
Greenfield, Susan (1999) *Brain Power: Working out the human mind.* Shaftesbury, Element Books.
Ratey, John (2001) *A User's Guide To The Brain.* London, Little, Brown.
http://brain.web-us.com/aboutthebrain.htm
http://www.context.org/ICLIB/IC06/Gilman1.htm
http://www.med.harvard.edu/publications/On_The_Brain/Volume4/Number4/F95Lang.html.
http://www.newhorizons.org/ofc_21cliusebrain.html

Brain LION model   The LION model is an acronymic guide to things that should help keep your brain in tiptop condition. LION stands for Love, Information, Oxygen, and Nutrition.

■ *love* for belief and positive thinking – Dr Bruce Perry, using PET scans, found that Romanian orphans who are fed, kept clean, but live with no loving human contact, have by the age of 3 brains that are 25 per cent less developed than normal. It seems that tender loving care is vital to develop the brain and keep it in tiptop shape.

■ *information* for stimulating the brain – Use it or lose it: you must challenge the brain with new information, ideas, pursuits and activities. A study has found that after learning all the routes necessary to be a London taxi-driver, the part of the brain involved in remembering routes was bigger than in other people (source: the London *Times*, 14 March 2000).

- *oxygen* for life – Exercise is good for your body as well as your brain. The brain uses up to 20 per cent of the oxygen required by the entire body when at rest.

- *nutrition* for preventive maintenance – What we feed the brain is a significant factor in its well-being. The brain burns 25 per cent of the calories we consume, although it accounts for only 2 per cent of the body's weight.

See also **Brain**; **Vitamins and learning**.

References
Buzan, Tony and Buzan, Barry (1993) *The Mind Map Book*. London, BBC Books.
Malone, Samuel A. (1997) *Mind Skills for Managers*. Aldershot, Gower.
Ratey, John (2001) *A User's Guide To The Brain*. London, Little, Brown.
http://www.newhorizons.org/wwart_dee3.htm
http://www.newhorizons.org/ofc_21cliusebrain.html
http://www.epub.org.br/cm/n01/memo/growth.htm

Brainstorming   Brainstorming is a technique used for generating ideas in which members of the brainstorming group freely express ideas as they think of them. Alex Osborn developed the technique in 1938. Initially, the emphasis is on generating as many ideas as possible without critical analysis. Later on, the ideas can be considered and evaluated. It is often recommended as a means of stimulating creativity when a group is experiencing difficulties in generating new ideas or solutions to apparently intractable problems.

To generate ideas, the group should freewheel, cross-fertilise and suspend judgement. Initially the emphasis should be on quantity rather than quality of ideas. According to Osborn (1957) this is because the quantity of ideas will eventually yield quality. The facilitator should play the role of an angel's advocate rather than a devil's advocate in the early stages to encourage ideas. Group participants should build on previous ideas – called piggybacking – and look for ways of combining two or more ideas to generate a third. Piggybacking is therefore a form of free association. Later on, the critical faculties can be engaged to eliminate unsuitable ideas. Learning maps can be used as a tool to generate ideas on an individual or group basis.

Within a training situation, the trainer can use the technique of brainstorming to generate ongoing ideas and encourage involvement and interaction by using open-ended questions like 'What are the advantages and disadvantages of . . .?' or 'What problems would you expect to arise from . . .?' The trainer can either ask participants to shout out their answer or invite group discussion and put the result on a flipchart for analysis.

Metaplanning is a term used for a type of structured brainstorming.

See also **Ideas generation**.

References

McFadzean, Elspeth (2000) 'Techniques to enhance creative thinking', *Team Performance Management: An international journal*, Volume 6, Number 3/4, pp62–72.

Malone, Samuel A. (1999). Success Skills for Managers. Dublin, Oak Tree Press.

Osborn, A. F. (1957) *Applied Imagination*. New York, Scribner.

Rickards, Tudor (1997) *Creativity and Problem Solving at Work*. Aldershot, Gower.

Brain waves   Brain waves are tiny electrical impulses in the brain. They can be recorded and measured on an electroencephalograph machine (EEG). Electrodes are attached to the scalp and the brain waves are recorded in cycles per second. The brain thinks at different frequencies depending on what it is doing. Brain waves vary significantly between states of wakefulness and sleep.

The four types of brain wave are:

■ *beta waves* – Beta waves are the most common, and they happen when we are alert, during normal mental activities such as thinking through and analysing situations. This is the state you are in while at work discussing, negotiating, decision-making, and problem-solving. Beta waves occur at the highest frequency of between 13 and 30 cycles per second – they are the fastest whereas delta waves are the slowest. If you feel yourself blocked by a problem, you are almost certainly in a beta mode.

■ *alpha waves* – Alpha waves occur when we are relaxed and experiencing pleasant feelings. They occur at 8 to 12 cycles per second. Such waves correspond to a state of relaxed alertness. A lack of alpha waves suggests anxiety and stress. People learn faster and remember more when in a state of relaxed alertness. Baroque music by Bach, Handel, or Telemann creates an atmosphere of focused concentration in the alpha brain wave state. Learning vocabulary, memorising facts or reading to Baroque music is highly effective. You have your best ideas when in the alpha state. This is the reason that some people get their best ideas while taking a bath. Orienstein found that when a person was doing maths, the EEG showed that the left hemisphere was active and in beta mode. Yet the EEG also showed an increase in alpha mode in the right hemisphere. Alpha mode would thus seem to allow for better integration of the two hemispheres of the brain. In general, the brain waves of clever people are more co-ordinated and coherent. This facilitates high levels of mental functioning.

■ *theta waves* – Theta waves occur during moments of reverie, often just before we are about to fall asleep or before we actually wake up. They occur at a low frequency of 4 to 7 cycles per second. During the theta waves you can almost feel your brain processing the experiences of the day. They may also occur during daydreaming. People often get their most creative and inspiring ideas during theta waves. So if you focus on a problem before you go to sleep, the mind will work on the problem and may have a solution ready when you wake. This is why it is a good idea to have a notepad at the ready to record it. Theta waves occur naturally during periods of meditation.

■ *delta waves* – Delta waves occur during deep dreamless sleep, and at $\frac{1}{2}$ to 3 cycles per second. It is not possible to learn during sleep [see the entry **Sleep**]. However, there is some evidence to suggest that learning up to the time we actually fall asleep can be very effective. It seems that sleep consolidates learning, and the less activity and interference between the learning and the sleep the better.

References
Greenfield, Susan (1996) *The Human Mind Explained: The control centre of the living machine*. London, Cassell.
http://www.happychild.org.uk/acc/tpr/amz/001wave.htm

Breaks as an aid to memory   Psychologists have found that the attention span at its longest averages about 20 minutes. This would suggest that during a one-hour study period we should take two mini-breaks of, say, five minutes and then a major break of 10 minutes at the end. Such an organisation of study time would maximise the reminiscence effect. Several shorter study sessions are always more effective than one long study session when learning new material.

During each break take some physical exercise or get out in the air for about five minutes. Remember: the brain needs oxygen to stay sharp. Also, vary the methods of learning – for example, read, take notes, create learning maps, review and reflect and rehearse key learning points out loud. Discuss material with a study buddy.

References
Malone, Samuel A. (1996) *Learning to Learn*. London, CIMA.
Ukens, Lorraine L. (2001) *What Smart Trainers Know*. San Francisco, Jossey-Bass Pfeiffer.

Briefing and debriefing   Briefing consists of informing learners about the objectives, structure, and content of the course programme, explaining how it relates to learner and business needs, and outlining the expectations of managers as to how the learning can be used to improve business or job performance. Debriefing is finding out after the event if the learners' and business expectations were met, and how each learner proposes to implement the knowledge and skills learned to the workplace. Learning from course programmes is not beneficial to a company unless the learning is transferred to the job and performance improves – hence the relevance of action learning, with its emphasis on real workplace problems.

References
Malone, Samuel A. (2000) *Learning Skills for Managers*. Dublin, Oak Tree Press.
Mumford, Alan (1997) *Management Development Strategies for Action*. London, IPD.

Business games   Business games are a great way to learn about business and management. Some of them promote conceptual thinking and provide participants with a business overview. They can be used to simulate the functional departments of a business and how they interact to achieve corporate goals. Players may take on the roles of functional managers and may be constrained to operate within financial budgets, time deadlines and other restrictions including those associated with marketing, competition, demographics and limited resources. Teams may compete against other teams representing other companies. The computer can simulate the complexities of modern business – and so business games have taken on a new reality. The effect of strategies, actions and decisions can be fed back to participants in the business game. Games may take several rounds to complete, the decisions taken in each round affecting the outcome of subsequent rounds. Teams are awarded points or bonuses for achieving maximum profitability and coming up with innovative managerial strategies.

Business games may be used to teach strategy and planning skills, functional skills such as marketing and finance, and human behaviour skills such as leadership and communication. Teambuilding, interpersonal relationships and problem-solving skills can also be developed. The lessons learned in a business game may be transferred to an actual business. Games are best when complementing training, to act as an example, or to reinforce key concepts.

Games must have a specific learning objective, or they may prove to be a waste of time.

They are widely used in colleges to teach management, marketing, finance and economics. For example, Curland and Fawcett (2001) report that a computer-driven management simulation game has been used with students to develop finance, accounting and operational management skills. It has likewise enabled a number of restaurant management teams to compete in a simulated marketplace over an extended period of time. The skills developed included menu-pricing, competitiveness, running a business, food costing, analysing profit and loss, group decision-making, turning each setback into an opportunity, structuring accounts and logical thought.

In the workplace, many companies prefer to design their own business games or customise existing ones. Some managers take the view that the word 'game' sounds childish and trivial for serious training.

See also **Simulations**.

References

Craig, Robert L. (1987) *Training and Development Handbook, 3rd edition. A Guide to Human Resource Development.* New York, McGraw-Hill.

Curland, Sue R. and Fawcett, S. Lyn (2001) 'Using simulation and gaming to develop financial skills in undergraduates', *International Journal of Contemporary Hospitality Management*, Volume 13, Number 3, pp116–119.

Feinstein, Andrew Hale, Mann, Stuart and Corsun, David L. 'Charting the experiential territory. Clarifying definitions and uses of computer simulation, games and role play', *The Journal of Management Development*, Volume 21, Number 10, pp732–744.

Gilgeous, Vic and D'Cruz, Mirabelle (1996). 'A study of business and management games', *Management Development Review*, Volume 9, Number 1, pp32–39.

Prior, John (1991) *A Handbook of Training and Development*. Aldershot, Gower.

Buzz group   A buzz group is a small group set up to discuss and respond to workshop or lecture issues. Such groups usually consist of between two and six people. The term 'buzz' comes from the sound of the groups in discussion. A spokesperson may be appointed in each group to report back to the whole workshop or lecture assembly. This is a way of making lectures interactive and interesting.

See also **Lecture method**.

References

Huczynski, Andrzej (2001) *Encyclopedia of Development Methods*. Aldershot, Gower.

C

CAP model of learning types   The CAP model is an acronymic guide to the three basic types of learning:

- *cognitive* or *mental* learning, as involved with analytical and problem-solving skills
- *affective* learning, depending on feelings and attitudes, as involved with interpersonal skills
- *psychomotor* learning, as involved with manual skills.

Learning objectives can be classified under these three headings.

    See also **Attitude**.

References
Binsted, Don and Armitage, Susan (1994) 'Facilitating management learning with interactive video' in the *Handbook of Management Development*, edited by Alan Mumford, Aldershot, Gower.
Davies, Ivor K. (1971) *The Management of Learning*. London, McGraw-Hill.

Career anchors   Career anchors are the motives or drivers that push you forward to achieve the goals you aim for in your career. They flow from within you and spur you into action. Such anchors may include the prospect of better income or promotion, power, challenge, achievement, autonomy, affiliation, recognition, security, higher status or improved lifestyle. Schein (1990) defines a career anchor as a pattern of self-perceived talents, motives and values that serve to guide, constrain, stabilise and integrate individual careers.

    Different people have different career anchors. Schein – who has designed a career anchor questionnaire – puts forward the case for flexible reward, and/or promotion recognition systems to address the different needs of individuals. For example, people with a lifestyle anchor are likely to place a high value on flexible benefits. On the other hand, people with a security/stability anchor will be more biased toward pension schemes and steady incremental pay scales. The career anchors of a trainer may include the opportunity to apply technical skills and make a major contribution to the success of the business. Many self-employed trainers are motivated by the desire for independence, authority, challenge, and variety.

References
Chia, Yew Ming (2003). 'Career drivers for junior auditors: an exploratory study', *Managerial Auditing Journal*, Volume 18, Number 2, pp100–111.
Megginson, David and Whitaker, Vivien (1996) *Cultivating Self-Development*. London, IPD.
Schein, E. H. (1990) *Career Anchors – Discovering Your Real Values*. San Diego, Calif., Pfeiffer.
Yarnall, Jane (1998) 'Career anchors: results of an organisational study in the UK', *Career Development International*, Volume 3, Number 2, pp56–61.

Career counselling

Career counselling may be provided to support the personal development of staff who may need advice on what options for career development and promotion are available within the company and what degree and diploma courses are supported by the educational support scheme. Employees also need to know what training and development opportunities are available, and what facilities are available for developing other skills such as those necessitated by lateral moves between functions or departments.

Mentors may provide career counselling.

References
Cochran, L. (1997) *Career Counselling*. London, Sage.
Fee, Kenneth (2001) *A Guide To Management Development Techniques*. London, Kogan Page.

Career development

Career development involves setting out a plan for your future career and gaining experience and training to meet your career goals. Development of this kind is usually achieved with the help of your employer or an outside training or educational establishment. For most of us our work provides the main source of personal and career development. Our jobs, apart from technical skills acquired, usually provide us with opportunities to meet other people in a social context and develop key communication and interpersonal relationship skills. Good employers may also provide recreational, educational, and training and development opportunities.

Promotion opportunities in most organisations are now limited in comparison with the past, but there remain unlimited opportunities for personal and career development. Also, the day of the job-for-life is gone and we should really be developing skills ourselves that will make us more employable in the market generally, or will take us into the ranks of the self-employed, rather than relying on our employer to do it for us. In other words, you must find the advice and career counselling that you need, network with people who can help you achieve your career goals, seek out training and development opportunities that will keep you marketable, and develop a personal development plan. Continuous improvement and lifelong learning should be part of your strategy.

Career development may also be seen as a process with stages similar to the product lifecycle of introduction, growth, maturity and decline. Each of these stages brings its own challenges. Adults may seek out learning experiences to cope with specific life-changing events such as marriage, divorce, a new job, promotion, redundancy, bereavement, or moving to a new location. The more life changes in a learner's life, the more likely he or she is to seek out new learning opportunities.

References
Burgoyne, John (1999) *Developing Yourself, Your Career and Your Organisation.* London, Lemos & Crane.
Jackson, Tricia (2000) *Career Development.* London, IPD.
Megginson, David and Whitaker, Vivien (1996) *Cultivating Self-Development.* London, IPD.

Career drivers   See **Career anchors**.

Case studies   Case studies are scenarios based on actual problems experienced by organisations that are used as a vehicle for discussion, analysis and solution in management training. Managers study a written narrative about a situation that has confronted an actual or fictitious organisation. Relevant production, marketing, finance, and human resource data are usually provided. The description of the problem may contain all the information needed to suggest a solution. Alternatively, it may leave out certain important facts so that different solutions can be generated depending on the assumptions made. Case studies offer a less costly alternative to simulation, often with greater learning benefits. They provide a good vehicle for the development and exercise of judgement and problem-solving skills.

A case study may include the history of an organisation, the key management players, production information such as a production plan, financial information such as past trading, profit-and-loss accounts, cash-flow statements and balance sheets, marketing information such as a marketing plan, and details about competition. The managers are then asked to devise a solution based on assumptions about resources, economic and legal constraints, and to develop an implementation plan. Later, they are given feedback on their solution to ensure successful transfer of learning to their own organisations.

Case studies can be analysed individually or in groups. Analysed in a group, case studies give participants an opportunity to develop interpersonal relationships and collaboration and team skills. The purpose of a case study may be to illustrate a point and help learners discover principles or solutions for themselves. Case studies can also be drawn up based on the managers' own organisation's problems.

Case studies are an important aspect of MBA programmes and other business degrees.

See also **Simulations**.

References
Craig, Robert L. (1987) *Training and Development Handbook, 3rd edition, A Guide to Human Resource Management*. New York, McGraw-Hill.
Fee, Kenneth (2001) *A Guide To Management Development Techniques*. London, Kogan Page.
Prior, John (1991) *A Handbook of Training and Development*. Aldershot, Gower.
Reid, Charles W. and Kleiner, Brian H. (1996) 'Which training methods are effective?', *Management Development Review*, Volume 9, Number 2, pp24–29.

Categorisation   Categorisation is a way of organising a list into meaningful groups. One reason for doing it is in order to remember it better. For example, a grocery list might be categorised into vegetables, fruit, dairy produce, meats, and so on.

See also **Organisation of information**.

References
Rupp, Rebecca (1998) *Committed to Memory: How we remember and why we forget*. London, Aurum Press.

Cerebellum   The cerebellum is the part of the brain tucked behind the top of the brainstem and connected to the medulla, pons, and midbrain by large bundles of nerves. Cerebellum literally means 'small brain' and has a function in co-ordination and balance. Brain imaging research shows that the cerebellum is active during tasks such as word-generation, tactile discrimination, and the maintaining of information in working memory.

An emerging view of the cerebellum is thus that it plays a role in intellectual as well as perceptual-motor performance.

See also **Cerebrum**.

References
Ratey, John (2001) *A User's Guide To The Brain*. London, Little, Brown.
Turkington, Carol (1996) *The Brain Encyclopedia*. New York, Checkmark Books.
http,//www.newhorizons.org/blab_leiner.html

Cerebrum   The cerebrum has through evolution grown over the rest of the brain and forms a wrinkled layer of grey matter called the cortex. It is involved with the more complex brain functions, such as higher thought and decision-making. The cerebrum is arranged in two hemispheres, one on each side and accordingly known as the right and left cerebral hemispheres. The right hemisphere of the cerebrum controls physical aspects of the left-hand side of the body and the left hemisphere controls physical aspects of the right-hand side of the body.

Each cerebral hemisphere is divided into four lobes: the frontal lobe, the perietal lobe, the temporal lobe and the occipital lobe. Functions involving memory are thought to take place within the first three of these lobes. Damage to a lobe causes physical and/or mental disorder and disability in accordance with which lobe is involved and the nature and precise location of the damage.

The cerebral cortex – the part of the brain involved with planning, problem-solving and decision-making – is more open to learning throughout our lifetimes than other parts of the brain.

See also **Brain hemispheres**; **Cerebellum**.

References

Beaumont, J. Graham (1994) *Brain Power: Unlock the power of your mind.* London, Grange Books.
Greenfield, Susan (1996) *The Human Mind Explained: The control centre of the living machine.* London, Cassell.
Turkington, Carol (1996) *The Brain Encyclopedia.* New York, Checkmark Books.
File,\\C,Program Files\Britannica\BCD\/Cache_0_PreviewRil.htm

Certification   A relevant certificate proves that the holder has passed an examination and has achieved the basic knowledge and skills needed for particular job requirements. Many employers recognise the value of established qualifications for which certificates and other forms of documentation are issued. Certificates and similar documents may also be used to determine the suitability of candidates for promotion.

Some large companies operate their own training programmes rather than rely on external certification. Other companies through educational support schemes encourage employees to undertake certificate, diploma, degree, and post-graduate programmes for personal and career development. A few multinationals have their own corporate universities.

It is always better to invest time in a qualification with wide acceptance and recognition than in one that has no official standing.

See also **Accreditation**; **Credit Accumulation Transfer Scheme (CATS)**.

References

Fee, Kenneth (2001) *A Guide to Management Development Techniques.* London, Kogan Page.
Jarvis, Peter (2002) *The Theory and Practice of Teaching.* London, Kogan Page.
Whiddett, Steve and Hollyforde, Sarah (1999) *The Competencies Handbook.* London, IPD

Chunking   Chunking is a method of improving short-term memory by grouping long numbers or long lists of data into smaller chunks. Studies show that there is room in short-term memory for only seven items, plus or minus two. In experiments to recall a series of unrelated numbers or words, some people will recall nine, others five, but most will recall seven. Chunking may well increase the capacity of your short-term memory. Although most people still can remember only seven numbers or words, they can group the items in a meaningful way to form a chunk of memory. Each chunk may then act as one item within the short-term memory.

For example, if you want to remember your cheque account number, say,

5634820642, it may be more memorable for you to break it down into chunks as 56 3482 0642.

See also **Grouping**.

References
Higbee, Kenneth L. (1990) *Your Memory: How it works and how to improve it*. London, Piatkus.
Rupp, Rebecca (1998). *Committed to Memory: How we remember and why we forget*. London, Aurum Press.
Samuel, David (1999) *Memory: How we use it, lose it and can improve it*. London, Phoenix.

CIRO model of evaluation

CIRO model of evaluation   The CIRO model is an acronymic guide to what is involved in the evaluation of training. Suggested by Warr, Bird and Rackham in 1970, the acronym CIRO stands for Context, Input, Reaction, and Output.

- *context* – This includes a training needs analysis and involves setting objectives at the immediate (knowledge, skills and attitudes), intermediate (behaviour), and ultimate (corporate) levels.

- *input* – This includes resource deployment and utilisation, establishing value for money and opportunity cost criteria.

- *reaction* – This involves getting the opinions of course participants, maybe through the use of a questionnaire or by asking them informally. This would be an equivalent to the first of Kirpatrick's four levels: the reaction level.

- *output* – This involves establishing outcomes at the three levels of immediate, intermediate and ultimate levels. These correspond to Kirkpatrick's last three levels.

The main strength of the CIRO model is that the objectives (context) and the training equipment (inputs) are considered. However, the model does not measure behavioural change. It is mainly used for measuring the effectiveness of management training programmes.

See also **Kirkpatrick's model of evaluation**.

References
Tennant, Charles, Boonkrong, Mahithorn and Roberts, Paul A. B. (2002) 'The design of a training programme measurement model', *Journal of European Industrial Training*, Volume 26, Number 5, pp230–240.
Warr, P., Bird, M. and Rackham, N. (1970). *The Evaluation of Management Training*. Aldershot, Gower.

Coaching

Coaching   Coaching is a systematic one-to-one on-the-job form of training usually by a manager on behalf of a member of his or her staff. Coaching may, however, also be carried out off-the-job. The manager demonstrates and guides the member of staff through the activity, procedure or job task. Coaching is job focused and performance related: it aims to improve knowledge, skills or abilities so that the person being coached becomes better at doing a given task.

The key skills of coaching include listening with empathy, goal-setting, planning, reframing, and establishing commitment. Managers trained in coaching skills can help staff resolve problems and improve their job performance. In the past few years a profession of coaching has emerged. There are now personal coaches who can be hired to improve an individual's business performance. Personal coaches help people with their relationships, finances, problem-solving, stress management, presentations, negotiations, life decisions and career choices. They may operate as catalysts to an individual manager's self-development.

Coaching can be used as part of an integrated management development programme and in management succession planning.

See also **Mentoring**.

References

Fee, Kenneth (2001) *A Guide To Management Development Techniques*. London, Kogan Page.

King, Paul and Eaton, John (1999) 'Coaching for results', *Industrial and Commercial Training*, Volume 31, Number 4, pp145–151.

Mumford, Alan (1997) *Management Development, Strategies for Action*. London, IPD.

Whitmore, John (2002) *Coaching for Performance*. London, Nicholas Brealey.

http,//www.mithya.com/learning/cncoaching.html

http,//www.noontimeu.com/article3.html

http,//coachingandmentoring.com/Articles/mentoring.html

http,//www.free-press.com/journals/gajal/articles/publish/gajal-article-069.htm

Cognitivist theory of learning

Cognitivists are interested in how the mind makes sense of the environment. Perception, insight, imagination, meaning, and how information is processed, stored and retrieved, and the importance of language to our thinking process are key elements in the contribution of cognitive theory to learning. Rather than being passive, the human mind interprets information and gives meaning to events based on prior knowledge, experience and expectations.

Gestalt theory, which is part of cognitive theory, proposed looking at the whole rather than its parts, at patterns and conceptual frameworks rather than isolated events. For Gestalists, the locus of control (the mind's 'authority figure') lies with the individual. On the other hand, for behaviourists it lies with the environment.

Modern developments in cognitive theory include models of the memory system and of comprehension, computer simulations and artificial intelligence. Cognitivist principles are being applied to screen design in computers, for example, in the use of icons and hypertext. Cognitivist principles have also been applied to training such as the use of discussion groups (especially for problem-solving), presentations, written assignments and reflective reports.

Cognitive psychology offers several key principles to learning that can be recalled via the acronym PROFIT, which stands for Prior knowledge, Relationships, Organisation, Feedback, Individual differences, and Task perception.

- *prior knowledge* – To facilitate learning it is important that new information is linked to prior knowledge and experience.

- *relationships* – The whole is greater than the sum of its parts. Subjects have an inherent structure. Learners should try to see the links between key ideas and concepts. An important aspect of cognitive learning is insight, which arises when a person suddenly sees the link between concepts, understands an issue or perceives a solution to a problem. Learning maps can facilitate this process.

- *organisation* – Organised materials are easier to learn and remember.

- *feedback* – Learners need to know about their success or failure at the learning task as soon after the event as possible. Knowledge of results is a motivator and a type of reinforcement.

- *individual differences* – Different learning styles can influence the outcome of learning. Learning should be designed to cater for the different learning styles of learners.

- *task perception* – Learners have different perceptions and pick out different aspects of the environment. Learning should be designed and presented to engage as many of the senses as possible.

Key theorists of the cognitivist theory of learning include Kurt Lewin, Robert Gagne, Jerome S. Bruner and Jean Piaget.

See also **Behaviourist theory of learning; Constructivist theory of learning; Humanist theory of learning; Social theory of learning**.

References

Cheetham, Graham and Chivers, Geoff (2001) 'How professionals learn in practice: an investigation of informal learning amongst people working in professions', *Journal of European Industrial Training*, Volume 25, Number 5, pp247–292.

Merriam, Sharon B and Caffarella, Rosemary S. (1999) *Learning in Adulthood: A comprehensive guide*, 2nd edition. San Francisco, Jossey-Bass.

Yeo, Roland (2002) 'Learning within organisations: linking the theoretical and empirical perspectives', *Journal of Workplace Learning*, Volume 14, Number 3, pp109–122.

http,//www.learnativity.com/edpsych.html

http,//www.infed.org/biblio/learning-cognitive.htm

Comfort zones   Comfort zones are areas of thinking and experience to which we confine ourselves so as not to feel threatened, uneasy or 'out of our depth'. Only people who know they do not know everything will be curious enough to find things out by moving outside their comfort zones. Personal development comes from venturing beyond and expanding our comfort zones. People who succeed take risks and welcome new personal development opportunities. John F. Kennedy said, 'There are risks and costs to a programme of action. But they are far less than the long-range risks and costs of comfortable inaction.' Silberman (2001) maintains that we must move out of our comfort zones if we want to improve our interpersonal intelligence or people quotient (PQ).

Progress and growth are impossible if you always do things the way you've always done them. Being stuck in a rut will not help you advance in your career. First weigh up the considerations and then take the risks. Try to learn new things each year. Set yourself personal challenges daily. Continuous personal development and improvement should be your aim. Take up new challenges. Broaden your experience, reactivate your mind and put yourself in a stronger position for promotion in the future. Study new subjects for mental challenge and stimulation. Reading is a great way of keeping your brain in shape.

References
Malone, Samuel A. (1999) *Success Skills for Managers*. Dublin, Oak Tree Press.
Silberman, Mel (2001) 'Developing interpersonal intelligence in the workplace', *Industrial and Commercial Training*, Volume 33, Number 7, pp266–270.
Tracy, Brian (1993) *Maximum Achievement*. New York, Simon & Schuster.

Commitment   In a learning context, commitment is dedication to the learning task. According to Disraeli, 'The secret of success is constancy to purpose.' You must be committed to doing the things necessary to achieve your learning goals regardless of how difficult they may appear to be. Ghandi's lifelong commitment to non-violent protest as a means of achieving political objectives contributed hugely to the end of British rule in India. Edison said that genius is 1 per cent inspiration and 99 per cent perspiration. Obstacles often act as a spur to greater learning and achievement. Mary Anning was one of the world's first successful palaeontologists. At the end of the 18th century she was left to fend for herself when her father died. At the age of 12 she discovered and successfully excavated the skeleton of a complete ichthyosaurus. She also discovered the first complete plesiosaurus and the first pterodactyl. Her success was due to her persistence, knowledge and vision.

References
Malone, Samuel A. (1999) *Success Skills for Managers*. Dublin, Oak Tree Press.
Tracy, Brian (1993) *Maximum Achievement*. New York, Simon & Schuster.
http,//www.happychild.org.uk/acc/tpr/gtm.0103mann.htm

Community of practice   A community of practice in an organisation is a group of people who have, and who share, special knowledge about a particular function or service within the organisation. The group need not be made up of personnel from the same department, and the special knowledge may be shared informally. In fact, the sharing of knowledge is often done while simply chatting.

For example, customer service representatives who repair photocopiers might share experiences during informal meetings over breakfast, lunch and coffee. The group might swap stories about malfunctioning machines. The knowledge shared often goes beyond the codified knowledge in the repair manual. These informal exchanges are often worth more than several hours of formal training. Such tacit knowledge is created out of the experience of work and constitutes a type of social capital.

Some people make the distinction between 'know-what' and 'know-how'. Know-how includes the ability to put know-what into practice. HRM should put in place the conditions for creating and sustaining communities of practice. This is not easy to do because such groups tend to be self-selecting and informal.

References

Carter, Chris and Scarbrough, Harry (2001) 'Towards a second generation of KM? The people management challenge', *Education and Training*, Volume 43, Number 4/5, pp215–224.

Competencies   A competency is a combination of skills, knowledge, behaviours, and attitudes expressed in a way that can be observed and noted with a view to certification. It has been defined as a feature of a person's ability to perform a job effectively.

The Training Agency (1988) defines *competences* as 'Things that a person who works in a given occupational area should be able to do. Each one is an action, behaviour or outcome that the person should be able to demonstrate'. This definition has a behavioural emphasis and measures the output of learning.

The US approach in addition includes the underlying values or characteristics that contribute to the role. Boyatzis (1982) in *The Competent Manager* defines *competencies* as 'Those characteristics that differentiate superior from average and poor performance . . . motives, traits, skills, aspects of one's self-image or social role, or body of knowledge'. The US definition has a cognitive emphasis and is an input approach to designing learning.

The approaches have tended to merge in UK companies because of the influence of multinationals. In a work situation, competencies reflect the underlying characteristics of an employee that result in an acceptable or superior performance. Job descriptions are lists of the general tasks, or functions, and responsibilities of a position, whereas competencies list the abilities needed to conduct those tasks or functions. Hirsh and Strebler (1994) maintain that although different people argue over definitions, the notion of competence seems to have three recurring features:

- A competence exists in the context of a particular job or job role within a particular organisation.

- Competences are positively associated with superior performance.

- Competences can be described in terms of specific observed behaviours.

These days there is a competency approach to training. Competency models are emerging in many of the professions including accountancy, teaching and nursing. The approach has been heavily influenced by notions of scientific management, with its emphasis on measurement and work elements. In order to measure, things have to be broken down into small steps. This can lead to a focus on the parts rather than the whole, on the trivial rather than the important. The overall significance of the learning may be lost sight of.

Many training programmes now emphasise outcomes that show competencies of various kinds, rather than stressing that the course content may be interesting or enjoyable. In other words, the emphasis is on what the course participants will be able to do as a result of the training.

The six core competencies of management roles common to most organisations are:

- teamworking

- people management

- communication

- leadership

- problem-solving

- planning and organising.

Abraham *et al* (2001) found that the six competencies most critical to success in management were:

- leadership

- customer focus

- orientation towards results

- solving problems

- communication

- teamworking.

They also found that many firms are not appraising these competencies in their managerial performance appraisal processes.

Competencies for trainers would include:

- presentation skills

- an ability to set learning goals and objectives

- communication skills

- interpersonal relationship skills, including providing positive reinforcement

- computer literacy

- general business knowledge

- an ability to use questions to involve course participants

- an ability to identify training needs, design training programmes and evaluate outcomes

- an ability to blend different training techniques.

See also **Accreditation; Credit Accumulation Transfer Scheme (CATS); National Vocational Qualifications (NVQs); Self-efficacy**.

References
Abraham, Steven E., Karns, Lanny A., Shaw, Kenneth and Mena, Manuel A. (2001) 'Managerial competencies and the managerial performance appraisal process', *Journal of Management Development*, Volume 20, Number 10, pp842–852.
Armstrong, Michael (2000) *A Handbook of Human Resource Management Practice*. London, Kogan Page.
Brophy, Monica and Kiely, Tony (2002) 'Competencies: a new sector', *Journal of European Industrial Training*, Volume 26, Number 2/3/4, pp165–176.
Burgoyne, John (1999) *Developing Yourself, Your Career and Your Organisation*. London, Lemos & Crane.
Fee, Kenneth (2001) *A Guide To Management Development Techniques*. London, Kogan Page.
Garavan, Thomas N., Costine, Pat and Heraty, Noreen (1997). *Training and Development in Ireland*. Dublin, Oak Tree Press.
Hirsh, Wendy and Strebler, Marie (1994) 'Defining managerial skills and competences' in the *Handbook of Management Development*, edited by Alan Mumford, Aldershot, Gower.
Hoffmann, Terence (1999) 'The meanings of competency', *Journal of European Industrial Training*, Volume 23, Number 6, pp275–286.
Roberts, Gareth (2002) *Recruitment and Selection: A competency approach*. London, CIPD.
http,//www.infed.org/b-comp.htm
http,//scholar.lib.vt.edu/ejournals/JVTE/v12n2/leach.html

Comprehension Comprehension is an intelligent grasp of the meaning of a situation or action. It is the ability to translate information into meaningful ideas. Memorisation without comprehension is of little value. There is no learning without comprehension.

The basic principles behind comprehension can be recalled by means of the acronym MICRO, which stands for Meaning, Interest, Critical issue, Rapport, and Overview.

- *meaning* – The more meaningful you find information, the easier it is to learn it.

- *interest* – The more interest you take in a subject, the easier it is to learn it.

- *critical issue* – The more you identify critical or key issues and separate them from unimportant detail, the easier it is to learn even a complex subject.

- *rapport* – The greater your rapport with the subject or the better you know a subject, the easier it is to learn more about it.

■ *overview* – Seeing the big picture and linking new information to it is important to learning.

See also **Understanding**.

References
Malone, Samuel A. (1996) *Learning to Learn*. London, CIMA
Swiercinsky, Dennis P. (1995) *Fifty Ways You Can Improve Your Memory*. Mission, World Wisdom Inc.
http,//www.pvc.maricopa.edu/lac/guest/memory.html

Computer-based training (CBT)   CBT relies on computer-assisted instruction techniques to train adults for specific skills such as proficiency on a keyboard or accountancy. Comparative studies suggest that the learning effectiveness of CBT is superior to that of conventional training – people learn faster and retain more: some studies show a 50 per cent reduction in the time required to learn. This is because the learner can:

■ choose his or her own pace of learning, and so take the most efficient path to learning the content

■ interact and receive feedback – the courseware is specially designed to provide reinforcement by giving plenty of practice. In some courses learners are not allowed to progress until earlier stages have been mastered.

Although technology is an important tool in communication and learning, however, it cannot replace the quality and personal touch that human interaction brings to learning. Nor can computers teach ethics, morality, compassion, social skills and personal responsibility. In addition there may be a significant cost in hardware and software.

References
Malone, Samuel A. (1997) *How To Set Up and Manage a Corporate Learning Centre*. Aldershot, Gower.
Reid, Charles W. and Kleiner, Brian H. (1996) 'Which training methods are effective?', *Management Development Review*, Volume 9, Number 2, pp24–29
Sloman, Martyn (2001) *The E-learning Revolution*. London, CIPD.

Concentration   Concentration may be defined as focused attention. Concentration is learning how to cope with, manage and eliminate distractions. Distractions can be categorised as internal distractions and external distractions. Internal distractions include daydreams, wishful thinking and spontaneous thoughts. External distractions relate to the physical environment in which you are studying.

According to psychologist Mihaly Csikszentmihalyi, the highest level of concentration achievable is 'flow'. It corresponds to a state in which you are totally absorbed in an activity. It is an intensified state of concentration, or focused attention. People in this state are highly centred on the task in hand, and often literally forget the passage of time. People who achieve 'flow' are usually very interested in the task, they love doing the task, and the task consumes all their mental and physical energy and focus.

Use creative visualisation to get rid of irrelevant thoughts, concerns, daydreams and negative feelings. Visualise yourself learning successfully. Psych yourself up to the learning task by saying to yourself, 'My concentration is very sharp; I am fully concentrated; every day in every way my concentration gets better and better.' Nothing will focus your concentration more than the actual process of beginning the learning task.

Newton's most famous work, the *Principia Mathematica* (1687), is often said to be the single most important book published in science. When he was asked how he made the astonishing discoveries in the book, he replied 'By thinking on it continually.'

Michelangelo (1475–1564) was a sculptor, painter and architect, a man of genius comparable to the great Leonardo da Vinci. Michelangelo had a remarkable ability to concentrate his thoughts and energy on the task in hand. Often while working he would eat very little, would sleep on the floor beside his unfinished painting or statue, and continue to wear the same clothes until he finished his work.

The brain requires sufficient quantities of vitamin B2 (riboflavin) to help in concentration. Vitamin B2 is found in chicken, almonds, spinach, milk and dairy products. Conversely, a lack of iron in the food you eat will cause feelings of listlessness and so affect your ability to concentrate. Meat products, green vegetables and nuts are rich in iron.

See also **Attention**; **Attention span**; **Flow**.

References
Hermann, Douglas J. (1995) *Super Memory: A quick-action programme for memory improvement*. London, Blandford.
Malone, Samuel A. (2000) *Learning Skills for Managers*. Dublin, Oak Tree Press.
http,//www.pvc.maricopa.edu/lac/guest/memory.html

Conference   A conference is the meeting together of a group of people from the same organisation or from different organisations to discuss and explore issues of common concern. Problem identification, discussion and solution are often the objectives of a conference. However, a conference is also used to exchange information and to improve co-operation. It is possible to meet people from different organisations with different experiences and perspectives. Conferences are also a great source for networking opportunities. Many academic, professional and trade bodies hold annual conferences to update their members.

References
Fee, Kenneth (2001) *A Guide To Management Development Techniques*. London, Kogan Page.
Malone, Samuel A. (2000) *Learning Skills for Managers*. Dublin, Oak Tree Press.

Confidence   Confidence is the belief that you will do what you mean to do – in the learning context, the belief that you have the innate ability to learn in formal and informal situations. Conversely, lack of confidence is synonymous with self-doubt, negative attitudes and self-imposed psychological limitations. Confidence and the need for respect are crucial in providing a foundation for learning. In Maslow's famous 'hierarchy of needs', considerable importance is given to self-esteem and self-actualisation, or becoming what you are capable of becoming.

Self-confidence is the first requisite for undertaking great deeds. Build on your strengths and work to eliminate your weaknesses. Think about the successes you've had in life rather than the failures. See mistakes as learning opportunities and convert threats to challenges. In examinations start with the easiest questions before working your way to the more difficult ones – this ensures that your level of confidence will increase as the exam progresses. Trainers have an important role in nurturing the self-confidence of learners who attend their programmes.

See also **Beliefs**.

References
Davies, Philippa (1996) *Total Confidence: The complete guide to self-assurance and personal success.* London, Piatkus.
Malone, Samuel A. (1999) *Success Skills for Managers.* Dublin, Oak Tree Press.

Constructivist theory of learning   The constructivist theory suggests that learners construct their own knowledge from their experience, mental models and beliefs. This implies that what is learned depends on the way you look at things. The theory was put forward by John Dewey and other innovators. They maintained that meaningful learning relies on active engagement in planning, problem-solving, communicating, and creating, rather than on rote memorisation and repetition. Learning is a process by which people make sense of their environment and personal history. The acquisition of new knowledge is affected and shaped by prior knowledge, interaction with others, experience, and inherited predispositions. Our ability to learn is also influenced by logic, emotion, intuition, and motivation.

According to the constructivist view, knowledge is relative rather than absolute. New paradigms replace old as new theories and discoveries are made. The basic philosophy underlying this view is that knowledge must be presented in a meaningful context to facilitate effective learning.

The trainer's role is thus to act as a learning facilitator, to engage the interest of learners and to get them actively to seek out and discover knowledge. In the decontextualised setting of the training room, the responsibility of the trainer is to relate the learning to the practical work situations to which the learners will return. Learners are primarily responsible for their own learning.

The constructivist theory of learning has been applied to experiential learning, self-directed learning, discovery learning, and notions of the role of reflection in learning. Life experience is seen as a resource and stimulus to learning. Practical activities supported by group discussion form the core of many training and development programmes. Adult training is a process of negotiation involving the construction and exchange of relevant information. We must talk and debate with others to test our understanding.

See also **Behaviourist theory of learning**; **Cognitivist theory of learning**; **Humanist theory of learning**; **Social theory of learning**.

References
Mezirow, Jack (1991) *Transformative Dimensions of Adult Learning.* San Francisco, Jossey-Bass.
Merriam, Sharon B. and Caffarella, Rosemary S. (1999) *Learning in Adulthood: A comprehensive guide*, 2nd edition. San Francisco, Jossey Bass.
Wells, G. and Chang-Wells, G. L.. (1992) *Constructing Knowledge Together: Classrooms as centres of inquiry and literacy.* Portsmouth, NH, Heinemann.
http,//www.21learn.org/publ/edleadership1999.html
http,//www.21learn.org/acti/trlearning.html
http,//www.learnativity.com/edpsych.html

Continuous assessment
Continuous assessment, if not actually continuous, is the assessment of a trainee or learner at frequent intervals during a course. This may be complementary to, or instead of, end-of-term exams.

See also **Continuous professional development (CPD)**.

References
Jarvis, Peter (2002) *The Theory and Practice of Teaching.* London, Kogan Page.

Continuous improvement and learning
Continuous improvement and learning is a training ideal that could theoretically become part of the ideal culture of an organisation.

You should never be satisfied with your current level of learning and memory but should try to improve all the time. You should view your life and work as an ongoing learning programme. Your goal should be to work smarter not harder. Through observation, experimentation, reflection and continuous feedback, you can improve your learning performance. You will need standards of excellence and learning objectives for comparison purposes.

Senior managers should act as role models for their staff by exemplifying continuous learning. Some senior managers are reluctant to reveal that they need to continue learning. They often feel they have nothing more to learn.

Quality improvement teams are an excellent way to achieve continuous incremental improvement and learning because they unlock human and intellectual potential. Organisations should establish structures, processes and programmes for continuous learning and promote a culture of self-development and lifelong learning. Employees should be encouraged and facilitated to develop learning-to-learn skills. These provide the foundation for lifelong learning.

See also **Learning-to-learn skills**; **Learning organisation**.

References
Malone, Samuel A. (2000). *Learning Skills for Managers*. Dublin, Oak Tree Press.
Mumford, Alan (1997) *Management Development Strategies for Action*. London, IPD.
Mumford, Alan (1994) 'Effectiveness in management development' in the *Handbook of Management Development*, edited by Alan Mumford, Aldershot, Gower.
http,//www.mapnp.org/library/trng_dev/design/cont_lrn.htm

Continuous professional development (CPD)

Most professional bodies now run continuous development programmes for their members to help them keep up to date through structured learning experiences. These structured learning experiences can be run in-company or by the professional institutes themselves. Such schemes also help trainers, developers, and managers to develop professional staff in their organisations.

CPD interventions help maintain and improve personal and organisational effectiveness in a rapidly changing work environment. CPD means lifelong learning with a strong element of self-direction and self-management.

References
Fee, Kenneth (2001) *A Guide To Management Development Techniques*. London, Kogan Page.
Malone, Samuel A. (2000) *Learning Skills for Managers*. Dublin, Oak Tree Press.
http,//www.free-press.com/journals/gajal/articles/publish/gajal-article-079.htm

Co-operative learning

Co-operative learning – also known as collaborative learning – is what takes place when a trainer trains by helping learners to help each other, and therefore corresponds to group, team or project learning. Individuals often learn better collaborating with others than they would on their own. Co-operative learning allows course participants with different skills and experiences to discuss and share ideas, to help each other and arrive at group decisions. They can also network and adopt useful role models. They may go on to develop or refine their teambuilding, communication, interpersonal relations, empathy, social awareness, and problem-solving skills.

Intense competition produces anxiety, which can interfere with learning. Learners are more attentive, comprehend better, produce more work, and are more favourable to the training method when they work co-operatively in groups rather than compete as individuals. Trainers should, however, be aware that co-operative learning has pitfalls as well as benefits.

To avoid the pitfalls the trainers should:

- set clear terms of reference and time limits for group tasks
- help groups establish and differentiate roles and tasks

- keep in touch with groups as the work progresses

- actively facilitate the whole learning process

- inform each group what outcomes are expected at the end of the process.

Some colleges now encourage students to co-operate on personal assignments to reap the benefits of collaborative learning.

See also **Study buddies**; **Study circles**.

References
Cheetham, Graham and Chivers, Geoff (2001) 'How professionals learn in practice: an investigation of informal learning amongst people working in professions', *Journal of European Industrial Training*, Volume 25, Number 5, pp247–292.
Malone, Samuel A. (2000) *Learning Skills for Managers*. Dublin, Oak Tree Press.
http,//www.ets.uidano.edu/aded5/4/adultlearner/dm109.htm

Corporate university   El-Tannir (2002) defines a corporate university as 'a function or department in the company that develops the skills for employees, and integrates them into the strategic orientation of the corporation with strong emphasis on leadership and improved work-related performance'. Such 'universities' have emerged over the past few years as part of the concept of the 'learning organisation'. The increased availability of web-based learning has accelerated the process, providing organisations with a huge learning resource for virtual learning, not only for their own employees but also for their customers and suppliers. Some people argue that corporate universities are merely existing training and development departments within companies repackaged or rebranded. Others see them as a way of facilitating lifelong learning rather than one-off training events and awarding qualifications based on competence. They also provide opportunities for greater collaboration and alliances between industry and educational establishments.

Some companies are developing special MBA programmes with the help of business schools. It is believed that there are about 1,800 corporate universities in the world including Motorola, Cisco and, in the UK, Unipart.

References
Adam, Debra (2001) 'Learning from experience – making the most of work-based learning', *International Journal of Contemporary Hospitality Management*, Volume 13, Number 5, pp235–240
El-Tannir, Akram A. (2002) 'The corporate university model for continuous learning, training and development', *Education and Training*, Volume 44, Number 2, pp76–81.
Fee, Kenneth (2001) *A Guide To Management Development Techniques*. London, Kogan Page.
Rossett, Allison (2002) *The ASTD E-Learning Handbook*. New York, McGraw-Hill.
Sloman, Martyn (2001) *The E-learning Revolution*. London, CIPD.

Corpus callosum   The corpus callosum is a thick bundle of nerve fibres in the brain which provides a communication link between the two cerebral hemispheres lying above it on each side.

See **Left-brained**; **Right-brained**.

References
Greenfield, Susan (1999) *Brain Power*. Shaftesbury, Element Books.
Turkington, Carol (1996) *The Brain Encyclopedia*. New York, Checkmark Books.

CRAMP model of on-the-job learning skills

The CRAMP model is an acronymic guide to the type of skills that most of us have to develop for learning on-the-job. Devised by the Industrial Training Research Unit Ltd, the acronym CRAMP stands for Comprehension, Reflex action, Attitude, Memorisation, and Procedural learning.

■ *comprehension* – You need an understanding of how business works and how the economy operates – more specifically, how your department interfaces with the other departments within the company, and how the company interfaces with competitors in the industry. Such knowledge underlies decision-making and problem-solving.

■ *reflex action* – You need to acquire skill in work activities and be quick in perception of what is going on around you (also known as kinesthetic abilities). That is, you need skill, speed and dexterity in doing job tasks – keyboarding skills are a good example of such abilities in combination. This is one of the seven intelligences listed by Howard Gardner.

■ *attitude* – You need to become aware of the culture of your company as reflected in the way it conducts business and treats customers and staff. Personally, a positive attitude will be reflected in the service you provide. If a company treats its staff well, they in turn will treat the customers well.

■ *memorisation* – You need to memorise the names of people in other departments that you have dealings with, and those in branches or other companies within the organisation, and you need to memorise codes, prices, safety regulations and company policies and rules.

■ *procedural learning* – You need to know how the policies, processes, systems and procedures in the company operate: this will enable you to do your job more efficiently and effectively.

References
Malone, Samuel A. (2000). *Learning Skills for Managers*. Dublin, Oak Tree Press.
Prior, John (1991) *A Handbook of Training and Development*. Aldershot, Gower, published in association with the Institute of Training and Development.

Creativity

Creativity is creating something that wasn't there before – including seeing novel relationships between things, ideas and people. The creativity is often in the novel combination of existing ideas or thinking about things in an unconventional way. The single most important element in the creative process is thus originality or uniqueness.

Creativity is a key part of learning. We can learn from our own creativity and from studying the creativity of others. Learning how to use your creativity is a most important aspect of learning-to-learn skills. A notable creative genius was the scientist Thomas Edison who patented over 1,000 commercial products including the electric light bulb and gramophone.

Creativity is not the same as intelligence. A person can be far more creative than intelligent, or far more intelligent than creative. Entrepreneurs, illustrators, actors, musicians, fashion designers, landscapers and artists are some of the people who have to be creative in their jobs. In the modern dynamic business environment, employees and managers need to be creative and innovative to come up with new ideas and improvements on products and processes. This is why training in creativity is so important.

Barriers to creativity can be recalled by means of the acronym SCALABLE, which stands for Self-imposed barriers, Conformity, Afraid to challenge, Looking a fool, Anxiety, Belief in oneself, Looking for one answer, Evaluating too quickly.

- *self-imposed barriers* – Preconceptions in our imagination often act as self-imposed barriers. Sometimes you have to go outside the box to get a new perspective.

- *conformity*, or coming up only with the answer expected – It is the unusual or unexpected that tends to be or to trigger off the best ideas. Both Isaac Newton and Albert Einstein believed that playfulness was an essential part of creativity. Humour can often stimulate groups to develop creative ideas.

- *afraid to challenge the obvious* – Sometimes you have to force yourself to go beyond the familiar or obvious if you want to come up with novel ideas.

- *looking a fool* in front of other people – People are often constrained by what they feel other people will think of them.

- *anxiety* – Too much and too little stress can inhibit creativity. An optimum amount of stress is needed for best results.'Ice-breakers' and energisers can be used to relax people and stimulate them to be more creative.

- *belief* – Without belief in your own unique ability to generate worthwhile ideas you are unlikely to get far.

- *looking for the one right answer* – Our logical minds are always looking for the one right answer, whereas in real life there are many alternative ways of doing things and solving problems.

- *evaluating too quickly* – Hasty conclusions stifle innovative solutions: sleep on it and let your subconscious process the problem for best results.

New ideas may be triggered off by means of the acronym CAMPERS, which stands for Combine ideas, Adapt a product, Modify a product, Put to other uses, Eliminate unnecessary parts, Rearrange, and Simplify.

- *combine two different ideas* to create a new whole – For example, drug development requires the best ideas of biologists, chemists, geneticists and clinicians. Their insights combine and create novel solutions none of the scientists could come up with on his or her own.

- *adapt an existing product* to meet the customised needs of a customer – For example, cars can be customised to meet the unique requirements of a customer.

- *modify an existing product* to meet a new purpose – For example, cameras have undergone many changes during the past few years. Today, we have compact, disposable, Polaroid, digital and video cameras.

- *put to uses other than the original intention* – For example, memory cards are now used instead of film for storing pictures in a camera.

- *eliminate unnecessary parts* or procedures – For example, you might redesign a form by eliminating information that is no longer required.

- *rearrange* to create a new synthesis – For example, supermarkets are now offering financial services which were previously only the remit of banks.

- *simplify* an existing procedure by reducing unnecessary complexity – James Dyson, the English inventor, introduced his revolutionary bagless vacuum cleaner on to the UK market in 1993.

The stages of creativity are:

- preparation – Define the problem and get the facts.

- effort – Generate suggestions and ideas, alternatives or options.

- incubation – Think them through and sleep on it.

- insight – The sudden breakthrough, the 'Aha!' feeling or Eureka!

- evaluation – Test it against logic and practicability. Will it work?

Edward De Bono, the inventor of lateral thinking, has suggested the following approach – known as the 'the Six Thinking Hats' – to make teams more creative:

- White-hat thinking – This is about getting facts, figures and information to solve a problem or make a decision. A white-hat thinker might say, 'Let's get all the facts before we go any further.'

- Red-hat thinking – This is concerned with hunches, feelings, intuition and emotions. The red hat allows people to express their feelings without any need to justify them. A red-hat thinker might say, 'I've got a hunch this idea will work.'

- Black-hat thinking – This is about caution, negativity, logic and critical judgement. It is useful because it helps people avoid silly mistakes. A black-hat thinker might say, 'The board will never accept this proposal because it is too expensive.'

- Yellow-hat thinking – This is for logic, optimism, and taking a positive point of view. The yellow hat looks for the benefits and for ways of making ideas work. A yellow-hat thinker might say, 'It's true that this system will take some time to work, but it will revolutionise our business and reduce our costs.'

- Green-hat thinking – This is about creativity and progressing things forward. The green hat gives the go-ahead to generate alternatives and explore ideas. A green-hat thinker would say, 'We need to explore new possibilities.'

- Blue-hat thinking – This is about managing the thinking process so that it becomes more productive. The chairperson or facilitator of the meeting usually wears this hat. The blue-hat thinker would say, 'Let's review where we are before we go any further.'

Edward De Bono has also put forward another interesting idea to avoid closed thinking. To keep things open we should categorise ideas into 'Plus', 'Minus', and 'Interesting'.

Williams (2001) reports that creativity can be taught.

See also **Analogies**; **Brainstorming**; **Ideas generation**; **Metaphors**.

References

De Bono, Edward (1990) *Six Thinking Hats*. London, Penguin Books.
McFadzean, Elspeth (2000) 'Techniques to enhance creative thinking', *Team Performance Management, An international journal*, Volume 6, Number 3/4, pp62–72.
Rickards, Tudor (1997) *Creativity and Problem Solving at Work*. Aldershot, Gower.
Rawlinson. J. G. (1970). *Creative Thinking And Brainstorming*. London, British Institute of Management.
Stine, Marie Jean (2000) *Super Brain: Six keys to unlocking your hidden genius*. New York, Prentice Hall.
Williams, Scott (2001) 'Increasing employees' creativity by training their managers', *Industrial and Commercial Training*, Volume 33, Number 2, pp63–68.
http,//www.21learn.org/arch/articles/fritz.html
file,//C,\Program Files\Britannica\BCD\Cache_13_PreviewRil.htm

Credit Accumulation Transfer Scheme (CATS)
CATS is a scheme in which educational institutions recognise each other's programmes for credits towards exemptions from similar programmes. Credits may also be awarded for

learning demonstrated in practice. Hamill and Sutherland (1994) report that the Credit Accumulation Transfer Scheme was introduced by the Council for National Academic Awards (CNAA) in 1986. The principal aims of the CAT Scheme were:

- to provide additional opportunities for students to develop

- to introduce greater flexibility into the curriculum

- to enable organisations to negotiate provision to suit their training needs

- to allow the award of credit for prior learning or learning undertaken outside educational institutions.

The chief advantage of the CAT Scheme approach is that the levels of credit required are universally agreed. For example, CIPD diploma-holders may be awarded credit points towards a degree or Master's qualification. There are two forms of recognition:

- Accreditation of Prior Learning (APL) may be given by a college, based on successful completion of recognised formal programmes. Relevant in-company programmes may be acceptable.

- Accreditation of Prior Experiential Learning (APEL) may be given, based on work experience evidenced by a portfolio of relevant documentation. The evidence should cover each element, satisfying each performance criterion, across the range specified. Assessed skills acquired on-the-job may count towards a formal qualification. In such circumstances qualifications may be completed faster.

These schemes are in line with lifelong learning and continuing professional development (CPD). They make further education more accessible to working adults pursuing part-time certificate, diploma, degree and post-graduate qualifications.

See also **National Vocational Qualifications (NVQs)**.

References

Adams, Debra (2001) 'Learning from experience – making the most of work-based learning', *International Journal of Comtemporary Hospitality Management*, Volume 13, Number 5, pp235–240
Hamill, John and Sutherland, John (1994) 'Accrediting prior learning, Part 1: Its nature and potential', *Education and Training*, Volume 36, Number 4, pp27–30.
Reid, Margaret Anne, Barrington, Harry and Kenney, John (1992) *Training Interventions*. London, IPM.

Criterion-referenced instruction (CRI)

CRI is a comprehensive set of methods for the design and delivery of training programmes. The framework was developed by Robert Mager.

The main aspects are:

- goal/task analysis – This identifies what is to be learned.

- performance objectives – These represent an exact specification of the outcomes to be achieved and the criteria for evaluation of those outcomes.

- criterion-referenced testing – The learning is evaluated against the knowledge/skills specified in the objectives.

- learning models – These are developed in relation to specific objectives.

Although applicable to any form of learning, CRI has been applied mostly to technical training.

References
Craig, Robert L. (1987) *A Training and Development Handbook, 3rd edition, A Guide To Human Resource Development.* New York, McGraw-Hill.
http,//tip.psychology.org/mager.html

Critical incident technique

The critical incident technique focuses on those tasks or job behaviours that have a critical effect on the success or failure of a job. Developed during World War II by John Flanagan, an American psychologist, its purpose was to investigate why errors were made during bombing missions over Germany and to discover ways of improving the training of the aircrew to eliminate such errors.

Flanagan (1954) first described his technique as a set of procedures for collecting direct observations of behaviour to solve practical problems and develop broad psychological principles. An incident is defined as any observable human activity sufficiently complete to permit inferences and predictions to be made about the person who is carrying out the activity. To be critical, an incident must occur in a situation where the purpose and consequences are clear to the observer. It is particularly valuable when constraints on training time force the trainer to concentrate on the vital or critical aspects of job performance. For example: a simple thing like a procedural check might be essential in a process where the repercussions of a mistake in the process may be very costly or indeed fatal. On the other hand, too many checks are inefficient and only add cost.

Critical incident techniques can be used for:

- describing skilled performance in terms of effective and ineffective behaviour

- identifying effective behaviours to be included in training programmes

- conducting a job analysis for performance appraisal

- identifying key learning skills

- identifying sources of errors so that corrective action can be taken to eliminate them

- identifying behaviours that please or displease customers when dealing with the company

- identifying human relations problems in the organisation, such as poor communication, interdepartmental conflicts, personality conflicts and inappropriate decision-making and problem-solving skills.

Data collection relating to critical incidents can be carried out in many ways, including personal interviews, focus group interviews and direct observation.

References

Edvardsson, Bo and Roos, Inger (2001) 'Critical incident techniques: towards a framework for analysing the criticality of critical incidents', *International Journal of Service Industry Management*, Volume 12, Number 3, pp251–268.

Flanagan, J. C. (1954) 'The critical incident technique', *Psychological Bulletin*, Volume 51, Number 4, pp327–358.

Garavan, Thomas N., Costine, Pat and Heraty, Noreen (1997) *Training and Development in Ireland*. Dublin, Oak Tree Press.

Truelove, Steve (1992) *A Handbook of Training and Development*. Oxford, Blackwell Business.

Cross-functional learning   See **Projects**.

Crystallised intelligence   Crystallised intelligence is intelligence acquired through education, culture, upbringing and knowledge. Examples of crystallised intelligence include vocabulary, numerical reasoning and the ability to evaluate one's own experience. Tests of crystallised intelligence are not timed.

Wisdom, which is an example of crystallised intelligence, improves with the years. That is why judges and chief executives tend to be middle-aged and older. Fluid intelligence shows a steady decline from adolescence to middle age, but this can be compensated for by an increase in crystallised intelligence.

See also **Fluid intelligence**.

References

Malone, Samuel A. (2000) *Learning Skills for Managers*. Dublin, Oak Tree Press.

Whalley, Lawrence (2001) *The Ageing Brain*. London, Weidenfeld & Nicolson.

File,//C,\Program Files\Britannica\BCD\Cache_5_PreviewRil.htm

Cues   Cues are devices you use to help you remember something. For example, a learning map may be used as a device to organise material and remember it better when making a presentation. Mnemonics are cues to help us remember lists of items. With the right cue, the information can be retrieved from memory.

The reason we cannot remember something may well be that the wrong cue has been used. An example of cue-dependent forgetting is when a person can't remember a fact until something 'jogs' his or her memory.

Cue cards containing formulae, key learning points or mnemonics, reviewed frequently, are a great memory booster for exams.

References
Gruneberg, Michael M. and Hermann, Douglas J. (1997) *Your Memory for Life*. London, Blandford.
Malone, Samuel A. (1996) *Learning to Learn*. London, CIMA.

Curiosity   Curiosity is the highly beneficial attitude of childlike desire to know why things are as they are. Children do have an inherent curiosity about everything and an amazing capacity to learn. They have the habit of prefacing everything they say with the marvellous word 'Why?' It is a characteristic that can be embarrassing to adults who sometimes cannot answer the questions posed, and who rather than admit their ignorance often respond in a discouraging fashion. Consequently the child eventually gives up asking questions, and natural curiosity is stifled rather than encouraged.

As Francis Bacon said, 'Wonder is the seed of knowledge.' To become successful learners we must rediscover this natural curiosity for knowledge and learning. Seeking out answers to questions is an active form of learning, as opposed to a passive form, and is thus more effective and meaningful.

As a trainer you should arouse learners' curiosity and get each learner open and ready for learning. To do this you must:

- give people case studies or challenging problems to solve in teams

- run question-and-answer sessions

- encourage people to ask questions

- design and run self-discovery learning projects for learners

- ask course participants to explore issues.

See also **Discovery learning**.

References
Malone, Samuel A. (2000) *Learning Skills for Managers*. Dublin, Oak Tree Press.
Meier, David (2000) *The Accelerated Learning Handbook*. New York, McGraw-Hill.

Cybernetic model of learning   The cybernetic model sees learning as comprising four parts: input, processing, output, and a feedback loop. The feedback loop provides information about the effects of the output. The principle of feedback loops is also used in single-loop and double-loop learning.

Some psychologists, making an analogy with computers, believe we have only serial processing capability. This means that we can deal with only one piece of information at a time. Others believe we have some parallel processing capacity, which means we can perform several mental tasks at the same time. Whatever the truth, it does suggest that our capacity to process information is limited.

See also **Information overload; Miller's seven plus or minus two rule**.

References

Cheetham, Graham and Chivers, Geoff (2001) 'How professionals learn in practice: an investigation of informal learning amongst people working in professions', *Journal of European Industrial Training*, Volume 25, Number 5, pp247–292.

D

Deep learning Deep learning occurs when learners seek meaning and understanding in study, reflect on what they read and hear, draw conclusions, and make the knowledge their own by relating it to prior knowledge, experience and goals. Memory plus comprehension equals effective learning.

Deep learning is needed if you want to move from mere knowledge to understanding. It is a type of transformational learning. Students are more likely to engage in deep learning if they have a liking for and an interest in the subject under study, if they have developed critical thinking skills such as problem-solving, decision-making, and conflict resolution, and if they believe they have control over their own learning. Prior knowledge and experience may affect the learning strategy adopted. For example, where previous knowledge is inadequate, learners are more likely to adopt surface approaches.

Some scientific studies suggest that strength of memory depends on how deeply information is processed, not on how long it is processed. This means reflecting and elaborating on the information to make it meaningful by linking it with something you know already. For example, you will learn a telephone number quicker if you notice that the numbers include (for example) your home address, the numbers on your car's registration plate, the date of a famous historical event or the date of your partner's birthday. Trainers can promote deep learning by emphasising principles and concepts rather than facts. Encouraging learners to use learning maps also helps the process by showing the relationships between key concepts. Trainers should also use advance organisers, and anchor ideas to learners' personal experience and prior knowledge.

See also **Double-loop learning**; **Surface learning**; **Transformational learning**.

References
Hassall, Trevor and Joyce, John (2001) 'Approaches to learning of management accounting students', *Education and Training*, Volume 43, Number 3, pp145–153.

Knasel, Eddy, Meed, John and Rossetti, Anna (2000) *Learn for Your Life: A blueprint for continuous learning.* London, Pearson Education.
Warburton, Kevin (2003) 'Deep learning and education for sustainability', *International Journal of Sustainability in Higher Education*, Volume 4, Number 1, pp44–56.
http,//www.newhorizons.org/lrnbus_marchese.html
http,//www.web-us.com/memory/improving_memory.htm

Déjà vu   Déjà vu is a mysterious feeling of having experienced something before.

Demonstrations   A demonstration is a physical example of an application or a procedure, delivered with commentary by an expert, so that people watching can do it themselves afterwards. As a method of teaching it is sometimes called the tell-show-and-do method.

To be a good demonstrator, you must be competent in the techniques of demonstration, know how people learn, know how to explain things clearly, have a friendly but directive teaching style, know how to handle questions, and know how to analyse participants' problems, provide feedback and give positive reinforcement.

A manager will benefit by learning how to break down a task into logical teachable units and how to present them in a clear and understandable way. This method is highly appropriate to teaching the use of software packages on a PC.

References
Fee, Kenneth (2001) *A Guide To Management Development Techniques.* London, Kogan Page.
Malone, Samuel A. (2000) *Learning Skills for Managers.* Dublin, Oak Tree Press.
Taylor, C. (1988) *The Art and Science of Lecture Demonstration.* London, Adam Hilger.

De-roling   De-roling is a way of signalling the end of a particular role in role-play. One signal indicates the end of the time period permitted, and a second indicates the completion of the task set. Depending on the type of roles, badges or coats might be removed to signify closure. Some people find it difficult to shed roles, and de-roling is thus necessary to help them come out of the role.

See also **Role-play**; **Role reversal**.

References
Thiagarajan, Sivasailam and Stolovich, Harold D. (1978) *Instructional Simulation Games.* New Jersey, Educational Technology Publications.

Development   Development is the process of preparing a person to take on more onerous responsibilities or equip him or her for future promotion within the organisation. Training, on the other hand, is a planned and systematic way of improving a person's knowledge, skills and attitudes so that he or she can perform the current job more competently. Development thus has a longer-term orientation than training.

Development is also the outcome of transformational learning. Through development we adopt new perspectives, become more discriminating and are able to deal with a broader range of experiences and challenges.

References
Fee, Kenneth (2001) *A Guide to Management Development Techniques.* London, Kogan Page.
Jackson, Tricia (2000) *Career Development.* London, IPD.
Mumford, Alan (1997) *Management Development Strategies for Action.* London, IPD.

Development centres   A development centre – which is an event, not a location – focuses on the development of managers rather than on selection, as an assessment centre does. Managers will be more relaxed and willing to avail themselves of the services of the centre if they know that the emphasis is on career counselling and identifying their own development needs rather than on the assessment or evaluation of management potential.

The output of a development centre is feedback in the form of a personal development plan, which will also go towards assisting managers to develop their career plans. In other words, it will help managers identify their development needs, draw up learning objectives, design personal development plans, monitor progress and identify their learning styles. Managers may thus identify their own unique aptitudes and potential, clarify their strengths and note any weaknesses that must be addressed. Psychological profiling may be used to do this. Participants may be offered further training and development or assigned a mentor to support their subsequent development.

The development centre philosophy is in line with empowerment, by which managers take responsibility for their own development and career progression.

See also **Assessment centres**.

References
Fee, Kenneth (2001) *A Guide To Management Development Techniques.* London, Kogan Page.
Mumford, Alan (1997) *Management Devevelopment, Strategies for Action.* London, IPD.
Wilson, Dean (1996) 'The future for development centres', *Career Development International*, Volume 1, Number 6, pp4–11.

Diagnostic instruments   Diagnostic instruments are devices for self-analysis, self-awareness and learning. They come usually in the form of questionnaires that you complete to find out your strengths and weaknesses in a particular area. From a manager's perspective they provide useful feedback to help him or her learn more effectively.

Make sure the instruments you use are from a reliable source and have been validated. The application and interpretation of some diagnostic instruments needs the guidance of an occupational psychologist.

The Honey and Mumford Learning Styles Questionnaire can determine which are your learning styles. The four styles are: *activist, reflector, theorist* and *pragmatist.*

Psychometric tests may be taken to determine attitude or abilities in specific areas. They are based on the assumption that certain qualities such as personality, attitudes, competencies, preferences and values can be measured with reasonable scientific accuracy. Such tests are often used to determine people's suitability for certain jobs.

The Myers-Briggs ® Type Indicator is a psychometric test that assesses four dimensions of personality. These are: *extroversion* or *introversion*; *sensing* or *intuiting*; *thinking* or *feeling*; and *judging* or *perceiving*. The model helps you become aware of the type of person you are and what particular strengths you have to offer.

There are several instruments for diagnosing team roles. These include Belbin's, the Margerison-McCann Team Management Index and the Strength Deployment Inventory. Although they are designed specifically for teams, they also provide important insights for personal development. The McBer Management Styles Questionnaire helps you become aware of your leadership style. The six styles are: *coercive*, *authoritative*, *affiliative*, *democratic*, *pace-setting* and *coaching*.

As well as getting feedback from your manager, you may also get feedback from your work colleagues. This is called 360-degree feedback. Some companies may include customers, suppliers, and other stakeholders in the feedback process.

See also **Learning styles questionnaire (LSQ)**; **Myers-Briggs ® Type Indicator**.

References
Burgoyne, John (1999) *Developing Yourself, Your Career and Your Organisation.* London, Lemos & Crane.
Fee, Kenneth (2001) *A Guide To Management Development Techniques.* London, Kogan Page.
Mumford, Alan (1997) *Management Development, Strategies for Action.* London, IPD.
http,//www.anbar.co.uk/courseware/mba121-003.htm

Discovery learning   Discovery learning places the responsibility for learning on the learner. Trainees are given just enough information to discover accurately for themselves how to perform tasks. The trainer must be discreet enough to know when his or her help is required and when he or she should withdraw into the background. In a formal setting, discovery learning is done through case studies, simulations, role-play and reflection. Learners must discuss and debate what they are learning, write about it, reflect on it, relate it to their prior experience and apply it to their jobs. Learners learn by finding out principles and relationships for themselves. The more relevant the learning, the more likely it is to be applied. The trainer becomes a facilitator and designer of the learning process that encourages this approach for the learner. Selected examples are presented first, and principles only when the learner has understood the concepts. It can be used with groups as well as individuals. However, it can be costly in terms of time. Perhaps accordingly, this is probably the most successful method for training older people in industry.

Curiosity is a great learning motivator. Learning is not a spectator sport. The emphasis in this approach is on the learner to discover and formulate his or her own understanding of a topic. This has two benefits:

■ People have to decide what to do – and this helps to register the learning in long-term memory.

■ People learn at their own pace – and this means they can sort out any problems. They learn for themselves rather than being taught directly by a trainer.

See also **Curiosity**.

References
Bicknell-Holmes, Tracy and Hoffman, Paul Seth (2000) 'Elicit, engage, experience, explore: discovery learning in library instruction', *Reference Services Review*, Volume 28, Number 4, pp313–322.
Fee, Kenneth (2001) *A Guide To Management Development Techniques*. London, Kogan Page.
Prior, John (1991) *A Handbook of Training and Development*. Aldershot, Gower, published in association with the Institute of Training and Development.

Distance learning   Distance learning takes place at a distance from the preparer and presenter of the learning material. The terms 'flexible learning', 'open learning' and 'distance learning' are used interchangeably and mean more or less the same thing. They come in a variety of formats including correspondence courses, telecourses, interactive television, and web-based instruction. The material is of a high quality and is produced with the needs of the learner in mind.

Correspondence courses were the original distance learning programmes. They were essentially text-based and were widely used by the accountancy and other business professions. The courses offered by the Open University are probably the best-known examples of distance learning. The development of information and communications technology has made it possible to offer these and other programmes over the Internet supported by audiovisual content.

The main advantages of distance learning are flexibility, cost and time savings, and staff motivation. People learn at their own time, place, and pace and retain more information, and learners are more likely to take responsibility for their own learning and be proactive in their own development. Distance learning presupposes that students have the discipline, time management and study skills needed to organise themselves. This is not always the case, however, and the attrition rate for such courses is high.

In the case of companies that prepare their own correspondence material for training, such material remains a valuable resource for the company. Distance learning can be supported by workshops and coaching.

See also **Open learning**.

References
Evans, Chris and Fan, Jing Ping (2002) 'Lifelong learning through the Virtual University', *Campus-Wide Information Systems*, Volume 19, Number 4, pp127–134.
Fee, Kenneth (2001) *A Guide To Management Development Techniques*. London, Kogan Page.
Malone, Samuel A. (1997) *How to Set Up and Manage a Corporate Learning Centre*. Aldershot, Gower.
Tarr, Madeleine (1998) 'Distance learning – bringing out the best in training', *Industrial and Commercial Training*, Volume 30, Number 3, pp104–106.
White, Alasdair (1998) *The Essential Guide To Developing Your Staff*. London, Piatkus.
http,//www.careerexplorer.net/articles/distancesolution.asp

Double-loop learning

Double-loop learning, also known as generative learning, involves creativity and innovation, going beyond just adapting to change to being ahead of, anticipating change. The generative process leads to a total reframing of an organisation's or a person's experiences, and learning from that process. For a company it may involve developing a new business, new products or new markets. At a personal level a religious conversion or an alcoholic's conversion to a sober lifestyle are examples.

Double-loop learning is a type of transformational learning, reframing or paradigm shift. In double-loop learning the person or company re-evaluates the nature of the objectives, underlying norms and policies, and the values and beliefs surrounding them. Existing ways of doing things are examined and alternative ways explored and tested, and new ways implemented if appropriate.

This type of learning involves drastically changing a person's values, attitudes and beliefs. In the case of a company, it involves changing the organisation's culture, redefining its vision and mission, the wholesale revision of systems, and alterations in strategy.

In single-loop learning, the problem is addressed purely at the operational levels, whereas in double-loop learning there is a reconsideration of policy and more strategic goals. Single-loop learning is analogous to a thermostat adjusting to a pre-set temperature, while double-loop is analogous to the questioning of whether the thermostat is set at the right temperature.

Double-loop learning is necessary for an organisation to survive in a rapidly changing environment.

See also **Single-loop learning**; **Transformational learning**.

References
Argyris, Chris (1999) *On Organisational Learning*. Oxford, Blackwell Business.
Butler, Jim (1994) 'Learning design for effective executive programme' in the *Handbook of Management Development*, edited by Alan Mumford, Aldershot, Gower.
http,//www.infed.org/thinkers/argyris.htm
http,//www.infed.org/thinkers/el-schon.htm
http,//www.newhorizons.org/article_oxford1.html

E

Educational psychologist   Educational psychologists are concerned with the diagnosis of educational potential, problems of individual adjustment and, increasingly, the social aspects of educational life and school organisation. The educational psychologist may also be concerned with teaching aids, teaching methods, the study of cognitive development and other ways of helping people learn more effectively. Research in educational psychology encompasses such diverse topics as gender differences in ability and learning, ways to help dyslexics read and learn better, and the effects of stress on learning.

See also **Experimental psychologist**.

References
http,//www.findarticles.com/cf_0/g2602/0002/2602000219/print.jhtml

E-learning   E-learning ('electronic learning') is learning that is organised through the Internet or an intranet. Some colleges offer certificate, diploma, degree and post-graduate programmes via this medium. 'Web-based training' is the term used to describe training packages offered on the Internet. Virtual classrooms may be used to link course participants in different locations with their tutor. Learning material may be presented using multimedia. Chat rooms may be used to enable people to talk to each other. This can be augmented by video or audio conferencing.

E-learning may not be suitable for everyone but it can be integrated with other forms of learning. This is called blended learning.

The benefits of E-learning include:

■ Learning can be more focused on the needs of the learner and presented on a just-in-time basis.

■ Learning can be enhanced through the use of multimedia.

■ Learning can be provided off-the-job in the learner's own home or elsewhere.

- Learners can interact with other learners and with their tutor.

- Learning is self-paced and generally at times to suit the learner.

Cost savings and convenience are the strongest drivers for the corporate uptake of e-learning. Forrester Research identified the perceived benefits of e-learning in a sample of the Fortune Top 2,500 companies as: cost savings, availability anywhere any time, provision of just-in-time learning, increased instructor availability, ease of use, fast distribution, self-paced learning, and ease of changes in content. The perceived obstacles were: lack of interactivity, cultural resistance, bandwidth limitations, difficulty in measuring return on investment, browser problems, firewalls, and problems with standards. Forrester recommends more evaluation, more individual tracking and more use of intranet tailoring, plus increased richness of content.

On the downside, e-learning is but one of a succession of supposed panaceas for learning that include programmed instruction, audio, video, television, computer-based instruction and the Internet. All of these have failed to live up to the hype. They partly facilitate learning but are not complete solutions in themselves. At the end of the day it is not possible to replace trainer contact and the social interaction of collaborative learning satisfactorily with technology.

See also **Video conferencing**.

References

Fry, Kate (2001) 'E-learning markets and providers, some issues and prospects', *Education and Training*, Volume 43, Number 4/5, pp233–239.
Malone, Samuel A. (2003) *How to Set Up and Manage a Corporate Learning Centre*, new edition. Aldershot, Gower.
Sloman, Martyn (2001) *The E-learning Revolution*. London, CIPD.

Emotional intelligence   Aristotle was aware of the importance of what is now known as emotional intelligence: he said that those who possess the rare skill 'to be angry with the right person, to the right degree, at the right time, for the right purpose, and in the right way are at an advantage in any domain of life'. Emotional intelligence is part of both intrapersonal and interpersonal intelligence and plays a significant role in social development.

Emotion is the trigger mechanism for almost everything that we do. Emotion drives attention, which in turn drives learning, memory and behaviour. The term 'emotional quotient' (EQ) is now used to quantify emotional intelligence.

Goleman (1995) describes five major aspects of emotional intelligence as:

- knowing one's emotions

- managing one's emotions

- motivating oneself

- recognising emotions in others

- handling relationships.

Emotional intelligence is one of the key factors to career and personal success. Goleman (1995) indicates that intelligence (as measured by IQ) at best contributes only about 20 per cent of the factors that determine success in life. Leaders tend to be more intelligent than the average group member, but not the most intelligent. Emotional intelligence is the ability to handle one's own emotions through self-awareness, be able to motivate oneself to get things done, be able to recognise emotions in others, and be able effectively to manage yourself and relate to other people. The importance of the role that plays in effective learning is now accepted.

Insensitive managers low in emotional intelligence often manage through fear, criticism, bullying, threats and coercion. Competent managers are persuasive, assertive, decisive, sensitive and good communicators. With training, practice and determination, emotional intelligence can be developed throughout life. Although the core emotional capabilities are laid down in early childhood, the brain is plastic and capable of being developed and changed. Psychologists and salespeople are usually very sensitive to the needs of others; poets and mystics are in tune with their own feelings and emotions. Some autistic or psychopathological people are completely insensitive to the emotional needs of others. Trainers need skills in conflict management, negotiation, listening, facilitation, assertiveness and stress management to be successful.

Socrates said, 'Know thyself,' by which he meant that we have to understand our emotions and learn how to control them. We need to temper our emotions with reason. Emotion without reason and control is a recipe for disaster. On the other hand, we don't want to become like *Star Trek*'s Mr Spock, who has no emotion but lives by pure reason. A more harmonious balance between reason and emotion would help us lead more productive and fulfilling lives.

The psychologist Edward Thorndike defined three types of intelligence as far back as in 1927, including social and emotional intelligence.

- abstract intelligence – This is the type of intelligence measured by IQ tests. It involves understanding and manipulating verbal and mathematical concepts.

- concrete intelligence – This involves understanding and manipulating objects and shapes.

- social intelligence – This is the equivalent to emotional intelligence. It involves understanding and relating well to people, and is clearly important in any type of teamwork.

The key points of emotional intelligence, as based on Goleman's research, can be recalled by means of the acronym FARCE, which stands for Feelings, Attitude, Relationships, Control, and Empathy.

- *feelings* – Self-awareness and self-understanding are a crucial part of emotional intelligence. How can we understand other people if we don't understand ourselves? People who know themselves are more in control of their lives and have a sure sense of their identity and self-worth and where they are going in life. Knowing yourself puts you in a better position to understand and empathise with others.

- *attitude* – Psychologists have defined attitude as 'an internal emotional orientation that explains the actions' of a person. Attitude has a major influence on behaviour. People with a positive attitude can often recover quickly from illness and the ups and downs of life. Negative thinkers find it difficult to shake off feelings of anxiety and doom and gloom. Positive thinkers see weaknesses as potential strengths and threats as opportunities. They see problems as challenges to be overcome and mistakes as learning opportunities.

- *relationships* – Being good at interpersonal relationships is useful in any occupation, but especially for those who deal a lot with people. For example, managers need to demonstrate good communication, inspirational, empathy, leadership and teambuilding skills if they want to succeed in their careers. They must be able to manage difficult employees and handle conflict situations. Some people with a high IQ often lead an unsuccessful life because of their self-centredness, high expectations and inability to relate effectively with others.

- *control* – Being in control of your emotions means that you can postpone gratification and stifle impulsive behaviour. Self-control means being aware of your inner feelings and recognising when your reactions are exaggerated, out of control and non-productive. People with out-of-control emotions do things that impact negatively on themselves and others during their lives.

- *empathy* – Empathy is being tuned into other people's feelings. In 1850, William Hazlett said, 'To get others to come into our ways of thinking, we must go over to theirs; and it is necessary to follow in order to lead.' Americans have a saying, 'Before you criticise someone, walk a mile in his shoes.' Empathy means that in your imagination you become the other person. Empathy is the foundation of emotional intelligence. It builds openness, mutual respect and trust in relationships. These skills are particularly needed in the caring professions, such as religion, nursing and psychology. By being kind and empathetic you build cordial and lasting relationships with your friends, work colleagues and with your customers. Empathetic people listen and empathise, but do not drown people with sympathy.

Nick Zenuik, a former senior executive with the Ford Motor Company, once said, 'Emotional intelligence is the hidden competitive advantage. If you take care of the soft stuff, the hard stuff takes care of itself.'

See also **Emotions and learning**; **Intelligence tests**; **Learning**.

References

Armstrong, Thomas (1993) *Seven Kinds of Smart: Identifying and developing your many intelligences.* London, Plume.

Dulewicz, Victor and Higgs, Malcolm (2000) 'Emotional intelligence – a review and evaluation study', *Journal of Managerial Psychology*, Volume 15, Number 4, pp341–372.

Goleman, Daniel (1995). *Emotional Intelligence.* London, Bloomsbury.

Langley, Andrew (2000) 'Emotional intelligence – a new evaluation for management development', *Career Development International*, Volume 5, Number 3, pp177–183.

http,//www.managementfirst.com/training_and_development/art_eq.htm

Emotions and learning   Learning is a very emotional process. To learn we must see, feel, experience and do. Surprise, happiness, fear, anger, disgust, and sadness, are our primary emotions. Embarrassment, jealousy, and guilt, are some of our secondary or social emotions.

The seat of the emotions is the limbic system of the brain. It is connected to the frontal lobes, which have an important role in learning. Learning can therefore be enhanced or speeded up if there is an emotional involvement with the subject to be learned. For example, students have no problem learning about things that interest them, such as football, movie stars or rock musicians. The more emotions are involved, the more information is registered in the brain. On the other hand, people don't like learning something they find boring. People learn things that they feel are useful and interesting, and that meet their current wants and needs.

Logic engages the left-hand side of the brain whereas emotions engage the right-hand side of the brain. Emotions drive attention, which in turn drives learning, memory, problem-solving and concentration. Scientists as far back as Sir Francis Bacon (1561–1626) believed that events linked with emotions were best remembered.

Some studies suggest that emotion exerts state-dependent effects on recall – that we shall best be able to recall a memory if we are in the same mood as when we experienced the original event. Emotions can help focus and intensify the level of concentration. We are more likely to remember situations in which our emotions are heightened, such as waiting for an important decision to be made or an important letter to arrive, or our wedding day. Most of us will never forget the events of 11 September 2001 when the Twin Towers were destroyed by terrorist activity in New York. Information that is processed by both the right and left sides of the brain is more likely to be remembered. Action learning, which employs visual, auditory and tactile senses, facilitates integrated learning and may engage the emotions. Teamworking and business games may have the same effect.

References

Baddeley, Alan (1991) *Human Memory: Theory and practice.* London, Lawrence Erlbaum Associates.
Beaver, Diana (1994) *Lazy Learning: Making the most of the brains you were born with.* Shaftesbury, Element Books.
Ostrander, Sheila and Schroeder, Lynn (1999) *Super-Learning 2000.* London, Souvenir Press.
Rose, Colin and Nicholl, Malcolm J. (1997) *Accelerated Learning for the 21st Century.* London, Piatkus.
http,//www.newhorizons.org/blab_sylwester01.htm
http,//www.brain.com/about/article.cfm?id=21106&cat_id=400
http,//www.findarticles.com/cf_0/m1254/6_32/67884315/print.jhtml

Empowerment   In a management context, empowerment is allocating staff members with the tools and resources to further the interests of the organisation. It assumes that management is prepared to share power, and that the employees in turn are prepared to take responsibility for it. Empowerment is a mechanism for investing responsibility in individuals and teams. It is the process of fostering beliefs of self-efficacy among employees. This implies both removing sources of powerlessness and providing employees with positive feedback and support. It encourages employees to be self-directed learners and to take responsibility for their own learning, thus providing them with more job satisfaction. It encourages team learning and knowledge-sharing.

A company or group cannot become a learning organisation without a commitment to empowerment – without delegating the power to solve problems independently. Continuous improvement depends on the initiative workers get from being empowered. The result is a self-reinforcing cycle: empowerment results in improvements and learning which further empowers. Empowerment is a principal goal of most forms of employee involvement.

See also **Learning organisation**.

References

Field, Laurie (1997) 'Impediments to empowerment and learning within organisations', *The Learning Organisation*, Volume 4, Number 4, pp149–158.
Malone, Samuel A. (1999) *Success Skills for Managers.* Dublin, Oak Tree Press.
Smith, Jane (1996) *Empowering People.* London, Kogan Page.

Empty-chair technique   The empty chair technique involves imagining a person about whom you have unresolved feelings (perhaps your manager) sitting on a chair opposite you, and having a conversation with him or her to thrash matters out. Still in the imagination, the roles are then reversed: you imagine what the other person would say to you in response. The result should at least be an increased understanding of the other person's viewpoint. The imagined conversation can be continued, back and forth, for as long as is useful.

It is a technique that has been borrowed from Gestalt therapy for use in training situations.

See also **Role-play**; **Role reversal**.

References
http,//danielson.laurentian.ca/drnotes/4516cn10.htm

Encoding   In a learning context, encoding is a term for the process by which information is recorded in memory. For example, a person memorises a word through vision, sound and meaning. You see the words and note how it is structured and spelt; you pronounce the word and you understand its meaning. All three aspects must be addressed if you want to get the word into long-term memory. To remember a person you must encode how they look, the sound of their voice, and some contextual information relating to them such as their name, interests, occupation and nationality.

One method to transfer information from short-term to long-term memory is to use elaborative encoding. Elaborative encoding involves any mnemonic process that helps you connect new information to information you already have, such as an acronym or story sequence to connect the items you want to recall, or the memory-placement system as developed by the ancient Greeks (by which you mentally store items in known physical locations).

Recent scanning research shows that the brain activity associated with encoding occurs in the left cerebral hemisphere.

References
Schwartz, Barry and Reisberg, Barry (1991) Learning and Memory. New York, WW Norton.
http,//www.web-us.com/memory/theories_and_processes.htm

Energisers   Energisers are exercises or games that raise the level of physical and mental alertness in course participants. They are particularly suitable for afternoon sessions when people's concentration levels are falling.

Enthusiasm for learning   To be successful in learning – as indeed to be successful in anything – you need plenty of enthusiasm. The main factors that contribute to enthusiasm in learning may be recalled by means of the acronym DREAM, which stands for Desire, Relevancy, Expectation, Anticipation, and Motivation.

- *desire* – You must really want to learn. Desire comes from an enthusiasm for the subject and an ambition to become an expert in the particular field.

- *relevancy* – The learning must be relevant to your present needs. For example, if you work as a middle manager, an MBA or professional qualification would be most relevant to your current and future career prospects. You must also be able to see how the knowledge learned can be applied on a day-to-day basis in the work situation. Application reinforces the knowledge and makes the learning more meaningful.

- *expectation* – You must have high expectations of success. Ask and you will receive. Seek and you shall find. Knock and the door will be opened to you. Believe and you will achieve. The self-belief must be matched by hard work and dedication to learning.

- *anticipation* – Anticipate in your mind's eye the feelings you will experience when you are successful. Constantly keep this in front of you. Imagine the pride you will feel and the respect you will gain from work colleagues when you eventually achieve that MBA!

- *motivation* – There are two types of motivation: towards and away from. Towards motivation is better, for this motivation works on the prospect of achieving the MBA and the success in your career that the achievement is likely to bring you. Away from motivation can also be useful, but centres on the pain of rejection and lack of progress that you are likely to encounter in your career if you *don't* get that MBA! Obviously, a combination of towards and away from motivation brings the best of both worlds.

References
Malone, Samuel A. (200) Learning Skills for Managers. Dublin, Oak Tree Press.

Environments for learning
An environment that is non-threatening and friendly facilitates learning. A learning organisation supports learning. A bureaucratic culture inhibits and does not promote learning. For many people Baroque music played at a low level in the background creates the right mindset for learning.

A trainer exhibits psychological support for a learner by:

- displaying a caring attitude so that participants feel appreciated, safe and supported; learning is more likely to take place in a caring and trusting environment

- valuing learners' views, experience, uniqueness, and participation – the trainer may learn as much from the learners as they do from the trainer: the law of reciprocity states that if the trainer displays trust and respect for the learners, they in turn will trust and respect the trainer

- displaying enthusiasm for learning: enthusiasm is contagious – the trainer must remember that he or she is the role model

- actively listening – the reason you have two ears and one mouth is so that you can listen twice as much as you speak: the trainer should provide regular feedback so that participants know how they are doing

- encouraging an open atmosphere in which participants can learn from each other – an atmosphere of openness, transparency and involvement: such an environment fosters intellectual freedom and encourages experimentation and creativity

- making it evident that learning from mistakes is a perfectly valid way to learn using genuine praise as a positive reinforcement to learning

- encouraging participants to take responsibility for their own learning

- making the learning challenging for participants – best is to challenge learners to go just beyond their present level of ability; if challenged too much, people give up – if challenged too little, they become bored

- making sure the physical learning environment is suited to the task – this includes the physical layout of the room, the acoustics, temperature and sightlines.

References
Honey, Peter and Mumford, Alan (1996) *How to Manage your Learning Environment*. Maidenhead, Peter Honey.
Malone, Samuel A. (2000) *Learning Skills for Managers*. Dublin, Oak Tree Press.
http,//ericacve.org/docs/adt-lrng.htm
http,//www.newhorizons.org/article_billington1.html

Episodic memory   The episodic memory is the mind's sequencer: it places events in time and facts in order. It provides sequence to the memories of episodes in our lives, such as our first day at school, our first date and our wedding day. In many societies, storytelling and the oral tradition as passed on through the elders is an example of using episodic memory. PET studies show that episodic memory is processed on the right side of the brain.

References
Baddeley, Alan (1991) *Human Memory: Theory and practice*. Hove, Lawrence Erlbaum Associates.
Rupp, Rebecca (1998) *Committed to Memory: How we remember and why we forget*. London, Aurum Press.

Estrogen and memory   See **Oestrogen and memory**.

Evaluation   In a training context, evaluation corresponds to assessing the financial, social and cost-effectiveness of a training course. Evaluation of training is normally distinguished from validation, which is concerned with training effectiveness in the form of the achievement of training objectives. The great majority of organisations do not systematically evaluate training. The only form of evaluation carried out by most organisations is by collecting end-of-course reactions.

In practice trainers rarely have the time, budget resources or evaluation expertise to do scientific evaluations. They concentrate on running programmes rather than verifying that such programmes are effective or good value for money.

So why evaluate? Some of the main arguments include:

- to justify costs incurred – Training competes for scarce budgetary resources with other functions within the business. In times of economic recession the training budget is usually the first to be cut. The training function must be able to present a favourable cost/benefit analysis to resist those cuts.

- to improve training design – Without evaluation it is difficult to see which training programmes should be retained and improved and which should be discarded.

- to improve training methods – There are different approaches to training such as on-the-job, off-the-job, learning centres, and e-learning. Without comparative analysis and evaluation techniques it is impossible to make rational decisions about the training method to employ and the cost-effectiveness of each.

- to keep up with other functions in the use of evaluation techniques – For example, the finance function has a whole range of evaluation techniques such as capital investment appraisal (discounted cash-flow), return-on-investment ratio analysis and break even analysis. Training, in comparison, has few.

A systematic evaluation model would include:

- a needs analysis to identify exactly what training or learning is required to achieve business objectives

- the formulation of training and learning objectives

- design of training and learning events intended to meet those objectives: such events could be on-the-job or off-the-job, formal or informal, or a combination of these approaches

- an evaluation of training – Has the training worked? Have objectives been achieved? Has the learning been transferred to the work situation? Has the performance, efficiency, productivity, and profitability of the organisation improved as a result? What cost/benefit is the training department to the organisation? How can the training be improved?

There are three types of evaluation techniques:

- interviews – Trainers, course participants or course participants' managers can be interviewed before, during, or after the training. Interviews can be structured or unstructured.

- questionnaires – Questionnaires can be used to evaluate at several levels. They can be qualitative or quantitative and involve self-assessment or objective measures.

- quantitative measures – Quantitative and statistical measures include the use of control groups, and experimental and quasi-experimental designs. It has to be said that experimental control groups, statistical analysis and similar methods are more discussed in academic journals than put into practice.

McCarthy and Garavan (2001) report that 360-degree feedback is useful for identifying training needs and for the evaluation of training outcomes, but is typically aimed only at managers.

See also **CIRO model of evaluation**; **Kirkpatrick's model of evaluation**; **NOTES model of training**.

References

Bramley, Peter (1996) *Evaluating Training*. London, IPD.

McCarthy, A. M. and Garavan, Thomas N. (2001) '360-degree feedback process, performance improvement and employee career development', *Journal of Industrial Training*, Volume 25, Number 1, pp5–32.

http,//cleo.murdoch.edu.au/gen/aset/ajet5/su89p89.html

http,//hale.pepperdine.edu/~cscunha/Pages/KIRK.HTM

Expert   Some authorities consider that it takes about 10 years of study to become an expert in a subject. Howard Gardner, the American educational psychologist, defines 'experts' as those who think about a concept by drawing on insights from several forms of intelligence.

Experts employ a mixture of analytical and intuitive thinking. Where there is no time for analysis, more reliance is put on intuition. Where there is time, greater analysis is likely to be applied. Experts tend to draw on repertoires of solutions built up over the years. Experts have an uncanny ability to focus on what is important. The terms 'expert' and 'specialist' should not be confused.

Cognitive scientists, among others, make a distinction between experts and specialists:

- Specialists know their subject inside out. They have great depth of knowledge in their specialism, uncluttered by a need to consider viewpoints from other specialisms. They tackle problems within the limits of their specialism. A specialist has been defined as a person who knows more and more about less and less. They thus often come across as arrogant and insensitive.

- Experts, on the other hand, are continually seeking out new knowledge to increase their level of expertise. They are keen to develop themselves and take on new challenges. The expert is open to new ideas irrespective of where they come from. Experts thus tend to be more creative than specialists. They are quick to grasp the overall situation and do not just concentrate on one part.

Dreyfus (1986) suggests that people go through five stages to become an expert: the novice stage, the stage of the advanced beginner, the competent stage, the proficient stage, and the expert stage. This is a model that is somewhat similar to the learning stages model.

In the modern world of dynamic change, people have to move out of their specialisms and become multi-disciplined, creative, innovative and adaptable. This ability is particularly required for the application of new technology in such areas as multimedia communications and the Internet.

See also **Artificial intelligence (AI)**.

References
Cheetham, Graham and Chivers, Geoff (2001) 'How professionals learn in practice: an investigation of informal learning amongst people working in professions', *Journal of European Industrial Training*, Volume 25, Number 5, pp247–292.
Dreyfus, Hubert L. and Dreyfus, Stuart E. (1986) *Mind over Machine: The power of human intuition and expertise in the era of the computer.* Oxford, Blackwell.
http,//www.21learn.org/publ/abbott_expertise.html
http,//www.21learn.org/acti/trlearning.html

Expert systems   Whatis.com defines an expert system thus:

❝ An expert system is a computer program that simulates the judgement and behaviour of a human or an organisation that has expert knowledge and experience in a particular field. Typically, such a system contains a knowledge base containing accumulated experience and a set of rules for applying the knowledge base to each particular situation that is described to the program. Sophisticated expert systems can be enhanced with additions to the knowledge base or to the set of rules. ❞

Expert systems are computer programs that mimic what experts do. Artificial intelligence (AI) and expert systems are used extensively in all areas of business. Expert systems should be an integral part of knowledge management. Capturing expertise and putting it online is critical to the success of any knowledge management system.

Microsoft, Xerox and Compaq are just some of the companies that have used expert systems to help them with their business. Expert systems can in certain cases make medical diagnoses as good as any doctor's. A computer beat even the world chess champion Gary Kasparov in 1997. Computers are used to predict the weather and share prices. AI-generated music is now commonplace. AI robots are used by the army for bomb disposal and have been used in space exploration. In industry, AI robots can do boring, dirty, repetitious, or dangerous jobs, sometimes in places that human can't reach.

See also **Knowledge management**.

References
Beaumont, J. Graham (1994) *Brain Power: Unlock the power of your mind.* London, Grange Books.
Liebowitz, Jay (1998). 'Expert systems: an integral part of knowledge management', *Kybernetes*, Volume 27, Number 2, pp170–175.

Malone, Samuel A. (2000) *Learning Skills for Managers.* Dublin, Oak Tree Press.
http,//www.freelock.com/technical/expert.pnp

Experiential learning   Experiential learning is learning acquired through action and practice. Aristotle said, 'What we have to learn to do, we learn by doing.' Confucius said, 'I hear and I forget, I see and I remember, I do and I understand.' We learn by interacting with others while engaged in meaningful tasks.

The experiential learning cycle suggests that we learn from our experiences by reflecting on them, drawing conclusions and then doing things differently. Carl Rogers said there were two types of learning: cognitive (meaningless) and experiential (significant). Cognitive learning is acquiring academic knowledge, such as vocabulary or multiplication tables. Experiential learning is acquiring applicable knowledge such as about the technicalities of personal computers.

According to Rogers, learning is facilitated when:

- the learner participates in the learning process and has control over its nature and direction – self-initiated learning is the most effective

- the learning is mainly concerned with practical, social, personal or research problems of interest to the learner

- the learner evaluates his or her own progress and/or success.

People learn best from their own experience – provided that that experience can be examined rationally and reflected on, and conclusions can be tested. Many universities grant credit for adults' experiential learning. Experience represents a valuable resource that trainers can draw on. Most trainers are aware of the importance of experiential methods such as business games, simulations, case studies, psychodrama, role-play and work-based projects. Action learning is a type of experiential learning.

There may be times when experiential techniques are not appropriate, such as when the learners know very little about the topic. Here the trainer may make short formal inputs in the form of lecturettes. In practice the learning process may not be as neat as that enunciated in the learning cycle.

The role of the trainer is to:

- set a positive climate for learning

- clarify learning objectives and how they meet the needs of learners

- organise and provide the resources to facilitate learning

- meet the emotional and intellectual needs of learners

- share feelings and thoughts as well as the knowledge content of the subject

- encourage mutual aid and support between learners

■ use the wisdom, experience and knowledge of course participants as a rich learning resource.

See also **Action learning**; **Learning cycle**.

References
Argyris, Chris (1999) *On Organisational Learning*. Oxford, Blackwell Business.
Cheetham, Graham and Chivers, Graham (2001) 'How professionals learn in practice: an investigation of informal learning amongst people working in professions', *Journal of European Industrial Training*, Volume 25, Number 5, pp247–292.
Fee, Kenneth (2001) *A Guide To Management Development Techniques*. London, Kogan Page.
Feinstein, Andrew Hale, Mann, Stuart and Corsun, David L. 'Charting the experiential territory. Clarifying definitions and uses of computer simulation, games and role play', *The Journal of Management Development*, Volume 21, Number 10, pp732–744.
http,//tip.psychology.org/rogers.html
http,//ni.edu/ace/Resources/Documents/AdultLearning.html
http,//www.infed.org/thinkers/el-lewin.htm
http,//www.infed.org/thinkers/el-rogers.htm

Experimental psychologist   Experimental psychologists usually work in laboratories and study various aspects of human and animal intelligence, memory, perception and attention. They may also study how people learn, think and solve problems.

Much of the work of experimental psychologists has related to animal species, particularly the white rat. Many theories about behaviour – particularly theories of learning and memory – have arisen from experiments with animals.

Experimental psychologists' theories about learning have helped us to understand how people learn, why some people find difficulty in learning, and how to help people to learn more effectively.

See also **Educational psychologist**.

References
Myers, David G. (1995) Psychology. New York, Worth.

Explicit knowledge   Explicit knowledge is knowledge that has been captured and recorded in formal language so that it can be shared, communicated, and used elsewhere. Explicit knowledge is tangible, teachable and thus easy for competitors to imitate. Knowledge in an employee's head realises its commercial potential only when it becomes explicit. At this stage it becomes organisational knowledge.

Product specifications for a machine are an example of explicit knowledge.

See also **Implicit knowledge**; **Tacit knowledge**.

References
Nonaka, Ikujiro and Takeuchi, Hirotaka (1995) *The Knowledge Creating Company, How Japanese companies create the dynamics of innovation*. Oxford, Oxford University Press.
http,//www.infed.org/thinkers/senge.htm

Extrovert learners   Extrovert learners do not enjoy learning on their own and prefer to be part of a learning group. In general, extrovert learners:

- like to experiment and try out new skills and approaches – they do not feel they have learned something until they have experienced how it works: they like action learning

- like to learn collaboratively in groups – they develop their thinking skills through discussion and debate with others; they refine their interpersonal relationship skills through interaction and feedback from others

- prefer to learn things that make a visible and tangible difference

- get bored if they spend too much time learning on their own.

See also **Introvert learners**.

F

Facilitation   Facilitation is what a trainer does as the 'guiding authority' in a group exercise or discussion or in any situation where the trainer's role is to act as a resource to be called upon by learners as needed. Facilitation is the art of drawing out the wisdom, knowledge, and experience already existing but lying untapped in the minds of the learners.

It takes a paradigm shift on the part of the trainer to go from instruction to facilitation. Some trainers may not want to make the transition because they feel their position is being undermined. A Chinese proverb says 'Teachers open the door. You enter by yourself.' Galileo advised that 'you cannot teach a man anything; you can only help him find it within himself.' Carl Rogers maintained that we cannot teach another person directly; we can only facilitate this learning. The art of the facilitator is thus to help a learner realise his or her capacity to learn.

Qualities and attitudes important in the facilitation of learning may be recalled by means of the acronym CHEST, which stands for Critical reflection, Honesty, Empathy, Self-directed learning, and Trust.

- *critical reflection* – People learn through action and reflection. Trainers should help learners realise that values, attitudes, beliefs and behaviours are culturally transmitted, that they are relative and can be changed.

- *honesty* – Trainers should be themselves. Sham and pretence are out. To connect on a person-to-person basis the trainer must be genuine, open, honest and real.

- *empathy* – The trainer should be able to put himself or herself in the place of the learner and experience the learning from a learner's perspective. Learners want to be understood from their own point of view rather than from the trainer's point of view. They do not like to be evaluated and judged.

- *self-directed learning* – The aim of facilitation is to create self-directed and empowered learners. Learners should see themselves as proactive and in control of their learning opportunities. Part of the process may be imparting learning-to-learn skills.

■ *trust* – The trainer must be the type of person whom the learner can accept and trust. Acceptance and trust is a two-way process. To win this trust the trainer must value and respect the learner.

Mentors also need facilitation skills.

See also **Mentoring**.

References
Bentley, Trevor (2000) *Facilitation.* Stroud, the space between.
http,//www.infed.org/thinkers/et-rogers.htm
http,//www.newhorizons.org/lrnbus_marchese.html

False memory syndrome   False memory syndrome is a condition in which what is remembered is – for one reason or another, but often in the presence of a figure of authority – not what actually happened.

Loftus (1994) conducted studies on over 20,000 subjects. She found evidence to suggest that memory is both fragile and unreliable. Her work supported the notion that eyewitness accounts of events are often inaccurate – and that false memories can be created through suggestion in 25 per cent of the population. Loftus's work questions the validity of memories that are recovered under coaching or questioning. She has shown that experiencing violent and traumatic events decreases the accuracy of memory. Loftus theorises that memory is suggestible and becomes less reliable over time. One of her classic studies is known as 'Lost in the shopping mall'. Here she proved that children and teenagers could be induced to remember being lost in a mall at an early age by questioning, even though it had never happened.

False memory syndrome is a controversial topic in the field of psychotherapy. Currently, research is also investigating schematic gap-filling, in which people compensate for gaps in their memories of a sequence of events by inventing things that might logically be expected to have occurred in the sequence. The mind has a natural tendency to fill gaps in patterns. People then 'remember' such events as if they actually happened.

References
Loftus, Elizabeth F. (1994) *The Myth of Repressed Memory, False Memories and Allegations of Sexual Abuse.* New York, St Martin's Press.
http,//www.fmsonline.org/
http,//faculty.washington.edu/eloftus/Articles/witchhunt.html
http,//www.findarticles.com/cf_0/g2602/0003/2602000371/print.jhtml
http,//www.findarticles.com/cf_0/g2699/0005/2699000545/print.jhtml

Feedback   Feedback is information on how you've been doing. Knowledge of results is feedback on your performance as a learner. A manager who receives timely, accurate and clear feedback from a mentor or senior manager is in a position to learn from experience and take corrective action for the future. Feedback may be received from senior managers, peers, customers and suppliers – 360-degree feedback is a useful technique in this regard.

It is difficult to make improvements if you are unaware of where you are going wrong and how you stand in relation to your stakeholders. In practice, many managers do not give any feedback to employees on their performance, or do not give feedback as often as they should.

The core elements of effective feedback may be recalled by means of the acronym SAT, which stands for Specific, Actionable, and Timely.

- *specific* – Feedback must be specific, not general. It must relate to a particular task, behaviour or performance, and not to personal attributes. Constructive feedback is an important source of self-knowledge, continuous improvement and learning.

- *actionable* – The feedback should be capable of being put into practice by the recipient.

- *timely* – For effective learning, feedback should be timely and given as near to the event as possible or it loses its effectiveness. It should also be frequent.

The normal performance appraisal, held annually or semi-annually in many firms, does not meet the timely criteria for effective feedback. This would suggest that performance appraisal should be a continuous process of on-the-job feedback rather than a one-off yearly event. Research has demonstrated that knowledge of results alone is not likely to change a person's work habits but to be successful must be tied in with the individual's goals.

See also **Knowledge of results**.

References
Cheetham, Graham and Chivers, Graham (2001) 'How professionals learn in practice: an investigation of informal learning amongst people working in professions', *Journal of European Industrial Training*, Volume 25, Number 5, pp247–292.
Malone, Samuel A. (2000) *Learning Skills for Managers*. Dublin, Oak Tree Press.
Thorne, Kaye and Mackey, David (2001) *Everything You Ever Needed To Know About Training*. London, Kogan Page.

FIBRES model of memory　　The FIBRES model is an acronymic guide to positive elements of memory. It stands for Frequency, Intensity, Belonging, Recency and primacy, Effect, and Standing out.

- *frequency* – This means that the more often one learns, the better one knows what is learned. Overlearn, so that in the examination room you won't have difficulty recalling information, even if under stress.

- *intensity* – Intensity, motivation, interest and confidence are all interlinked. Each reinforces the other. The more success you have, the more confident and motivated you become. Similarly, the more enthusiastic you are about a topic, the better your recall.

- *belonging* – This means understanding how what you are learning fits into a greater mass of information (an attitude to learning that is sometimes called the 'holistic method'). The mind likes to get an overview of a topic before it starts filling in the details. Just as with a jigsaw puzzle we look at the illustration and then start working from the outer edges and work our way inwards. We are using a telescopic approach going from less detail to more detail. Psychologists call this the 'Gestalt' approach. Learning maps are an application of this idea.

- *recency and primacy* – Recency means we remember best what we did last, that is, most recently. Primacy means we remember best what we did first, rather than what came subsequently. We remember our first day at school, our first day at work, our first love affair, etc. This is the novelty concept and the reason why as a child you learned so well.

- *effect* – High expectations from yourself or from others will enhance your ability to learn. Teachers who expect high results from their students usually elicit better performances.

- *standing out* – We tend to remember things that are unique and outstanding. This is known as the Von Restorff effect.

See also **MUD model of learning**.

References
Malone, Samuel A. (1996) *Learning to Learn*. London, CIMA.

Fishbowl   The Fishbowl is a sort of role-play scenario that typically involves a selection of training course participants in some activity in the centre of a room while other participants in an outer circle observe what is going on. Those in the centre are the 'goldfish'. The role of the participants in the outer circle is to watch closely and provide feedback about their behaviour and effectiveness for the goldfish in the centre. The observers and observed may then change places.

Flexible learning   Flexible learning describes any method or environment that enables learners to learn what, when, where and how they want to. Distance learning and computer-based learning are types of flexible learning.

See also **Distance learning**.

References
Malone, Samuel A. (1997) *How to Set Up and Manage a Corporate Learning Centre.* Aldershot, Gower.

Flow Psychologist Mihalyi Csikszentmihalyi has suggested that optimal learning occurs when you achieve your 'flow' state of total concentration. This is a distinctive state of mind and feeling in which learning is effortless and enjoyable. The flow zone is also known as the stretch zone because it takes you out of your comfort zone.

Learn from your failures and mistakes and take actions that stretch you beyond your comfort zone. When you are stretched you gain access to your creativity and passion. You need to stretch beyond your limits and discover new abilities and possibilities. You need to look for the opportunity to learn new skills and new subjects – you need to put yourself under some pressure.

In the flow zone you will learn more, acquire new skills, increase your self-esteem and self-confidence and equip yourself to take on even more challenging work. In this zone you have the energy and confidence to keep going. This is the zone you're in when learning new skills.

Csikszentmihalyi has studied the conditions which give rise to a state of flow. He concludes that a state of flow is achieved when:

- the challenge is just slightly greater than the skill required to achieve it

- clear goals have been established

- feedback is immediate

- there is no concern about possible failure.

When these conditions are met, the attention on the task becomes focused and fully engaged, and the passage of time may literally be forgotten.

See also **Concentration**.

References
Csikszentmihalyi, Mihaly (1991) *Flow: The psychology of optimal experience.* New York, HarperCollins.
http,//www.newhorizons.org/lrnbus_marchese.html
http,//www.newhorizons.org/trm_lwilson1.html

Fluid intelligence Fluid intelligence is the natural intellectual ability to perceive complex relationships, form concepts and use short-term memory. It is measured by tests for rote memory, basic reasoning, figure relationships and memory span. Tests of fluid intelligence are timed and should be free from cultural bias. Some fluid intelligence abilities such as short-term memory decline with age, but the rate of decline is minimal and is more than compensated for by the increase in crystallised intelligence.

Short-term memory decline can be offset by the use of mnemonics and other memory devices. Although fluid intelligence may decline with age, it can be improved by the application of appropriate learning strategies.

See also **Crystallised intelligence**.

References
Whalley, Lawrence (2001) *The Ageing Brain*. London, Weidenfeld & Nicolson.

Force field analysis   Force field analysis – a technique originally developed by Kurt Lewin, a social scientist – is a systematic examination of those elements that seek to encourage learning (known in this context as driving forces) and those elements that discourage learning (known similarly as resisters). It aims to measure the relative strengths of progressive driving forces and inhibiting resisters. Learning is facilitated through the reduction or elimination of the resisting forces.

Learning, like work, is goal-driven. People who want to get ahead will therefore put effort into personal achievement. Some theorists suggest that motivation emerges from the interaction of two factors, expectancy and valence:

■ Expectancy consists of two components: the expectation of personal success in the learning activity, and the expectation that success will bring positive results.

■ Valence refers to the sum of positive or negative values that people assign to learning. For example, involvement in learning activities may lead to promotion but it can also interfere with family or recreational activities.

Learning force field analysis

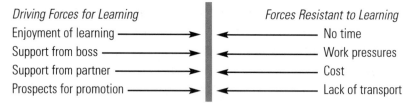

Driving Forces for Learning · *Forces Resistant to Learning*

Enjoyment of learning ———→ ←——— No time
Support from boss ———→ ←——— Work pressures
Support from partner ———→ ←——— Cost
Prospects for promotion ———→ ←——— Lack of transport

Source: adapted from Lewin (1951)

Driving forces are those forces that create the momentum for learning to occur. They tend to start a change and keep it going. Resistant forces put up resistance to or decrease the driving forces. A level of equilibrium is reached when the sum of the driving forces is equal to the sum of the resistant forces. This level of equilibrium, or present level of learning, can be increased or decreased by changing the relationship between the driving and the resisting forces. In the present example some of the resistant forces could be addressed by asking for time off to study and paying the cost on successful completion of the exams.

References
Lewin, Kurt (1951) *Field Theory in Social Science*. New York, Harper & Brothers.
Smither, Robert D., Houston, John M. and McIntire, Sandra D. (1996) *Organisation Development: Strategies for changing environments*. New York, HarperCollins.

Forgetting curve   Some experts have calculated that we forget 50 per cent of what we learn immediately, 80 per cent within 24 hours, 90 per cent within 48 hours and almost everything within a week unless we review and revise. Forgetting has a survival value. We forget information that is no longer of use to us and replace it with currently useful information that helps us to survive. Memory research indicates that the rate of forgetting is the same for normal individuals who put in the same amount of learning application or effort.

There are various theories on why people forget:

- decay – Memory gradually fades away with the passage of time and with non-use.

- repression – Forgetting occurs because unpleasant memories are repressed.

- memory distortion – We tend to remember things the way we want to remember them. We distort things to make them the way we think they ought to be.

- interference – What comes before and what comes after affect memories.

- cue dependency – The right cue is often needed to retrieve certain memories. Mnemonic strategies can be used for this purpose.

- displacement – Information is displaced by new information from long-term memory storage. Information may also be modified by new information rather than displaced by it.

- retrieval failure – We all forget names occasionally even though we know we know the names but can't recall them when we urgently want to. This is known as the tip-of-the-tongue phenomenon. A lost word or name usually pops back into the mind some time later when we are relaxed and under less pressure to remember.

Mood has a powerful effect on retrieval. We are more likely to remember happy events when we are happy and sad events when we are sad.

See also **Barriers to memory**.

References
Baddeley, Alan (1991). *Human Memory: Theory and practice*. Hove, Lawrence Erlbaum Associates.
Rupp, Rebecca (1998) *Committed To Memory: How we remember and why we forget*. London, Aurum Press.
http,//www.web-us.com/memory/memory_encoding.htm
http,//www.web-us.com/brain/brainmemoryrythms.htm
http,//www.web-us.com/memory/generic_ltm_memory.htm

http,//www.web-us.com/memory/hermann_ebbinghaus.htm
file,//C,\Program Files\Britannica\BCD\Cache_5_PreviewRil.htm

Formal learning   Formal learning is usually off-the-job learning in the form of training programmes or degree programmes or attendance at a corporate learning centre.

See also **Informal learning**.

References
Mumford, Alan (1997) *Management Development Strategies for Action.* London, IPD.

G

Games   A game is a structured activity in which players compete abiding by rules to achieve a goal. Well-known examples are chess and Monopoly. Games by their nature are competitive, have rules, involve scoring, and end after a certain period of time. Games have been designed for use in marketing and management training. They may be used as a vehicle for looking at competition, strategy, teamworking, leadership, organisation or planning.

The main benefits of games are that they are fun and often energise a training session. Different lessons can be drawn from the processes or behaviours that take place during a game. For example, the game Desert Survival requires learners to work out survival tactics individually and then as a group. The explicit objective is to learn how to survive. An implicit objective is to show that co-operation enhances the chances of survival. The trainer should set the scene at the start of the game and through discussion bring out the key learning points at the end.

The dangers involved in using games are:

- Participants may reject them as superficial or childish, and unrelated to the real-life experience of work.

- Because some of the objectives may be hidden, the lessons of the games may be lost on the participants.

- Some participants may have experienced the game before.

- Some participants may get so carried away with the game that they get upset if they lose.

See also **Simulations**.

References
Graig, L. Robert (1987) *A Training and Development Handbook, 3rd edition. A Guide to Human Resource Development.* New York, McGraw-Hill, sponsored by The American Society for Training and Development.

Reid, Charles W. and Kleiner, Brian H. (1996) 'Which training methods are effective?', *Management Development Review*, Volume 9, Number 2, pp24–29.

Gender differences   In a learning context, although the brains of men and women are very similar, some differences have been discovered. (These findings do not show that the brain of one sex is better than that of the other – they just show that the two are different.)

- The brain of a male is about 10 per cent bigger than the brain of a female. In a way, this is to be expected in that men on average are taller and bigger than women. However, relative brain size does not make a difference. The number of connections between brain cells, rather than size, are what mostly determine intelligence. Jonathan Swift's brain weighed 2 kilograms (4.4 pounds). However, Albert Einstein had a normal-sized brain of about 1.4 kilograms (3 pounds), while Anatole France, who won the Nobel Prize for literature, had a brain that weighed only 1 kilogram (2.2 pounds).

- Psychological testing consistently shows that the average man performs better than the average woman on spatial tasks, such as visualising objects in three dimensions. This may account for the fact that there are many more male mathematicians, airplane pilots, bush guides, mechanical engineers, architects and racing-car drivers than female ones. Women, on the other hand, do better than men in tests involving writing, reading and vocabulary. But this average difference in ability is small. Many men are better at language than the average for women, and many women have better spatial skills than the average for men. The male has a thicker right hemisphere, which may account for his reported edge in visual and spatial tasks such as reading a map. On the other hand, the female has a thicker left hemisphere, which may account for her edge in fluency and language skills.

- There is a brain region in the cortex called inferior parietal lobule which is significantly larger in men than in women. Furthermore, the left side of the inferior parietal lobule is larger in men than the right side. In women, this asymmetry is reversed. This is the area that was larger in Albert Einstein's brain, and is larger in other physicists and mathematicians, which suggests that the inferior parietal lobule correlates highly with mental mathematical abilities.

- Studies have shown that two areas in the frontal and temporal lobes relating to language, known as Broca's and Wernicke's areas, are significantly larger in women. This provides some biological evidence for women's superiority in verbal skills.

- Females are better than males at fine motor control, which would suggest that they would make superior surgeons.

■ Imaging technology studies of men and women reading or thinking about words show differences. These studies have found that men generally use only their left cerebral hemisphere for processing language, but women use both hemispheres. An interesting fact is that it has also been found that oriental people who use pictographic written language tend also to use both sides of the brain, regardless of gender.

■ The male has fewer brain cells than the female and loses brain cells three times faster.

■ In line with mortality statistics, the brain of a female survives on average about eight years longer than the brain of a male. The female has a larger corpus callosum, which may suggest that her brain is more integrated and holistic. This may account for 'feminine intuition' and make women more emotionally intelligent.

■ Men's brains are more specialised and are more vulnerable to dyslexia and hyperactivity. The more specialised brain of the male may account for men's supposed superiority in maths, engineering and science. There are more left-handed men than women, and boys with learning difficulties far outnumber girls. Some scientists believe that if a foetus produces excess testosterone, it stunts the growth of the left hemisphere, causing left-handedness and learning disorders.

■ Men tend to have more difficulty recovering from strokes or brain injuries.

■ Males are four times more likely to have a stammer than females.

■ Females are more likely to get Alzheimer's disease than males. This may be only because they live longer.

■ Females are better at tests that involve generating ideas.

■ Females score better than males on some tests of social judgement, empathy and co-operation. The 'Father of sociobiology', Edward O. Wilson of Harvard University, said that women tend to have better empathy, verbal, and social skills than men. On the other hand, men tend to be more aggressive than women and have better spatial and mathematical skills.

■ Tests show that women generally can recall lists of words or paragraphs better than men can.

■ Evolution may have helped differentiate the brains of men and women. In early times men were traditionally the hunters while women gathered food near the home and cared for the children. This may account for men's superior spatial and navigation skills. Men use strength to compete with other men while women use language to gain social advantage through debate and persuasion.

■ Hormones also play a significant role in differentiating the brains of males and females.

Theorists in adult learning have suggested two different learning styles that are somewhat gender-related:

■ the autonomous, separate or independent path, which typifies the majority of men and also applies to some women

■ the relational, connected, or interdependent path, which typifies the majority of women and also applies to some men.

According to the Myers-Briggs ® Type Indicator, about two-thirds of women have profiles in which feeling predominates, whereas two-thirds of men have profiles in which thinking predominates. The learning styles questionnaire (LSQ) shows little significant gender differences in learning styles.

References
Carter, Rita (1998) *Mapping the Mind*. London, Phoenix.
Conlon, Roberta (1999) *States of Mind: New discoveries about how our brains make us who we are*. New York, The Dana Press.
Malone, Samuel A. (2000) *Learning Skills for Managers*. Dublin, Oak Tree Press.
Ratey, John (2001) *A User's Guide To The Brain*. London, Little, Brown.
Rogers, Lesley (1999) *Sexing The Brain*. London, Phoenix.
Tarleton State University, *Brain Differences in Males and Females*.
http,//ww.tarleton.edu/~sandrson/Brain%20Differences.doc.
http,//www.happychild.org.uk/acc/tpr/amz/0012menw.htm
http,//www.brain.com/about/article.cfm?id=21006&cat_id=12
http,//www.epub.org.br/cm/h11/mente/eisntein/cerebro-homens.html
http,//www.sciencenet.org.uk/database/Biology/Brain/b0038/c.html
http,//faculty.washington.edu/chudler/heshe.html
http,//www.oregoncounseling.org/ArticlesPapers/D...DifferencesMenWomen.ht

Genius   A genius is a person of extraordinary intellectual power. There are two aspects to genius – intelligence and creativity. The US psychologist Lewis M. Terman set the IQ for 'potential genius' at 140 or over. This score is reached by only about 1 in 250 of the general population. To the British scientist Sir Francis Galton, 'genius' referred to creative ability demonstrated by actual achievement. Galton in his *Hereditary Genius* (1869) presented clear statistical evidence that genius, as measured by outstanding accomplishment, tends to run in families. Scientists differ as to the contribution of 'nature or nurture' to the making of genius.

Thinking strategies that may help you to approach the level of genius may be recalled by means of the acronym SHAMROCK, which stands for Serendipity, Hatching ideas, Alternatives, Metaphorical thinking, Recording, Opposite thinking, Combining ideas, and Knowing how to connect.

■ *serendipity* – Serendipity means making pleasant discoveries by accident. The strength of genius is that they have through years of research and observation prepared themselves to see and exploit the chance event. B. F. Skinner said that if you chance on something interesting, drop everything else and study it. Alexander Fleming was not the first physician studying bacteria to notice the mould on an exposed culture. However, he was the first to follow through on the phenomenon that eventually led to penicillin.

- *hatching numerous ideas* – A characteristic of geniuses is that they generate lots of ideas. It often took only one good idea to make them famous. Nevertheless, their output is usually prodigious. Einstein is famous for his Theory of Relativity, but he published 248 other papers. Thomas Edison, inventor of the electric light-bulb and phonograph, was the holder of 1,093 US patents. He is reputed to have said that genius was 99 per cent perspiration and 1 per cent inspiration. It seems there are many failed ideas on the road to fame and success.

- *alternatives* – Geniuses look at problems in many different ways. They generate different perspectives on a problem to deepen their understanding of the issues involved. A paradigm shift or challenging the conventional wisdom is often needed to solve a problem.

- *metaphorical thinking* – Being able to draw inspiration from and see similarities between different things is the mark of genius. Alexander Graham Bell got his inspiration for the telephone from studying the human ear. Einstein got the inspiration for many of his ideas by drawing analogies with everyday events such as rowing a boat or observing a train while standing on a platform.

- *recording* – A characteristic of geniuses is that they keep diaries or learning logs about their experiences. Many successful people in history have kept diaries and journals, including da Vinci, Darwin, Faraday, Galileo, and Newton. They often use diagrams, drawings, and sketches to record their ideas. Einstein preferred to think in visual ways using diagrams. He believed that visual means rather than words and numbers played a significant role in his thinking process.

- *opposite thinking* – Geniuses are often able to see a connection between two opposite or incompatible subjects, suspend judgement while the mind moves to a new plane, and exploit the result. Thomas Edison combined wiring in parallel circuits with high-resistance filaments to produce his electric light-bulb. The combination of these two things was considered impossible at the time by conventional thinkers.

- *combining ideas* – Geniuses are constantly combining and remembering ideas, images and thoughts in different ways, using both their conscious and subconscious minds. The Austrian monk Gregor Mendel combined mathematics and biology to create the modern science of genetics. Einstein combined the known concepts of energy, mass and the speed of light to come up with his Theory of Relativity expressed by the equation $E = mc^2$.

■ *knowing how to connect the unconnected* – Geniuses have the ability to make juxtapositions between dissimilar objects.

References
Buzan, Tony and Keene, Raymond (1994). *Buzan's Book of Genius and how to Unleash Your Own.* London, Stanley Paul.
DePorter, Bobbi and Hernacki, Mike (1993) *Quantum Learning: Unleash the genius within you.* London, Piatkus.
File,//C,\Program Files\Britannica\BCD\Cache_8_PreviewRil.htm
File,//C,\Program Files\Britannica\BCD\Cache_9_PreviewRil.htm
http,//www.newhorizons.org/wwart_michalko1.html

Gestalt

Gestalt   The word *Gestalt* is German for 'shape', 'pattern' or 'form': Gestalt is a branch of cognitive psychology in which the basic theory emphasises our ability to perceive patterns as wholes – indeed, to perceive that 'The whole is more than the sum of the parts.' This is sometimes called the holistic approach, and in the learning context refers to a group of techniques associated with Gestalt psychology.

Learning should be seen as holistic rather than fragmented. The learner should be seen as a whole person with physical, mental and emotional capacities. The systems approach is a similar concept. Awareness is thus expanded on an overall rather than a piecemeal basis. A common term for this approach is the 'helicopter viewpoint'.

Gestalt techniques have been used in organisational development and team-building interventions. Gestalt therapy helps people become whole or complete by becoming more self-aware.

See also **Whole method**.

References
Cheetham, Graham and Chivers, Geoff (2001) 'How professionals learn in practice: an investigation of informal learning amongst people working in professions', *Journal of European Industrial Training*, Volume 25, Number 5, pp247–292.
Clarke, N. F. and Fraser, T. (1982) *The Gestalt Approach: An introduction for managers and trainers.* Horsham, Roffey Park Management Centre.
Huczynski, Andrzej (2001) *Encyclopedia of Development Methods.* Aldershot, Gower.
Sternberg, Robert J. (1995) *In Search of the Human Mind.* New York, Harcourt Brace College Publishers.

Goals

Goals   There is no motivation without a goal. Goals should be strongly desired, visualised clearly, and broken down into achievable and manageable tasks. Thomas Edison, the inventor of the phonograph, and probably one of the most prolific inventors of all time, was remarkably persistent in the pursuit of imaginative goals. He described invention as '99 per cent perspiration and 1 per cent inspiration'. Goals or objectives are essential for any training or learning task. Overall objectives should be set for a training programme and for each learning session of the programme. Objectives should be expressed in behavioural terms.

One of the advantages of goals is that having a goal activates our reticular activating system (RAS). The RAS is a network-like structure of brain cells that acts as a sentry or lookout. It spots and brings to our attention only information that is relevant to the achievement of our goals. So when you are given an assignment to write on a particular topic, you begin to notice (as, strangely, you never did previously) people, books, articles and resources pertinent to the subject matter that will help you achieve your goal.

See also **Behavioral objectives**.

References
Alder, Harry (1996) *NLP for Managers: How to achieve excellence at work*. London, Piatkus.
Malone, Samuel A. (1999) *Success Skills for Managers*. Dublin, Oak Tree Press.

Graveyard slot   The 'graveyard slot' is the training period immediately after lunch when concentration is low and bodily energy is diverted to digesting food rather than energising the brain. It is a challenge to trainers to keep people focused and interested on the topic during this session. Practical activities rather than lectures should be the theme of this session. Case studies, role-play, buzz groups, energisers, and brainstorming sessions should help people keep focused and alert.

Group dynamics   Group dynamics describes the way people interact and interrelate in groups – and the way groups relate to other groups. In the context of training, task and process skills and managing conflict are an important aspect of group dynamics. Teamworking is emphasised in modern organisations.

See also **Group learning**.

Reference
Luthans, Fred (1995) *Organisational Behaviour*. New York, McGraw-Hill.

Grouping   Grouping similar concepts, related ideas and topics is a useful way of organising material. For example, grouping the digits can increase your short-term memory for telephone numbers. This normally has a maximum capacity of about nine digits. Organising a list into groups will often help you understand the relationship between concepts better. Classification systems help us to organise information for easier retrieval and better recall.

See also **Miller's seven plus or minus two rule**.

References
Higbee, Kenneth L. (1990) *Your Memory: How it works and how to improve it*. London, Piatkus.
Rupp, Rebecca (1998) *Committed To Memory: How we remember and why we forget*. London, Aurum Press.
http,//www.web-us.com/memory/improving_memory.htm

Group learning We are social animals and so most of us prefer to learn collaboratively in groups rather than on our own. Adults need to work in groups to move beyond understanding to application, analysis, synthesis, and evaluation. Small group activities provide an opportunity to share, reflect, and generalise learning experiences. Groups provide an opportunity to practise and learn important social skills. A trainer can capitalise on this by forming discussion groups. The trainer may need to take on the role of facilitator to support effective group learning. Roles played by the facilitator may include those of resource person, mentor, coach, catalyst, reinforcer, and evaluator (Smith 2000). The trainer may use an icebreaker exercise initially to establish rapport within the group.

See also **Group dynamics**; **Team learning**.

References
Senge, Peter (1993) *The Fifth Discipline, The art and practice of the learning organisation.* London, Century Business.
Smith, E. (2000) 'Applying knowledge-enabling methods in the classroom and in the workplace', *Journal of Workplace Learning, Employee Counselling Today*, p12(6).
http,//www.emerald.com/brev/08612fbl.htm.

Group norms A work group establishes 'norms' or acceptable levels and methods of behaviour, to which all members of the group are expected to conform. People who refuse to conform may be ostracised and made to feel uncomfortable so that they eventually either conform or leave the group. This group attitude will have a negative effect on the organisation if it sets unreasonably low production norms. Norms can be negative or positive, and can thus either be detrimental to or enhance learning.

References
Cole, G. A. (1995) *Organisational Behaviour.* London, DP Publications.

H

Habits Habits are difficult to change. It is well known that people who are proficient at typing with two fingers find it much more difficult to learn to touch-type properly than those who have never used a keyboard. However, if we want different results we must change our habits. By changing the way we perceive and do things we discover new abilities, approaches and possibilities. One way of improving your memory is to establish good habits or routines. If you believe in a place for everything and everything in its place, then you won't forget where you left something. However, if you do forget where you put your keys, retracing your steps may be a help in finding them.

References
O'Connor, Joseph and Seymour, John (1990) *Neuro-Linguistic Programming*. London, Aquarian/Thorsons.
Malone, Samuel A. (2000) *Success Skills for Managers*. Dublin, Oak Tree Press.

Handouts These can be a good *aide-mémoire* if course participants want to refer to them any time after the course is over. People who attend course programmes expect handouts. In practice, however, very few people refer to them again.

Handouts can also be used as pre-course reading material. They should be given out about a week in advance. This enables the trainer to concentrate on the explanation of key concepts and difficult points and to encourage discussion. Key point handouts distributed before the course starts encourage learners to take notes to elaborate on the points made. Reading lists can also be given to encourage learners in the use of books for independent learning and research.

References
Howe, M. J. A. and Singer, L. (1975) 'Presentation and students' activities in meaningful learning', *British Journal of Educational Psychology*, Volume 7, pp52–61.

Happiness sheets 'Happiness sheets' or 'happy sheets' is the term often used by trainers for end-of-training-course assessment sheets. Positive feedback about the programme is frequently more an indication of how much participants enjoyed themselves socially and how good the catering facilities were than how effective the training was. Nevertheless, there is some value in happiness sheets in that they do provide feedback in the form of participants' perceptions on the benefits or otherwise of the training course.

Reference
Bramley, Peter (1996) *Evaluating Training.* London, IPD.

Hawthorne effect   The Hawthorne effect – sometimes called the attention factor – is a term used to describe the situation in learning where improvement is due to the introduction of a new technique – and to the interest this attracts – as much as to the technique itself. The name is derived from experiments conducted by Elton Mayo on incentives in the Hawthorne works of the Western Electric Company during the 1930s.

References
Cole, G. A. (1995) *Organisational Behaviour.* London, DP Publications.

Herrmann's model of learning styles   Ned Herrmann's model (1988) is well designed and easy to use, and describes four types of learner: the analyser, the organiser, the sensor, and the explorer.

- *the analyser* – The analyser learns by obtaining and quantifying facts. He applies analysis and logic, thinking through ideas, building cases and forming theories. This type of learner likes formal lectures, facts, case studies, books and bibliographies.

- *the organiser* – The organiser learns by categorising and structuring text. He evaluates and tests theories. He acquires skills through practice, and by implementing the content of courses. This learner responds to planning, programmed learning, structure and lectures.

- *the sensor* – The sensor learns by listening and sharing ideas. He identifies emotionally with the content. This learner likes experiential opportunities, movement, music and group discussion and interaction.

- *the explorer* – The explorer learns by taking the initiative and exploring hidden possibilities. He or she likes to use intuition, construct concepts and synthesise content. This learner enjoys spontaneity, experimentation, visual displays, aesthetics and being involved.

See also **Learning styles**.

Herzberg's motivation-hygiene theory   Frederick Herzberg's theory was essentially about job satisfaction. Some factors at work gave specific pleasure to employees; other factors at work although they did not give particular pleasure would have aroused displeasure had they not been present. The first factors he called 'motivators', and the second, demotivating factors, he called 'hygiene factors'

The motivators include:

- Reward and recognition.

- Opportunities for self-development

- Making learners responsible for their own learning.

- Giving learners a sense of achievement.

- Professional presentation.

- Good time-keeping.

The demotivators include:

- Threats and insults by the trainer.

- Poor trainer preparation, planning and presentation.

- Poor time-keeping by the trainer.

- Overuse of technical jargon by the trainer.

- Poor interpersonal relationships with learners.

- Poor learning environment.

See also **Motivation and learning**.

References
Cole, G. A. (1995) *Organisational Behaviour.* London, DP Publications.

Hippocampus   The hippocampus – named after its curving shape which reminded neuroscientists of a seahorse – is part of the limbic system of the brain and plays an important role in memory. It seems to be particularly important in learning and remembering spatial information, as for example in the ability to follow road routes. The hippocampus is not fully developed in infancy, which is a possible reason for our inability to remember incidents from our very early life.

Damage to the hippocampus interferes with the ability to form any new long-term memory, but short-term memory remains intact. When we are stressed our adrenal glands tend to produce more of a hormone called cortisol (or hydrocortisone). Cortisol facilitates the fight-or-flight response in the short term. However, long-term secretion through stress may damage the hippocampus and impair memory.

See also **Limbic system**.

References
Ratey, John (2001) *A User's Guide To The Brain*. London, Little, Brown.
Turkington, Carol (1996) *The Brain Encyclopedia*. New York, Checkmark Books.
http,//www.epub.org.br/cm/n01/memo/mechanisms.htm

Holistic   A holistic way of thinking seeks to encompass and integrate multiple perspectives and experience rather than defining human possibilities narrowly. Gardner's theory of multiple intelligences indicates that every person's intelligence and abilities are far more complex than standardised IQ tests would indicate. In the holistic view of education and training, peoples' moral, emotional, physical, psychological and spiritual needs should be catered for in addition to their intellectual needs. This means that when acquiring knowledge through experience learners should engage all seven capacities of thinking, hearing, imaging, feeling, remembering, sensing and will.

By using real-life experiences, current events, case studies, co-operative learning and role-play, trainers can kindle a love of learning. By encouraging reflection and questioning rather than mere rote memorisation, trainers can promote an enquiring mind, the development of intelligence and effective learning.

References
Sternberg, Robert J. (1995) *In Search of the Human Mind*. New York, Harcourt Brace College Publishers.
http,//www.infed.org/biblio/holisticeducation.htm

Humanist theory of learning   The humanist theory considers learning from the viewpoint of the human potential for growth. Unlike behaviourists, humanists do not accept that either the environment or the subconscious determines behaviour. People have free will and can determine their own destiny. People have unlimited potential for growth and development. Learning occurs primarily through reflection on personal experience. Reflection leads to insights and understanding of others and ourselves.

Humanism facilitates collaborative learning in which trainers and learners jointly agree methods of identifying training needs, learning objectives, training methods and evaluation approaches. The approaches used include asking stimulating questions, project work, debriefing sessions, action planning, self-assessment, visualisation and guided reflection. We learn more effectively if we feel secure, respected, esteemed and empowered. Learning is undermined if we feel threatened, anxious, hostile, or demeaned.

In summary, the assumptions underlying the humanist approach to learning are:

- People are inherently good.

- People are free and autonomous and are capable of making decisions. The motivation for learning is primarily from within.

- The potential for personal growth and development is virtually unlimited.

- Self-concept plays an important part in personal development.

- People move towards becoming self-actualised.

- People are responsible to themselves and others. They are capable of evaluating their own learning.

- The whole person should be involved in learning. Feelings and emotions as well as thinking are part of the learning process.

The humanist philosophy underpins much of adult learning theory, such as self-directed learning and the value of experience in learning. To Abraham Maslow, self-actualisation was the goal of learning, and it was for trainers and educators to strive to bring this about. Similarly, Carl Rogers was concerned with personal growth and development.

See also **Behaviourist theory of learning; Cognitivist theory of learning; Constructivist theory of learning; Social theory of learning**.

References
Merriam, Sharon B. and Caffarella, Rosemary S. (1999) *Learning in Adulthood: A comprehensive guide*, 2nd edition. San Francisco, Jossey–Bass.
http,//www.learnativity.com/edpsych.html
http,//www.infed.org/biblio/learning-humanistic.htm

Human resource development   Human resource (or resources) development (HRD) is a term that is sometimes used as an alternative for training and development. It is that part of the personnel management function concerned with training and developing employees. Handy maintains that the term 'human resource' is inappropriate. He says that people are not human resources. They are living individuals with the right to be different.

See also **Management development**.

References
Megginson, David, Banfield, Paul and Joy-Mathews, Jennifer (1999) *Human Resource Development*. London, Kogan Page.

Humour   Humour can be useful: you are more likely to remember something if you put it into a humorous context. Use funny associations to make the image absurd or nonsensical. In the training room key learning points may be got across more effectively through jokes, puns, satire, funny stories, and anecdotes. Relaxed alertness that facilitates effective learning is helped by humour. Cartoons can be used in visuals to illustrate learning points and create a relaxed atmosphere. Facial expression and movement can be used to convey humour and create a non-threatening learning environment. Funny rhymes can be created to facilitate the memorisation and learning of key points. As we know, laughter is contagious and helps relax participants at a training course. Good trainers should not take themselves too seriously and should look for the humour in unexpected setbacks and challenges. Management and organisational life is a rich source of day-to-day humorous events. These can be used to illustrate and make learning points more memorable. But avoid sexist humour or any humour that may cause offence.

References

Huczynski, Andrzej (2001) *Encyclopedia of Development Methods.* Aldershot, Gower.
Parkin, Margaret (1998) *Tales for Trainers.* London, Kogan Page.
http,//www.newhorizons.org/recn_mi.html

Hypothalamus   The hypothalamus is part of the brain near the top of the brainstem and close to the pituitary gland. It monitors basic body needs such as food and water intake and regulates body temperature. The balance between need and satisfaction is called homeostasis. When we get hungry, the homeostatic balance is out of equilibrium. Eating restores the balance. The hypothalamus acts like a thermostat in controlling appetites and body heat by switching the controls of hunger, thirst and temperature on and off in response to body chemistry.

References

Ratey, John (2001) *A User's Guide To The Brain.* London, Little, Brown.
Turkington, Carol (1996) *The Brain Encyclopedia.* New York, Checkmark Books.

Ice-breaker   An ice-breaker is an introductory chat, group discussion or exercise used by trainers to 'break the ice' or dissolve barriers between participants and to speed up the onset of informality and group cohesion. For example, participants may be asked to spend a few minutes in pairs telling each other something about themselves. One well-known ice-breaker is to ask people to tell the group something unusual about themselves. Later on it may be a good test of everyone's memory to see if they can recall what was said during these introductions.

References
Thorne, Kaye and Mackey, David (2001) *Everything You Ever Needed To Know About Training.* London, Kogan Page.

Ideas generation   It may be useful for trainers to ask learners to generate ideas in order to involve participants and to explore issues about a topic. The trainer might therefore start the ball rolling by saying, 'In how many different ways can we . . .?'
    See also **Brainstorming**; **Creativity**.

References
Thorne, Kaye and Mackey, David (2001) *Everything You Ever Needed To Know About Training.* London, Kogan Page.

Imaging and imagination   The stronger the image of what you want to remember, the greater is your ability to recall it. Use your imagination to create the most effective memory techniques for you, to suit your particular learning style. Albert Einstein said, 'Imagination is more important than knowledge.' Your imagination is vital to good memory. The more you use it, the better your memory will be. Images created by someone else are not as effective because they do not reflect the way that you think and learn. You are more likely to remember topics linked to your own interactive colourful images. A hallmark of intellectual skill is the ability to use imagery.

Albert Einstein claimed that images came to him before the formulation of equations. Many other famous people also claim that imagery plays a major role in their thinking. In success theory it is claimed that what the mind can conceive, the body can achieve. Imagery plays an important role in helping us achieve our goals in life. Visual memory is superior to verbal memory. A picture is worth more than a thousand words. In the course of evolution the brain's visual cortex has become highly developed.

See also **Visualisation**.

References

Meir, David (2000) *The Accelerated Learning Handbook*. New York, McGraw-Hill.
http,//www.durbinhypnosis.com/adams.htm
http,//www.findarticles.com/cf_0/m0961/2001_Annual/73232717/print.jhtml

Imaging technology   Through the use of modern imaging technology it is now possible to study the workings of the body – including the brain – in a non-invasive way. Scientists can, for instance, study the brain while it is engaged in mental activities like thinking, problem-solving and learning by using positron emission tomography (PET) or functional magnetic resonance imaging (fMRI). The latter involves powerful magnetic fields and radio waves that scan the brain and other body structures.

These techniques are increasing scientific understanding of memory, learning and how the brain processes information. They are also able to pinpoint the locations in the brain where the activities are taking place. Differences between the brains of males and females can be observed and studied.

References

Greenfield, Susan (1996) *The Human Mind Explained: The control centre of the living machine*. London, Cassell.
Ratey, John (2001) *A User's Guide to the Brain*. London, Little, Brown.
http,//www.findarticles.com/cf_0/m0961/2001_Annual/73232717/print.jhtml

Implicit knowledge   Implicit knowledge is knowledge that is not generally available to others because it exists in someone's head: it is intangible, tacit, observable primarily in action, and may be complex and difficult to obtain in any kind of verbal form from the person who possesses it. It is the type of knowledge that a master craftsman passes on to an apprentice. It is the type of knowledge that a trainee doctor acquires during an internship. Implicit knowledge acquires commercial value only when it becomes explicit.

See also **Explicit knowledge; Tacit knowledge**.

References

Nonaka, Ikujiro and Takeuchi, Hirotaka (1995) *The Knowledge Creating Company, How Japanese companies create the dynamics of innovation*. Oxford, Oxford University Press.
http,//www.infed.org/thinkers/senge.htm

Incremental learning   Incremental learning usually means gradual step-by-step progress in the acquisition of usable information, steadily taking in more knowledge to support the models and frameworks that have already been learned. No major new insights result from this type of learning, primarily because it means building on existing learning.

For example, you may be fairly competent in making presentations. Many people stop there and don't bother to pursue excellence. However, you can always improve by adopting an attitude of continuous incremental improvement. There is always room for doing better, and there is always more to learn about any particular job. Maybe the organisation of your presentation could be improved by having a better introduction and a more positive conclusion. In between, you might use your tone, pitch, and delivery to create interest and variety. Being competent in one Windows-based software package means you can transfer the knowledge to another Windows-based package and learn it quite easily by building on your existing knowledge.

See also **Transformational learning**.

References
Malone, Samuel A. (2000) *Learning Skills for Managers*. Dublin, Oak Tree Press.
Mumford, Alan (1997) *Management Development Strategies for Action*. London, IPD.

Induction   Induction is the process of introducing the company and its culture and systems to a new employee, and incidentally of introducing the new employee to the company. The purpose is to familiarise the new employee with the workings of the organisation and facilitate a smooth integration. Induction provides background information about the company relating to management, organisation, culture, mission, vision, objectives, products manufactured or services provided, welfare facilities, holidays, promotion prospects. It demonstrates how the new employee's duties fit in with the overall scheme of things. It enables new staff members to become oriented to the business environment in which they now take part, to the company's policies and practices. It also ensures that initial work is performed to required standards. In addition to formal classroom-style training and on-the-job training, induction training may involve tours of the business, introductions to staff, videos of the manufacturing process and talks by senior managers.

References
Garavan, Thomas N., Costine, Pat and Heraty, Noreen (1997) *Training and Development in Ireland*. Dublin, Oak Tree Press.

Informal learning   Informal learning is the type of learning that happens on-the-job on a day-to-day basis. It tends to be conversation-based rather than follow a set curriculum, and in many cases probably accounts for most of a person's learning during a lifetime. The purpose of formal learning should be to provide the knowledge, concepts and capabilities to help us learn informally and to inculcate the desire to do so. Through informal learning we accumulate knowledge, skills, attitudes and insights from daily exposure to work, personal experiences and interaction with others. Informal learning can be acquired from newspapers, magazines, television, CDs, DVDs, the Internet and other computer media.

Informal learning is a type of self-education or self-directed learning. This is the best type of learning, provided it is reflected on and lessons are learned for future application. More learning must take place in the workplace and the home where it can be immediately employed to improve and add value to organisational and personal lives. The most effective aspect of management development is through informal on-the-job learning. The Institute for Research on Learning found that formal learning (courses and workshops) is the source of only about 20 per cent of the learning that takes place in organisations. This finding highlights the importance of informal learning.

Cheetham and Chivers (2001) have come up with a very useful model of informal learning for people who work in the professions. The general learning mechanisms identified were:

- practice, repetition and rehearsal – Practice makes perfect, and practice makes permanent. Generally the more often we do something, the better we become at it.

- reflection – Reflection is important to effective learning.

- observation and copying – Most of us learn by observing others. Modelling, role-play and shadowing can be effective here.

- extra-occupational transfer – People can benefit from learning in activities outside the workplace, the results of which can be used on-the-job.

- stretching activities – Things we haven't done before can be regarded as good development opportunities.

- perspective-changing/-switching – Reframing or seeing things from different viewpoints.

- mentor/coach interaction – Many successful managers admit that they owe their success to effective mentors.

- unconscious absorption or 'osmosis' – When working closely with other experts we sometimes unconsciously pick up some of their expertise.

- the use of psychological devices/mental tricks – Positive thinking, visualisation and reframing are some of the devices that successful managers adopt.

- articulation – Putting things down in writing clarifies one's thinking.

- collaboration – The effect of synergy is often achieved when working with others.

See also **Formal learning**; **Intuitive learning**.

References
Cheetham, Graham and Chivers, Geoff (2001) 'How professionals learn in practice: an investigation of informal learning amongst people working in professions', *Journal of European Industrial Training*, Volume 25, Number 5, pp247–292.
Mumford, Alan (1997) *Management Development Strategies for Action.* London, IPD.
http,//www.infed.org/biblio/inf-lrn.htm
http,//www.internettime.com/itimegroup/articles/knowledgeplatform.htm

Information overload   There is a tendency among managers and organisations to request and then process excessive amounts of information, with the result that organisational efficiency may be adversely affected – such managers and organisations may be described as suffering from information overload. Information overload is the condition in which the amount of information being processed is greater than can usefully be dealt with. This may lead to such negative outcomes as excessive cost, errors in processing and curtailment of the time required for the proper evaluation of alternatives when making decisions. With the Internet, information overload through the sheer complexity and number of sources of information has become a common reality.

Trainers should also be aware that learners may suffer from information overload if the trainer tries to cram too much information into a learning session. Information overload may cause a temporary barrier to the learners' ability to learn effectively. It is well known that our short-term memory can cope only with between five and nine pieces of information at a time.

See also **Cybernetic model of learning**; **Miller's seven plus or minus two rule**.

References
Cheetham, Graham and Chivers, Geoff (2001) 'How professionals learn in practice: an investigation of informal learning amongst people working in professions', *Journal of European Industrial Training*, Volume 25, Number 5, pp247–292.

Inhibitors to learning   This term is often used in the context of the 'learning organisation', and refers to factors that represent barriers to an organisation's intake of the kind of information that may give it a cutting edge in its market. The culture of an organisation can be a major inhibitor to learning. Because culture is difficult to identify and to change, as an inhibitor it is therefore a silent, almost invisible barrier that is at the same time very powerful. Learning tends to be discouraged in a bureaucracy. Inhibitors also appear at the strategic and structural levels. Strategic inhibitors include having no clear goals or direction for the organisation. Structural inhibitors include disruptive command-and-control management styles.

References

Argyris, Chris (1999) On Organisational Learning. Oxford, Blackwell Business.

Instructional model   An instructional model provides a guide intended to help a trainer suit his or her training style to the learning needs of the learning group to be trained. Many models hold that the trainer should vary his or her instructional style depending on the maturity of the learners. The maturity of a learner depends on:

- education and experience

- the capacity to set learning goals

- a willingness to accept responsibility for his or her own learning.

In a way an instructional model is comparable with models of leadership style. The following is based on Hersey and Blanchard's situational leadership model:

Leadership style

High	Learners of intermediate self-direction who have both skill and the basic knowledge and view themselves as being ready and able to explore specific subject areas.	Learners of moderate self-direction who are motivated and confident but largely ignorant of the subject matter.
	Learners of high self-direction who are both willing and able to plan, execute and evaluate their own learning with or without the help of a trainer.	Learners of low self-direction who need trainers to tell them what to do.

Low   Direction   High
          High   *Moderate*   *Low*
◄───►
                              Maturity of followers

Source: adapted from the Hersey-Blanchard situational model (1982)

According to this model there are four types of learner, each of which demands different treatment by a trainer:

- learners low in self-direction – Because of their lack of maturity and subject knowledge, these learners need the trainer's total attention. For example, new employees.

- moderately self-directed learners – These learners are motivated and confident but still need a significant input from the trainer because they know very little about the subject.

- learners who are intermediate in self-direction – These learners have both the skill and basic knowledge and see themselves being capable of exploring the subject further with the guidance of the trainer.

- learners high in self-direction – These learners are both confident and willing and able to plan, do, and evaluate their own learning with or without the help of a trainer. The trainer becomes a facilitator of learning.

Collins *et al* (1989) alternatively offer a six-stage progressive model of instruction:

1 modelling by an expert

2 coaching – the learner tries it out and the coach provides feedback on performance

3 'scaffolding' – the coach provides adequate support which is gradually reduced as the learner becomes more proficient

4 articulation – the learners can describe their problem-solving or reasoning process

5 reflection – the learners compare their problem-solving or reasoning process with that of the coach

6 exploration – the learners solve problems without support.

References
Cheetham, Graham and Chivers, Geoff (2001) 'How professionals learn in practice: an investigation of informal learning amongst people working in organisations', *Journal of European Industrial Training*, Volume 25, Number 5, pp247–292.
Collins, A., Brown, J. S. and Newman, S. E. (1989) 'Cognitive apprenticeships: teaching the crafts of reading, writing and mathematics', in Resnick, L. B. (ed.) *Knowing, Learning and Instruction, Essays in Honor of Robert Glaser*, Hillsdale, NJ, Lawrence Erlbaum Associates.
Hersey, P. and Blanchard, K. (1982) *The Management of Organisational Behavior*. New York, Prentice Hall.
Luthans, Fred (1995) *Organisational Behavior*, 7th edition. New York, McGraw-Hill.

Instructional style   Instructional styles can be didactic or facilitative or stages in between. There is no one best style. It really depends on the situation. A formally direct style may be necessary when making a demonstration or when getting across factual information. When dealing with adults who have their own experience and knowledge to bring to the training, a facilitative style is naturally more appropriate.

A trainer can learn as much from learning adults as they can from him or her

See also **Instructional model**.

Intellectual capital   The intellectual capital of an organisation corresponds to the knowledge and information, the skills, culture, inventiveness and research capabilities that it possesses. What a company knows is its competitive advantage. The physical assets of organisations – such as Internet companies, accountancy practices, advertising agencies and law firms – are negligible compared with the intellectual capital employed. Employees often know more about the technical aspects of their work than do the managers who manage them. For example, in the financial services industry many managers admit that they do not fully understand the derivatives and other exotic financial instruments that their staff trade on a daily basis.

One of the big drawbacks of downsizing is that some of the intellectual capital of the organisation goes out of the door with the departing employees. Organisations can never preserve their intellectual capital unless they make it explicit. Mergers and acquisitions are often prompted more by the prospect of acquiring intellectual capital than by physical assets. This intellectual capital can be eroded if key employees leave. In companies at the cutting edge of technology, the intellectual and creative ability of the research and development staff is crucial. If they decided to leave, it could have dire implications for the company.

See also **Intellectual property**.

References

Drummond, Helga (2000) *An Introduction to Organisational Behaviour*. Oxford, Oxford University Press.
Wexler, Mark N. (2002) 'Organisational memory and intellectual capital', *Journal of Intellectual Capital*, Volume 3, Number 4, pp393–414.
http,//www.internettime.com/itimegroup/articles/knowledgeplatform.htm

Intellectual property   A company's intellectual property corresponds to the knowledge and the rights of possession over that knowledge which the company may call upon the law to protect. A business may claim inviolable copyright, patent or trade-mark in respect of a particular product, process or design and against unauthorised imitation.

Intellectual property is a type of intangible asset capable of generating a stream of financial revenue for a company, and should thus be recognised as a capital resource on the balance sheet.

See also **Intellectual capital**.

Intelligence tests   In a world in which psychologists have found that the average intelligence of successive generations is rising, the most widely used intelligence tests include the Stanford-Binet Test and the Wechsler Intelligence Scales. Critics maintain that these tests are limited and are now very old-fashioned in concept. The original Binet test dates back to the first decade of the twentieth century, and the

Wechsler Scale derives from the 1940s. Although there have been cosmetic changes, the technology of 'measuring intelligence' has hardly changed in 100 years.

Any test designed to measure intelligence depends upon a definition of 'intelligence' as ability in abstract reasoning, forming concepts, problem-solving, dealing with new situations, and so on. Such tests generally contain a number of graded tasks which individuals have to tackle either orally or in a written format. Some, but not all, provide results in terms of an IQ ('intelligence quotient'), of which the principal use is as a diagnostic instrument to predict success in educational and/or occupational contexts.

In an organisation intelligence tests may be used in the selection process as a way of screening and reducing the number of candidates called for interview. Such a test may also be a way of ascertaining the suitability of someone for further development, perhaps for sponsorship on an MBA programme.

Critics say that intelligence tests favour groups from more affluent backgrounds and discriminate against less privileged racial, ethnic or social groups, and that they emphasise analytical skills far more than interpersonal, creative and practical skills. The critics claim that the reason IQ tests are good at predicting academic performances is because analytical skills are the ones most valued in formal education. Psychologists have therefore attempted to develop culture-free tests.

Gardner considered IQ tests to be a poor measure of real intelligence [see **SIMILAR model of intelligences**]. And indeed, many people who failed IQ tests have gone on to distinguish themselves in life. For example, the renowned mathematician Henri Poincaré did so poorly on the Binet IQ test that he was thought to be stupid. Robert J. Sternberg, IBM Professor of Psychology and Education at Yale University, admits that as a child he did poorly on IQ tests.

The French psychologist Alfred Binet recognised that mental ability is complex. The test that he initiated has been developed into the refined instruments of today. The practice is to sample a wide variety of mental abilities and combine scores on these performances into a suitable composite score – usually the Intelligence Quotient (IQ). IQ is an age-related measure of intelligence level. It is defined as 100 times the mental age (MA, determined by a standardised test) divided by the chronological age (CA). Note that this procedure establishes the average IQ.

The concept of mental age has fallen into disrepute. Few tests now involve the computation of mental age – yet many tests yield an IQ score. An average score is 100; a score of 130 or above is considered gifted; whereas a score below 70 is considered backward or retarded. However, such a test may obscure almost as much as it reveals of the true potential of a person. Suppose two people take a single-score test composed equally of verbal and numerical questions. One answers only a few numerical questions correctly but gets almost every verbal question right. The other picks up a few points on the verbal side but answers all numerical questions correctly. If both people get the same score, they will be classed as having the same IQ – yet they have different abilities.

Properly-designed IQ tests follow objective statistical rules. An IQ test is not a test of acquired knowledge. It attempts to measure the ability to manipulate the elements of a problem in such a way as to find a solution that has not been part of formal training. General mental ability is only one kind of intelligence. Many people possess specialised abilities – verbal, numerical, perceptual, spatial, and so on, which can also be measured by special tests. Elevated to the status of skills, these abilities are vital in specialised walks of life and in the professional and academic fields.

Although there are no differences in overall intelligence between the sexes, there are differences on some of the specialised abilities. Women are superior to men in verbal and memory skills. Men have the edge when it comes to perceptual and spatial skills.

Since its inception, the dominant use of the intelligence test has been as a predictor of scholastic success. There should be little surprise, therefore, that the 'adaptive and successful' behaviours have been precisely those of reasoning, judging, learning, dealing with novelty, abstracting, and so forth. Generally, people who score well on IQ tests do better at school and university. They also tend to enter the higher professions. However, success in life also depends on other qualities such as ambition, dedication, persistence, hard work and luck. It is now well established that intelligence is not fixed but an open dynamic system that can develop throughout life.

See also **Emotional intelligence**; **SIMILAR model of intelligences**.

References
Myers, David G. (1995) *Psychology*. New York, Worth.
Sternberg, Robert J. (1995) *In Search of the Human Mind*. New York, Harcourt Brace College Publishers.
http,//www.21learn.org/arch/articles/sternberg.html
http,//www.21learn.org/publ/edleadership1997.html
file,//C,\Program Files\Britannica\BCD\Cache_11_PreviewRil.htm
http,//www.theatlantic.com//issues/99feb/intel.htm
http,//www.theatlantic.com//issues/99feb/intel2.htm
http,//www.theatlantic.com//issues/99feb/intel3.htm

Intensity   The more intense your interest in a topic, the more likely you are to remember it. Hobbies are areas that people have a fund of knowledge about because they are interested and naturally review their knowledge. Develop an interest in your topic for better learning and recall. Read around your topic. At the very least, if business is your interest, read an appropriate professional journal and the business pages in the newspapers. Interest creates motivation and counteracts boredom. Integrate what you want to remember into your everyday activities. Information is forgotten quickly if not actively reflected on and used. Intensity, motivation, interest and confidence are all interlinked. Each reinforces the others. The more success you have, the more confident and motivated you become. Similarly, the more enthusiastic you are about a topic, the better your ability to learn and recall.

See also **Interest**.

References
Higbee, Kenneth L. (1990) Your Memory: How it works and how to improve it. London, Piatkus.

Interest   People who are interested in a topic find it easier to learn it. Interest engages attention. You pay attention to things you are interested in. We remember so much more about people, places and subjects that interest us. Make the material more interesting and of value to you and your recall will improve. Leonardo da Vinci said, 'Just as eating against one's will is injurious to health, so study without a liking for it spoils the memory, and it retains nothing it takes in.'

See also **Intensity**.

References
Swiercinsky, Dennis P. (1995) *Fifty Ways You Can Improve Your Memory.* Mission, World Wisdom Inc.

Internet   The Internet is a complex of linked computer networks, worldwide in scope, that facilitates data communication services such as e-mail, the World Wide Web, chat rooms, and newsgroups. It consists of millions of computers and tens of millions of users. The World Wide Web has seen the emergence of e-commerce by which companies promote and sell their products. We can access people from all over the world on the Internet. The Internet has eliminated the need for a physical presence and created the facilities for virtual learning. There are unlimited learning and developmental opportunities on the Internet. Training and even degree programmes can now be accessed on a wide range of topics on the net. The 'learndirect' e-learning network – part of the University for Industry – brings training and learning opportunities directly into the workplace.

See also **Corporate university; Intranet**.

References
Pollitt, David (2002) 'Pod transforms learning at K. Stevens', *Education and Training*, Volume 44, Number 7, pp328–329.
Pollitt, David (2002) 'Executives "plug in" to electronic commerce', *Education and Training*, Volume 22, Number 7, pp330–331.
El-Tannir, Akram A. (2002) 'The corporate university model for continuous learning, training and development', *Education and Training*, Volume 44, Number 2, pp76–81.
Sloman, Martyn (2001) *The E-learning Revolution.* London, CIPD.

Interpersonal intelligence   Interpersonal intelligence is one of the seven intelligences discerned by Howard Gardner in his book *Frames of Mind* (1984). People with this intelligence are good at interpersonal relationships. They have a good sense of empathy and get along very well with others. They like to have many friends, talk to people and join groups. Well-known examples would include the late Diana, Princess of Wales, and TV personalities Oprah Winfrey and Terry Wogan. They tend to be extroverts. Salespeople, trainers, social directors, travel agents, and human resource people such as interviewers, counsellors and negotiators need this ability to survive in their jobs.

The interpersonal learner learns best by sharing, comparing, relating, co-operating, influencing, negotiating, resolving conflicts and interviewing. To enhance this ability get involved in teams, debating societies, teach others, lead discussions, coach and mentor others, conduct interviews and seminars, engage in small-talk with shop assistants and socialise as much as possible. We all have this intelligence to a lesser or greater extent. It is up to each person to develop it further.

Silberman (2001) maintains that whereas IQ will get you hired, you need PQ ('people quotient' – a supposed measure of interpersonal intelligence) to get you promoted.

See also **SIMILAR model of intelligences**.

References

Armstrong, Thomas (1993) *Seven Kinds of Smart: Identifying and developing your many intelligences.* London, Plume.
Gardner, Howard (1993). *Frames of Mind: The theory of multiple intelligences.* London, Fontana.
Goleman, D. (1996) *Emotional Intelligence: Why can it matter more than IQ?* London, Bloomsbury.
Silberman, Mel (2001) 'Developing interpersonal intelligence in the workplace', *Industrial and Commercial Training*, Volume 33, Number 7, pp266–270.
Vincent, Annette and Ross, Dianne (2001) 'Personalise training: determine learning styles, personality types and multiple intelligences online', *The Learning Company*, Volume 8, Number 1, pp36–43.
http,//www.famu.edu/sjmga/ggrow/7ln/Personal.html

Intranet   A private electronic communications system available via semi-independent terminals only to employees and managers of one organisation. It is a medium that makes the organisation's intellectual capital accessible to staff. The term 'extranet' is applied when the system is opened up to stakeholders outside the company such as suppliers and customers. The potential of the intranet as a learning medium is enormous. It can also be used to support teleworking.

See also **Internet**.

References

Sloman, Martyn (2001) *The E-learning Revolution.* London, CIPD.

Intrapersonal intelligence   Intrapersonal intelligence is one of the seven intelligences discerned by Howard Gardner in his book *Frames of Mind* (1984). People with this intelligence tend to be introverts. In learning style models they are called reflectors. They tend to be introspective, focusing on inner feelings and intuitions. People with intrapersonal intelligence have a high level of self-understanding. They know their own strengths and weaknesses, motivations, interests, goals and feelings. Monks and others in the contemplative religious life tend to have developed this ability to a high degree. Freud's science of psychoanalysis emerged from his great capacity for introspection. For Jung, people were either introverts or extroverts. Writers, philosophers, therapists, entrepreneurs and psychologists need this ability to be successful in their careers. Well-known examples would include Plato, Aristotle and Socrates.

To enhance this sort of intelligence in yourself, reflect on your life's experiences on a daily basis and record them in a diary. We all have this intelligence to a lesser or greater extent. The intrapersonal learner learns best from individual projects, research and computer-based training. Use guided imagery to solve problems.

See also **SIMILAR model of intelligences**.

References

Armstrong, Thomas (1993) *Seven Kinds of Smart: Identifying and developing your many intelligences*, London, Plume.
Gardner, Howard (1993) *Frames of Mind: The theory of multiple intelligences*. London, Fontana.
Vincent, Annette and Ross, Dianne (2001) 'Personalise training: determine learning styles, personality types and multiple intelligence online', *The Learning Company*, Volume 8, Number 1, pp36–43.
http,//www.famu.edu/sjmga/ggrow/ggrow/7ln/Personal.html

In-tray exercises   In in-tray exercises, which may be used in management training, a real or conceptual in-tray contains a typical day's work in the form of memos, reports, fax, e-mails and diary notes, all of which have to be dealt with by the manager. The exercise can be made more realistic by including interruptions in the form of telephone calls, personal callers, urgent meetings, disciplinary problems, and so on. In-tray exercises test a manager's ability to solve problems, work under pressure and prioritise tasks as in the real world. They can be used to test technical, administrative, managerial, financial, time-management and interpersonal skills. Learners receive feedback on the possible consequences of their chosen courses of action.

In-tray exercises are an integral part of the assessment centre approach.

References

Prior, John (1991) *A Handbook of Training and Development*. Aldershot, Gower, published in association with the Institute of Training and Development.

Introvert learners Introvert learners prefer to learn on their own rather than in a group. In general introvert learners:

■ like to reflect on new skills and approaches before trying them out

■ like to learn in private even when part of a group – their silence and lack of participation should not be interpreted as lack of interest: comments when they do come are often very worthwhile and insightful

- enjoy learning for learning's sake – new information may be seen as coming in useful at some future date

- usually feel stressed after a lot of interaction.

See also **Extrovert learners**.

Intuitive learning   Intuitive learning is learning unconsciously from experience – just 'picking things up'. The subconscious mind learns more than the conscious mind, and it does so seemingly effortlessly. There is much we do not understand about the subconscious mind, but it seems that it tirelessly recognises and records everything we see, say and do, 24 hours a day. It is learning without reflection. Learning happens inevitably from experiencing.

We are truly learning machines. We are learning all the time, whether we are aware of it or not. It is a natural outcome of experience. Mumford says that people who learn in this way are content that learning occurs as if through some natural process of osmosis. Individuals are clearly aware that they have learned something but they cannot articulate what.

See also **Accidental learning**.

References

Mumford, Alan (1997) *Management Development Strategies for Action*, 3rd edition. London, IPD.

Involvement   To maximise learners' retention of your training you must maximise the learners' involvement. Techniques of involvement include discussion tasks, case studies and role-play. Lack of involvement may lead to lack of concentration and boredom.

J

Job aids   Job aids are instructional items located in the workplace to help an employee recall information presented during training. Job aids facilitate the learning process and reduce training time. They are best for teaching job skills and are particularly valuable when integrated into a training programme. They may be printed on posters or cue cards, or be presented online.

See also **Just-in-time learning**.

References
Garavan, Thomas N., Costine, Pat and Heraty, Noreen (1997). *Training and Development in Ireland.* Dublin, Oak Tree Press.

Job analysis   The *Glossary of Training Terms* (Department of Employment, 1978) describes job analysis as 'the process of examining a job in detail in order to identify its component tasks'. A job analysis identifies the knowledge, skills and attitudes required by the job-holder, and describes the duties, activities and responsibilities involved in the position.

References
Garavan, Thomas N., Costine, Pat and Heraty, Noreen (1997) *Training and Development in Ireland.* Dublin, Oak Tree Press.

Job enlargement   Job enlargement is a means of presenting a new challenge to an employee by giving him or her a greater variety of tasks to do. It does provide some learning opportunites and some job satisfaction but is obviously not as stretching as job enrichment. It amounts to a type of on-the-job learning.

See also **Job enrichment**; **Job rotation**.

References
Cole, G. A. (1995) *Organisational Behaviour.* London, DP Publications.

Job enrichment   Job enrichment is a means of presenting a new challenge to an employee by giving him or her more responsible and more demanding tasks to do. As well as representing a great source of learning, this provides opportunities for achievement, recognition, esteem and responsibility. It amounts to a type of on-the-job learning.

In brain research it has been established that an intellectually enriched environment improves brain capacity.

See also **Job enlargement**; **Job rotation**.

References
Cole, G. A. (1995) *Organisational Behaviour*. London, DP Publications.
http,//www.newhorizons.org/blab_diamond3.html

Job rotation   Job rotation allocates managers a series of lateral job assignments in different parts of the organisation for a period of time from three months to twelve months. A switch between a line job and a functional job is particularly insightful. Here the manager learns the difference between the hands-on action-oriented approach required in a line job in comparison with the more laid-back reflective and strategic style necessary in a staff role.

The primary objective of job rotation is to improve managers' problem-solving and decision-making skills while at the same time giving them an overall perspective of the company and the interface between departments. Job rotation helps managers to crystallise their career paths and improves job satisfaction and motivation. To maximise the effectiveness of job rotation, managers should be given the appropriate level of responsibility to use new skills and make decisions. Job rotation amounts to a type of on-the-job learning.

Ideally, mentors who are available for coaching, counselling and advice should support the job rotation programme. Role rotation within teams also provides opportunities for learning, as people struggle to master an unfamiliar role. On a more limited scale, task rotation within a section can provide wider experience and developmental opportunities.

Job rotation may be part of a professional accountancy training programme making sure that potential accountants are exposed to the required range of financial, management and business experience.

See also **Job enlargement**; **Job enrichment**.

References
Cole, G. A. (1995) *Organisational Behaviour*. London, DP Publications.

Johari window   The Johari window – named after its designers, Joe Luft and Harry Ingram – was created to help people understand how they interact with others, and how disclosing personal information can improve rapport. It is a two-by-two table that contrasts areas of public and private information about an individual.

Self

	Known	Unknown
Known	Public Area	Blind Area
Unknown	Closed Area	Unknown Area

Others (label on left, rows: Known / Unknown)

Source: Loft (1961)

■ The first box of the window is the public area. This represents information known to both oneself and others. The information includes one's manner of speech, marital status and favourite pastimes. This is the type of information that facilitates communication and rapport. According to the model, the more information that is in the public area, the greater the degree of rapport. This requires a great deal of trust.

■ The second box of the window is the blind area. Information in this box is known to others but not to oneself. For example, staff may well know that their manager is usually in a bad mood early in the morning but that by the afternoon his mood has improved for the better. So if they want to get approval for something, the best time to look for it is in the afternoon. People with large blind areas can be difficult to deal with. They are often grumpy and insensitive to others. They often lack rapport and can be manipulated by sycophants.

■ The third box of the window is the closed area. It represents information known to oneself but not shared with others. This area may include personal feelings about others, your opinion of the boss and information about your personal life. People keep information in the closed area because they feel that disclosure would damage their reputation and undermine their position. Where trust in an organisation is low, the closed area is large and the public area is small. On the other hand, where trust is high in the organisation, the closed area is small and the public area is large.

■ The fourth box of the window is the unknown area. Information in this box is unknown to oneself and to others. It includes unconscious motivations, repressed feelings and past memories. Some psychologists believe that information from the unknown area has an important impact on the ways people behave in all areas. In the USA the A. K. Rice Institute offers group relations workshops designed to help people understand the unconscious ways in which they respond to issues of power, authority and gender within organisations.

Obviously, the Johari window can be very useful as a personal development tool. Correctly used it can help us learn to become more open, transparent and sensitive to the needs of others. When we meet people for the first time, we are reluctant to disclose much about ourselves and the open window is very small. As trust develops we disclose more and more about ourselves. Our background, history, beliefs and attitudes become known. Thus the open window becomes larger and the closed window becomes smaller. To increase the open window further it is necessary to reduce the blind area. This can be achieved by being more open and honest and by seeking and accepting feedback from other people. As the open area grows and the hidden and blind areas diminish, it is likely that the unknown area will reduce as well. This will lead to greater self-awareness and rapport with others.

Most organisations encourage the expansion, rather than the contraction, of the closed area. Companies tend to hire hands rather than hearts, and to show only superficial concern for people's personal and domestic lives. They expect you to do your job, collect your pay, keep your mouth shut and keep your troubles to yourself. Dealing with personal issues is often viewed as a minefield.

References
Loft, J. (1961) 'The Johari Window', *Human Relations Training News*, 5, pp6–7.
Smither, Robert D., Houston, John M. and McIntire, Sandra D. (1996). *Organisation Development: Strategies for changing environments*. New York, HarperCollins.

Jug-and-mug approach   The 'jug-and-mug' approach is trainers' slang for an attitude to training that might fit the headlines 'Expert pours knowledge into passive receptacle'. It is an approach that sees the brain as an empty vessel and the job of the trainer or teacher to fill it with useful information. It represents the antithesis of a learner-centred approach. Under the jug-and-mug approach the trainer adopts the role of instructor rather than facilitator. Such an approach tends to create learned helplessness in people, by which the learner becomes totally dependent on the trainer rather than taking responsibility for his or her own learning.

Lectures may have their place in a learning situation, especially where learners have no knowledge of the topic, but simply talking at learners doesn't achieve learning at a deep level. Training should equip people for further self-initiated development beyond the content of a training programme. As Plutarch said, 'The mind is not a vessel to be filled but a fire to be ignited.'

See also **Action learning**; **Activity-based learning (ABL)**; **Transmission model**.

Junior boards   A junior board may be set up to shadow the board of directors in order to give younger managers some insight into how the company is governed, how strategies are developed, how decisions are made, and how policies are formulated. The junior board learns how to take a strategic view of the business and the policy-making process. It may be given the same information on which to base its decisions as the senior board. The decisions the junior board would take can be benchmarked against the actual decisions taken by the senior board.

The main purpose of the junior board is to develop rising stars for future senior management positions within the company. Because junior boards have no real power, responsibility or accountability, this method of developing managers is not widely used.

References
Mumford, Alan (1997). *Management Development Strategies for Action*, 3rd edition. London, IPD.

Just-in-time learning (JITL)   Just-in-time learning implies being able to access learning just when you need it to solve a particular workplace problem – the right information, in the right place, at the right time, for the right problem. Learning is thus more focused on the company's business. Just-in-time learning is highly motivational because it is applied to an immediate problem with immediate results. Computers can be used to facilitate this process. A knowledge platform can be built to capture critical corporate information. Just-in-time learning is available as the need arises.

This is the opposite of just-in-case learning which we get during our formal education or on subsequent training programmes. Just-in-case learning is quickly forgotten because it has no immediate application. Just-in-time learning is a form of active learning through which relevant information is acquired and critical thinking and problem-solving skills are developed at the same time.

See also **Job aids**.

References
El-Tannir, Akram A. (2002 'The corporate university model for continuous learning, training and development', *Education and Training*, Volume 44, Number 2, pp76–81.
Malone, Samuel A. (2000) *Learning Skills for Managers*. Dublin, Oak Tree Press.
http,//www.internettime.com/itimegroup/articles/knowledgeplatform.htm

K

Key words Key words are cues that relate to concepts. Psychologists have long established that effective learners learn concepts and broad principles rather than cluttering their minds with detail. So key words are those words that bring to mind the main concepts of the text. The more concrete they are, the more memorable. They are usually nouns. They are words that trigger off a whole range of other words and images. They are the hooks on which other words can be hung and chained together. Concrete words that convert to visual images are on the whole more easily remembered than abstract words for which imagery is difficult. Key words form the basis of learning maps.

See also **Learning map**.

References
Buzan, Tony and Buzan, Barry (1993) *The Mind Map Book*. London, BBC Books.
Malone, Samuel A. (1996). *Learning to Learn*. London, CIMA.

Kinesthetic intellegence Kinesthetic intelligence is one of the seven intelligences discerned by Howard Gardner in his book *Frames of Mind* (1984). 'Kinesthetic' describes learning through doing, moving and touching. Athletes, racing-drivers, dancers, masseurs, chiropractors, osteopaths, mime artists, gymnasts and sculptors all have this intelligence. Surgeons need fine-tuned kinesthetic skills to carry out operations, and skilled tradespeople need highly developed manual skills. Well-known famous examples of people with kinesthetic intelligence would include Thomas Edison, Michael Flatley, Fred Astaire, George Best, Charlie Chaplin and Muhammad Ali.

People with this ability have a hands-on approach and tend to be mechanically-minded. Experiential learning enhances this ability. The action learning approach to management development uses this intelligence. Get learners to perform the job, role-play, demonstrate to others, and simulate real situations. To enhance this ability, use body language, take notes, make models, walk up and down as you learn, learn on the job, and practise. The importance of practice to success was emphasised by Gary

Player, who is reputed to have said, 'The more I practise, the luckier I get.' Practice makes perfect. We all have this intelligence to a lesser or greater degree.

See also **SIMILAR model of intelligences**.

References

Armstrong, Thomas (1993) *Seven Kinds of Smart: Identifying and developing your many intelligences*. London, Plume.

Gardner, Howard (1993). *Frames of Mind: The theory of multiple intelligences*. London, Fontana.

Vincent, Annette and Ross, Dianne (2001) 'Personalize training: determine learning styles, personality types and multiple intelligences online', *The Learning Organisation*, Volume 8, Number 1, pp36–43.

Stine, Jean Marie (2000) *Super Brain Power: Six keys to unlocking your hidden genius*. New York, Prentice Hall.

http,//www.famu.edu/sjmga/ggrow/7ln/Bodily.html

Kirpatrick's model of evaluation

Kirkpatrick's model divides the evaluation of training into four levels corresponding to reaction, learning, behaviour and results.

- At the reaction level, 'reactionnaires' are used to collect opinions about the learning. Learning can be categorised into knowledge, skills and attitudes. This is a measure of customer satisfaction taken immediately on the conclusion of the course programme. At best it provides subjective impressions and should not be considered proof of learning.

- Knowledge can be evaluated by exams, multiple-choice questions and programmed learning. Skills can be tested by practical demonstration. Attitudes can be measured by psychometric tests. A pre-test and post-test check should be carried out so that any learning can be attributed to the training programme. In theory, a control group should be used for comparison with the actual training group. In practice, this is rarely done because of the cost and logistics involved.

- Behaviour can be evaluated by 'before' and 'after' measures. The organisational climate must support the transfer of training. The need for transfer of training should be built in at the training design stage. Course participants should be encouraged to draw up action plans for transferring the skills learned on the course to their own work. If they don't use it, they'll lose it, making the training nothing but a complete waste of time and money. Has on-the-job behaviour changed as a result of the training? Ongoing performance appraisal may be useful in this context, including 360-degree feedback.

- Results may be evaluated at the departmental or corporate levels by cost/benefit analysis. Has the efficiency, effectiveness, productivity and profitability of the company improved as a result of the training? All evaluation should begin with an identification of needs analysis. Training needs should ultimately be linked to corporate objectives via session objectives, programme objectives, section objectives and departmental objectives. Secondary data – such as reductions in downtime, accident rates, absenteeism, customer feedback, assembly-line rejects, staff turnover and employee grievances – may all be partly or totally attributable to training.

The main strength of this model is the focus on the change in behaviour. However, the model does not consider the measurement of other critical areas before training, such as objectives, contents and equipment needed for training. Evaluation gets progressively more difficult, costly and time-consuming to do as you move from reaction to learning, to behaviour, and finally to results.

See also **CIRO model of evaluation**; **Evaluation**; **NOTES model of training**; **Training objectives**.

References

Kirkpatrick, D. L. (1976) *Evaluation of Training: A training and development handbook.* New York, McGraw-Hill.

Sadler-Smith, Eugene (1996) 'Learning styles: a holistic approach', *Journal of Industrial Training*, Volume 20, Number 7, pp29–36.

Tennant, Charles, Boonkrong, Mahithorn and Roberts, Paul A. B. (2002) 'The design of a training programme measurement model', *Journal of European Industrial Training*, Volume 26, Number 5, pp230–240.

Knowledge   Knowledge has been described as representations of facts and concepts to help us plan for the future and solve problems. It is useful to distinguish between 'knowing how' from 'knowing what'. Intelligence is all about knowing how to use knowledge. 'Knowing how' enables us to use our past experiences to shape our future. There is a saying which maintains that practice without theory is blind and theory without practice is useless. Knowledge is not something a learner absorbs. Knowledge is something a learner creates. Clarke and Rollo (2001) highlight the difference between data, information, and knowledge:

- Data is sets of discrete objective facts, presented without judgement or context. Data becomes information when categorised, analysed, summarised and placed in context, becoming intelligible to the recipient.

- Information is data endowed with relevance and purpose. Information develops into knowledge when used to make comparisons, assess consequences, establish connections and engage in dialogue. Information is used in decision-making.

- Knowledge is information that comes with insights, framed experience, intuition, judgement and values. In some sense, knowledge represents truth and therefore offers a reliable basis for action. Knowledge is the body of understanding and skills that is constructed mentally by people. It increases through reflection and interaction with other people.

Learners need time to make sense of knowledge through reflection, integration, application and reinforcement. Learning is quickly lost if there is no opportunity for immediate application.

See also **Attitude**; **Skills**; **Wisdom**.

References

Clarke, Thomas and Rollo, Christine (2001) 'Corporate initiatives in knowledge management', *Education and Training*, Volume 43, Number 4/5, pp206–214.

Knowledge conversion model

The knowledge conversion model highlights the importance of capturing implicit knowledge and making it explicit so that it can be used elsewhere in the organisation or sold outside to others. Devised by Ikujiro Nonaka and Hirotaka Takeuchi, the model is illustrated below:

KNOWLEDGE CONVERSION MODEL

Tacit knowledge to explicit knowledge

Tacit knowledge	Socialisation	Externalisation
from		
explicit knowledge	Internalisation	Combination

Source: Ikujiro Nonaka and Hirotaka Takeuchi (1995)

- *Socialisation* is the process by which tacit knowledge is passed from one person to another. Tacit knowledge is knowledge that is understood but not expressed in writing. The key to tacit knowledge is shared experience. For example, a craft apprentice learns by watching the master craftsman. Learning is through demonstration, observation, imitation and practice. The apprentice is socialised into the craft. However, socialisation is a rather limited form of knowledge creation. The knowledge is transferred to the apprentice without either the apprentice or the master gaining any systematic insight into their craft knowledge. The knowledge does not become explicit or captured in any tangible form, and as a result the company is unable to use it elsewhere. Made explicit, the knowledge becomes intellectual property, which could be used to train other apprentices or generate revenue on a consultancy basis for the company. Socialisation yields sympathetic knowledge, such as shared mental models or technical skills.

- *Externalisation* or articulation is the process by which tacit knowledge is made into explicit knowledge. This happens when the master craftman is able to articulate his knowledge so that it can be recorded and used to train others without the craftsman's being present. Articulation is often through stories, metaphors, analogies, concepts, hypotheses or models. Externalistion opens up all sorts of possibilities for the company. For example, the knowledge might be made into a software program. It has now become intellectual property that can be used by trainees or sold to external clients. Explicit or recorded information can be discussed, debated, reflected and improved upon. Externalisation creates technical knowledge.

■ *Internalisation* is what happens when explicit knowledge is shared with others so that they make it part of their own store of knowledge and experience through reflection. In other words, they have internalised the explicit knowledge and made it tacit. It is closely related to learning by doing. Internalisation supports true understanding. It is like learning to drive, which becomes second nature. Internalisation gives rise to operational knowledge such as new production processes.

■ *Combination* is the process by which explicit knowledge is integrated with more explicit knowledge. Individuals exchange and combine knowledge through documents, meetings, telephone and computer networks. Reconfiguration of existing information can lead to new knowledge. For example, a management accountant may combine knowledge from different parts of the company and put it in a new format such as monthly accounts to assist managers to make better decisions. All that has happened is that existing knowledge has been recombined and reorganised in a different way. This does not add to the organisation's total knowledge. Combination gives rise to systemic knowledge such as a new product prototype.

See also **Knowledge management**.

References
Clarke, Thomas and Rollo, Christine (2001) 'Corporate initiatives in knowledge management', *Education and Training*, Volume 43, Number 4/5, pp206–214.
Nonaka, Ikujiro and Takeuchi, Hirotaka (1995) *The Knowledge Creating Company: How Japanese companies create the dynamics of innovation.* Oxford, Oxford University Press.

Knowledge management
Knowledge management refers to the systematic management of knowledge in an organisation which realises that knowledge can provide its most important competitive edge. Productivity is determined more by intelligence and systems than by fixed assets such as buildings and machinery. In the past few hundred years we have gone from a farm-based economy to a factory-based economy, and now, very rapidly, to a computer-based economy. For the first time since the Industrial Revolution the world's richest man, Bill Gates, is a knowledge-worker rather than an industrial tycoon. Automation, robotics and computer-controlled machines have revolutionised manufacturing technology. Information and communications technology has revolutionised our ability to create, store, retrieve, manage and transmit information.

Knowledge management systems are especially important in today's business environment where many organisations are re-engineering, downsizing, and losing senior managers due to early retirement. Such systems can capture the institutional memory of the organisation before this intellectual capital is lost. In the knowledge organisation, employees become valuable capital assets acquiring knowledge, synthesising it, and passing that knowledge throughout the company. We should learn from the past so that we do not have to reinvent the wheel. Most organisations safeguard their financial assets but few give knowledge management the priority it deserves.

Knowledge can be tacit or explicit. Tacit knowledge is the knowledge in the heads of managers and employees acquired through experience and reflection. Managerial skills are learned on-the-job and are often difficult to articulate to others. Explicit knowledge is recorded in writing or held on a computer. Explicit knowledge includes management information systems, procedures, rules and regulations, reports and minutes of meetings. One of the objectives of knowledge management is to convert tacit knowledge into explicit knowledge. Tacit knowledge has been described as 'knowledge that goes home every night'. As such, if people leave the organisation, it just walks out of the door with them. Tacit knowledge rather than explicit knowledge often supports creativity and innovation.

It is difficult and expensive to convert tacit knowledge to explicit knowledge, but it may be very worthwhile. Tacit knowledge that is captured and recorded can be studied and passed on to others and converted into software packages. These software packages can in turn be used to train others or, indeed, sold commercially.

More than 70 per cent of jobs in the developed world depend on brain-power rather than brawn. Today, engineers and other professionals find that a significant proportion of their knowledge is obsolete within five years. It is estimated that 80 per cent of children in primary schools will enter jobs and careers that don't exist now, involving technology that hasn't yet been invented. The amount of information in the world is doubling every five to 10 years. In the past land, labour, materials and machines were the key factors of production. Today it is knowledge, information, ideas and creativity. Hence the need for lifelong learning to equip people for change and new job opportunities.

Liebowitz and Beckman (1998) describe a process involving eight steps for knowledge management:

1   identify – Determine core competencies, sourcing strategy, and knowledge domains.

2   capture – Formalise existing knowledge.

3   select – Assess the value, accuracy and relevance of knowledge.

4 store – Use various knowledge formats to store corporate knowledge in the knowledge management system.

5 share – Distribute knowledge automatically to users based on interest and work; use virtual teams to collaborate on knowledge work.

6 apply – Retrieve and use knowledge in making decisions, solving problems, automating or supporting work, job aids, and training.

7 create – Use research, experiments, and creative thinking to discover new knowledge.

8 sell – Develop and market new knowledge-based products and services.

See also **Expert systems**.

References

Byrne, Roger (2001) 'Employees, capital or commodity?', *Career Development International*, Volume 006, Number 06, pp324–330.

Fee, Kenneth (2001) *A Guide To Management Development Techniques*. London, Kogan Page.

Liebowitz, Jay (1998) 'Expert systems: an integral part of knowledge management', *Kybernetes*, Volume 27, Number 2, pp170–175.

Liebowitz, Jay and Beckham, T. (1998) *Knowledge Organisations: What every manager should know*. Boca Raton, Fla., CRC Press.

Nonaka, Ikujiro and Takeuchi, Hirotaka (1995) *The Knowledge Creating Company: How Japanese companies create the dynamics of innovation*. Oxford, Oxford University Press.

http,//www.managementfirst.com/articles/t_beyond_training.htm

Knowledge of results   Knowledge of results is a major part of feedback. It is very difficult to learn unless you get feedback on how you are progressing in relation to benchmarks and in relation to others. Getting feedback on how successful you are has high motivational value, especially when the news is good. Knowledge of results must come as soon after the learning event as possible. The longer the time between the learning event and the feedback, especially if favourable, the less chance there is of the results' being motivational. On the other hand, knowledge of failure, particularly if it is frequent, can be equally devastating. The learning steps in a training programme should be short and correspond to a gradual build-up in the level of difficulty in order to facilitate a generally high level of success and frequent feedback.

See also **Feedback**.

References

Garavan, Thomas N., Costine, Pat and Heraty, Noreen (1997) *Training and Development in Ireland*. Dublin, Oak Tree Press.

Kolb's learning styles model   David Kolb has created a well-known model of learning styles focused around two separate learning activities, perception and processing.

Perception can be divided into opposites:

- concrete experience, such as feeling, touching, seeing and hearing
- abstract conceptualisation, as when using mental or visual concepts.

After the information is perceived, it must then be processed. Information may be processed in either of two ways:

- active experimentation, such as doing something with the information
- reflective observation, such as thinking about the information.

There are four learning dimensions in this model. They may be recalled by means of the acronym COAT, which stands for Concrete experience, Observation and reflection, Abstract conceptualisation, and Testing.

- *concrete experience* – Such learners learn from specific (concrete) experiences, relating to and empathising with people, and being sensitive to feelings. The trainer should get these learners involved in project work.

- *observation and reflection* – Such learners learn from careful observation before making a judgement, viewing things from different perspectives, and exploring meaning and understanding. These learners should be encouraged to use learning logs or journals, or to brainstorm.

- *abstract conceptualisation* – Such learners learn by analysing ideas, systematic planning and doing things only when what's involved is thoroughly understood. Lectures, handouts and analogies work well for these learners.

- *testing in new situations or active experimentation* – Such learners learn by getting things done, risk-taking and influencing people through action. The trainer should get these learners to do simulations, case studies and classwork.

Combining these four dimensions, Kolb derives the following learning model:

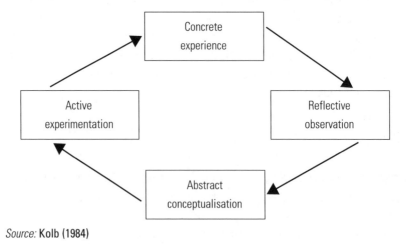

Source: **Kolb (1984)**

Kolb's learning cycle is therefore concrete experience, reflective observation, abstract conceptualisation and active experimentation.

But learners are ordinarily more complex than to belong to any single one of the dimensions listed above. According to Kolb there are four types of learners, each combining two dimensions:

- the converger – abstract conceptualisation plus active experimentation. You are a hands-on learner. You like to apply your learning in real-life situations. You tend to be unemotional and have narrow interests.

- the diverger – concrete experience plus reflective observation. You perceive things from different angles. You prefer to observe rather than take action. You like to collect and categorise information. You use imaginative problem-solving approaches. You are interested in people and have broad cultural interests. You are a sensitive learner.

- the assimilator – abstract conceptualisation plus reflective observation. You have a strong ability to create theoretical models. You excel in inductive reasoning. You prefer abstract concepts to people.

- the accommodator – concrete experience plus active experimentation. Your greatest strength is doing things. You are more of a risk-taker. You perform well in response to immediate problems. You solve problems intuitively.

References

Buckley, Roger and Caple, Jim (1992) *The Theory and Practice of Training*, 2nd edition. London, Kogan Page.

Kolb, D. A. (1984) *Experiential Learning: Experiences as the source of learning and development.* New Jersey, Prentice Hall.

http,//www.cyg.net/~jblackmo/diglib/styl-a.html

http,//www.infed.org/biblio/b-explrn.htm

http,//www.reviewing.co.uk/research/learning.cycles.htm

http,//www.aitech.ac.jp/~iteslj/Articles/Kelly_Experiential/

http,//granite.cyg.net/~jblackmo/diglib/styl-d.html

http,//www.algonquinc.on.ca/edtech/gened/styles.html

Korsakoff's psychosis 　Korsakoff's psychosis is a memory disorder usually caused by the chronic abuse of alcohol and an associated failure to eat properly, resulting in a lack of thiamine or vitamin B1. Most seriously affected is short-term memory, including the ability to learn new information. Long-term memory may remain unaffected, so that a sufferer may remember what happened 20 years ago but not be able to remember what happened 20 minutes previously. One of the hallmarks of Korsakoff's psychosis is the sufferer's complete unawareness of the memory deficiency and a tendency to invent immediate past history.

See also **Alcohol and learning**.

References

Noll, Richard and Turkington, Carol (1994). *The Encyclopedia of Memory and Memory Disorders.* New York, Facts on File Inc.

http,//www.findarticles.com/cf_0/g2601/0007/2601000799/print.jhtml

L

Law of reversed effort The 'law of reversed effort' is a slightly tongue-in-cheek description of how, sometimes when you are trying to remember something, the more you try to remember it the less you succeed. Relax! Worrying about an elusive name, word or tune will only make it more difficult for you to remember. If you dismiss it from your mind and start to do other things, the chances are that what you are trying to remember will unexpectedly jump into your mind.

See also **Tip of the tongue**.

References
Higbee, Kenneth L. (1990) *Your memory: How it works and how to improve it.* London, Piatkus.

Laws of learning There are quite a few 'laws' related to the subject of learning:

- *the law of association* – Adult learners learn by linking, connecting, and associating new knowledge to prior knowledge and existing experience. Techniques like learning maps, previewing and the SQ3R method act as advance organisers by facilitating the acquisition of new concepts, knowledge and information.

- *the law of effect* – You are more likely to learn and pursue your learning on a longer-term basis if the learning is rewarded, and is pleasant, satisfying, and enjoyable. Behaviour that has led to a desirable or rewarding outcome tends to be repeated. Behaviour that has led to a punishing outcome tends not to be repeated. Remember the term 'information overload'. If as a trainer you try to cover too much in one learning session, your audience will become confused and unable to cope. Concentrate on the essentials, rather than clouding the issue with too much detail. Take frequent breaks for rest, review and reflection. Be aware of biorhythms.

- *the law of exercise*, also known as *the law of frequency* – The more often you do something, the more proficient you become in doing it. Knowledge of positive results must follow for reinforcement to take place. Practice makes perfect, and practice makes permanent. Overlearn for true mastery.

- *the law of disuse* – If you don't practise a skill or recall and rehearse knowledge, it will eventually be forgotten. Forgetting has nothing to do with age. It's just a consequence of not reviewing. The forgetting curve is a well-established and proven theory in learning. The period immediately following the learning process is the most important time for reinforcing knowledge. Learners should also be encouraged to reflect in order to consolidate and integrate new learning with their existing knowledge and experience. Learning maps which concentrate on essentials should form part of the review plan. For most people, remembering can be enhanced threefold by the use of visuals.

- *the law of intensity* – Intensively engage the hearing, seeing and doing senses. You must engage the emotional part of the brain known as the limbic system if you want to learn effectively. If the learning experience is dramatic, exciting and memorable it is more likely to be remembered than if it is routine and boring. Consider for a moment what you remember about your holidays – very little, except the unique, outstanding and funny incidents. Good trainers have a reputation for bringing their subject alive. They do this by relating their enthusiasm to the learner's experience and by the use of discussion, example, anecdote, analogy, metaphor, story, illustrations and good visuals. The greater and more intense the interest of your learners, the more effective the learning process will be.

- *the law of primacy* – New things or things that you do first are remembered better. This is the novelty concept at work. Likewise, you remember that which is unique and outstanding. Also, those actions you do last are more lasting. This is known as *the law of recency*. You probably remember what you had for dinner yesterday but are unable to recall what you had for dinner two weeks ago. In-between things are more inclined to be forgotten. The more participation and involvement you create for your learners, the more likely they are to learn and remember. Actively engage all their abilities, including seeing, discussing and doing, during the process.

- *the law of readiness* – You can take the horse to the water, but you can't make it drink. Adults must be able, willing, eager and ready to learn. Unless an adult is inherently motivated and ready to learn, the best efforts of a tutor or trainer will be to no avail. Trainers should always emphasise the importance of the topic, how it relates to the experience and goals of the learner, and how it can be used to improve job performance or career prospects. Case studies, simulations, demonstrations, role-play, management games, practical exercises, questionnaires and group discussion will all make the learning experience more realistic and relevant to adult learners. They will also promote the transfer of learning to on-the-job situations. Frequent summarisation during the learning session helps reflection, retention and recall. The more variety there is in your approaches to learners' learning, the better.

- *the law of vividness* – We tend to remember striking or spectacular impressions rather than the ordinary. Few of us will not remember 11 September 2001 and the terrorist attack with passenger aircraft on the twin towers of the Trade Center in New York and the Pentagon in Arlington, Virginia. Similarly, you are more likely to remember what you did on your last birthday rather than what you did the day before.

See also **Association**.

References
Malone, Samuel A. (2000) *Learning* Skills for Managers. Dublin, Oak Tree Press.
Tracy, Brian (1993) *Maximum Achievement*. New York, Simon & Schuster.
http,//www.premiumhealth.com/memory/htiym2.htm

Learned optimism   Learned optimism is an attitude of determined positivity. Some people always see the optimistic, bright side to things and regard the glass as 'half full'. Others always take a pessimistic view and regard the glass as 'half empty'. Some people see possibilities in a situation, whereas others discern solely limitations and obstacles. Some people are knocked back only temporarily when something goes wrong, whereas others see it as a recurring pattern of bad luck. A pessimist has destructive thoughts about the normal setbacks of life. The optimist has learned to deal with these setbacks by constructive solution-centred thoughts. How you explain things to yourself determines how you view the world.

Seligman (1998) says this has three elements:

- permanence – Setbacks can be perceived either as always happening to you or as just one-off events.

- pervasiveness – Misfortunes can be perceived either as discrete phenomena or as pervading your whole life.

- personalisation – You may see yourself either as having control over events or as being at the mercy of forces over which you have no control.

The type of things you say to yourself when confronted with setbacks determines whether you are an optimist or a pessimist.

See also **Positive thinking**.

References
Seligman, Martin (1998). *Learned Optimism. How to Change Your Mind and Your Life.* London, Pocket Books.

Learner-centred training   In learner-centred training the emphasis is on the needs of the learner rather than on the skills and knowledge of the trainer. The approach is similar to the marketing concept which encourages the salesperson to determine what the customer actually needs rather than just promoting the organisation's goods and services.

Learner types   Types of learner correspond to the four learning styles – activist, reflector, theorist and pragmatist – which together comprise a useful generic model for understanding the differences between them. In practice we all have a unique combination of these styles, which effectively means that there are as many learning styles as learners.

See also **Activist**; **Learning styles**; **Pragmatist**; **Reflector**; **Theorist**.

References
Mumford, Alan (1997) *Management Development, Strategies for Action.* London, IPD.

Learning   Learning is the process which brings about persistent change in behaviour. Learning gives a person increased competence to deal successfully with his or her environment as by acquiring knowledge, skills and attitudes. To bring about this change as a trainer it is essential to understand the learner, the knowledge and the learning process. Take into account the learner's emotions and intellectual ability. Clearly define the level of knowledge to be learned and the expected outcomes.

As people learn there is a physical transformation in the brain. Neural pathways are laid down and more connections are made. Neuroscientists believe that learning occurs through a change in the strength of certain synaptic connections in the brain. A frequently-used synapse becomes stronger, whereas an infrequently-used one may grow weaker over time. In autopsies on infants, scientists have found that newborn babies have relatively few connections between nerve cells but older babies have more, indicating that in the meantime they have learned more about the world.

The process of learning takes a person with basic ability to a particular level of skill through instruction, experience and guided practice. The more you know about a topic, the easier it is to learn, remember and understand new information about it. Your existing level of knowledge facilitates the linking and association of additional knowledge. Knowledge and practice are closely interlinked. Knowledge changes the thinking process. The thinking process influences behaviour. Knowledge thus has a direct bearing on practice.

Learning is enhanced by challenge and inhibited by threat. Exposure to information may result in partial learning even if you had no intention of learning from it. Learning is both a conscious and an unconscious process. Learning involves both focused attention and peripheral perception. If you subsequently decide to learn the topic, you may then learn it more easily. Supervisors and managers who must train staff should understand the learning process. It will help them to become more effective instructors, coaches, trainers and learning facilitators.

Learning is like a journey:

- First, you decide where you want to go (learning objectives).

- Second, you devise a means of getting there (design a learning programme, attend a training course, or prepare a personal development plan).

- Third, you organise it so that you know when you have arrived (evaluation of the learning).

Techniques to help you learn more effectively include:

- learning maps – Use learning maps to integrate existing knowledge and experience with new learning. They will help you to see how the parts make up the whole.

- ensuring that you understand the material before you learn

- the SQ3R method of effective reading

- memorising techniques such as the use of mnemonics – Simplify complicated material by using key words. Practise retrieving information using mnemonic strategies.

- accelerated learning – Applying the principles of accelerated learning will speed up the learning process.

- engaging the emotional part of the brain known as the limbic system

- personalising your learning by generating your own examples to demonstrate understanding and consolidate memory

- monitoring your comprehension when learning by saying to yourself, 'Do I really understand this?' – Make sure that what you're learning makes sense to you. The learning process consists of discovering meanings and building up patterns of knowledge and meaningful relations.

- visualisation – Use your imagination to think in pictures, colours, shapes and movement. Remember: a picture is worth more than a thousand words. Use flowcharts and block diagrams to summarise key learning points.

- organising and classifying information for more effective learning – giving meaningful structure to concepts helps to implant them in long-term memory. Prioritise information by concentrating on the key issues.

References
Cotton, Julie (1995) *The Theory of Learners: An introduction.* London, Kogan Page.
DePorter, Bobbi (1998) *Quantum Business: Achieving success through quantum learning.* London, Piatkus.
Malone, Samuel A. (2000) *Learning Skills for Managers.* Dublin, Oak Tree Press.
http,//www.newhorizons.org/lrnbus_marchese.html
http,//www.supermemo.com/articles/20rules.htm

Learning and change   According to Reg Revans, for an organisation to survive, its rate of learning must be equal to or greater than the rate of change in its external environment, or

$$L > C$$

where L is learning and C is change. If the organisation's rate of learning in relation to environmental change is behind and is not being monitored for corrective action, the organisation will not survive.

We change the way we think over time. We add and adapt beliefs, values, attitudes, knowledge, understanding and wisdom with the passage of time. Not only does thinking change but the body changes as well. Every cell in the body is changed after seven years. Yet as adults we are often resistant to change. Continuous incremental improvement and lifelong learning should be our goal if we wish to survive and prosper in the modern dynamic world. Research shows that participation in learning opportunities is frequently linked to changes in life circumstances such as changes in jobs, the break-up of relationships, having children, bereavement and retirement.

References
Argyris, Chris (1999) *On Organisational Learning.* Oxford, Blackwell Business.
Mumford, Alan (1997) *Management Development, Strategies for Action.* London, IPD.

Learning blocks   See **Barriers to learning**.

Learning by objectives   Learning objectives are needed so that you can compare actual results against objectives and take corrective action if needed to reach your goals. Without a mechanism of benchmarks, comparison and feedback it would be impossible to gauge how you are progressing and whether you were going wrong. Learning objectives provide a purpose and sense of direction. They help you organise and direct your learning activities. All learning sessions should start with a statement of learning objectives.

There are three basic things to consider as a trainer when setting learning objectives:

- What is the learner required to do?

- What standard or level of performance should be set?

- Under what conditions should learning take place? The resources for the learning and the constraints and context in which the learning takes place should be identified.

The importance of objectives in successful learning cannot be overstated.

Bloom (1956) categorised learning objectives under six headings:

- *knowledge* – Have you acquired the knowledge that you set out to acquire? Can you remember, recognise and recall information?

- *comprehension* – Knowledge without understanding is not very useful. Have you acquired the conceptual framework for the knowledge, and do you understand its significance and relevance in the work situation? Practice without theory is blind.

- *application* – Are you able to apply the knowledge, facts, rules and principles to your general life or work situation? In business you must have a practical bias. Theory without practice is not very useful. It is one thing to read and study about the theory of driving. It is another thing to put it into practice.

- *analysis* – Can you break down the knowledge into component parts? Can you identify motives? Can you classify, compare and contrast? Chunking is often necessary to achieve understanding.

- *synthesis* – Can you recombine the component parts of the knowledge so that you are able to grasp the complete picture? Can you combine ideas to form a new whole?

- *evaluation* – Have you achieved your learning objectives? Have you learned from your mistakes? Can you develop opinions, judgements and decisions? Can you prioritise?

See also **Behavioural objectives; Bloom's learning model.**

References
Malone, Samuel A. (2000). *Learning Skills for Managers.* Dublin, Oak Tree Press.
Bloom, B. S (1956) *The Taxonomy of Education Objectives. Handbook One, Cognitive Domain.* New York, McKay.
http,//members.spree.com/teach2prime/objectives.htm
http,//www.hcc.hawaii.edu/intranet/committees/FacDevCom/gui.../questype.ht

Learning centre   A learning centre is a place within a company which provides learning resources for staff training and development and personal development. It is a tangible resource to meet the lifelong learning needs of staff.

Learning centre courses make learning accessible, easy, self-paced and interesting. The courses are designed around different forms of media. They range from textbooks, audio- and videotapes to CD-ROMs, DVDs, intranet and the Internet. However, unlike teacher-centred conventional learning, the responsibility for the learning is solely with the learner. Access to the learning centre computer resources can be facilitated via the corporate intranet to individual workstations, so allowing for just-in-time learning.

Learning resources in a corporate learning centre commonly include:

- text-based course materials – These may encompass course programme notes donated by staff from courses they have attended in the past, correspondence-course material or manuals containing human resource development material and exercises.

- books – Depending on the needs of the particular organisation, a wide range of books including management, information technology and engineering textbooks may be stocked. The centre may operate a library system lending books out to staff. The centre may also be linked up to other libraries.

- videos – Videos are available that feature all aspects of business life and personal development needs. These can be viewed in the centre or loaned out to staff to be viewed at home.

- audios and CDs – Audios and CDs now cover all aspects of business and personal development. The big advantage of audio and CD is that you can listen to them while driving or stuck in traffic. You might cover the equivalent of a university course in a year or two while commuting to and from work – a much more productive use of your time.

- CD-ROMs/DVDs – Every aspect of business and information technology is now available on CD-ROM and/or DVD. Complete course programmes are available on the medium. The advantage is that you can use the programmes at home at times to suit your needs.

- access to the learning resources of the Internet.

See also **Learning management systems**.

References
Malone, Samuel A. (1997) *How to Set Up and Manage a Corporate Learning Centre.* Aldershot, Gower.
http,//www.newhorizons.org/obsdeck_dickinson23htm.htm

Learning climate   Honey and Mumford (1996) describe a learning climate as one in which the behaviours and practices involved in continuous development are actively encouraged. They go on to outline four key activities which managers should undertake to develop a learning climate within an organisation:

- role modelling behaviours and practices

- planning and providing learning opportunities

- building learning into organisational processes

- acting as learning champions.

At the individual level this would include learning-to-learn skills, commitment to lifelong learning and continuous improvement. At the team level it would include shared vision and goals, co-operative learning, challenging attitudes, continuous improvement and management facilitation and support. At the organisational level it would include mission, vision, corporate goals and strategies, structures and practices to support learning.

References
Honey, Peter and Mumford, Alan (1996) *How to Manage Your Learning Environment*. Maidenhead, Peter Honey.

Learning climate questionnaire (LCQ)   The LCQ was developed by Bartram *et al* (1993) and purports to assess how well an organisation supports workplace learning and development. It is based on seven dimensions:

- management relations and style

- time available

- autonomy and responsibility

- team style

- opportunities for development

- guidance available

- satisfaction with the workplace environment.

It is important that managers act as role models by 'walking the talk' through their own commitment to self-development and learning, and by putting the structures and incentives in place for learning.

Honey and Mumford (Mumford, 1997) have developed a similar instrument called the Learning Environment Questionnaire. Other learning climate questionnaires have been developed by Pedler and Burgoyne (1991) and Pearn *et al* (1995).

References
Bartram, D., Foster, J., Lindley, P. A., Brown, A. J. and Nixon, S. (1993) *Learning Climate Questionnaire (LCQ), A User's Guide*. Hull, Newland Park Associates.
Mumford, Alan (1997) *Management Development, Strategies for Action*. London, IPD.
Pearn, M., Roderick, C. and Mulrooney, C. (1995) *Learning Organisations in Practice*. London, McGraw-Hill.
Pedler, M. J. and Burgoyne, J. C. (1991) *The Learning Company*. London, McGraw-Hill

Learning community   A learning community is a nurturing, supportive, collaborative, interactive educational environment in which a group of people come together to meet specific learning needs and to share resources and skills.

Characteristics of learning groups include:

- They offer a holistic approach to education and provide opportunities for greater interaction between students and faculty/trainers. Experiential and action learning are used.

- They foster a sense of collaboration and community.

- By clustering courses they provide lecturers/trainers and students with a more coherent and enriched learning environment.

- They develop critical thinking and team-building skills in students.

- They encourage autonomous learning by which learners are encouraged to identify their own learning needs, draw up a learning plan and evaluate progress towards their learning objectives.

- There is a strong emphasis on personal growth and development.

- They are student-centred and encourage learners to develop learning-to-learn skills by emphasising the range of learning resources available for exploration.

References
Revans, Reg (1998) *An ABC of Action Learning*, London. Lemos & Crane.
http,//www.21learn.org/arch/articles/colin.kay.html

Learning contract   A learning contract is a written agreement between a manager and a staff member concerning what the staff member is going to learn, how he or she is going to learn it, within what time period, how he or she is going to apply the learning to the job, and how the learning is going to be reviewed. It should contain specific learning objectives.

Critical elements of the learning contract can be recalled by means of the acronym LORE, which stands for Learning task, Objectives, Resources, and Evidence of achievement.

- *learning* – The learning task is described.

- *objectives for learning* – The objectives for the learning and the criteria of good practice are established.

- *resources* – The resources needed are determined and an action plan is drawn up.

- *evidence of achievement* – An evaluation process is set up to establish that the learning has been achieved.

The learning contract is a means of helping learners to structure their learning activities systematically. It helps to clearly identify the learning opportunities in work. It also identifies the systems and supports available to the learner for learning. At the same time, the learner takes responsibility for his or her own learning. And the learning is designed to address and solve real organisational problems.

Learning goals are identified by asking a series of questions, such as:

- Where am I now? Determine your existing position and the resources for learning that you currently possess. Identify learning constraints and what you need to do to overcome them.

- Where do I want to be? How are you going to learn? What are your learning objectives? What do you want to learn?

- How can I get there? What learning resources and strategies do you need to achieve your goals?

- How will I know when I've achieved my learning objectives? What criteria will be used for evaluating the learning experience?

The advantages of a learning contract are that:

- They help get the commitment of the manager and the staff member. It is known that participation in setting learning objectives increases the learner's commitment to the learning process and the likelihood of success.

- Learners learn at their own pace.

- It systematically identifies and plans learning experiences on an individual basis.

- The staff member is proactively involved with the manager in deciding his or her own learning objectives and experiences.

- The expectations of both management and staff concerning learning are clearly laid out.

- It makes the learner responsible for his or her own learning.

- It can cater for the personal learning style of the learner.

See also **Learning log**; **Learning sets**.

References
Fee, Kenneth (2001) *A Guide To Management Development Techniques*. London, Kogan Page.
Mumford, Alan (1993) *How Managers Can Develop Managers*. Aldershot, Gower.
Revans, Reg (1998) *An ABC of Action Learning*. London, Lemos & Crane.
http,//fohweb.macarthur.uws.edu.au/ot/samplelc.htm
http,//fohweb.macarthur.uws.edu.au/ot/lc.htm
http,//www.tobincls.com/responsibility.htm

Learning curve   A learning curve is a measure of the increase in speed at which learning is achieved after the repetition of identical or similar learning events. Such curves have represented a source of study among experimental psychologists since the 1920s and 1930s. In the US aircraft industry at that time an 80 per cent learning curve was found to apply. This means that the cumulative average time to produce an aircraft fell by 20 per cent for each doubling of output of that type of aircraft. Since then the learning curve concept has been extended to other industries.

The learning curve is a graph that can be drawn to represent the pattern of learning in many production and construction tasks. The learning curve effect particularly applies to a group of workers who do the same job repetitively with the same equipment and machinery.

It has been found that the time required to do most tasks of a repetitive nature gets shorter as people acquire experience and develop better methods of doing the work. The cumulative average time per unit produced is assumed to fall by a constant percentage every time total output of the product doubles. In learning, there is usually a rapid advance at the beginning, which then levels out into a plateau, which takes off again before flattening out into another plateau. However, not all learning curves follow this pattern. Some people may experience very slow progress at the beginning of a learning task.

Understanding the nature of learning curves is important for a manager. The obvious message is that the pace of improvement in a skill or knowledge area is not constant. It will be rapid and dramatic at times and at other times very slow or at a standstill. The learning curve has also important implications for manufacturing processes. Any change in production schedules and processes initially reduces efficiency because it involves some learning or relearning. For similar reasons, the cost characteristics of new products tend to improve with the passage of time as machine speeds, labour efficiency and material usage improve and the learning curve gets steeper.

From a personal development viewpoint, any new learning challenge will have periods of rapid progress, of no progress and of slow progress. To be a successful learner you must persist through the periods of no progress and slow progress and realise that this is the norm for most learners.

The learning curve can also have an impact on company strategy, because it can have important implications for a company's costs. A company that moves into a new market, and has its production staff move up the learning curve ahead of its competitors, will be more productive, and can compete more effectively on price.

References
Moingeon, Bertrand and Edmondson, Amy (1996) *Organisational Learning and Competitive Advantage.* London, Sage.
Starkey, Ken (1996) *How Organisations Learn.* London, International Thomson Business Press.

Learning cycle   The learning cycle may be said to correspond with the sequence of doing something, reflecting or thinking about it, understanding and concluding, and then doing it differently and/or better. It is similar to the continuous improvement cycle of 'plan, do, check, act'.

See also **Kolb's learning styles model**.

References
Mumford, Alan (1997) *Management Development, Strategies for Action.* London, IPD.
http,www.reviewing.co.uk/research/learning.cycles.htm

Learning domains   Learning domains are fundamental aspects of mental ability that are used in learning. They can be broadly classified under three main headings which may be recalled by the acronym CAP, standing for Cognitive, Affective, and Psychomotor.

- *cognitive* – The cognitive (a word that derives from the Latin *cognitus* 'known') domain is concerned with information and knowledge. Knowledge is acquired through the application of perception, memory, reasoning and judgement. Knowledge is best delivered through lectures or presentations. It is usually evaluated by written tests.

- *affective* – Affective abilities are concerned with beliefs, values, attitudes, feelings and emotions. Role-play and discussion influence them. Attitudes can be difficult to change.

- *psychomotor* – Psychomotor abilities are concerned with manual skills. Manual skills are mostly acquired through imitation and practice. Evaluation is through a performance or skill test. The acquisition of skills is easy to observe and measure.

References
Merriam, Sharon B. and Caffarella, Rosemary S. (1999) *Learning in Adulthood: A comprehensive guide.* San Francisco, Jossey-Bass.
http,//www.hcc.hawaii.edu/intranet/committees/Fac/DevCom/gui...domains.ht

Learning events   Robert Gagne (1977) suggested that the act of learning involves a chain of eight events, some internal to the learner and others external. The eight events are:

- the initial motivation or expectation of learning – If you expect to learn you are more likely to learn.

- apprehending, distinguishing the material from other information

- acquisition – The learner codes the knowledge for input to memory. Mnemonic strategies might be useful here.

- retention – The learner stores the knowledge in the short-term or long-term memory. Repetition, reflection and review may be appropriate at this stage.

- recall – The learner recalls the knowledge as required. In exams the ability to recall information is paramount to passing the exam. Difficulties of retrieval may be due to inadequate input strategies in the first instance.

- generalisation – The learner transfers the knowledge to new situations, facilitating the development of strategies for dealing with them.

- performance, putting the strategies into practice

- feedback – The learner obtains feedback on his or her performance and takes corrective action as appropriate.

Where there is failure to learn, Gagne argues, it will happen at one of these eight events. It is the task of the tutors to find out which. It may be that the learning has failed to capture the learners' attention, or that it makes no sense to them, or they have failed to transfer it to long-term memory or they are unable to recall it. Analysing learning failure in this way helps teachers and trainers. It enables them to concentrate on the specific stage at which the learner appears to be going wrong. Frequently they discover that the fault does not lie with the learner but relates to the way the learning task has been organised, presented and/or explained.

References
Gagne, Robert M. (1977) *The Conditions of Learning*, 3rd edition. New York. Holt-Saunders International.

Learning from mistakes Learning from experience – including from mistakes – is the most important of all the life skills. Somebody once said that inside every mistake there are lessons waiting to get out. We learn well and fast when we experience the consequences of what we do – and don't do! Doing it right first time should be our goal. Nevertheless, it is part of the human condition that mistakes will happen. Elbert Hubbard said that 'Constant effort and frequent mistakes are the stepping-stones to genius.'

Learned helplessness is a term for the state of mind people get into when they make several mistakes while doing a particular task and then decide that the task is just beyond them. They stop trying. This is tantamount to saying that you can't learn from your mistakes. Take responsibility for your mistakes and don't start blaming yourself or others.

Research has found that pointing out people's mistakes just causes them to make more mistakes. On the other hand, telling people they are doing something right encourages them to be right more often. Blame discourages a person from objectively examining a mistake and the circumstances surrounding it.

As a child you learned to walk by trial and error. Every time you fell down, you got up again. This probably happened plenty of times before you mastered the skill of walking. Failure never entered your mind. As adults we often give up learning something new after one or two attempts. The fear of failure has become part of our consciousness. Yet we know that people who have become experts in their field did so by practising over and over again, and quitting never entered their minds.

Some organisations have a 'blame culture': people in authority are more interested in attributing blame for a mistake than finding out why the mistake happened in the first place. Organisations should tolerate a certain degree of failure because it is a necessary part of personal growth. In fact, however, highly successful organisations and people tend to become arrogant. They have never failed and therefore never had the opportunity to learn from failure. They fall into the trap of thinking they know all the answers and have nothing more to learn. We must learn from our mistakes so that they will not happen again. Knowing what doesn't work guides us towards what does work.

A company must capture, collate, and circulate details of mistakes so that employees can study them, learn from them and ensure that similar mistakes are not made again. Drucker (1993) claims that the most important ingredient for success is the ability to learn from our mistakes and apply the lessons in new and productive ways. High standards of performance should be the norm. Mistakes should be the exception rather than the rule. The training department should design case studies around mistakes for use on training courses.

One approach might be to reflect on your mistakes by carrying out a cause-and-effect analysis:

- What kind or type of mistake has occurred?

- What is the effect of the mistake? What are its consequences?

- What was the cause of the mistake? Knowing the cause of a mistake is essential before you can take the proper steps to correct it.

- How can I correct my mistake?

- How can I prevent the mistake from happening again? Observation and experiment will tell you what works and what does not work. You must take the appropriate corrective action.

The history of invention and discovery is a history of learning from mistakes, transformational learning, continuous learning and improvement. The road to creativity is strewn with errors not ignored but objectively studied and analysed for the lessons to be learned from them.

In other words, the people who learn from their mistakes are the people who reflect on their mistakes. It is the reflection process that creates the learning.

The same approach should apply to organisations. Everybody is entitled to make mistakes – but they must learn from them so that they do not repeat the same mistake in the future. Why sack somebody after making an expensive mistake when everybody else can benefit from his or her hard-earned wisdom?

See also **Santayana review**.

References

Drucker, Peter (1993) *Post-Capitalist Society.* New York, Harper Business.
Gerber, Rod (2001) 'The concept of common sense in workplace learning and experience', *Education and Training,* Volume 43, Number 2, pp72–81.
Malone, Samuel A. (2000) *Learning Skills for Managers.* Dublin, Oak Tree Press.

Learning log   A learning log is a diary in which a learner's learning experiences are recorded for later reflection and review. A life unreflected on in this way is not very productive, from a learning point of view. The learning log encourages the learner to systematically apply the learning cycle of 'do, reflect, conclude, and do it again differently or better', according to whichever is his or her most appropriate learning style – ie as activist, reflector, theorist or pragmatist.

- The event has been/should be an opportunity for us to do/learn something (activist).

- The 'what happened' section gives us an opportunity to think and reflect on it (reflector).

- The 'conclusions' part is where we draw lessons, make sense of it and perceive the learning points (theorist).

- The 'action' part is where we explore how we will do it differently: we'll work out an action plan to determine what we are going to do and how we are going to do it (pragmatist).

The learning log ensures that we learn from our mistakes and continually improve. It must be integrated into the learning activity in which the managers are involved, whether on-the-job or off-the-job. It may be used to review and learn from (for example) how you conducted a meeting, gave a presentation or reacted to any critical incidents that occurred during the working day.

Participants on a course programme may be encouraged to keep a learning log of the major learning experiences of the course. From this people may see the relevance of the learning log for recording and reflecting on major learning events encountered when working on-the-job, or indeed reflecting on the process of learning itself. It may be used to review and learn from (for example) what you made of a lecture, case study or group discussion.

It might be a good idea to restrict your learning log to some learning skill you currently want to improve. This will focus your attention and make the prospect of keeping a learning log less daunting. Learning logs can be kept for retrospective learning events or prospective learning events.

Many successful people in history kept diaries and journals, including da Vinci, Darwin, Faraday, Edison and Newton. The surviving 5,000 pages of Leonardo's notebooks contain research into anatomy, mechanics, hydraulics, and a wide range of other sciences. The notebooks also detail many civil and engineering schemes, plus designs for numerous mechanical devices, including a bicycle and a helicopter. Although few of these designs were realised in his lifetime, they do show how accurate a vision of the future he had and what a meticulous note-taker he was. Edison produced 3 million pages of notes and letters.

Some professional bodies require the keeping of learning logs by students during their internship as proof of acquired relevant experience and to facilitate their transition to full membership.

See also **Learning contract**; **Learning sets**; **Learning styles**.

References
Fee, Kenneth (2001) *A Guide To Management Development Techniques*. London, Kogan Page.
Huczynski, Andrzej (2001) *Encyclopedia of Development Methods*. Aldershot, Gower.
Megginson, David and Whitaker, Vivien (1996) *Cultivating Self-Development*. London, IPD.
http,//fohweb.macarthur.uws.edu.au/lrndiary.htm
http,//www.anbar.co.uk/courseware/mba/121-005.htm

Learning management systems   Learning management systems is a term used in e-learning and corporate learning centres for the systems that do all the recording necessary (such as time, type and description of course, and booth allocated) for booking learners in to courses, tracking e-learning programmes, keeping tabs on learners' progress and registering loans and returns of books, audio-tapes, CDs, DVDs and video packages. They also provide comprehensive management information for individual training records and usage level of the courses.

See also **Learning centre**.

References
Holmes, Andrew (2002) *Lifelong Learning*. Oxford, Capstone.
Malone, Samuel A. (2003) *How to Set Up and Manage a Corporate Learning Centre*, revised edition. Aldershot, Gower.
Rossett, Allison (2002) *The ASTD E-Learning Handbook*. New York, McGraw-Hill.

Learning map   A learning map is a non-linear graphic representation of a subject in which the main feature is presented as a central image from which major themes radiate on branches containing secondary images and captions or key words. These branches may themselves have sub-branches stemming from them which present topics of lesser importance and their captions and key words. All together, with the central image at the centre the branches form a connected nodal structure.

Learning maps may be enhanced and enriched with colour, pictures, codes and dimensions to add interest. Such enhancements are reputed, *inter alia*, to aid memory and recall, to improve comprehension and conceptualisation, and not least to divert and entertain and motivate.

Learning maps are said to be brain-friendly: the brain stores information by association, in clusters, rather than in linear form.

Learning maps can be used for:

- illustrating lectures

- planning lectures

- time management

- project planning

- study

- creative exercise

- brainstorming

- planning writing assignments and theses

- taking the minutes of meetings

- report-writing

- facilitating reflection.

The uses of learning maps are constrained only by the imagination of the user. Software packages are available to help draw learning maps.

References
Buzan, Tony and Buzan, Barry (1993) *The Mind Map Book*. London, BBC Books.
Malone, Samuel A. (2000) *Learning Skills for Managers*. Dublin, Oak Tree Press.
Pattison, Sherry A. (2001) 'Staff meetings: an opportunity for accelerated training of employees', *Journal of Workplace Learning*, Volume 13, Number 4, pp172–179.
http,//world.std.com/~emagic/mindmap.html

Learning organisation   A learning organisation is an organisation that values learning and makes learning part of its mission and culture. Learning thus occurs at the individual, team and systems level. A learning organisation continually transforms and improves itself through the learning of its employees. The learning organisation makes experience explicit and transforms it into knowledge. It has the flexibility to provide learning where it's needed in the organisation. Learning is an ongoing rather than a one-off event. In the ideal organisation, every employee is committed to lifelong learning. They want to be better tomorrow than they are today, through learning. The organisation is devoted to continuous improvement of its products, services and processes through learning about learning. People learn from mistakes, and management-by-blame is discouraged. Employees experience better job satisfaction, customers experience better service and the organisation builds a more prosperous and lasting future for itself. An organisation's unique learning base is now the most important sustainable competitive advantage that it has. Its ability to learn faster than the competition keeps it ahead in the marketplace. After all, an organisation might be committed to training and development but could still be vulnerable if it does not respond rapidly enough to environmental changes.

One type of organisation Charles Handy, the management guru, anticipates is the 'triple-I organisation', which stands for Information, Intelligence and Ideas. Handy thus highlights the crucial importance of knowledge management to the success of modern organisations. He believes that employees should be obsessed with the pursuit of learning if they are going to keep up with the pace of change. He says that people are not 'human resources', they are living individuals with the right to be different.

Using the human brain as a metaphor for an organisation leads to three insights:

- Organisations are repositories of knowledge.

- Organisations can learn.

- Organisations are networks of information.

Peter Senge in his book *The Fifth Discipline* (1990) has come up with five core principles of a learning organisation:

- systems thinking – This is the ability to see the big picture. We tend to concentrate on the parts rather than the whole and thus fail to see the organisation as a dynamic process. We must have the ability to foresee long-term consequences when making decisions.

- personal mastery – This is the ability to continually clarify and deepen our personal vision, focus our energies, develop patience, and see reality objectively. It requires lifelong learning to achieve this end.

- mental models – These are the attitudes, beliefs, values, assumptions and images that influence the way we see the world. We must become aware of these mental models and subject them to scrutiny and change as appropriate.

- shared vision – Organisations will not be successful unless the followers buy into the visions of the leaders. Leaders' personal visions must be translated into shared visions for commitment and involvement rather than compliance.

■ team thinking – Teams are ideal places in which to learn. The result is good both for the organisation and for the personal development of team members. Team members enhance their communication, interpersonal relations, collaboration, problem-solving and decision-making skills.

References

Garratt, Bob (2001) *The Learning Organisation Developing Democracy at Work*. London, HarperCollins Business.

Matlay, Harry (2000) 'Organisational learning in small learning organisations: an empirical overview', *Education and Training*, Volume 42, Number 4/5, pp202–211.

Moingeon, Bertrand and Edmondson, Amy (1996) *Organisational Learning and Competitive Advantage*. London, Sage.

Pearn, Michael (1994) 'Tools for a learning organisation', *Management Development Review*, Volume 07, Number 4, pp9–13.

Senge, Peter M. (1993) *The Fifth Discipline: The art and practice of the learning organisation*. London, Century Business.

Senge, Peter, Kleiner, Art, Roberts, Charlotte, Ross, Richard B. and Smith, Bryan J. ((1996) *The Fifth Discipline Fieldbook. Strategies and Tools for Building a Learning Organisation*. London, Nicholas Brealey.

Starkey, Ken (1996) *How Organisations Learn*. London, International Thomson Business Press.

http,//www.infed.org/thinkers/senge.htm

http,//www.mithya.com/learning/designorg.html

http,//www.free-press.com/journals/gajal/articles/publish/gajal-article-046.htm

http,//gbr.pepperdine.edu/001/learning.html

http,//www.imc.org.uk/imc/riu/revans99/teare-final.html

Learning plateau   A learning plateau corresponds to a stage of the learning curve at which very little or no progress at all is made. It is important that learners realise that this is the norm and that they do not get discouraged or give up the learning task at this stage. Determination and persistence will see them successfully through in the end.

See also **Learning curve**.

References

Malone, Samuel A. (1996). *Learning to Learn*. London, CIMA.

Moingeon, Bertrand and Edmondson, Amy (1996) *Organisational Learning and Competitive Advantage*. London, Sage.

Learning portal   A learning portal – as used in e-learning – is a website that offers people working in an organisation access to a wide variety of training and learning resources. It may also provide online communication and collaboration for learners.

References

Sloman, Martyn (2001). *The E-learning Revolution: From propositions to action*. London, CIPD.

Learning preference Learning preference is the preference of a learner for one way of learning over another. For example, one learner may like lectures whereas another may prefer project work or role-play. Reichmann and Grasha (1974) identified three learning-preference types of learner:

- *Dependent learners* prefer instructor-led training. They like highly structured programmes such as lectures or tutorials.

- *Collaborative learners* prefer discussion and group work. They like case studies, role-play, business games and simulations.

- *Independent learners* like to structure their own learning using the trainer as a facilitator or resource. They like distance learning and computer-based learning.

Trainers should take the idea of learning preferences on board by ensuring a carefully balanced approach to the design of learning.

References

Reichmann, S. W. and Grasha, A. F. (1974) 'A rational approach to developing and assessing the construct validity of a study learning styles scale inventory', *Journal of Psychology*, Volume 87, pp213–223.
Sadler-Smith, Eugene (1996) 'Learning styles: a holistic approach', *Journal of European Industrial Training*, Volume 20, Number 7, pp29–36.

Learning process Learning can be viewed as a process which involves receiving technical information or developing skills. It may be seen as transferring information from short-term to long-term memory and thus as a physiological process which happens when connections are made between brain cells or neurons. We read books, listen to audios, watch videos, attend lectures, participate in seminars and workshops, and actively engage in work, in order to acquire new knowledge, skills or attitudes. Learning is often regarded as solitary and passive in nature, as if we are mere receptacles for the knowledge of the trainer or teacher. Learning is seen as a means of controlling or manipulating our environment more effectively.

The key to effective learning is that the learner must be actively involved in the learning process. Involvement may include doing the task being taught, taking notes, discussing issues and asking questions.

However, there are two other forms of learning that most adults find much more valuable and meaningful. These are 'social' and 'developmental' learning. Social learning is learning about others, learning about how to relate and communicate effectively. It is associated with what Howard Gardner called interpersonal intelligence. Developmental learning involves learning about oneself. It is what Howard Gardner would regard as a type of intrapersonal intelligence. Intuition and wisdom are examples.

References
Holmes, Andrew (2002) *Lifelong Learning.* Oxford, Capstone.
Malone, Samuel A. (2000) *Learning Skills for Managers.* Dublin, Oak Tree Press.
Reid, Charles W. and Kleiner, Brian W. (1996) 'Which training methods are effective?', *Management Development Review*, Volume 9, Number 2 pp24–29.

Learning pyramid   The learning pyramid was developed as a model by Mumford in his book *Management Development, Strategies for Action.* The learning pyramid has the individual learner at the top, and proceeds through one-to-one learning to group learning, and finally to the learning organisation. It demonstrates that the learning organisation starts with the individual learner.

References
Mumford, Alan (1997) *Management Development, Strategies for Action*, 3rd edition. London, IPD.

Learning sets   A learning set is a group of people who come together with the common purpose of learning and self-development. Ideally, this learning and self-development should have a payoff for the organisation. Each person in the learning set keeps a learning log in which he or she reviews learning experiences. The members of the learning set themselves facilitate the learning process. We need colleagues to support, challenge and improve our learning and problem-solving skills. The central task of the learning set is to successfully complete the task that they have taken on.

The learning set will itself need a facilitator so that everyone gets an opportunity to air views and receive feedback. Feedback does not necessarily mean the facilitating trainer's giving advice, however. The best help is often to ask penetrating questions and to make suggestions for consideration. Most people want to use facilitators as sounding-boards rather than as sources of advice.

Because of the time factor, it is generally suggested that six members are a good number for a set. It is through feedback and reflection that we learn. The learning set is based on a number of principles, including the fact that we learn best when supported and challenged by others, and that it is easier to accept feedback from peers rather than from superiors.

See also **Learning contract**; **Learning log**.

References
Megginson, David and Whitaker, Vivien (1996) *Cultivating Self-Development.* London, IPD.
Revans, Reg (1998) *An ABC of Action Learning.* London, Lemos & Crane.
http,//www.free-press.com/journals/gajal/articles/publish/gajal-article-028.htm
http,//www.imc.org.uk/imc/apc-1999/papers/cyril-atkinson-1.html

Learning stages   Psychologists have discovered that there are four stages in learning: learning may start at unconscious incompetence (not knowing that you don't know), proceed to conscious incompetence (knowing that you don't know), then move to conscious competence (remaining aware that you know what you know), and finally end up at unconscious competence (knowing what you know without having to think about it).

1   *unconscious incompetence* – This is the stage of learning at which you don't know that you don't know. You are just not aware of your own level of ignorance and lack of experience. On the other hand, you may believe that you know all there is to know – and if you think you know it all you will be less open to new learning, information and ideas. If you've never driven a car, for example, you will have no idea of what is involved. On the other hand, if you ever give driving lessons, you begin to appreciate just how much you know without realising it. It is very difficult to express it in words because it is tacit knowledge. This is why it is so difficult for an experienced, competent driver at the unconscious competence level to train somebody at the unconscious incompetence level. It is very difficult to make tacit knowledge explicit. The skills have become habitual, automatic responses and are thus very difficult to verbalise, organise and explain consciously. Many a happy marriage has come to grief because one partner has unwittingly agreed to teach the other how to drive without really thinking about how difficult and traumatic it can prove to be. Making tacit knowledge explicit is not an easy task. Einstein said 'The more I learn, the more I realise I don't know.'

2   *conscious incompetence* – This is the stage of learning where you know you don't know. To learn new things, you must move out of your comfort zone. This is the single most important step to take because it involves the broadening of your awareness. You start to learn how to drive. You become disillusioned and your confidence drops when you see how awkward you are. You feel you need to be an octopus to co-ordinate the movements required for steering, clutch, brake and accelerator, while at the same time watching the controls and the road. This is the stage at which you generally unnerve and challenge the patience of your instructor and other road users. You learn most at this time, but need confidence, persistence and determination to take you to the next stage. Motivation, encouragement, goals, action plans and taking responsibility for your own learning will get you there in the end. Some people get frustrated and lose confidence at this stage and give up. They don't realise that everybody goes through the same stages of the learning curve and experiences negative feelings, setbacks, frustrations and difficulties. There is no gain without some pain. Determination will see you through.

3   *conscious competence* – This is the stage at which you can drive the car but you have to think what you're doing all the time – at which you strive to master what you know you can do. It takes all your concentration and energy. However, your

confidence increases in line with your skill. You are proficient but not a master of the art. You may even pass the driving test at this stage, but you must make a conscious effort to reach the required standard. Overconfidence may be a problem, leading to the taking of unnecessary risks. The result of this is a high rate of accidents for newly qualified young drivers, which is confirmed by road accident statistics.

4   *unconscious competence* – At this stage you can drive, listen to the radio and converse at the same time. You are a self-contained learner. The movements involved in driving the car have become an automatic response. Your unconscious mind has taken over the routine, freeing your mind to concentrate on the rules of the road and the prevailing traffic conditions. Driving has become a habit. It is now part of what you are. However, the problem with habits is that there are bad habits and poor practice as well as good habits. Many a person over the years has unconsciously acquired poor driving habits, which may have to be unlearned and replaced with good habits.

See also **Learning styles**; **New learning**.

References

Holmes, Andrew (2002) *Lifelong Learning.* Oxford, Capstone.
O'Connor, Joseph and Seymour, John (1990) *Neuro-Linguistic Programming.* London, Aquarian/Thorsons.

Learning styles   People's individual learning styles are ordinarily determined by education, age, experience and personal preferences. As the brain develops it evolves its own unique neural networks and thus its own distinctive preferences in how it works. Some of these preferences have to do with which side of the brain we use the most, the environmental conditions for learning, and the way in which the learning is presented. If you know your particular learning preference, you are in a better position to improve and compensate for shortcomings in your less dominant styles of learning.

Honey and Mumford have identified four styles, known as the activist, the reflector, the theorist and the pragmatist [see **Activist**; **Pragmatist**; **Reflector**; **Theorist**]. They have further developed a model based on Kolb [see **Kolb's learning styles model**] and designed a learning style questionnaire. Another model based on the senses categorises learning styles as visual, auditory and kinesthetic [see **VAK model of learning**]. Ned Herrmann has also designed a learning styles model [see **Herrmann's model of learning styles**].

A model of learning styles is also derived from the Myers-Briggs ® Type Indicator. It can be recalled by means of the acronym VISAS, which stands for Visual/verbal, Inductive/deductive, Sensory/intuitive, Active/reflective, and Sequential/global.

Visual	**Verbal**
• likes information in the form of videos, films, CD-ROMs, pictures, diagrams, graphs, symbols, learning maps and demonstrations • learns better from what he/she sees rather than from what he/she hears or reads • says things like 'I see what you mean' or 'I get the picture'	• likes information in the form of spoken or written words • learns better from what he/she hears or reads rather than what he/she sees • says things like 'I hear you loud and clear' or 'That doesn't sound right to me'
Inductive	**Deductive**
• goes from observations and data to theories, rules or principles • examines the detail and decides what the big picture is • works from the particular to the general • likes to infer principles	• begins with the theory, concepts, rules or principles and then looks at the practice • works backwards from the results • goes from the general to the particular • likes to deduce consequences
Sensory	**Intuitive**
• selects information through the senses of sight, hearing and touch • likes learning facts and data • tends to be practical rather than innovative • solves problems by tried and trusted methodologies • dislikes surprises • can handle details, but dislikes complications • Doesn't like taking time-based tests	• is inclined to use intuition when generating possibilities and discovering relationships • likes to understand and see connections between information • likes theory, concepts, principles and models; good at abstractions and mathematical formulations • is creative rather than practical • likes innovation • dislikes routine and checking results • doesn't like details but can handle complications • may have trouble with tests; tends to start answering questions before reading the question thoroughly
Active	**Reflective**
• likes to learn while doing something active like talking or moving • likes to think out loud • likes to experiment and apply ideas • has the attitude of 'Let's try it out and see what happens' • may fail to look before he/she leaps and thus jump into tasks prematurely • likes to work in groups	• likes to learn through introspection and reflection • likes to think silently • likes theory, concepts, models and principles; is not happy until he/she understands the basis of something • likes to say 'Let's think about this' • prefers thinking to doing; as a result may indulge in procrastination and never get started • likes to work alone
Sequential	**Global**
• likes to learn in a logical step-by-step way • functions well with partial understanding • is good at analysis and convergent thinking • may get lost in the detail and fail to see the big picture	• likes to learn by getting an overview first • doesn't like partial understanding, but likes to see the big picture • is good at synthesis but often weak on details • likes solving complex problems

All paired combinations of these styles are possible but individual learners tend to have particular preferences. No combination is best. Thomas Edison (1847–1931), US physicist and prolific inventor, was sequential/sensory. Carl Friedrich Gauss (1777–1855), German mathematician was one of the greatest of all mathematicians: he was sequential/intuitive. Pablo Picasso (1881–1973) was a Spanish painter and sculptor: he was global/sensory. Albert Einstein (1879–1955), German-Swiss-US theoretical physicist who conceived the Theory of Relativity, was global/intuitive.

Trainers should be aware that:

■ Learners will learn better if the training style matches their learning style preference.

■ Learners will learn more effectively if they expand their learning styles.

■ If trainers accommodate more learning styles, successful learning is more likely.

■ Trainers should design learning activities that include specific and multiple learning styles as needed.

The evidence supporting learning styles inventories is not conclusive but they do remind trainers of the importance of not making generalised assumptions about learners. From the learners' viewpoint, they increase self-awareness enabling learners to exploit learning opportunities more effectively.

See also **Learning stages**.

References

Cheetham, Graham and Chivers, Geoff (2001) 'How professionals learn in practice: an investigation of informal learning amongst people working in professions', *Journal of European Industrial Training*, Volume, 25, Number 5, pp247–292.

DePorter, Bobbi and Hernacki, Mike (1993) *Quantum Learning: Unleash the genius within you.* London, Piatkus.

Mumford, Alan (1997) *Management Development, Strategies for Action*, 3rd edition. London, IPD.

http,//www.learnativity.com/learningstyles.html

http,//www.tamu-commerce.edu/coe/psy/697/styles.html

http,//www.algonquinc.on.ca/edtech/gened/styles.html

http,//silcon.com/~scmiller/lsweb/fourls.htm

http,//granite.cyg.net/~jblackmo/diglib/styl-c.html

http,//granite.cyg.net/~jblackmo/diglib/styl-d.html

http,//granite.cyg.net/~jblackmo/diglib/styl-e.html

Learning styles questionnaire (LSQ)   The idea of a learning styles questionnaire is naturally based on the concept of learning styles – the assumption that some individuals prefer learning in one way compared with another.

You can determine your learning styles by filling in Honey and Mumford's learning styles questionnaire, which takes about 20 minutes to complete and is very reliable for determining particular learning styles. Most people have a mix from Honey and Mumford's four named learning styles of activist, reflection, theorist and pragmatist.

It is important to find out your learning preferences so that you can take corrective action on your weaker styles. Draw up an action plan specifying the actions you need to take.

Also, when selecting people for jobs it might be a good idea to find out what particular learning styles they prefer in order to place them into suitable roles. Some jobs put an emphasis on certain learning styles rather than others. For example, general managers tend to be pragmatists and activists rather than reflectors and theorists. On the other hand, people in strategic planning and research and development would be expected to prefer strong reflector and theorist styles.

In a training situation, a course should be designed to appeal to all four learning styles or in certain cases to the preferential learning styles of individual participants. Course participants should therefore complete a learning styles questionnaire before a course to ascertain their individual learning styles. Managers should do likewise before they coach or mentor staff.

References

Honey, Peter and Alan Mumford (1986) *Using Your Learning Styles.* Berkshire, Peter Honey.
Mumford, Alan (1995) 'Putting learning styles to work: an integrated approach', *Industrial and Commercial Training*, Volume 27, Number 8, pp28–35.

Learning: three key variables   Jerome Bruner (1973) considers that in dealing with learning activities a teacher must take account of three important variables:

- the nature of the learner
- the nature of the knowledge to be learned
- the nature of the learning process.

Factors that influence individual learners' ability to learn include intelligence, emotion, motivation, age, gender and memory.

Trainers should be aware that:

- Training should focus on practical problems relevant to the needs of learners.
- Learners have a wide range of skills, abilities and attitudes, and these must be taken into account when planning training.
- Trainers should allow learners to proceed at their own unique pace.
- Trainers should help learners continuously assess their progress and provide feedback as part of the learning process.
- Trainers should draw on the learners' experience as an invaluable resource to facilitate future learning.

References

Bruner, J. S. (1973) *Beyond The Information Given.* New York, WWNorton.

Learning-to-learn skills   Learning-to-learn skills are those skills required to learn effectively in any learning situation, the skills required for lifelong learning. They include concentration, creativity, problem-solving, memory, mnemonic strategies, effective reading, time management, researching ability and the ability to produce learning maps. Reviewing learning and keeping a learning log are an important part of the process. A knowledge of learning styles equips learners to recognise and exploit learning opportunities and deal more effectively with learning situations that conflict with their personal learning styles. They can also take steps to improve their ability in those learning styles in which they are weak.

Peter Drucker maintains that the acquisition of learning-to-learn skills is vital for the future. By acquiring learning-to-learn skills you become an active rather than a passive consumer of education.

Knowledge quickly becomes out of date and must be updated constantly if we want to hold our own in the modern business environment. Transformational learning is needed to take advantage of new opportunities and to anticipate future changes. Your education and professional training, in themselves, will no longer equip you for the rest of your life. Many people on qualifying throw away their books, not realising that learning is now a lifelong process. They should keep their books as a core library and build on them as new ideas and developments arise. Jobs are no longer for life and people will change jobs many times in their lifetimes, often having to learn new and different skills in the process. The need for lifelong learning has been recognised by the professions with their continuing professional development/education programmes.

See also **Lifelong learning**.

References

Holmes, Andrew (2002) *Lifelong Learning.* Oxford, Capstone.
Malone, Samuel A. (1996) Learning to Learn. London, CIMA.
Mumford, Alan (1995) 'Putting learning styles to work: an integrated approach', *Industrial and Commercial Training*, Volume 27, Number 8, pp28–35.
Sadler-Smith, Eugene (1996) 'Learning styles: a holistic approach', *Journal of European Industrial Training*, Volume 20, Number 7, pp29–36.
http,/www.unc.edu/dept/unc_caps/TenTraps.html

Lecture method   The lecture method of training involves the trainer delivering a formal talk on a specific topic. It is meant to have clear learning outcomes – but because of the lack of participation and involvement of the audience, the lecture method is not very effective as a tool of learning. Lectures may be good at developing knowledge and comprehension but are poor at promoting application, analysis, synthesis and evaluation.

The solution to this is to stop the lecture at appropriate points and invite the learners to draw conclusions from the information presented. The discussion should be orchestrated towards the objectives of the training.

For large groups of people, however, the straight lecture can be an efficient and cost-effective way of getting information across. A variation is lecturettes which last between 10 and 20 minutes and may be used as cues for discussion on new topics.

Good presentation skills are needed to give lectures. The trainer should inspire the learners by enthusiasm for the topic, make it as interesting as possible, and grab attention by presenting it in a dynamic way. The lecture can be combined with slides and group discussion to make it more lively still. Lectures remain the preferred method of instruction in universities, particularly in business subjects.

References

Evans, Chris and Fan, Jing Ping (2002) 'Lifelong learning through the Virtual University', *Campus-Wide Information Systems*, Volume 19, Number 4, pp127–134.
Reid, Charles W. and Kleiner, Brian H. (1996) 'Which training methods are effective?', *Management Development Review*, Volume 9, Number 2, pp24–29.

Left-brained   The term 'left-brained' describes a person who is more logical than creative. This is because the logical and analytical functions tend to be carried out in the left-hand side of the brain. Damage to this side of the brain may result in poor performance in tests for verbal ability. The dominant cerebral hemisphere in right-handed people is always the left one. It controls the right side of the body.

See also **Right-brained**.

References

Ratey, John (2001) *A User's Guide To The Brain*. London, Little, Brown.
http,//www.mtsu.edu/~devstud/advisor/hemis.html

Lifelong learning   Changes in work organisation and management, such as de-layering, outsourcing, multiskilling, and flexible working, combined with more focus on markets, competition, consumption and lifestyle, has attracted organisations to the idea of lifelong learning. In the information age, the rapid rate of technological change means we have to update our learning and skills throughout our working lives. Lifelong learning is thus now the norm. To earn more we've got to learn more. Indeed, we must update our skills continually just to keep our existing job. In addition to skills, we also need more general knowledge and social skills to equip us to deal with the demands of the modern workplace. This means creating a climate and culture in which all employees accept the idea of continuous learning and development as standard.

Employees are an organisation's greatest resource. Employees should be encouraged to learn on-the-job and off-the-job. Employers must create economic and other incentives for employees to make the effort worthwhile. They should be encouraged to make lifelong learning and continuous personal improvement their goal. It was Henry Ford, the great populariser of the modern car who said, 'Anyone who stops learning is old, whether 21 or 80. Anyone who keeps learning stays young. The greatest thing in life is to keep your mind young.'

Educational support schemes should be put in place to encourage people to undertake formal studies at certificate, diploma and degree level. Post-graduate studies should be supported for junior, middle and senior management. Individual training plans should be put in place to identify training and development needs. A corporate learning centre should be established in the workplace as a visible sign of management support for lifelong learning. More intensive use of correspondence-based distance learning, web-based learning and virtual universities should also be encouraged.

The leading professional bodies have taken the concept of lifelong learning on board through their continuing professional development (CPD) programmes that are mandatory in some cases. Some experts estimate that the amount of information generated in the world doubles every seven years. In addition, about half of the information that most professionals learn will be out of date in five years. Learning how to acquire learning-to-learn skills that provide the foundation for lifelong learning is essential for success in personal and business life.

In the future, knowledge and creativity will be the most important competitive edge. This is recognised in the new discipline of knowledge management. To become an effective lifelong learner you must understand your preferred learning style. Forearmed with this knowledge you will be better able to set up learning situations that suit your particular style of learning.

Key features of lifelong learning are:

- equipping people with learning-to-learn skills
- helping people ascertain their particular style of learning
- encouraging people to take responsibility for their own learning
- providing the resources and creating the opportunities for learning
- continuous professional development
- supporting action learning
- having a mentoring scheme and coaching process in place
- encouraging people to draw up personal development plans
- ensuring that learning is a positive experience
- creating a partnership between in-house training departments and external educational establishments.

See also **Learning-to-learn skills**.

References
Evans, Chris and Fan, Jing Ping (2002) 'Lifelong learning throught the Virtual University', *Campus-Wide Information Systems*, Volume 19, Number 4, pp127–134.
Holmes, Andrew (2002) *Lifelong Learning*. Oxford, Capstone.
http,//www.infed.org/lifelonglearning/b-life.htm
http,//www.newhorizons.org/article_hermansn.html
http,//www.iftdo.org/article3.htm

Limbic system   The limbic system is an area in the centre of the brain that is associated with control of emotion and behaviour, especially perception, motivation, memory and thought. Parts of the limbic system are thought to be crucial for learning and short-term memory. Emotions have a profound effect on learning. Positive feelings speed learning. Negative feelings slow or stop learning. Get learners to collaborate rather than compete and learning will improve significantly.

Major structures within the limbic system include the hippocampus, cingulate gyrus and amygdala.

See also **Hippocampus**.

References
Ratey, John (2001) *A User's Guide To The Brain*. London, Little, Brown.
Turkington, Carol (1996) *The Brain Encyclopedia*. New York, Checkmark Books.

Linguistic intelligence   Linguistic intelligence is one of the seven intelligences discerned by Howard Gardner in his book *Frames of Mind*. People with this intelligence are good at reading, writing, talking, debating and learning languages. They tend to have a good vocabulary, be fluent speakers and good all-round communicators. Their ability in this respect is likely to increase right through life and into their fifties, sixties and seventies. They are good at remembering names, dates, places, facts and other detailed information. Poets, writers, actors, preachers and politicians tend to have highly developed linguistic skills. William Shakespeare, Winston Churchill, John F. Kennedy, Bill Clinton, Robin Williams and Isaac Asimov would typify linguistic intelligence. This skill is highly valued in most occupations and in life generally. Many politicians have this ability to a high degree.

To enhance this ability, learn from books, tapes, games, lectures and seminars. Do crosswords and word games and debate issues with friends. Write instructions for others to follow. Explain how to solve a problem, and solve problems collaboratively with a friend. Take up part-time lecturing or join Toastmasters. We all have this ability to a lesser or greater extent.

See also **SIMILAR model of intelligences**.

References
Armstrong, Thomas (1993) *Seven Kinds of Smart: Identifying and developing your many intelligences.* London, Plume.
Gardner, Howard (1993) *Frames of Mind: The theory of multiple intelligences.* London, Fontana.
Stine, Jean Marie (2000) *Super Brain Power: Six keys to unlocking your hidden genius.* New York, Prentice Hall.
Vincent, Annette and Ross, Dianne (2001) 'Personalize training: determine learning styles, personality types and multiple intelligence online', *The Learning Organisation*, Volume 8, Number 1, pp36–43.
http,//www.famu.edu/sjmga/ggrow/7ln/Linguistic.html

Link system of memorising

The link system is a basic method of memorising by which each item in a list is linked or associated with the next. This uses a vivid imagination to associate items together in sequence – just like a train with carriages attached. Use the MUSE principle when making the links: imagine some Movement, something Unusual, something with Slapstick, something wildly Exaggerated. In other words, see things in an action-related context; larger than life; millions of them; in a humorous situation or in colour. As an example, say you want to remember 'dog', 'television', 'pencil' and 'apple'. Just picture the dog devouring the TV, the TV with pencils stuck out of the screen, and apples with pencils stuck in them. The more active, vivid and unusual the association, the better you'll recall it.

The link system works on the principle that people remember stories best. The strength of the images and the logic of the sequence provide the cues for retrieval. The link system is very easy to learn and use – but may be unreliable if you are hoping to remember the exact sequence of events in a story.

See also **Association**; **PLAN model of memorising systems**.

References
Higbee, Kenneth L. (1990) *Your Memory: How it works and how to improve it.* London, Piatkus.
http,//www.markgiles.co.uk/method2.htm
http,//www.mindtools.com/link.html
http,//www.cs.nott.ac.uk/~rjw97c/longlist.htm

Locus method of memorising

In the locus method, items to be remembered are mentally located in an imaginary place. To recall the items a person simply recalls the location in which each item has been placed. The method dates back to around 500 BC.

See also **Place system of memorising**.

References
Higbee, Kenneth L. (1990) *Your Memory: How it works and how to improve it.* London, Piatkus.

Locus of control

The locus of control is where the mind perceives the control centre of our lives to be located. People with an internal locus of control feel they are in charge of their lives. They are responsible for their own learning. They adopt a can-do attitude, 'If it's going to be, it's up to me.' Learners who attribute failure to lack of aptitude generally do not persist when they fail. Their attitude is that if their ability is fixed, there is not much they can do about it. On the other hand, learners who believe their failure is due to lack of effort, tend to persist in the face of failure. Their attitude is that they are not trying hard enough.

Somebody once said that there were three types of people in the world: those who make things happen, those who watch things happen, and those who haven't a clue what's happening. Your aim should be to make things happen. If you don't control your life, other people will control it for you – and with their interests at heart rather than yours.

Take responsibility for your learning. Undertake that training programme or degree course now! People with an internal locus of control draw up their own personal development and career plans. They believe they can influence the direction of their lives by undertaking formal and informal learning programmes. They don't wait around for other people to do things – they do things for themselves. They take control of their own lives and destiny. An internal locus of control is central to the concept of self-empowerment through continuous learning and self-improvement.

On the other hand, people with an external locus of control feel that they are manipulated and controlled by forces outside themselves. Consequently, they accept little personal accountability. They let their careers drift along and blame lack of progress on external forces such as the government, the boss, fate, luck, astrology, circumstances and parents. If you spend your time waiting for others to help you in your career, you are going to be sorely disappointed.

Let's take as an example of how locus of control might relate to motivation and participation in adult education: a man who has just been made redundant. He may blame his unwanted unemployment on factors he has no control over, such as an economic downturn, his age or just pure bad luck. He has an external locus of control. A man with an internal locus of control might see the unwanted unemployment as due to his lack of experience, education or special expertise such as computer skills. Such a person is more likely to engage in further education and training to make himself more marketable. People with an active internal locus of control are more likely to find employment.

Holmes and Cartwright (1994) report that internally motivated workers have a strong internal locus of control and are usually more satisfied in their jobs. In addition, the 'internals' see their supervisors as democratic, believe they have greater autonomy and control, and stay in their jobs longer than do 'externals' within the same organisation. Top managers have high levels of intrinsic motivation and exhibit a strong internal locus of control. Similarly, Cox *et al* (1997) report that successful career women have a strong internal locus of control – they believe that they can control the direction of their careers.

References
Cox, Barbara, White, Charles and Cooper, Cary L. (1997) 'A portrait of successful women', *Women in Management Review*, Volume 12, Number 1, pp27–34.
Holmes, Teresa and Cartwright, Sue (1994) 'Mid-Career Change', *Employee Relations*, Volume 16, Number 7, pp58–72.
Malone, Samuel A. (1999) *Success Skills for Managers*. Dublin, Oak Tree Press.
Tracy, Brian (1993) *Maximum Achievement*. New York, Simon & Schuster.

Long-term memory

It is in the long-term memory that we store information that we need for a long period of time. There are thought to be two conditions under which information is transferred from short-term to long-term memory:

- if the information is rehearsed and reflected on long enough

- if the information is made meaningful.

The amount of information we can store in the long-term memory is amazing. Unlike short-term memory, the capacity of long-term memory is practically unlimited. Psychologist and memory expert Elizabeth Loftus estimates that long-term memory records as many as 1 quadrillion separate bits of information. Some of these memories can often be retrieved under hypnosis.

Researchers divide long-term memory into three types:

- procedural memory – the memory of how to do something such as swim or ride a bike

- semantic memory – the memory for factual information

- episodic memory – the memory for personal events such as your first day at school.

See also **Short-term memory**; **WISE model of memory types**.

References
Baddeley, Alan (1991) *Human Memory: Theory and practice*. Hove, Lawrence Erlbaum Associates.
http,//www.web-us.com/memory/memory_encoding.htm
http,//www.ntu.ac.uk/soc/bscpsych/memory/goodhead.htm
http,//www.ntu.ac.uk/soc/bscpsych/memory/horsley.htm

Lozanov

Georgi Lozanov, a Bulgarian, is the force behind Suggestology, a forerunner to the Accelerated Learning Movement. Suggestology is based on the theory that suggestions can and do affect the outcome of learning. His early programmes focused on the teaching of foreign languages. It is claimed that students learned between 100 and 1,000 new words a day, with 91 per cent retention or better. A qualified medical hypnotist, he argued that everything in a learning environment should suggest success. Music, body language, colour, posters, and play should be used to create a relaxed, non-threatening learning environment. Lozanov points out that rational consciousness is just the tip of the iceberg in terms of one's full mental capacity. People learn on many levels simultaneously both at the conscious and subconscious levels. People learn holistically through their minds and bodies. We learn verbally, intuitively and intellectually – all at the same time. The Society for Effective Affective Learning (SEAL) was founded in 1983 to promote Lozanov's work.

See also **Suggestology**.

References

DePorter, Bobbi and Hernacki, Mike (1993) *Quantum Learning: Unleash the genius within you.* London, Piatkus.

Ostrander, Sheila and Schroeder, Lynn (1999) *Super-Learning 2000.* London, Souvenir Press.

M

Management development Management development is the improvement of managerial effectiveness by means of a planned and deliberate learning process. Management development should involve a combination of on-the-job and off-job-approaches. The more real the off-the-job experience, the more effective it is.

See also **Human resource development**.

References

Malone, Samuel A. (2000) *Learning Skills for Managers*. Dublin, Oak Tree Press.

Mumford, Alan (1993) *How Managers Can Develop Managers*. Aldershot, Gower.

Mumford, Alan (1997) *Management Development, Strategies for Action*, 3rd edition. London, IPD.

http,//www.reviewing.co.uk/research/ple_sum.htm

Maslow See **Motivation and learning**.

Massed practice In the terminology of experimental psychologists, the scheduling of learning sessions can be either 'massed' (ie concentrated) or 'distributed' (ie spread over time). The more complex the material to be learned, the greater the benefit of distributed practice. Material learned by distributed practice tends to be retained longer than material learned by massed practice. Learning is more effective over a period of time than in a concentrated stint, and training with breaks at intervals is more beneficial than training without breaks.

References

Malone, Samuel A. (2000) *Learning Skills for Managers*. Dublin, Oak Tree Press.

Megginson's learning model David Megginson developed his learning model after reflecting on the fact that he was better at reacting to opportunities than at creating opportunities himself.

MEGGINSON'S LEARNING MODEL

	Low	High
High Planned learning	Warrior	Sage
Low	Sleeper	Adventurer

Low   *High*

Learning from experience

Source: **Megginson and Whitaker (1996)**

'Planned learning' in this model implies that learners take responsibility for the direction and control of their training and development. 'Learning from experience' implies that learners respond to their experience in a thoughtful and reflective way.

Four types of learner are highlighted in the model:

■ *sleepers* – Sleepers show little initiative or response to their experiences. They are low on planned learning and low on learning from experience. They lack an awareness of the need to exploit job activities as learning opportunities. They are ineffective learners. Sleepers have much to learn from warriors and adventurers.

■ *warriors* – Warriors plan their experiences but tend not to learn from them. This is because they don't review and reflect on their learning. Because of this in turn they tend not to learn from their mistakes. We describe planned learners as 'warriors' because they have focus, direction, clarity and persistence . . . but due to lack of reflection have little insight on their learning.

■ *adventurers* – Adventurers respond to and learn from opportunities that come their way, but tend not to create opportunities for themselves. This is because of a lack of planned or prospective learning. We call emergent learners 'adventurers' because they have curiosity, flexibility and opportunism, and because they live in the here-and-now. Adventurers are thus reactive rather than proactive.

■ *sages* – The sage is the ideal learner. Sages plan, reflect and learn from their experiences. Sages have personal development plans and an integrated approach to on-the-job and off-the-job training. Sages have the qualities of warriors and adventurers. They realise that formal and informal learning is complementary, and that both are essential to long-term management development.

References
Megginson, David and Whitaker, Vivien (1996) *Cultivating Self-Development.* London, IPD.

Memory   Psychologists recognise the existence of two main kinds of memory: short-term and long-term. All information received by the senses seems to enter the short-term memory where after a brief period it is either discarded or transferred to long-term memory. Obviously, the transfer of information to long-term memory is vital for learning.

Researchers believe that the parts of the brain concerned with memory are located in the temporal and frontal lobes, and the hippocampus. Researchers at the National Institute of Mental Health in the USA, using positron emission tomography (PET) to map neuron activity, found that short-term memory for facial features and for spatial relations are located in different areas of the prefrontal cortex.

People with particular talents tend to have very good memories. Mozart was reputed to be able to write down all the notes of a piece of music after hearing it for the first time. He could compose musical scores in his head and then write them down correctly. A small proportion of autistic people (people otherwise generally unresponsive to daily reality) have a similarly specialised memory for one or other talent. People with high IQs generally have excellent memories.

Neuro-lingusitic programming (NLP) claims that the way we aim our eyes affects which part of the brain we are accessing. If you can't remember something, instead of looking down, look up, because this accesses information from the memory.

It is now generally accepted that the memory process is facilitated if:

- the information is of interest to the learner and put to immediate practical use

- an item to be committed to memory is repeated and practised

- items to be committed to memory are linked, connected, and associated with existing knowledge and experience

- the interest in the topic is intense and emotional

- the item to be committed to memory comes first or last in a sequence

- an overview of a topic to be learned is obtained early on – hence the value of learning maps

- the information is immediately meaningful – learning such information takes only about one tenth of the effort required to learn a comparable amount of nonsense material

- you concentrate on the key points or important issues

- you visualise images – ie you see them in your mind's eye

- it is continually challenged with new subjects and skills, so developing and extending the neural connections

- you exercise regularly by walking in the fresh air, drink sufficient water, and get sufficient sleep: the brain needs oxygen to function effectively

- your diet includes a sufficient concentration of B vitamins – hazelnuts are especially rich in B vitamins; brazil nuts are rich in various B vitamins, vitamin E, magnesium, potassium and iron, which makes them an ideal food for those interested in improving the memory; the lipid (fat) lecithin, often described as a 'brain food', is mainly found in egg yolks, pulses and carrots and other root vegetables

- you relax – it is impossible to pay attention if you are tense and anxious; in addition, emotional or physical stress stimulates the release of stress hormones such as cortisol and adrenaline: constant exposure to stress kills off brain cells and causes memory loss

- you use mnemonic devices as appropriate, which will help you to associate facts with images.

See also **Long-term memory**; **Memory training**; **Short-term memory**.

References
Hermann, Douglas J. (1995) *Super Memory: A quick-action programme for memory improvement*. London, Blandford.
Higbee, Kenneth L. (1990) *Your Memory: How it works and how to improve it*. London, Piatkus.
Rupp, Rebecca (1998) *Committed to Memory: How we remember and why we forget*. London, Aurum Press.
http,//www.sdc.uwo.ca/learning/memory.html
http,//www.happychild.org.uk/acc/tpr/mem/0498supm.htm
http,//onhealth.com/ch1/live/ohlive/archive/item,55568.asp
http,//ericir.syr.edu/Projects/Newton11/memory.html
http,//www.epub.org.br/cm/n01/memo/improve_i.htm
file,//C,\Program Files\Britannica\BCD\Cache_6_PreviewRil.htm
http,//www.findarticles.com/cf_0/g2603/0005/2603000517/print.jhtml

Memory aids   Aids to memory can be classified as either of two types:

- *internal memory aids* – These include a range of mnemonic devices such as the PLAN model [see **PLAN model of memorising systems**] and rehearsal strategies.

- *external memory aids* – These include devices such as diaries, address books, to-do lists, electronic reminders and alarms.

Memory stages   The three stages of memory are:

- registration
- retention
- recall.

Registration is encoding or learning the material. Retention is storing or keeping the material 'on file' until needed. Recall is retrieving the information when needed.

If you can't remember something it may be because:

■ you failed to register the information in the first place

■ the information was never stored

■ the information was not stored in a way that makes it easy to find.

Most problems in remembering occur in the recall stage rather than in the registration and retention stages. Mnemonic devices may help you to recall information more efficiently.

See also **Memory**.

References
Hermann, Douglas J. (1995) *Super Memory: A quick-action programme for memory improvement.* London, Blandford.
Higbee, Kenneth L. (1990) *Your Memory: How it works and how to improve it.* London, Piatkus.
Rupp, Rebecca (1998) *Committed to Memory: How we remember and why we forget.* London, Aurum Press.

Memory training   Considerable evidence suggests that you can improve your ability to recall information using various memory techniques. These include:

■ mnemonics [see **Mnemonics**]

■ rehearsal [see **Repetition**]

■ relaxation [see **Relaxation**]

■ visual imagery [see **Visualisation**]

■ 'chunking' information [see **Chunking**]

■ paying attention [see **Attention**; **Attention span**]

■ learning maps [see **Learning map**]

■ positive expectation – if you believe you have a good memory, your mind will do everything to prove you right [see also **Attitude**].

References
Hermann, Douglas J. (1995) *Super Memory: A quick-action programme for memory improvement.* London, Blandford.
Higbee, Kenneth L. (1990) *Your Memory: How it works and how to improve it.* London, Piatkus.
Rupp, Rebecca (1998) *Committed to Memory: How we remember and why we forget.* London, Aurum Press.
http,//www.mindpub.com/art079.htm

Mental maps   Mental maps – also known as schemata or mental models – are personal models of reality: the way an individual sees the world. They allow people to categorise events, assess consequences and consider appropriate actions. Our upbringing, education, experience, beliefs, and values shape mental maps. When a craftsman produces an object, it is the result of an idea, image or pattern of what he wants to make. The artisan has a guiding plan or mental model. For example, a potter before he starts has a clear idea of what he wants to make. While the work progresses he may make changes, develop the original idea, but he is constrained by his original mental model. When we look at an object or a person or formulate an idea or an opinion, our view is highly influenced by our prior experiences, expectations and emotions. We share aspects of our mental maps with other people, but no two people have identical mental maps.

Mental maps are relevant to learning and development. Development can be viewed as a process of changing our mental maps. We outgrow our mental maps, but only through choice. We become rigid or creative in our thinking. Either way, our future models are not inevitable. Instead they reflect the clarity of our vision, mission, attitudes, values and beliefs as of today.

Transformational learning, similar to paradigm shifts, occur when you radically change your mental map of the world. In negotiation, this might be a change from a win–lose approach to a win–win approach. In leadership, it might be a move from an autocratic to a democratic style. To be an effective communicator, it is important to realise that people do not share common mental maps. Empathy is the ability to get inside another's mental map. In neuro-linguistic programming they say that the map is not the territory. This means that your map of reality is not reality itself.

See also **Mental set**; **Schema**.

References
Russell, Peter (1979) *The Brain Book*. London, Routledge & Kegan Paul.

Mental rehearsal   Mental rehearsal is running through in your mind an activity which you know you should be able to do or do better. It involves creating images, sounds, and feelings in your mind. It is one of the techniques of neuro-linguistic programming (NLP). Psychologists have found that mental rehearsal is nearly as effective for the mind as doing the actual event. Imaging one's own body movements 'lights up' many of the same brain areas as actual performance of these movements.

Mental rehearsal is a type of prospective learning. It is used extensively in sports psychology. Jack Nicklaus and other golfers use visualisation to enhance their game. They mentally rehearse every shot in their minds before going on the golf course. Two-time US Olympic pentathlon champion Marilyn King came back from a serious accident which left her bedridden for some time. She used mental rehearsal while convalescing. Mary Lou Retton, US 1984 Olympic gold medal gymnast, used mental rehearsal to practise her routine the night before she struck gold. Napoleon Bonaparte is said to have mentally rehearsed his battles beforehand. Thomas S. Whetstone of the University of Louisville found (1996) that police officers who mentally rehearsed target-shooting for 40 minutes at home had better shooting scores than those who did little or no mental rehearsal at home.

You might mentally rehearse a presentation that you will be giving to the senior management team in the near future. Visualise yourself in the room in which you are to make the presentation and in your mind rehearse the process that you will go through. See yourself acting confidently and getting a favourable response from the audience. See yourself handling questions in a confident manner. Use positive affirmations to programme your mind for success. Say to yourself, 'I am a confident speaker.'

Mental rehearsal is a proactive activity. You are thinking ahead and anticipating any problems that may arise. You can then put contingency plans in place to cater for these problems if they happen.

References

O'Connor, Joseph and Seymour, John (1994) *Training with NLP Skills for Managers, Trainers and Communicators*. London, Thorsons.
Whetstone, T. S. (1996) 'Mental practice enhances recruit police officers' acquisition of critical psychomotor skills', *Police Studies*, Volume 19, Number 1, pp19–43.
http,//www.findarticles.com/cf_0/m0961/2001_Annual/73232717/print.jhtml

Mental set   If you have just bought a new car, your mind will immediately start picking out similar cars on the road – this is an example of what psychologists call a mental set. The mind tends to pick out whatever it is 'set' for. It seems we are programmed to see and hear whatever interests us amid all other distracting sights and sounds.

People with a particular belief system are programmed to notice those facts that support their belief and ignore those that don't. A teacher's expectation of a student's ability can influence learning outcomes. If a teacher is told that his students are academically bright, he will react to them in a more positive way – and the students are likely therefore to perform better than if he were told that they were academically poor. This is also an example of a self-fulfilling prophecy.

When studying, it is important to establish a strong mental set in the form of learning objectives and questions that you want answers for.

See also **Mental maps**; **Schema**.

References

Malone, Samuel A. (2000) *Learning Skills for Managers*. Dublin, Oak Tree Press.
Ukens, Lorraine L. (2001) *What Smart Trainers Know*. San Francisco, Jossey-Bass Pfeiffer.

Mentoring   Mentors are people who can advise, support, coach, and counsel learners in their career aspirations. Mentors can be part of your personal as well as your business life. They can be formal or informal. Many successful business people attribute their success to having being mentored at an early stage in their careers. A mentor may act as a role model, sounding-board and confidant.

Mentoring is not anything new. It has a pedigree going back to ancient Greek tutelage. In the Middle Ages the apprentice copied and learned from the master craftsman. Mentoring differs from coaching in that mentoring is general rather than specific, is long-term rather than short-term in focus, and is delivered by someone other than the line manager. Mentoring is a great opportunity to help someone fulfil his or her potential while at the same time developing a whole range of skills.

Mentoring is as much a learning opportunity for the mentor as it is for the mentee. The mentor may develop counselling, listening, questioning and empathy skills by establishing and maintaining the relationship with the mentee. The mentor will learn how adults learn, how their learning styles differ, and how to develop people. The mentor will learn how to be facilitative and objective rather than directive and partisan in the mentoring relationship. The mentor will develop creative problem-solving skills by enabling the mentee to generate alternative and novel solutions for consideration. The mentor will develop influencing and negotiating skills in dealings with senior management on behalf of the mentee. Compatibility is an important ingredient in successful mentoring.

Usual reasons for asking someone to act as mentor include:

- *training and development:* training and developing staff to meet the operational needs of the organisation – This is a practical and work-focused reason. There is disenchantment with traditional training and a need for more relevancy.

- *succession:* the succession needs of the organisation – As part of the human resource development plan there may be a need to identify potential managerial talent to fill middle and senior management positions in the future. Retirements, resignations, technological change, market growth, downsizing, mergers and takeovers create vacancies and succession needs in organisations. Mentoring is an important technique for developing leaders.

- *induction:* to induct trainees into the culture of the company – A well-run mentoring programme engages the hearts and minds of those involved and enhances the commitment and morale of staff. Mentoring is particularly suitable as part of a graduate development programme.

- *the learning organisation:* as a visible sign of support for the learning organisation – These and other training initiatives show that senior management are prepared to 'to walk the talk' about becoming a learning organisation and display concern for the development of staff.

- *equal opportunities:* as part of an equality agenda, to advance the needs of women or minority groups – The proportion of women compared to men in middle and senior management positions remains very low in relation to their numbers in the workforce.

■ *knowledge management*: to pass on the tacit knowledge of experienced managers and their judgement, perspective and wisdom to the next generation – On the retirement of senior managers or in downsizing situations, there is always the danger that their expertise may be lost to the organisation.

■ *realising people's potential* – Mentoring is a practical planned way of helping people reach their potential. Few people possess the skill necessary to identify their own learning and development needs. Mentees are encouraged to make personal development plans and think about their career progression in the company. Many young people leave organisations after a relatively short time because they feel frustrated, ignored and underutilised. A mentoring programme may help to meet the modern expectations of participation, empowerment and job satisfaction.

■ *business competitiveness* – Mentoring may enhance company competitiveness by improving personal efficiency, job performance, decision-making and, ultimately, the bottom line – profits. At the end of the day a cost/benefit analysis should demonstrate that the benefits of the mentoring scheme are greater than the costs.

■ *education*: to support mature staff in the organisation who are undertaking company-financed educational initiatives such as MBA programmes or professional qualifications.

Some government agencies offer entrepreneurial mentoring programmes to stimulate economic development.

See also **Coaching**.

References

Bisk, Leonard (2002) 'Formal entrepreneurial mentoring: the efficacy of third-party-managed programs', *Career Development International*, Volume 7, Number 5, pp262–270.

Cheetham, Graham and Chivers, Geoff (2001) 'How professionals learn in practice: an investigation of informal learning amongst people working in professions', *Journal of European Industrial Training*, Volume 25, Number 5, pp247–292.

Clutterbuck, David (1998) *Everyone Needs A Mentor*, 2nd edition. London, IPD.

Shea, Gordon F. (1997) *Mentoring*. London, Kogan Page.

http,//coachingandmentoring.com/Articles/mentoring.html

http,//www.free-press.com/journals/gajal/articles/gajal-article-034.htm

http,//www.usenix.org/sage/mentor/mentor_guidelines.html

Meta-learning　　Meta-learning – also known as metacognition – is learning how to learn. Thinking about one's thinking creates the foundation for learning to learn. There is accumulating evidence from brain research that thinking skills can be learned.

People are designed by evolution to learn and adapt to their environment. The brain is an open and dynamic learning system. What mental processes do we use when we solve problems? Are we aware of the reasoning, assumptions, evidence and justification underlying our beliefs? People have different learning styles. As learners, what are our strengths and weaknesses? What learning strategies have successfully worked for us in the past? Some people learn by reading, some by watching, some by listening, and some through experimentation using a hands-on approach. It is important to know what is the best method or combination of methods for our own learning. If you understand how you think and learn, you can refine and improve your learning skills.

Metacognition is probably the most important lifelong learning skill. Key aspects to metacognition include:

- knowing the difference between understanding and memorising, and knowing which mental strategies to use as and when appropriate

- the ability to recognise difficult subjects, where to start, and how much time to spend on them

- the ability to identify particular difficulties in the learning material, order them, and try to resolve them.

- knowing when we don't understand something and knowing when to seek the help of an expert

- knowing when the expert's explanation solves our learning problem.

References
Ukens, Lorraine L. (2001) *What Smart Trainers Know.* San Francisco, Jossey-Bass Pfeiffer.
http,//www.learnativity.com/edpsych.com
http,//www.mathmatters.net/math7.htm

Metamemory   Metamemory is what you know about your own memory. If you know how your memory works, and especially if you know how well or how badly it works, you are in a better position to improve it. People improve their memories by using visual imagination, mnemonics and rehearsal strategies. We can employ the strategy that suits our needs, and monitor progress.

References
Parkin, Alan J. (1993) *Memory Phenomena: Experiment and theory.* Oxford, Blackwell.

Metaphors   A metaphor is the representation of one thing in terms of another. Metaphors are useful in learning since they connect complex concepts to understandable objects and events.

Metaphors can be drawn from science, nature, industry, sport, literature and history.

For example, the voltage in electrical current can be compared to the flow of water down a hose. With the right attachments you can vary the speed, volume, and force of water. The same thing happens with electricity.

An infant's brain has been compared to a computer waiting to be programmed. A more appropriate metaphor sees the brain as a biological self-adjusting organism that grows and reshapes itself in response to challenge and new learning. The downside is that parts of it may wither through disuse.

Machinery has been a common metaphor used to understand the workings of modern society. We refer to the machinery of government, re-engineering corporations, and even input-output models for educational systems. It is now clear that biological and social systems are open, and that the machine metaphor is inappropriate as a way of understanding such systems.

Metaphors have been used as methods for training, communication and teaching since human history began. Andrew Ortony (1993) says there are three main reasons for using metaphors in a learning context:

- to achieve compactness in how we communicate – Metaphors can be clear, concise and effective, and can be used to provide universal understanding.

- to include vividness in our language – Metaphors can engage our emotions by creating appropriate symbols and images.

- to help us express the otherwise inexpressible – In a learning situation they may be used to clarify and simplify difficult ideas and concepts.

Aristotle considered the use of metaphor a sign of genius. He believed that people who had the capacity to perceive similarities between two different things and link them together were possessors of a special gift.

References
Alder, Harry (1994) 'The technology of creativity', *Management Decision*, Volume 32, Number 4, pp23–29.
Parkin, Margaret (1998) *Tales for Trainers: Using stories and metaphors to facilitate learning*. London, Kogan Page.

Miller's seven plus or minus two rule   George Miller has posited that our short-term memory can hold only between five and nine items at any one time without special rehearsal. Miller, from Harvard, set this principle out in a famous paper entitled 'The magic number seven, plus or minus two'. However, you can improve your short-term memory span by 'chunking' items together.

References
Miller, George A. (1956) 'The magical number seven, plus or minus two: some limits on our capacity for processing information'. *Psychological Review*, Volume 2, pp81–97.

Mind maps   See **Learning map**.

Mnemonics   The term 'mnemonics' is derived from the ancient Greek *mnēmonikos* 'to do with remembering' (from *mnēmōn* 'keeping in mind'). Mnemonic techniques have been practised since well before 500 BC. Studies have consistently shown how useful mnemonic strategies are in retrieving information from memory. They can be either verbal or visual or both – verbal mnemonics use words and rhyme to make associations, and visual mnemonics use visual imagery to link the information.

For example:

- Psychology students remember Freud's personality theory by the little rhyme, 'Id is just a kid.'

- You probably remember the following from school – the rule for remembering ei or ie: '*I* before *e* except after *c*, or when sounded like *a* as in neighbour and weigh'.

- If you have difficulty remembering which way to turn a screwdriver, the following little ditty may help: 'Righty tighty, lefty loosey'.

- If you have difficulty remembering which way to turn the key of your front door when leaving or returning, this may help: 'Left to leave, right to return'.

- If you want to improve your performance, you could remember the formula $P = L + B$, where P is performance, L is learning, and B is behaviour.

- The mnemonic ABC encapsulates the basis of behaviourism. A stands for antecedent, B for behaviour, and C for consequence. Behaviour is triggered by an antecedent and results in a consequence.

The well-known acronym STAR is used in the nuclear industry to help operators remember the problem-solving process:

- Stop!

- Think!

- Act! and

- Review.

The human brain has evolved to deal with information in a multifaceted way, combining sound, vision, touch, smell, spatial awareness, emotion and language. However, a great deal of information is presented to us via a single source – the written page. The purpose of mnemonics is to awaken all the senses so that information we need to remember is registered strongly on our memories. A useful acronym for this purpose is MUSE, which stands for Movement, Unusualness, Slapstick content, and Exaggeration.

- *movement* – Adding movement to an image makes it more vivid, exciting and memorable.

- *unusualness* – Bizarre or weird (or maybe rude) images are easy to remember.

- *slapstick* – Funny situations are easier to remember than normal ones.

- *exaggeration* – Exaggerate the size and number of the items for better recall. Vivid, colourful images are easier to remember than drab ones.

See also **Acronyms**; **Acrostic**; **PLAN model of memorising systems**.

References
Hermann, Douglas J. (1995) *Super Memory: A quick-action programme for memory improvement*. London, Blandford.
Higbee, Kenneth L. (1990) *Your Memory: How it works and how to improve it*. London, Piatkus.
Malone, Samuel A. (1996) *Learning to Learn*. London, CIMA.
Rupp, Rebecca (1998) *Committed to Memory: How we remember and why we forget*. London, Aurum Press.
http,//www.ldonline.org/ld_indepth/teaching_techniques/mnemonic_strategies.html
http,//www.mindtools.com/mnemexam.html
http,//www.mindtools.com/mnemeffc.html
http,//www.csu.edu.au/divisions/studserv/memory1.htm
http,//www.peterhoneylearning.com/Article//2

Modelling   Modelling – also known as observational learning – is learning a new behaviour simply by watching and profiting from another's successes or mistakes. As children we learn to walk and talk by observing those around us. Learning from observation is a natural process. On a daily basis the example and behaviours of our role models influence us. We can model ourselves on examples of human excellence.

In management development, 'shadowing' is a technique based on the principle of modelling. The idea is to model a manager who displays excellent managerial skills. The model must be a person whom we love, trust, respect, and admire. As Goethe said in 1825, 'Everywhere, we learn only for those whom we love.'

Some model themselves on many different people rather than on just one person. People can also be influenced by negative role models – examples of how *not* to behave. For example, your manager might have an inappropriate leadership style which you find is counterproductive.

Apprentices learn by observing or modelling their behaviour on that of the craftsman. The craftsman teaches by demonstrating, coaching and facilitating until the apprentice becomes a self-directed learner. At this stage there are two outcomes for apprentices:

- The apprentices have internalised or made the learning their own. They are now equipped to do the task or solve the problem on their own.

- The apprentices have generalised what they have learned. This enables them to apply the learning to similar situations or use the learning as a starting point for further learning.

We are likely to model ourselves on others if they:

- show unusual competence

- are seen as having something in common with ourselves

- are role models, walk the talk or do what they say they will do – we are unlikely to be influenced (for example) by a health educator who is obese, smokes too much and avoids physical exercise

- are enthusiastic and committed.

Albert Bandura (1986) also identifies two levels at which people regard others as role models:

- imitation, in which one person simply tries to copy the behaviour of another

- identification, in which a person tries to be the same kind of person as another.

See also **Observational learning**.

References
Bandura, Albert (1986) *Social Foundations of Thought and Action: A social cognitive theory.* New Jersey, Prentice Hall.

Beaver, Diana (1994) *Lazy Learning: Making the most of the brains you were born with.* Shaftesbury, Element Books.

Cheetham, Graham and Chivers, Geoff (2001) 'How professionals learn in practice: an investigation of informal learning amongst people working in professions', *Journal of European Industrial Training,* Volume 25, Number 5, pp247–292.

O'Connor, Joseph and Seymour, John (1990). *Introducing NLP: Psychological skills for understanding and influencing people.* London, Aquarian/Thorsons.

DePorter, Bobbi and Hernacki, Mike (1993) *Quantum Learning: Unleash the genius within you.* London, Piatkus.

http,//www.infed.org/foundations/commitment.htm

file,//C,\Program Files\Britannica\BCD\Cache_15_PreviewRil.htm

Modular training   Modular training involves separate training programmes (modules) designed as an integrated series that leads to certain level of qualifications or attainment. Each module covers a specific area of the course. Modules can be chosen depending on the needs or preferences of trainees. Each module is self-contained and has its own learning objectives. Modules for self-study may be supplemented by audios and videos.

References
Prior, John (1991) *A Handbook of Training and Development.* Aldershot, Gower.

Motivation and learning   Motivation for learning may be intrinsic, coming from within, or extrinsic, coming from without. Intrinsic motivation is the stronger because it corresponds to the desire to learn to meet your own goals and needs rather than the expectations or goals of others such as parents or peers. Sources of extrinsic motivation include promotion prospects, fear of redundancy, managerial pressure, and peer competition. Meaningful learning is more likely to occur when learners engage with the subject for its own sake, rather than to satisfy an extrinsic demand. Ultimately, learning should be driven by a search for meaning and purpose.

Learners are more highly motivated if their organisation supports learning and if they have responsibility for their own learning. Employees who are set clear goals frequently improve their performance and heighten their job satisfaction. Goals are more likely to be achieved if they are clearly visualised and broken down into manageable parts or sub-goals. High but realistic expectations are most effective. For example, all the ingredients for successful learning are often designed into computer-based training. These include motivational objectives, learner responsibility and opportunities for feedback of results.

Abraham Maslow's hierarchy of needs – a prioritised checklist of what people need, want and expect from their employment – can be adapted to form a motivational model for learning.

- At the physical and safety level, a stimulating, secure, supportive and safe environment must be provided for learning. Appropriate equipment and resources for learning must be made available. The learner must have opportunities to practise the new behaviour.

- At the emotional level, the learner must be made responsible for his or her learning but at the same time must be given recognition, respect, acceptance and a sense of belonging through collaborative learning. The learner must be encouraged to picture the new behaviour he or she wishes to adopt.

- At the intellectual level, the learning should be varied, stimulating and challenging. The learner may seek knowledge for its own sake or to satisfy an inquiring mind. Learning material should be difficult enough to offer challenge to participants but not be too difficult so that he or she becomes frustrated.

- At the self-actualising level, the learning must be meaningful, provide a sense of purpose and be a vehicle for self-expression and self-development. The learner may be looking for professional advancement, promotion or higher status. The trainer should explain how the content and objectives of the course will help participants achieve their learning, professional and/or personal goals. The learner should try to discern his or her vocation in life. People are not at peace with themselves unless they find their true calling. Maslow believed that 95 per cent of people are capable of self-actualisation in their older years, but that only 1 per cent ever achieved it.

In general, people have a high motivation to learn if:

- they accept they have a need to learn – In the context of work this usually means they accept that they have a performance problem, a skills gap, or a need to improve promotion prospects through developmental activities.

- they believe that they have the potential ability to learn the required skill – Some people may accept that they have a need but at the same time are not confident that they can improve on their performance. For example, many older people often lack the self-belief to learn information and communications technology skills.

- they believe that learning a particular skill is a priority – If they do, they will allocate the required time and resources to achieve the learning task. As Goethe said, 'Whatever you can do or dream you can, begin it. Boldness has genius, power and magic in it. Begin it now.'

- they need to meet the external expectation of their manager, who wants them to acquire a particular skill to equip them to do their job more effectively

- they are learning through pure interest, to satisfy personal curiosity or to challenge their brains.

Cyril Houle, in *The Inquiring Mind* in 1961, categorised the reasons people engaged in adult education programmes as:

- goals – They use education as a way of achieving their goals.

- activity – They participate because of the social aspect of learning.

- learning – They enjoy learning for its own sake.

Other studies show that adult learners get involved in learning because of life transitions such as caused by the stage of life they have reached and family and career events. The need to make sense of one's life experiences is often the incentive to take part in a learning opportunity in the first place.

    See also **Herzberg's motivation-hygiene theory.**

References

Houle, Cyril O. (1961) *The Inquiring Mind.* Madison, Wis., University of Wisconsin Press.

Kinman Gail and Kinman, Russell (2001) 'The role of motivation to learn in management education', *Journal of Workplace Learning*, Volume 13, Number 4, pp132–144.

Reid, Margaret Anne, Barrington, Harry and Kennedy, John (1992) *Training Interventions.* London, IPM.

http,//www.learnativity.com/motivation.html

file,\\C,Program Files\Britannica\BCD\Cache_14_PreviewRil.htm

file,\\C,\Program Files\Britannica\BCD\Cache_24_PreviewRil.htm

http,//www.csu.edu.au/division/studserv/motivbro.htm

http,//www.hcc.hawaii.edu/intranet/committees/FacDevCom/guid…/maslow.ht

http,//www.hcc.hawaii.edu/intranet/committees/FacDevCom/guideb…/motiv.ht

http,//www.hcc.hawaii.edu/intranet/committees/FacDevCom/gui…/motivate.ht

MUD model of learning　The MUD model is an acronymic guide to how things can be learned, the acronym MUD stands for Memory, Understanding and Doing, and is based on a mnemonic by G. Gibbs in his book *How Do I Learn?* (1973).

- Memorising involves association, repetition, review, paraphrasing and self-testing. Don't memorise a formula without understanding it first. This understanding will help you recreate the formula if your memory fails you. You may achieve adequate comprehension of a concept, but may be unable to recall the facts associated with it. Hence the need for review and reflection.

- Understanding is about making sense of information, extracting meaning and relating information to the realities of everyday life. We gain a greater understanding of the world through the application and reinterpretation of knowledge. Understanding involves questioning, comparing, contrasting, analysis, synthesis, evaluation, acquiring insights and problem-solving. Professional and university examinations test students' capacity to demonstrate their analytical and problem-solving abilities rather than rote memorisation. So identify the key learning points, organise your material, and make sure that you understand what you are committing to memory.

- Doing involves a physical activity of some sort, with practice sessions to achieve perfection. There is an old saying that there can be no learning without action, and no action without learning. It is about developing skills and methods and testing ideas in the real live world. Confucius said, 'I hear and I forget. I see and I remember. I do and I understand.' Being actively involved in a learning task engraves it on your memory and helps you understand it. Remember the 'say and do' principle – research shows that we remember only 10 per cent of what we read, 20 per cent of what we see, but a full 90 per cent of what we say and do. Aristotle echoed this when he said 'What we have to do, we learn by doing.' He also said that theory should be followed by experimental verification. However, Artistotle didn't always follow his own precepts and check his theories. His erroneous theory that heavier bodies fall faster was not subjected to experimental verfication for nigh on 2,000 years until Galileo disproved it. You don't become a competent footballer by studying a 'how-to' book and memorising the rules. The important knowledge is tacit. You learn the sport by getting out there on the field, in competition with an opposing side, and playing with experienced players. The same applies to any craft or profession.

Obviously, if you really want to remember something you should understand it. Memory is but one of the ingredients of effective learning. There is no learning without memory and no memory without learning.

See also **FIBRES** model of memory.

References
Cotton, Julie (1995) *The Theory of Learners*. London, Kogan Page.
Gibbs, G. (1973) *How Do I Learn?* London, FEU.
Malone, Samuel A. (1996) *Learning to Learn*. London, CIMA.

Multiple intelligence   See **SIMILAR** model of intelligences.

Multiskilling   Multiskilling is the creation and allocation of work that requires employees regularly to exchange and/or share tasks. No job is undertaken exclusively by an individual. Multiskilling requires appropriate training and creates a more flexible workforce. Craftworkers may see it as erosion of their skills, and the unions may oppose it for similar reasons.

References
Malone, Samuel A. (2000) *Learning Skills for Managers*. Dublin, Oak Tree Press.

MUSE model of memory   The MUSE model is an acronymic guide to ways of memorising things for easy recall. The acronym stands for Movement, Unusualness, Slapstick and Exaggeration.

In other words, if you want to remember something, visualise it in an unusual action context, using vivid imagination, colour, exaggeration, and humour. Be creative, be inspired – which of course was what the ancient Greek Muses were all about.

References
Malone, Samuel A. (1996) *Learning to Learn*. London, CIMA.

Musical intelligence   Musical intelligence is one of the seven intelligences discerned by Howard Gardner in his book *Frames of Mind* (1984). Mozart obviously enjoyed this ability to an exceptional degree. Most of the rest of us exercise this talent to a lesser extent by listening to music, singing and humming along to a tune. People with musical intelligence are good at picking up sounds, remembering melodies, noticing pitches/rhythms and keeping time. Composers, song-writers, musicians, singers, and pop artists have this ability. Beethoven, Elton John, the Beatles, Frank Sinatra, Elvis Presley and Luciano Pavarotti would be prime examples.

Research has shown that for many people listening to music can enhance both the creative and learning process because a complexity of melody and harmony supports complexity of thinking. To increase this ability, try relaxing to music and studying or reading to Baroque music playing softly in the background. We all have this intelligence to a lesser or greater degree.

Set what you want to learn to music. Rhythm and music will make it easier to remember. Use music to reduce stress and create poems and songs to memorise and learn information. Advertisers link information to music for more effective recall.

See also **SIMILAR model of intelligences**.

References
Armstrong, Thomas (1993) *Seven Kinds of Smart: Identifying and developing your many intelligences.* London, Plume.
Gardner, Howard (1993) *Frames of Mind: The theory of multiple intelligences.* London, Fontana.
Vincent, Annette and Ross, Dianne (2001) 'Personalise training: determine learning styles, personality types and multiple intelligence online', *The Learning Organisation*, Volume 8, Number 1, pp36–43.
http,//www.famu.edu/sjmga/ggrow/7ln/Musical.html

Music and learning   Scientists are finding out that the human brain may be pre-wired for music and that some intelligences may be enhanced by music. Studies show that children who learn to play music tend to do better at mathematics. This may be because music involves proportions, ratios and sequences, all of which form the foundation for mathematical reasoning. Scientists have discovered that Baroque music can assist in regulating heatbeat and blood pressure and for many people helps to create a stress-free learning environment. It has also been found that lively harmonic music, such as that of Mozart, Beethoven and Brahms, stimulates the brain. Setting information to music may help many of us to remember better.

The front part of the corpus callosum – the part of the brain that connects the two hemispheres – is more developed in musicians than other professions. To be successful, musicians need to integrate the emotional right brain with the analytical left brain. Imaging technology shows that when people listen to music the right hemisphere of the brain is activated. When people read music the left hemisphere of the brain is activated in the same area involved in analytical and mathematical thinking. One report has disclosed that the foremost designers and engineers in Silicon Valley are almost all practising musicians. Scientists have also discovered that mental rehearsal combined with physical practice at music improves performance better than physical practice alone.

Trainers can use music to create a positive learning atmosphere by playing appropriate music as course participants enter the training room, during breaks, and at the end of training sessions. Music may be used to help focus concentration, improve memory, enhance imagination, develop rapport, and reduce tension. 'Music is the electrical soil in which the spirit lives, thinks and invents' – Ludwig van Beethoven.

References
Beaver, Diana (1994) *Lazy Learning: Making the most of the brains you were born with.* Shaftesbury, Element Books.
Begley, Sharon (2000) 'Music on the mind', *Newsweek*, 24 July.
DePorter, Bobbi and Hernacki, Mike (1993) *Quantum Learning: Unleash the genius within you.* London, Piatkus.
Meir, Dave (2000) *The Accelerated Learning Handbook.* New York, McGraw-Hill.

Pattison, Sherry A. (2001) 'Staff meetings: an opportunity for accelerated training of employees', *Journal of Workplace Learning*, Volume 13, Number 4, pp172–179.
http,//www.newhorizons.org/arts_dickinson.htm
http,//www.newhorizons.org/arts_brewer.htm

Myers-Briggs ® Type Indicator   The Myers-Briggs ® Type Indicator is a framework against which it is possible to plot any individual's personality as a 'type'. It is based on Carl Jung's theory of personality type, which assumes that personality can be divided into four independent scales: energising, attending, deciding, and living. Each scale is measurable as a preference between two opposites, making a total of 16 possible different personality combinations.

The scales are:

- Energising (orientation to life) – From where does a person draw energy for living?
  Extroversion (E)
  The outside world of people, activities and things. Extrovert learners like explaining things to others and like to get involved in collaborative learning. They like action learning.
  Introversion (I)
  The internal world of concepts, ideas, emotions and impressions. Introvert learners like to develop frameworks that integrate or connect the subject matter. They are thoughtful and self-sufficient. They like to see the big picture. Learning maps and flowcharts will help them do this.

- Attending (perception) – What a person pays attention to.
  Sensing (S)
  Preference for taking in information through the five senses; what is real and actual. Sensing learners like logically structured lectures. They have a realistic, practical and detailed focus.
  Intuition (N)
  Preference for taking in information through a sixth sense; what might be. Intuitive learners like to focus on the future and discover patterns and possibilities. They like abstract thinking, are imaginative and creative. They trust their feelings and intuition and like to see the big picture.

- Deciding (decision-making) – How a person makes decisions.
  Thinking (T)
  Information is organised and structured in a logical, objective way. Thinking learners like to see cause-and-effect relationships. They are objective and critical. They like clear learning objectives.
  Feeling (F)
  Information is structured in a personal, value-oriented way. Feeling learners are

more subjective than objective. They are good at persuasion and settling differences within groups. They prefer collaborative learning.

■ Living (attitude to the outside world) – The type of lifestyle adopted.
Judgement (J)
Preference for living a planned, organised life. Judging learners like to get on with things, and want to know only the essentials. They often have difficulty in completing a task. They thus need notetaking, time management and organisation skills.

Perception (P)
Preference for living a spontaneous and flexible life. Perceptive learners are curious, open, interested and adaptable. They often leave things to the last minute. They need to chunk complex tasks into sub-tasks and set deadlines for each. Deadlines keep them on target and sub-tasks provide them with feedback.

The Myers-Briggs ® Type Indicator has been widely used to classify student learning styles across various disciplines. One study of second-level students showed that those with the highest grades are a combination of 'introverted, intuitive, thinking and judging' personality types. Those with the lowest grades were a combination of 'extroverted, sensing, feeling, and perceiving' personality types. These latter might do better academically if the learning in colleges was activity-based rather than lecture-based. Research has found that there is a mismatch between university faculty styles and student learning styles. Generally, lecturers like to focus on theory whereas students prefer practical applications and examples before examining the theory.

See also **Diagnostic instruments**; **Learning styles**; **VAK model of learning**.

References

Higgs, Malcolm (2001) 'Is there a relationship between the Myers-Briggs ® Type Indicator and emotional intelligence?', *Journal of Management Psychology*, Volume 16, Number 7, pp509–533.

Megginson, David and Whitaker, Vivien (1996) *Cultivating Self-Development*. London, IPD.

Vincent, Annette and Ross, Dianne (2001) 'Personalise training: determine learning styles, personality types and multiple intelligences online', *The Learning Organisation*, Volume 8, Number 1, pp36–43.

http,//www.atl.ualberta.ca/articles/idesign/learnchar.cim
http,//www.newhorizons.org/arts_research.html
http,//www.fln.vcu.edu/lntensive/LearningStrategies.html
http,//www.gsu.edu/~dscnjb/wwwmbti.html

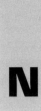

N

Names The easiest way to create rapport is to use a person's name frequently during a conversation. The sound of a person's name is like music to their ears. Yet most people find it difficult to remember names. Publius Scipio, the Roman general, was on the other hand reputed to have been able to remember the names of all 35,000 soldiers in his army. Simonides remembered the people who were killed when a banqueting hall collapsed by associating them with the places where they had sat.

Research suggests that last names tend to be harder to remember than first names. This is probably because they are less common. Generally, it is easier to recognise a person than to remember the person's name. Face recognition takes place in a region in the right brain that specialises in spatial recognition. But with a little concentrated effort and practice you can remember the names of those people you want to remember.

In this regard you may wish to make use of the acronymic guide MEMORY, which stands for Minutes, Evaluate, Make an effort, Organise, Repeat, and Your curiosity.

■ *minutes, not seconds* – When you meet someone for the first time, take some moments to absorb his or her name. This takes concentrated attention, reflection and practice. Most people are so conscious of themselves, and what they are going to say next, that they fail to hear the other person's name properly. The reason we don't remember a person's name is that we haven't encoded it into long-term memory in the first place. Short-term memory holds a name for only a few seconds and then forgets it unless it is repeated and reinforced and reviewed for long-term memory recall. We need to rehearse frequently in order to register names in our memory. Ask the person to repeat his or her name and spell it if necessary.

■ *evaluate* – Ask questions about the name. Inquire about the name's background. Names usually have a history attached to them. Where did the name originally come from? What does it mean? All these questions will help you to imprint the name in your mind and put it into a contextual framework.

- *make an effort* – Use the name frequently during the conversation. Make sure you address the person by name when saying your goodbyes. Link the face to the name in a memorable fashion. For example, you can link the name to a person you know already with the same name. Imagine in your mind's eye the two people shaking hands with each other. You can also imagine the name of the person you want to remember written across his or her forehead in bold capital letters. Another technique is to select a distinctive feature, transform the person's name into a noun with a similar sound, and then link the feature to the noun. For example, Byrne might be burn. If the distinctive feature of Mr Byrne is his nose, you could picture fire coming down his nostrils causing his nose to burn.

- *organise* – You could exchange business cards if these are available. Otherwise, write the name into your diary and a few key points about the individual to help you place him or her in context in the future.

- *repeat and review* – Occasionally look up your diary and bring the person to mind so that if you meet him or her again, you will remember the name. Use your powers of imagination and visualisation to recall his or her face and general appearance.

- *your curiosity will aid recall* – Exercise your own curiosity about the person and build up a dossier by inquiring with others who may know something about him or her. Background family information will help you put the name in context. Look up the telephone number in the directory and see if he or she is listed. If he or she is a member of a professional body, looking up a membership directory will reinforce the name.

References
Hermann, Douglas J. (1995) *Super Memory: A quick-action programme for memory improvement.* London, Blandford.
Higbee, Kenneth L. (1990) *Your Memory: How it works and how to improve it.* London, Piatkus.
Rupp Rebecca (1998) *Committed to Memory: How we remember and why we forget.* London, Aurum Press.
http,//www.mark.giles.co.uk/method4.htm
http,//www.mindtools.com/remnames.html

National Vocational Qualifications (NVQs)   The NVQs comprise a system of nationally-approved competence-based qualifications in England and Wales. The equivalents in Scotland are the SVQs The awarding body is the National Council for Vocational Qualifications (NCVQ).

Many organisations in the UK use NVQs for developing their employees by relating training programmes directly to their work. Rather than examinations on learning and theory, NVQs are assessments which focus on the attainment of competencies in the workplace. Companies can have their own NVQ centre or use a local centre. Competence is defined as the ability to perform a task successfully. The intention is that there will be national standards of competence for all occupations.

NVQs are mainly concerned with vocational or technical subjects. They are organised in five levels, from basic to professional. Each NVQ is framed around a number of units of competence. Each unit of competence is built up from elements of competence. Performance criteria and range statements support each element of competence.

NVQs can be taken in colleges of further education, on a full-time or part-time basis, or as approved on-the-job training. They are awarded after a period of vocational training and formal assessment. Flexibility and accessibility are key aspects of the scheme. People may thus be given credits for prior work experience or for successful completion of prior relevant formal programmes.

A lower-level qualification called General National Vocational Qualifications (GNVQs) prepares students in school or college either for direct entry into the labour market or for entry into higher education. This qualification is in three levels – foundation, intermediate and advanced. The Government has referred to advanced GNVQs as 'vocational A-levels'. Matlay and Addis (2002) report that NVQs have peaked in larger organisations and have declined considerably in the case of smaller businesses. There still remain market and accreditation barriers to wider employer acceptance.

See also **Credit Accumulation Transfer Scheme (CATS)**.

References
Matlay, Harry and Addis, Mark (2002) 'Competence-based training, vocational qualifications and learning targets: some lessons for the Learning and Skills Council', *Education and Training*, Volume 44, Number 6, pp250–260.
Morgan, Arthur (2002) 'The utilisaton of NVQs in higher education', *Education and Training*, Volume 44, Number 2, pp90–98.
Reid, Margaret Anne; Barrington, Harry and Kenney, John (1992) *Training Interventions*. London, IPM.
Shackleton, J. R. and Walsh, S. (1995) 'The UK's National Vocational Qualifications: the story so far', *Journal of European Industrial Training*, Volume 19, Number 11, pp14–27.

Natural intelligence The natural intelligence is the eighth of the intelligences discerned by Howard Gardner. People with this intelligence are tuned into the natural and ecological world. Gardiner describes the naturalist as the individual who 'is able to recognise flora or fauna, to make other consequential distinctions in the natural world, and to use this ability productively in hunting, farming and biological science'. Farmers, botanists, fishermen, conservationists, biologists, environmentalists and Green Party members would all have strong naturalist intelligence. A famous example would be Charles Darwin. Darwin's theory of evolution by natural selection is probably the major intellectual contribution of the 19th century.

Cultural groups possessing and valuing this form of intelligence include many Native American nations and Australian Aboriginal peoples.

References

Armstrong, Thomas (1993) *Seven Kinds of Smart: Identifying and developing your many intelligences.* London, Plume.

Gardner, Howard (1993) *Frames of Mind: The theory of multiple intelligences.* London, Fontana.

http,//www.newhorizons.org/trm_hoerrmi.html

http,//www.newhorizons.org/gng_mmeyer1.html

http,//www.newhorizons.org.gng_lwilson2.html

Nature versus nurture debate

There has always been considerable controversy over the relative contributions of 'nature' or biological forces (eg genetic and physiological effects) and of 'nurture' or environmental forces (eg social conditions and experience) to the development of a person's psychological qualities and learning abilities. This is called the nature versus nurture controversy. It is clear that hereditary factors provide the raw materials from which our personality is constructed. However, the extent to which these factors are stunted and frustrated or developed is dependent to a great degree on environmental factors. In the Confucian societies of East Asia, individual differences in endowment are assumed to be modest. Differences in achievement are thought to be due largely to effort.

Personality traits and types are strongly determined by genetic factors. This has been shown many times by studying identical twins separated early in life, comparing identical and fraternal twins, and studying adopted children and family resemblances. The IQs of identical twins are more similar than the IQs of fraternal twins. Contrary to common sense, the IQs of biologically related people grow closer in the latter years of life. Some psychologists think the relative importance of heredity and environment is approximately two parts heredity to one part environment. Follow-up studies of infants in adulthood certainly verify the fact that adult personality is clearly foreshadowed at a very tender age. There may indeed be permanent or semi-permanent structures of personality.

The strong influence of genetic factors on personality suggests that personality may have a strong biological basis. Habitual differences in the level of activity in the cortex of the brain seem to be largely responsible for the patterns of behaviour we label as extrovert and introvert. Differences in emotional stability seem to be related to the activity of the limbic system in the brain. Hormones too are intimately linked to personality. Antisocial behaviour is more frequent in extroverts, neurotic behaviour more frequent in introverts. Both types of conduct are more frequent in emotionally unstable people. Introverts do much better than extroverts in secondary school and at university. Emotionally unstable people are strongly disadvantaged in higher education.

A newly born infant has physical and psychological needs. Harry Stock Sullivan, a psychologist, called these 'the need for satisfaction' (physical) and the 'the need for security' (psychological). Habits, traits and attitudes are subconsciously imprinted on us from our parents and family members who act as our role models. As we mature, these attitudes and values are often modified by later experiences but they are never entirely removed. Our relationship with other people also affects our personality. One psychologist said that 'Personality is defined by the character of one's interpersonal relationships.' So there seems to be some truth in the saying, 'Show me your friends, and I'll tell you who you are.'

This might seem to give a deterministic view of personality. However, people are not deprived of choice. Time, heredity, environment and our early relationships may have limited our personality type options, but options are still there. Brain research confirms that intelligence is not a static structure but an open, dynamic system that can continue to develop throughout life. As we get older the range of choices expands. This is particularly true in the area of relationships. Parental relationships are fundamental in the function of our personality, but other relationships – particularly those with authority figures – are critical to the development of a mature person.

See also **Plasticity of the brain**.

References
Sternberg, Robert J. (1995) In Search of the Human Mind. New York, Harcourt Brace College Publishers.
http,//www.newhorizons.org/trm_guild.htm
http,//www.newhorizons.org/report_confprice.html

Needs analysis   Needs analysis is an investigative technique used by trainers to identify the training needs of people. There is no point in teaching things that people don't want or need to know. In an organisational setting learning or training needs should be related to corporate objectives as well as personal development plans and job requirements.

See also **NOTES model of training**.

References
Boydell, Tom and Leary, Malcolm (1996) *Identifying Training Needs*. London, IPD.
Ukens, Lorraine L. (2001) *What Smart Trainers Know*. San Francisco, Jossey-Bass Pfeiffer.

Negative reinforcement   Negative reinforcement is anything that makes you even more determined to avoid something that is going to lead to what you know will be unpleasant consequences. Negative reinforcement – especially in the form of punishment for wrongdoing – is useful in trying to change modes of behaviour.

The result of negative reinforcement is extinction. That is, the trainer uses negative reinforcement until the inappropriate behaviour disappears.

See also **Positive reinforcement**.

References
Hardingham, Alison (1998) *Psychology for Trainers*. London, IPD.
Ukens, Lorraine L. (2001) *What Smart Trainers Know*. San Francisco, Jossey-Bass Pfeiffer.

Networking   Networking – working in a freely contributing group – with others is a great source of learning. You might network informally with people in your own organisation, and formally with people outside and with peers in your professional body, and indeed with people from other backgrounds or professions. In addition to your circle of friends, consider creating a learning network to include perhaps a coach, mentor, role model, lecturer, trainer, learning set, and so on. Clubs and associations are often formed to help people share common interests and problems. Networking may also be used to find out about vacancies in other organisations. In these times of rapid change and sudden company closures you never know when you might need to use your networks for this purpose. Benefits of networking include sharing expertise, mutual learning, comparing notes, help with problem-solving and reassurance that you are doing something right.

References
Cheetham, Graham and Chivers, Geoff (2001) 'How professionals learn in practice: an investigation of informal learning amongst people working in professions', *Journal of European Industrial Training*, Volume 25, Number 5, pp247–292.
Fee, Kenneth (2001) *A Guide To Management Development Techniques*. London, Kogan Page.
Megginson, David, Banfield, Paul and Joy-Matthews, Jennifer (1999) *Human Resource Development*. London, Kogan Page.

Neuro-linguistic programming (NLP)   NLP makes use of a combination of behavioural and cognitive principles, and corresponds to a technique for ensuring that your mind and thoughts are at all times directed towards the positive – that your 'neural language' is programmed towards a desirable future.

You can model your behaviour on that of people you admire (and in NLP this applies especially to the non-verbal form of communication known as body language). Alternatively, anti-role-models can also be a source of modelling, provided you do the opposite of what they do, so programming yourself not to copy them. Visualising goals and outcomes are more likely to motivate you to succeed.

NLP may be used for:

- sales training

- communications training

- counselling and coaching

- management training

- interpersonal relationship training

- personal development

- training and presentation skills.

The key beliefs for success according to NLP are:

- Everything happens for a purpose.

- The mind and body affect each other.

- The meaning of communication is the response you get.

- There is no such thing as failure, only results. So learn from your mistakes.

- Whatever happens, take responsibility. You are responsible for your own learning.

- People are your greatest resource for learning.

- Work is play. To be successful at your work, find work that you enjoy doing.

- There is no success in learning without commitment. You must commit time and resources to the learning task.

- It's not what you know, it's what you do with what you know that makes the difference.

- You learn from excellent people by finding out the difference that makes the difference.

- You have all the ability you need to succeed.

- The map is not the territory. Perception is not reality.

Some critics say that the claimed benefits of NLP have not been supported by empirical research.

References

Cheetam, Graham and Chivers, Geoff (2001) 'How professionals learn in practice: an investigation of informal learning amongst people working in professions', *Journal of European Industrial Training*, Volume 25, Number 5, pp247–292.

Dowlen, Ashley (1996) 'NLP – help or hype? Investigating the uses of neuro-linguistic programming in management learning', *Career Development International*, Volume 1, Number 1, pp27–34.

O'Connor, Joseph and Seymour, John (1990) *Introducing NLP: Psychological skills for understanding and influencing people*. London, Aquarian/Thorsons.

New learning   In learning – really learning – something new, you go from a state of unconscious incompetence (not knowing that you don't know) to a state of unconscious competence (not having to think about knowing). You go through an 'S' curve of progress in which, after an initial slow period of learning, you make rapid progress until you come to a plateau. At this point it is important to stick to the task, because eventually you will progress to a higher plane of learning.

New learning is hard work and requires determination and persistence for success. Repetition and practice is needed to consolidate the new learning. For example, learning keyboarding skills requires putting together many skilled finger movements and combinations. These movements are guided by the letters or word that we want to input. At first, you have to input letter by letter. With practice, you learn to input word by word or phrase by phrase. In verbal learning, such as memorising a poem, we learn sequences of words. We then combine these sequences into an organised whole. Such learning requires considerable practice, and we must overlearn if we want to become truly proficient. Overlearning is learning beyond the stage that you feel you know the topic.

Psychologists believe new learning can benefit from old learning because of three factors:

- the positive transfer of learning – Suppose you learn two tasks. If Task 2 is easier to learn after Task 1, then positive transfer has occurred. However, if Task 2 is more difficult to learn after Task 1, negative transfer has occurred.

- general principles that we learn in one task may be applied to another task

- good learning habits we learn in one task may help us to learn another.

See also **Learning stages**; **Unlearning**.

References

Malone, Samuel A. (2000). *Learning Skills for Managers*. Dublin, Oak Tree Press.

Non-verbal communication   Meaning can be communicated non-verbally – ie through body language – as well as by words. A good trainer becomes an observer of human behaviour by studying posture, voice intonation, gestures, eye movements, facial expressions and reactions. An important aspect of learning is modelling your behaviour on the behaviour of others. In neuro-linguistic programming, people get into the same state of mind by matching body language: this creates rapport. However, you should do this in a subtle and sensitive way, or instead of building rapport you could create resentment. Research indicates that meaning is conveyed 7 per cent through words, 38 per cent through tone of voice, and 55 per cent through body language. This shows how important body language is to the communications process.

References

Mullins, Laurie J. (1996) *Management and Organisational Behaviour*, 4th edition. London, Pitman.
O'Connor, Joseph and Seymour, John (1990) *Introducing NLP: Psychological skills for understanding and influencing people*. London, Aquarian/Thorsons.

Note-taking   There are some excellent reasons for taking notes when learning:

- Notes speed up the task of revision.

- The preparation of notes keeps you actively involved in your studies. They help you focus your concentration.

- Research has shown that students who take and use notes do much better in examinations than students who don't.

- When attending training courses or lectures, note-taking is a good test of your listening, comprehension and short-term memory-retention skills.

In addition, notes are a permanent record of your work and progress and a boost to your morale. They are essential to the task of doing assignments or writing a thesis.

See also **Learning map**.

References
Malone, Samuel A. (1996) *Learning to Learn*. London, CIMA
http,//www.csu.edu.au/division/studserv/notetake.htm

NOTES model of training   The NOTES model is an acronymic guide to assist in remembering the elements of successful training. The acronym stands for Needs analysis, Objectives, Training design, Evaluation, and Styles of learning.

- *needs analysis* – Before you contemplate any training, you must first of all identify exactly the training needs of the potential participants. This can be established through a training survey.

- *objectives* – Having identified the training needs, you must define the overall objectives for the training and set down learning objectives for each session.

- *training design* – Having completed the first three stages, you must now design the training programme and the type of training techniques you intend to use to maximise learning. This may be a combination of on-the-job and off-the-job training methods.

- *evaluation* – Having completed the training, you must evaluate the training to see that overall training objectives and session-learning objectives have been achieved. More importantly, you should feed back the results into the training design so that it can be improved next time around.

- *styles of learning* – Determining the learning style of proposed participants before you undertake the training will help you design training in harmony with their unique learning styles. The trainer should match his learning style with those of the course participants.

See also **Evaluation**; **Kirkpatrick's model of evaluation**; **Learning styles**.

References
Malone, Samuel A. (2000) *Learning Skills for Managers*. Dublin, Oak Tree Press.

Not-invented-here syndrome   The not-invented-here syndrome is behaviour that marks a rejection by individuals and groups of innovation and change for the sole reason that the innovations and changes were not of their own devising.

People are more likely to be committed to changes that they have themselves suggested or have been involved in or consulted about.

Novelty   See **Von Restorff effect**.

Number rhyme system of memory   The number rhyme system is a well-known method of memorising used in scores of memory books. It is a very simple way to remember lists of items in a specific order. The small investment in time to memorise the cues can be repaid many times over in the form of an enhanced memory. Items missed become obvious as gaps in the list. The numbers are represented by things that rhyme with the number. Items to be remembered are then linked to these hooks or cues for recall.

The cues are: 1 is gun; 2 is shoe; 3 is tree; 4 is door; 5 is hive; 6 is sticks; 7 is heaven; 8 is gate; 9 is wine; 10 is hen. You can expand the range of the system by using mnemonic expanders. For example, you might increase the original ten hooks 'in ice' to give you a series of hooks from 11 to 20 – 11 is thus represented as a gun frozen in ice, 12 is a shoe frozen in ice, and so on. You might then have the original ten hooks covered 'in oil' to give you a series of hooks from 21 to 30.

See also **Number shape system of memory**; **PLAN model of memorising systems**.

References
Hermann, Douglas J. (1995) *Super Memory: A quick-action programme for memory improvement.* London, Blandford.
Higbee, Kenneth L. (1990) *Your Memory: How it works and how to improve it.* London, Piatkus.
Rupp, Rebecca (1998) *Committed to Memory: How we remember and why we forget.* London, Aurum Press.
http,//www.markgiles.co.uk/method1.htm
http,//www.mindtools.com/norhyme.html

Number shape system of memory   The number shape system is a method of memorising in which a number is represented by an image shaped like the number. The system may be used to remember lists, whether of things or numbers.

The images might for example be: 1 is a pole; 2 is a swan; 3 is a butterfly; 4 is a sailing boat; 5 is a sickle; 6 is a golf club; 7 is the bow of a ship; 8 is an hourglass; 9 is a walking stick; 10 is a bat and ball. (If you find that these images do not work for you, change them for something more meaningful.) The images are memory hooks on which you can then hang the items you want to remember.

The number shape technique is a very effective way of remembering lists. The shapes or cues are easy to remember – but take a little bit of effort initially to memorise. You can also use this technique to recall dates or numbers. To recall 26, for instance, you could visualise a swan with a golf club in its mouth.

See also **Number rhyme system of memory**; **PLAN model of memorising systems**.

References
Hermann, Douglas J. (1995) *Super Memory: A quick-action programme for memory improvement.* London, Blandford.
Higbee, Kenneth L. (1990) *Your Memory: How it works and how to improve it.* London, Piatkus.
Rupp, Rebecca (1998) *Committed to Memory: How we remember and why we forget.* London, Aurum Press.
http,//www.mindtools.com/noshape.html

Nutrition   Nutrition is important in a learning context. It is now known that an adequate supply of nutrients and vitamins is needed for peak body and brain performance. This is nothing new. It was Plato who said in around 400 BC that a healthy body promotes a healthy mind, and a healthy mind a healthy body. A balanced diet and exercise are essential for a healthy brain and body. A healthy diet stabilises levels of blood sugar, which is the only source of fuel for the brain. Low blood sugar causes poor concentration and prevents memories from being laid down.

Research shows that food low in protein and high in carbohydrates boosts alertness and performance in the brain. Some vitamins, such as vitamin B1 (thiamine), folic acid and B12, are essential for the proper functioning of memory. They are found in bread and cereals, vegetables and fruits. Research suggests that vitamins C and E have a role in keeping the memory sharp. Phosphatidylserine (PS) is known to improve memory. Primrose oil, when ingested, can also apparently help to keep at bay the kind of memory loss associated with advancing age.

Six glasses of water a day help to maintain your memory, especially in older people. Dehydration can generate confusion and other mental problems. It's not a good idea to eat large amounts of food immediately before beginning a learning task. Loading up the stomach impairs performance and distracts the mind during the critical registration and remembering phase. For this reason, memory experts advise eating only a light meal before giving a speech, running a training course, taking a test or attending class.

See also **Vitamins and learning**.

References
Carper, Jean (2000) *Your Miracle Brain.* London, Thorsons.

O

Objectives   See **Goals**.

Observational learning   Observational learning is learning simply by watching someone else doing something. It is common knowledge that children learn by watching their parents, other adults and their peers. The extent to which children and adults learn behaviours through imitation is influenced not only by the observed behaviour but also by its consequences. Behaviour that is rewarded is more likely to be adopted than behaviour that is punished. Behaviour that produces successful outcomes is more likely to be adopted than behaviour that doesn't. This type of learning benefits from another's successes or mistakes.

On-the-job learning such as shadowing is a type of observational learning. A significant element of apprenticeship training is still through observational learning or modelling. The apprentice learns by observing the master craftsman at work. There are four important aspects to apprenticeship:

- modelling – The apprentice observes the master craftsman demonstrating explicitly how to do different tasks. The apprentice learns mostly by observation.

- 'scaffolding' – This is the support system the master craftsman provides for the apprentice. It includes demonstrating, coaching and encouragement.

- fading – This is where the support is gradually removed and more responsibility given as the apprentice acquires experience, judgement, expertise and confidence.

- coaching – This happens during the entire apprenticeship process. The master craftsman coaches the apprentice in a wide range of skills until the apprentice is capable of working on his or her own.

Observational learning is an important type of learning because there is no compulsion to adopt the behaviour observed. It is also possible to learn by finding out how not to do something. Observational learning plays a key role in the development of competences.

See also **Modelling**.

References

Cheetham, Graham and Chivers, Geoff (2001) 'How professionals learn in practice: an investigation of informal learning amongst people working in professions', *Journal of European Industrial Training*, Volume 25, Number 5, pp247–292.

DePorter, Bobbi and Hernacki, Mike (1993) *Quantum Learning: Unleash the genius within you.* London, Piatkus.

Oestrogen and memory   Research has found that oestrogen hormones may play a protective role against memory loss and Alzheimer's disease, and may also improve brain function. In one study, women who took oestrogen after the menopause were found to be 40 per cent less likely to suffer from Alzheimer's. Oestrogen hormones also reduce the risk of heart disease and osteoporosis ('brittle bones'). However, taking oestrogen supplements is not without risk – supplements used on a regular basis after the menopause have been linked to the incidence of breast cancer.

References

Turkington, Carol (1996) *The Brain Encyclopedia.* New York, Checkmark Books.

Off-the-job learning   Off-the-job learning is a term usually applied to formal training courses and degree programmes that are held in establishments away from the workplace. Off-the-job learning includes lectures, case studies, in-tray exercises, management games, role-play and behaviour modelling. Individualised off-the-job training is seldom carried out because of the high cost. The big problem with off-the-job learning is that the skills learned may not be transferred to the job on return to work.

The diagram below illustrates a variety of learning methods.

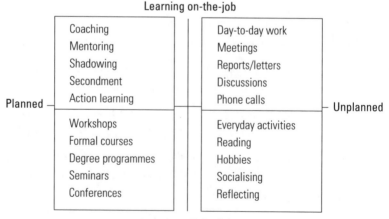

Learning on-the-job

Planned	Coaching Mentoring Shadowing Secondment Action learning	Day-to-day work Meetings Reports/letters Discussions Phone calls	Unplanned
	Workshops Formal courses Degree programmes Seminars Conferences	Everyday activities Reading Hobbies Socialising Reflecting	

Learning off-the-job

Source: unknown – adapted.

See also **On-the-job learning**.

References
Mumford, Alan (1997) *Management Development, Strategies for Action.* London, IPD.
Reid, Charles W. and Kleiner, Brian H. (1996) 'Which training methods are effective?', *Management Development Review,* Volume 9, Number 2, pp24–29.
Reid, Margaret Anne, Barrington, Harry and Kenney, John (1992) *Training Interventions.* London IPM.

OHP   'OHP' is standard trainer-speak for 'overhead projector' as used in talks and demonstrations to project transparencies (slides) on to a screen. It can be used in normal lighting conditions so that the trainer can maintain eye contact with the course participants. Software packages such as (Microsoft) PowerPoint may be used to produce transparencies.

On-the-job learning   On-the-job learning is precisely learning while on the job, and thus includes everyday work experience, job rotation, coaching and mentoring. On-the-job learning almost always involves decision-making and problem-solving, social interaction with peers and subordinates, real-life presentations, and an opportunity to perform the job rather than just discuss or write about it. It can be planned as part of an integrated training and development programme, or unplanned. Those involved in on-the-job training should undergo training as trainers.

A systematic approach to on-the-job learning includes the following steps:

1   Prepare the trainee. State the objectives of the training. Ascertain whether or not the trainee requires any prior training. Explain safety and quality issues that are pertinent to the shop floor. Explain how the training will be done and what outcomes are expected. Solicit any questions and put the trainee at ease.

2   Present the training. This may be done at the desk or workbench. Give an overview of the topic before going on to cover the detailed steps. This may include a demonstration. Finally, review the topic by summarising the key learning points.

3   Get the trainee to demonstrate his or her knowledge and provide feedback on his or her performance. Reinforce if correct, or alternatively give further training.

4   Get the trainee to reflect on and evaluate his or her own performance. Compare the self-evaluation with your evaluation, and note any differences and the reasons.

On-the-job learning is the best way to learn, provided the work is meaningful and reflection is an integrated part of the process. People should be shown how their work contributes to the overall objectives of the company. As well as acquiring know-how, people should know why. Lifelong learning and continuous incremental improvement should be part of everyday work. For this, the average worker needs communication, collaborative, interpersonal, empathy, interpretative, participative, numeracy, problem-solving, decision-making and team-building skills. He or she must also be able to access relevant information quickly when necessary, and be able to handle company forms and documents. All of these skills can be developed in the workplace.

See also **Off-the-job learning**.

References

Malone, Samuel A. (2000) *Learning Skills for Managers*. Dublin, Oak Tree Press.
Reid, Margaret Anne, Barrington, Harry and Kenney, John (1992) *Training Interventions*. London, IPM.
http,//www.qualitymag.com/articles/1999/nov99/1199tt.asp

Open learning   Open learning is learning for which there are no pre-qualifications (such as age, status, or previous exam results) necessary to do the programme. It also implies flexibility in

- where to learn – suggesting learning may take place at home

- when to learn – suggesting possibly in the morning, at lunchtime or in the evening

- how to learn – suggesting a mixture of methods, such as text, CBT, CD-ROM, DVD, audio and video

- the pace at which to learn, as decided by the adult learner.

In practice, many 'open learning' programmes run by educational or training establishments set minimum academic standards and other criteria for admission.

See also **Distance learning**.

References

Davis, Hayley J. (1996) 'A review of open and distance learning within management development', *Journal of Management Development*, Volume 15, Number 4, pp20–34.
Malone, Samuel A. (1997) *How to Set Up and Manage a Corporate Learning Centre*. Aldershot, Gower.

Operant conditioning   Operant conditioning – which was B. F. Skinner's major contribution to our understanding of learning – put simply, means rewarding behaviour you want to be repeated (positive reinforcement), and ignoring or punishing behaviour you don't want to be repeated (negative reinforcement). Behaviour that is reinforced or rewarded is more likely to be repeated again in similar circumstances.

See also **Programmed learning; Transmission model**.

References

Gagne, Robert M. (1977) *The Conditions of Learning*. New York, Holt, Rinehart & Winston.

Organisation of information   In the context of memorising information, it is easier to recall information that has been organised or structured in some way. For example, imagine how difficult it would be to remember a random list of 65 letters. Yet you could memorise the first sentence of this entry with little difficulty and it contains well over 65 letters. The difference is that the information is meaningful. Organising what you want to learn into groups or categories will help you remember it better. It would be very difficult to find a book in a library if all the books were not arranged in some way. If you always put your keys in a particular drawer – that's a mnemonic. If you structure activities, they are easier to remember. As the saying goes, 'a place for everything and everything in its place'. Being organised will help you become a more effective learner. Having goals, drawing up action plans, good time management, prioritising, and concentrating on the here and now, will help you achieve your learning objectives.

See also **Categorisation**; **Chunking**.

References
Hermann, Douglas J. (1995) *Super Memory: A quick-action programme for memory improvement*. London, Blandford.
Higbee, Kenneth L. (1990) *Your Memory: How it works and how to improve it*. London, Piatkus.
Rupp, Rebecca (1998) Committed to Memory: How we remember and why we forget. London, Aurum Press.
http,//www.csu.edu.au/division/studserv/motivbro.htm

Outdoor experiential training (OET)

OET – possibly even better known as 'Outward Bound' training – was originally developed in the army for the training of officers, but now more often involves a group of managers who engage in challenging outdoor activities, such as hill climbing, white-water rafting or tree climbing to learn about their personal styles of interaction and tolerance limits, or to improve problem-solving skills, leadership skills and/or followership skills.

One particular form of OET is intended temporarily to eliminate behaviours typical of a manager's role at work. Consequently, while on the programme participants are expected to avoid formal dress and the use of titles or any signs of deference that they may enjoy in their own organisation. During the OET, which can last from one to five days, status symbols are eliminated and social barriers are broken down. Managers get to know each other as individuals rather than as roles or titles. The leadership qualities of participants often come to the fore. Confidence and self-reliance is developed and participants become aware of their own strengths and weaknesses and discover latent talents. Some research suggests that groups who participate in OET are more cohesive and effective for several months after the experience.

References
Burnett, D. and James, K. (1994) 'Using the outdoors to facilitate personal change in managers', *Journal of Management Development*, Volume 13, Number 9, pp14–24.
Truelove, Steve (1992) *A Handbook of Training and Development*. Oxford, Blackwell.

Overlearning

Overlearning is deliberately learning beyond the stage that you feel you know the topic. Such learning requires considerable practice, mental rehearsal, review and repetition – but overlearning is essential to become truly proficient. It is the way we learned multiplication tables and the alphabet at school. Forgetting is less likely to occur if overlearning takes place. This is because the learning has become an automatic response to appropriate stimuli. Students when preparing for examinations are often therefore recommended to overlearn key topics. In such stressful conditions overlearning helps learners react automatically.

References

Cheetham, Graham and Chivers, Geoff (2001) 'How professionals learn in practice: an investigation of informal learning amongst people working in professions', *Journal of European Industrial Training*, Volume 25, Number 5, pp247–292.

Malone, Samuel A. (1996) *Learning to Learn*. London, CIMA.

Reid, Margaret Anne, Barrington, Harry and Kenney, John (1992) *Training Interventions*. London, IPM.

P

Paradigm shift   A paradigm shift is a substantial change in the way a person perceives the world, and in the way he or she explains what is going on around him or her. It tends to happen suddenly, and may be traumatic to the individual and/or to those who are familiar with him or her.

A radical change of perspective is often needed. Einstein's Theory of Relativity required a paradigm shift that entailed a move on from Newton's theorising on physics in general. Science operates within frameworks of theoretical models or paradigms. An example of a paradigm is Darwin's principle of natural selection by the survival of the fittest. A paradigm shift involves not only learning new facts but also unlearning and discarding much of what is already known.

William Harvey (1578–1657) was the English physician who through questioning, experimentation and reflection discovered the circulation of blood around the whole of the human body. He set out to question Galen's account of the threefold circulation of the blood that was the accepted paradigm of the time and had been for 1,500 years.

Before 1954, breaking the four-minute barrier when running a mile was thought to be impossible. Then along came Roger Bannister. Today it is routine for a good runner to run a mile in less than four minutes. In Gutenberg's time (1400–1468) many books were still being laboriously copied by hand. His invention of movable type for use on the printing press revolutionised the spread of knowledge. Today, Bill Gates of Microsoft is having a similar effect on information and communications technology. Not too long ago we believed the brain was 'hard-wired'. Now we know that the brain is shaped through experience and learning.

See also **Transformational learning**.

References
McFadzean, Elspeth (2000) 'Techniques to enhance creative thinking', *Team Performance Management, An International Journal*, Volume 6, Number 3/4, pp62–72.
Malone, Samuel A. (2000) *Learning Skills for Managers*. Dublin, Oak Tree Press.

Smith, A. (1975) *The Power of the Mind*. New York, Ballantine Books.
http,//www.newhorizons.org/ofc_cliusebrain.html

Pedagogy

Pedagogy is the science or art of teaching children. The term has recently been adopted as contrasting with the older concept of the 'pedagogue', the teacher who relied on directly addressing pupils sitting in a classroom, in that the new pedagogy employs diverse learning approaches such as reflective journal-writing, storytelling, metaphors, role-play and small group discussion. It also tries to accommodate the different learning styles of students.

References
Knowles, M. S. (1984) *Andragogy in Action*. San Francisco, Jossey Bass.
http,//www.learnativity.com/andragogy.html

Peg system of memory   See **PLAN model of memorising systems**.

Performance appraisal interview

A performance appraisal interview lets employees know how they are getting on in the job. The interview, which takes the form of a review, investigates each employee's strengths and weaknesses, the reasons for successes and failures, and ways in which the employee can improve in the future. Goals for future performance are jointly agreed for review at the next appraisal interview, and training and development needs are identified. Action plans should be drawn up to encourage improved performance.

The feedback from the performance appraisal interviews is a great learning opportunity. The training plans should be agreed, because training that is simply imposed by the manager may well demotivate the appraisee. Some experts maintain that discussion of training and development issues should be kept separate from assessment, promotion and remuneration.

Appraisal interviews are usually held half-yearly or yearly. Many companies operate 360-degree appraisal systems by which the views of others such as customers and suppliers are also taken into account. British Petroleum operates an upward appraisal system. This gives employees an opportunity to give feedback to managers on a wide range of issues such as empowerment and collaboration.

References
Gillen, Terry (1998) *The Appraisal Discussion*. London, IPD.
Mumford, Alan (1997) *Management Development, Strategies for Action*, 3rd edition. London, IPD.
Wilson, John P. and Western, Steven (2001) 'Performance appraisal: an obstacle to training and development?', *Career Development International*, Volume 6, Number 2, pp93–100.

Performance objectives

Performance objectives are the business goals of individual employees, of groups of employees, and of the organisation as a whole in terms of profits, sales levels, customer satisfaction, productivity and output, market share and shareholder value. The achievement or non-achievement of these objectives may be used to assess cost-effectiveness of the individuals, the groups and the organisation, as measured on business performance criteria. Measurements of quantity, quality, timeliness, and yield are often used.

Performance objectives are usually part of a performance management system. They may be linked to critical success factors – the outcomes essential to achieve the performance objectives. The critical success factors in turn must be linked to key tasks done to bring about the outcome. These in turn must be linked to performance standards so that you know you have achieved the required standards. Failure to achieve performance objectives may be due to insufficient training.

See also **Training objectives**.

References
Hutt, Geoff (1994) 'Incorporating quality performance objectives into performance appraisal systems', *TQM Magazine*, Volume 06, Number 1, pp8–12.

Peripheral vision   Your peripheral vision is what you see out of the corner of your eyes when you are looking at something else. You use peripheral vision every day when driving. Without moving your eyes, you notice that a child is about to step off the footpath and run across the road. At the same time you are concentrating and looking ahead.

In speed-reading it is possible to capitalise on this phenomenon by relying on your peripheral vision to read the left-hand and right-hand edges of each line of text while your eyes actually focus on the central part. This speeds up reading.

References
Buzan, Tony (1997) *The Speed-Reading Book*. London, BBC Books.
Malone, Samuel A. (1996) *Learning to Learn*. London, CIMA.
Redway, Kathryn (1995) *Beat the Bumph: Cut clutter, read rapidly and succeed in the information jungle*. London, Nicholas Brealey.

Personal development plan   A personal development plan (PDP) identifies your personal strengths and weaknesses, notes your training and development needs, and specifies goals for your self-development. Personal development plans promote self-responsibility and a sense of ownership for personal, educational, training and career development.

A PDP may be the output of an assessment centre, a development centre, a workshop or a performance appraisal scheme. Ideally, personal development plans should be linked to annual business plans and strategic plans. Once formulated, they should be implemented and followed through to completion. They should be updated each year or even more frequently.

You should draw up your own personal development plan, even if the company in which you work does not support the process. Most professional bodies now have continuing professional development (CPD) requirements for their members. CPD may be conducted within the context of a personal development plan.

References
Fee, Kenneth (2001) *A Guide To Management Development Techniques*. London, Kogan Page.
Jackson, Tricia (2000) *Career Development*. London, IPD.
Megginson, David and Whitaker, Vivien (1996) *Cultivating Self-Development*. London, IPD.

Phonetic system of memorising   The phonetic system of memorising converts numbers into words for easier recall. For example, suppose you wanted to remember that the Old Testament of the Bible contains 39 books. Under the phonetic system (see below) 3 is m and 9 is p – thus 'mp'. Insert a vowel-sound between the consonants – say, 'a' – and we get the word 'map'. Now visualise a map of the Old Testament world. Later, when we want to remember how many books there are in the Old Testament we recall the word 'map', which translates into 39.

The system links the numbers 1 to 0 with consonants or groups of consonants that are phonetically distinct (which is why 'm' represents a number by itself, whereas the number 8 is represented by the phonetically-related 'f', 'ph' and 'v', and 9 corresponds to 'p' and 'b'). This is why it is known as the phonetic system although its methodology has otherwise little to do with phonetics.

	letter(s) represented	easy way to remember
1	t d	t has one downstroke
2	n	n has two downstrokes
3	m	m has three downstrokes
4	r	r is the last letter of 'four'
5	l	l corresponds to the Roman numeral 50
6	j sh ch tch soft g	j looks like a (rough) 6 backwards
7	k hard c hard g	a k can be formed with two 7s
8	f ph v	a hand-written 8 is not unlike a script f
9	b p	p looks like a (poor) 9 backwards
0	s z soft c	z is the first letter of 'zero'

For the purpose of memorising, vowel sounds should be added as and when necessary to make pronounceable words. The number 914, for example, gives the possible combinations 'btr', 'bdr', 'ptr' and 'pdr', from which the most memorably pronounceable versions are probably 'batter', 'better' and 'butter' (although 'bidder', 'Peter', 'potter' and 'Pedro' are not far behind). Concrete images make the most memorable words, so 'butter' may be best. (Pay no attention to the doubling of the 't' – it's the overall pronunciation that is important for memorising.)

The system is particularly useful for recalling historical dates. To remember that Columbus discovered America in 1492, for instance, code the number 1 as 't', 4 as 'r', 9 as 'b', and 2 as 'n'. This coverts to 'trbn'. Add the appropriate vowel-sounds and this becomes 'turban'. Now link 'turban' to Columbus (imagine him wearing a turban) and you have a device for remembering the date.

But you can use this system to recall long telephone numbers. The number has to be chunked and then each chunk is converted into a word. The words are then associated together using a link or story technique.

The phonetic system is a major memory system which requires a significant investment in time to master. However, once learned it is very powerful. It is the chosen system of many of the mnemonists – those memory magicians whose feats of memory amaze and astound us on stage and screen.

See also **PLAN model of memorising systems**.

References
Higbee, Kenneth L. (1990) *Your Memory: How it works and how to improve it.* London, Piatkus.

Photographic memory   Few adults have a truly photographic – or eidetic – memory. Most young children, on the other hand, have a good memory for pictures and scenes on the printed page. However, as they grow up they lose this ability.

You can revive something of this ability by using your imagination and visualisation.

See also **Visualisation**.

References
Higbee, Kenneth L. (1990) *Your Memory: How it works and how to improve it.* London, Piatkus.

Physical exercise   Exercise improves cardiovascular condition, reduces stress and depression, and improves digestion and sleep – all of which helps memory. The brain needs oxygen. The simplest way of providing the brain with oxygen is through physical exercise. For older people a good brisk walk for about half an hour a day is sufficient. Other aerobic exercise such as swimming, cycling, jogging and playing tennis is equally good. One study found that after six months of aerobic exercise for 45 minutes three times a week, formerly sedentary people improved their mental performance by as much as 25 per cent.

References
Carper, Jean (2000) *Your Miracle Brain.* London, Thorsons.

Place system of memorising   The basic idea in the place system for memorising objects is to use the items of furniture or equipment in each room in your house – or to use prominent buildings on a familiar journey – as hooks to associate, connect or link things to. The hooks in your house might be door, lamp, window, clock, chair, table, plant, TV, cabinet, and fireplace. Associate the items you want to remember with these hooks. Then when you want to remember them you take a mental walk around your house, picking off the items as you go. It is easier to associate items with familiar pegs, and what could be more familiar than the items in your own house? The system is also expandable in relation to the number of rooms and items in each room in your home. Also, different locations can be used to recall different lists – for example, the journey you take each day to work or the route you take for your favourite walk. You could also use different towns that you are familiar with as locations to recall whatever items you want to remember.

For abstract items, you may have to substitute concrete images. An example of this would be, say, the principles of Justice, Liberty and Fraternity. To remember these, you might think of a judge, the Statue of Liberty and a group of relatives who have turned up unexpectedly. Visualise the judge sitting down on your favourite fireside chair, the Statue of Liberty on top of the TV, and your relatives sitting on the sofa.

'Places' need not be taken literally. You could also use parts of your body as memory-pegs. Twelve body pegs might be foot, knee, hips, stomach, shoulder, neck, chin, mouth, eyes, forehead, ears and hair. Similarly, you could use your car as a mnemonic device. A list of items to be remembered can be associated with these pegs.

Use the MUSE principle to imprint the items on your memory – that is, imbue your mental images with movement; unusualness; slapstick and exaggeration. The more vivid and bizarre the better.

The place technique is easy to learn and use and is very effective as a memory aid. However, some investment in time is needed in preparing journeys clearly in your mind (perhaps refamilarising yourself with the items of furniture in each room in your house).

See also **Locus method of memorising; PLAN model of memorising systems**.

References

Higbee, Kenneth L. (1990) *Your Memory: How it works and how to improve it.* London, Piatkus.
Rupp, Rebecca (1998) *Committed to Memory: How we remember and why we forget.* London, Aurum Press.
http,//www.markgiles.co.uk/method3.htm
http,//www.mindtools.com/romanrom.html
http,//www.mindtools.com/journey.html

PLAN model of memorising systems

The PLAN model is an acronymic guide to the main systems by which things can be memorised. They are:

- the *place* system
- a *link* system

- the *alphabet* system

- a *number* rhyme or number shape system.

People have different learning styles, different brains, different needs and different experiences. Pick the memory system that suits you.

See **Alphabet system**; **Link system of memorising**; **Number rhyme system of memory**; **Number shape system of memory**; **Place system of memorising**.

References
Malone, Samuel A. (2000) *Learning Skills for Managers*. Dublin, Oak Tree Press.
http.//www.csu.edu.au/division/studserv/memory2.htm

Plasticity of the brain   That the brain is 'plastic' – it can 'rewire' itself in response to environmental stimuli and learning – is now accepted. Individual brains therefore differ significantly, depending on a person's background and experience. The part of the brain used for remembering routes is bigger in London taxi-drivers than in other people. The fingers activate the same general area of the sensory cortex in everyone's brain, but this area is larger in people who use their fingers particularly often. Examples include musicians who play stringed instruments, or blind people who read Braille. In Wernicke's area of the brain, which deals with word understanding, the nerve cells have more connecting dendrites in college-educated people than in people with only a secondary education. So the brain is constantly adapting to serve us better in the things we do frequently. The brain is shaped by our experiences and learning, just as our muscles are strengthened by exercise.

Modern imaging techniques can show how learning stimulates the brain. PET scans show that the brains of people skilled in a particular field consume less energy when carrying out their duties than those just starting to learn them. The experienced brains have generated new synaptic connections, which improves their performance. Feed the brain with information and the connections between the brain cells increase. Starve your brain of information and the dendrites wither and die. Rats raised in an enriched environment had 25 per cent more connections between their brain cells than rats living in a cage with nothing to do or learn. In sensory deprivation experiments, in which people are kept in complete isolation, skills built up over a lifetime can quickly deteriorate. Your brain depends on stimulation from the environment and from social interaction with people. Passive observation is not enough; there must be interaction with the environment. Scientists have found that the brain's cortical thickness diminishes with an impoverished environment. Old people put in a retirement home without adequate mental stimulation and control over their own lives become senile and dependent. However, the opposite happens if they are challenged by new learning experiences and given responsibility for themselves.

Education is food for the brain. It is now known that, in general, well-educated people live longer than people with less education. The cerebral cortex grows rapidly in the first ten years of a child's life. By providing a stimulating, emotionally supporting, and enriched learning environment during this period, the growth of dendritic connections is facilitated. This merely supports what educationalists have long known – that providing a growing child with a wide variety of experiences enhances intellectual development. So mental exercise does far more than just increase your knowledge. It increases the size of your brain and the number of dendritic connections between your brain cells.

See also **Using your brain**.

References
Sternberg, Robert J. (1995) *In Search of the Human Mind.* New York, Harcourt Brace College Publishers.
http,//www.newhorizons.org/ofc_21cliusebrain.html

Positive reinforcement   Positive reinforcement is anything that determines you even more to achieve what will be a good result. Tutors may positively reinforce appropriate learning behaviour by praising. Positive reinforcement should be part of the training/learning process to ensure correct behaviour. Trainers should use it on a frequent and regular basis early in the training process to help learners retain what they have learned. Reinforcement can also come from the sense of satisfaction felt in having learned something new or difficult. This can set up a virtuous learning cycle as people seek additional satisfaction in a similar way. Managers can encourage appropriate behaviour by recognising and rewarding when learners apply skills learned on training programmes to the job.

You can provide positive reinforcement for yourself by the occasional treat after accomplishing personal learning goals.

See also **Negative reinforcement**; **Rewards**; **Virtuous learning cycle**.

References
Reid, Charles W. and Kleiner, Brian H. (1996) 'Which training methods are effective?', *Management Development Review*, Volume 9, Number 2, pp24–29.
Reid, Margaret Anne, Barrington, Harry and Kenney, John (1992) *Training Interventions.* London, IPM.

Positive thinking   Positive thinking leads to positive results. Believing that you are a good learner will help you become a more effective learner. In NLP, positive thinking is the technique of focusing on the successful completion of personal goals or outcomes. It is more constructive to concentrate on the positive or what we want, rather than on the negative or what we wish to avoid.

Positive thinking often manifests itself in good posture. Research shows that good posture results in sharper memories. This is because poor posture may affect blood flow to the brain.

Reprogramme your mind for positive thinking with the acronym SAVER, which stands for:

- **S**ubstitute positive thoughts for negative.
- **A**ffirm the new image.
- **V**isualise images of success.
- **E**motionalise the image for imprinting in long-term memory.
- **R**ehearse.

See also **Affirmations**; **Learned optimism**; **Self-esteem**.

References
Clements, Phil (1995) *Be Positive*. London, Kogan Page.
Malone, Samuel A. (2000) *Learning Skills for Managers*. Dublin, Oak Tree Press.

Positive transfer   Positive transfer is how trainers describe learning that has a beneficial effect not only in the performance of the trained activity but also in the performance of other similar activities through the learning and understanding gained in the training. For example, learning to play a game such as tennis may improve elements of hand–eye co-ordination which result in positive transfer when later learning squash, badminton or table tennis.

See also **Transfer of learning**.

References
Davies, Ivor K. (1971) *The Management of Learning*. New York, McGraw-Hill.

Practice and learning   Practice including mental rehearsal reinforces learning until eventually it becomes an automatic response. Obviously, the more time you spend on any subject, the better you will become at it. From a training point of view, participants on a course programme remember information better if they have practised using it frequently.

Review your training frequently so that key learning points are reinforced.

References
Davies, Ivor K. (1971) *The Management of Learning*. New York, McGraw-Hill.

Practical intelligence   Practical intelligence is a form of intelligence like those discerned by Howard Gardner in his book *Frames of Mind* (1984). People with practical intelligence prefer practice to theory – they can't wait to put theory into practice. They like to fix things or put things together. They may well enjoy servicing their own cars, gardening, carpentry, or other DIY efforts. As a child they may have liked to take things apart to see how they worked. They prefer to get on with work rather than talk about it. They have a curious mind with a very practical bent.

Managerial success depends a good deal on practical intelligence, as in how to manage oneself, delegate tasks, motivate and deal effectively with other people.

See also **Pragmatist; SIMILAR model of intelligences**.

References

Myers, David G. (1995) *Psychology*. New York, Worth.

Pragmatist   In the learning context, 'pragmatist' is one of the four styles of learning; activist, reflector, theorist and pragmatist. As the name suggests, pragmatists have a very practical bent. They can't wait to try out ideas, theories and techniques to see if they work in practice. They dislike too much theory. Unlike activists, they like to see a link between what they've learned and how they plan to use it on the job. They are thus more proactive than reactive. They are the type of people who come back from a course bursting with ideas and very keen to apply them. They see problems as opportunities, and threats as challenges. They know that there is always a better way of doing things. They believe in the philosophy of continuous incremental improvement. Pragmatists make good computer programmers.

In general, pragmatists learn best from:

- teaching on subjects that are relevant to the job

- experts who know how to do the job themselves

- practical ideas and techniques

- practising techniques

- practical guidelines

- implementing ideas

- action plans

- films demonstrating how things should be done.

To develop your pragmatist style you should collect practical techniques, produce action plans, experiment, model yourself on practical people, seek the advice of experts, and tackle do-it-yourself projects.

See also **Activist; Reflector; Theorist**.

References

Honey, Peter (1994) 'Styles of learning' in the *Handbook of Management Development*, edited by Alan Mumford, Aldershot, Gower.

Honey, Peter and Mumford, Alan (1986) *Using Your Learning Styles*. Berkshire, Peter Honey.

Mumford, Alan (1995) 'Putting learning styles to work: an integrated approach', *Industrial and Commercial Training*, Volume 27, Number 8, pp28–35.

Mumford, Alan (1997) *Management Development, Strategies for Action*, 3rd edition. London, IPD.

Praise   Praise can be a great motivator to stick to the task and go on learning. Blanchard and Johnson in their book *The One Minute Manager* talked about 'catching people doing something right'. Catching somebody making mistakes leads them to make more mistakes. Catching somebody doing something right encourages them to be right more often. This suggests that praise creates better morale and improved productivity. By and large, most people miss opportunities to give sincere praise to others. Even teachers and trainers are sometimes reluctant to give praise. Praise must be genuine and earned. It should be simple, direct, unambiguous and natural. Praise should be specific to a learning event.

Praise should be reserved for performance above the norm. Praise used to soften subsequent criticism is counterproductive. The praise should be given as soon after the event as possible. When we praise somebody sincerely, we expect it to have a positive effect. Yet our experience shows us that praise may have a lot of negative effects if perceived as insincere or patronising. Too much praise can also be counterproductive and may give the impression that low standards are acceptable. A good manager praises the good performance of his or her staff. But don't wait for others to praise you. Praise and treat yourself when you have accomplished some goal.

References
Malone, Samuel A. (2000) *Learning Skills for Managers*. Dublin, Oak Tree Press.
Ukens, Lorraine L. (2001) *What Smart Trainers Know*. San Francisco, Jossey-Bass Pfeiffer.
http,//www.mithya.com/learning/artaccomplishment.html

Primacy effect   The primacy effect corresponds with the fact that you tend to remember the first words on a list better than any others – except perhaps the very last on the same list. The entries in the middle of the list are usually forgotten unless they are made unique and outstanding in some way. The tendency to recall the last words is called the recency effect.

See also **Recency effect**.

References

Parkin, Alan J. (1993) *Memory Phenomena: Experiment and theory*. Oxford, Blackwell.

Proactive inhibition   Proactive inhibition occurs when previously learned information interferes with a person's ability to remember new material. For example, if you studied an economics chapter last week, and today you were studying for a management test, proactive inhibition would take place if the economics terms kept on popping into your mind when you were trying to recall the management terms. Similarly, a previously learned computer package may interfere with your progress in learning a new one. Previously learned keyboard strokes may not give the same results as a new package.

It is described as proactive because the interference comes in a forward direction from previously learned information. Interference in the reverse direction is known as retroactive inhibition.

See also **Retroactive inhibition**.

References

Baddeley, Alan (1991) *Human Memory: Theory and practice*. Hove, Lawrence Erlbaum Associates.

Problem-based learning (PBL)

PBL is a system of learning in which learners in a group formulate their own questions, determine the solution process, reflect on the quality of the information they research, and present their findings to the group. It is a type of collaborative learning. It helps learners to understand their own learning style and develop critical thinking skills in a group situation. The trainer acts as a facilitator rather than as an instructor.

References

Ball, Stephen (1995) 'Enriching student learning through innovative real-life exercises', *Education and Training*, Volume 37, Number 4, pp18–25.

Programmed learning

Programmed learning was developed by the American psychologist B. F. Skinner (1904–1990) and comprises a training technique in which the learner is presented with learning material in small chunks called 'frames'. Each frame is immediately followed by questions to be answered by the learner prior to moving on to more difficult material. If the questions are answered correctly, the learner is rewarded by being allowed to move on (positive reinforcement). If the questions are answered incorrectly the learner is punished (negative reinforcement) by being told to revisit previous steps.

Books and computer-based training programmes have been designed around the concept of programmed learning, which is an application of operant conditioning. Advantages include clear learning objectives, standardised logically sequenced material, different learning paths according to individual needs, and immediate feedback or knowledge of results. Disadvantages include the facts that it is not suitable for non-factual material, such as human relations topics, and that learners often get bored. The absence of social interaction is a major drawback of the technique

See also **Operant conditioning**.

References

Craig, Robert L. (1987) *A Training and Development Handbook, 3rd edition, A Guide To Human Resource Development*. New York, McGraw-Hill.

Malone, Samuel A. (1997) *How to Set Up and Manage a Corporate Learning Centre*. Aldershot, Gower.

Projects

A project is a means of cross-functional learning. Being part of a project or task force is a great way of learning on-the-job. Projects can range from a few days' duration to a few months'. They may, for example, involve the computerisation of a manual system, introducing new equipment, the relocation of offices, or improving some aspect of the business. Projects have a sponsor and should be guided by written terms of reference. They are normally conducted by teams and operate to deadlines. A formal report is issued at the end of the project, making recommendations. Projects provide many learning opportunities, including developing interpersonal relationship skills, learning how to co-operate in a team situation, working to a deadline, coping with unusual situations, developing report-writing skills, learning how to organise and run meetings, and gaining experience in an area in which you would not normally work.

Projects frequently afford an opportunity to work across a wide range of functions, thereby combining expertise across internal and external organisational boundaries. Some project teams are responsible for implementation as well as for making recommendations. This type of project provides the strongest form of development.

Project teams are often set up to manage change, including the change that follows acquisition or merger. The team members involved should be debriefed during and at the end of the project to see what learning opportunities have occurred and how those opportunities have contributed to individuals' development. Overseas projects offer a unique learning opportunity. Multinationals can offer this type of opportunity when managers are posted to overseas subsidiaries. Such a manager must learn how to manage in a country that has a culture different from his or her own. This of course has to be carried out against a backdrop of different social, economic and political institutions.

References

Adams, Debra (2001) 'Learning from experience – making the most of work-based learning', *International Journal of Contemporary Hospitality Management*, Volume 13, Number 5, pp235–240.
Malone, Samuel A. (2000) *Learning Skills for Managers*. Dublin, Oak Tree Press.
Mumford, Alan (1997) *Management Development, Strategies for Action*. London, IPD.

Prospective learning   Prospective learning is learning from future planned events. It is a type of proactive learning. The process of thinking about learning in advance means that you are more likely to learn when the event actually happens. You think of future events as learning opportunities.

The four-stage sequence in prospective learning (Mumford 1997) is:

1   Plan to learn.

2   Implement the plan.

3   Review the plan.

4   Draw conclusions.

Prospective learning includes planned management development on-the-job and off-the-job. On-the-job events might include forthcoming meetings, appraisals, projects, secondments, negotiation and presentations. Off-the-job events might include training courses, reading assignments, academic courses and using a corporate learning centre.

Before you go on a formal training programme you should do some preparation for the anticipated learning. Include formulating your learning goals, visualising learning outcomes and thinking ahead on how you are going to apply the learning in the workplace. You could be briefed by your manager about your expected and likely learning outcomes before the programme, and debriefed after the programme to see if your expectations were met and whether the learning outcomes have been realised. More importantly – how will the job improve as a result of the learning?

See also **Retrospective learning**.

References
Mumford, Alan (1997) *Management Development, Strategies for Action*, 3rd edition. London, IPD.

Psychological contract   The psychological contract is an unwritten extension of the (physical) contract of employment between employer and worker, and relates to the expectations that both parties have of each other for the duration of the employment. It amounts roughly to an agreement that employer and worker will both do their best for each other. Whereas the contract of employment deals with hours, pay and conditions, the psychological contract has more to do with concern for health and safety and with loyalty and commitment.

Psychological contracts may be said to have two components:

- transactional, involving the exchange of the employee's time, skill, knowledge, experience and satisfactory performance for monetary reward

- relational, involving such factors as the employee's commitment, loyalty and trust in return for competent management, job satisfaction, an input to decisions, recognition, a sense of achievement, relationships with colleagues, and a sense of belonging.

With the disappearance of the traditional permanent pensionable job, the psychological contract has changed. Employees now expect to change jobs many times during their lifetimes. Under the new psychological contract the employee hopes to be made more marketable and employable through continuous learning opportunities. The security previously provided by employers must now be provided by employees themselves. Employees are less loyal and more demanding of the organisation that they join. Employers, to compensate for the loss of the traditional permanent pensionable job, must offer better financial rewards, more challenging work, and more opportunities for training and development in order to prepare them for these moves.

In return employers expect employees to work hard and to be committed and loyal, even if only in the short term.

References
Burgoyne, John (1999) *Developing Yourself, Your Career and Your Organisation*. London, Lemos & Crane.
Jackson, Tricia (2000) *Career Development*. London, IPD.
Maguire, Heather (2002) 'Psychological contracts: are they still relevant?', *Career Development International*, Volume 7, Number 3, pp167–180.
Megginson, David, Banfield, Paul and Joy-Matthews, Jennifer (1999) *Human Resource Development*. London, Kogan Page.

Psychometric tests
Psychometric tests are selection tests that seek to quantify the psychological dimensions of job applicants by investigating intelligence, creativity, personality, motivation, and aptitudes. Psychometric tests thus assume that intelligence can be measured quantitatively. They are used to predict the suitability of candidates for jobs.

See also **Myers-Briggs ® Type Indicator**.

References
Armstrong, Michael (2000) *A Handbook of Human Resource Management Practice*, 7th edition. London, Kogan Page.

Pygmalion effect
The Pygmalion effect becomes visible when, after an inspirational teacher has made it clear he or she expects students to reach an exceptionally high standard, the students do then reach that standard. It shows that we are influenced by the expectations of others, and that our own expectations can be raised accordingly.

If our managers set high standards, we are often motivated to achieve them. Managers can draw out the best from their staff by leading by example, treating staff as intelligent, resourceful and empowered human beings. On the other hand, managers can draw out the worst in people by setting a bad example and treating staff as altogether lacking in intelligence, ideas and initiative.

Trainers' expectations have a powerful effect on course participants' performance. If you as trainer act as though you expect your course participants to be motivated, hard-working, and interested, they are more likely to live up to your expectations. Set realistic expectations for learners when you conduct discussions, role-play, brainstorming, case studies and other learning tasks. 'Realistic' means that your standards are high enough to motivate learners to produce their own best work but not too high to cause information overload and frustration. To develop the drive to achieve, course participants need to believe that achievement is possible – which means that you provide early opportunities for success.

References
Malone, Samuel A. (1996) *Learning to Learn*. London, CIMA.
Sternberg, Robert J. (1995) *In Search of the Human Mind*. New York, Harcourt Brace College Publishers.

Question-and-answer sessions   Question-and-answer sessions are often relegated to the end of a training session – but should be encouraged at any time during a training course.

Strategies for handling questions include:

■ Repeat the question, paraphrasing it. This ensures that you understand the question and that the entire group hears the question. This process also gives other course participants time to think about possible answers.

■ Redirect the question. You might redirect the question to another course participant or to the group in general. This approach encourages participation and acknowledges that the group is a good resource for learning. In addition, if you don't know the answer to the question, this may be a particularly useful strategy to adopt.

■ Ask probing questions that relate to the original question. This helps to explore issues in depth and highlights issues that may have been overlooked.

■ Promote discussion of the question among course participants. Form buzz groups to debate or brainstorm designated issues.

■ Admit when you do not know the answer to a question. However, always take responsibility for finding out the answer and reporting back to the group.

Strategies for asking questions include:

■ Ask open-ended as well as closed questions. An open-ended question encourages opening up, exploring alternatives, brainstorming of issues and discussion. A closed question encourages 'yes' or 'no' responses. Open-ended questions are prefaced by words such as 'who', 'what', 'when', 'where', 'how' and 'why'. Closed questions are appropriate when the trainer wants to check that learning has occurred as intended or to hold the attention of the group.

- Ask divergent as well as convergent questions. Divergent questions are appropriate when there are alternatives and options. Convergent questions are appropriate when there is only one right answer.

In order to encourage dialogue and participation you should create an accepting and open atmosphere by:

- asking for questions – Use silences and pauses as appropriate to give learners time to reflect and formulate questions.

- answering questions – Take time to answer questions adequately and never ignore a question. Ask the course participants if you have answered the question.

- listening to the question – Rephrase the question to ensure understanding.

- never putting down the questioner – Your job is to create a non-threatening learning environment by encouraging dialogue.

See also **Questions**.

References
Truelove, Steve (1992) *A Handbook of Training and Development*. Oxford, Blackwell.
http,//www.hcc.hawaii.edu/intranet/committees/FacDevCom/gui.../askquest.ht.

Questionnaires   Questionnaires or surveys may be used to identify training and learning needs and also to evaluate training. All training initiatives should be included, such as formal training courses, distance learning, coaching and mentoring. All users of training should be surveyed, including senior managers, functional managers, line managers and past delegates. Managers who rarely use training should be particularly surveyed to find out the reason why. The design, piloting and implementation of questionnaires, and the analysis of their results, are highly skilled activities and are best left to professionals.

References
Boydell, Tom and Leary, Malcolm (1996) *Identifying Training Needs*. London, IPD.
Ukens, Lorraine L. (2001) *What Smart Trainers Know*. San Francisco, Jossey-Bass Pfeiffer.

Questions   Asking questions is a great way of learning. People learn when their minds are seeking answers to questions. Invent open-ended questions that begin with 'what', 'why', 'when', 'how', 'where' and/or 'who'.

Some learning experts have applied the questioning approach to determining preferred learning styles. Questions like these might elicit such information:

- Who is interested in knowing the purpose and rationale of something before they move ahead? Why are they interested?

- Who is interested in data, information, research and theory behind the process?

- Who is interested in the mechanics of the process?

- Who is interested in practical applications and extensions?

One of the darkest periods of history was a time when questions were discouraged. It was really not until the end of the 18th century in northern Europe that scientific questions could once more be asked – and answered. Crick and Watson discovered the molecular structure of DNA (deoxyribonucleic acid) in 1953. They inaugurated a whole new science (molecular biology) by asking the right question: 'How do genes replicate and carry information?'

Pertinent incisive questions come before all great scientific discoveries. Before setting down to read serious matter, draw up a series of questions that you want answered. This will create the right mindset. Questions provide a sense of purpose. They focus our concentration. Our minds become unsettled until the information gaps are filled.

A curious mind is like a magnet drawing answers towards it. For personal development, the most productive questions are those that stimulate fresh ideas and insights rather than those that address the familiar. Questions create a tension between our existing level of knowledge and our desired level of knowledge. Learning abhors a vacuum, which inevitably you will seek to fill.

Questions can help you identify a problem, generate alternatives, make choices, discover new information, and see things from different perspectives. You can find out anything provided you ask the right questions. In action learning, participants learn to solve real work-based problems and exploit opportunities by asking the right questions. Maintaining a curious outlook is one way to enrich and develop yourself throughout life.

This process will also develop the connections between your brain cells. Some trainers have a tendency to talk too much rather than facilitate. You can counteract this tendency by asking open-ended questions to draw out course participants' knowledge and experience.

See also **Question-and-answer sessions**.

References
Malone, Samuel A. (2000) *Learning Skills for Managers*. Dublin, Oak Tree Press.
Ukens, Lorraine L. (2001) *What Smart Trainers Know*. San Francisco, Jossey-Bass Pfeiffer.
http,//www.newhorizons.org/wwart_johnston1.html
http,//www.hcc.hawaii.edu/intranet/committees/Fac/Dev/Com/guid…/effquest.ht

R

Readiness to learn   Adults are almost always ready to learn what they need to know in order to cope with work and personal responsibilities. This constitutes a good motivation to learn. Walking, language, motor co-ordination, and other skills are best learned by children when they are sufficiently developed mentally and physically to learn them, at critical periods in their development. Once a critical period is past, however, it may be very difficult or impossible to learn the skill effectively. A major skill in teaching children is to recognise when a critical period has come. Piaget has suggested the ages in children for which certain learning activities are appropriate.

Reference
Pedler, Mike and Aspinwall, Kath (1998) *A Concise Guide to the Learning Organisation.* London, Lemos & Crane.

Recall   Recall – also known as retrieval – can be improved by focusing on key words and using mnemonics. Neuro-linguistic programming claims that by raising the eyes we can access information from our memories. So when faced with a mental block, instead of staring at your desk, look up as you try to retrieve that crucial information.

The human body is more than 70 per cent water, and drinking six glasses of water a day will help keep you mentally alert and improve your recall.

Effective learning is based on repetition. Without repetition, whatever you learn will be quickly forgotten. But for repetition, active recall is essential. Active recall means that you recall information in response to questions. The more ways you have of encoding information, the more ways you will have of retrieving it. When encoding information use as many of the senses as possible – visual, auditory and kinesthetic. Reflection will help you to encode material.

Memory is aided by encoding and retrieving information in multiple ways. Recent scanning research shows that most brain activity associated with retrieval takes place in the right cerebral hemisphere. We may spend a lot of time learning but most of us spend little time practising the recall of the information that we have learned. You should spend at least as much time demonstrating what you know by recalling it as you did learning it.

Recall and recognition are not exactly the same. You may recognise information but need specific cues to recall it. Trying to recall a memory from long-term storage requires some guidance – just like looking for a book in a library. To some extent multiple-choice questions, where alternative answers to a question are offered and the individual is asked to select one answer, rely on recognition. However, with quantitative multiple-choice questions, where the solution has to be worked out mathematically and compared to the answers given, a high degree of recall is required. So the difference between conventional written examination questions and multiple-choice is that recall is most often employed in written exams and recognition in the multiple-choice.

See also **Review**.

References

Hermann, Douglas J. (1995) *Super Memory: A quick-action programme for memory improvement*. London, Blandford.

Malone, Samuel A. (2000) *Learning Skills for Managers*. Dublin, Oak Tree Press.

http,//www.supermemo.com/articles/power.htm

http,//www.web-us.com/memory/generic_ltm_memory.htm

http,//www.web-us.com/memory/theories_and_processes.htm

Recency effect   The recency effect corresponds to the fact that in remembering the entries on a list, you are likely to remember the last words on the list only marginally less well than you remember the first words. It is the words in between that will be forgotten. This is so, provided the recall begins immediately after the presentation of the list of words. If you wait for up to 15 seconds before recalling the words and cannot rehearse them, the recency effect seems to evaporate completely – although you will probably still remember the words at the beginning of the list (the 'primacy effect').

See also **Primacy effect**.

References

Parkin, Alan J. (1993) *Memory Phenomena: Experiment and theory*. Oxford, Blackwell.

Refabrication   Refabrication or confabulation corresponds to the unconscious invention of false memories. To compensate for the poor memory of something that happened a long time ago, we tend to fill in the gap with invented details. Refabricated memories seem real and are almost impossible to distinguish from the truth.

See also **False memory syndrome**.

References
Baddeley, Alan (1991) *Human Memory: Theory and practice.* Hove and London, Lawrence Erlbaum Associates.

Reflection   The reflective approach to learning is to follow the learning cycle of 'do something, think about it, conclude, and do it differently or better'. Reflection is the second stage of the learning cycle and follows an action. You reflect and think about observations, behaviour and performance with a view to doing it better in the future. Reflection is an important part of continuous learning and improvement and of the appraisal process. Keeping a personal development log would be part of the process.

See also **Action learning**; **Learning cycle**; **Learning sets**.

References
Knasel, Eddy, Meed, John and Rossetti, Anna (2000) *Learn For Your Life: A blueprint for continuous learning.* London, Pearson Education.
Mumford, Alan (1997) *Management Development, Strategies for Action.* London, IPD.
http,//www.nci.ac.uk/pima/DS/PDP4.HTM

Reflector   In the learning context, 'reflector' is one of the four styles of learning; activist, reflector, theorist and pragmatist. Plato said, 'The life which is unexamined is not worth living.' Learning begins when we reflect on our experiences. The purpose of education is to acquire wisdom by reflecting on important issues and questions. Reflections often result in new understanding: that is learning. Dewey's formula is 'Experience plus reflection equals learning'. 'Let's think it through first is the reflective learner's response.'

Learning is a consequence of thinking. The cerebral cortex, the part of the brain involved in complex thinking and learning, does not show significant growth with too much stimulation as it does with a moderate amount. The brain needs time to reflect on recaptured experience, to think about, evaluate, consolidate and understand information.

People for whom reflection is the preferred style of learning tend to think deeply about their experiences and consider them from different viewpoints. They are good at listening to others and like to consider the facts before they come to a conclusion. They tend to be cautious and have the philosophy of 'Look before you leap.' At meetings they seem to be quiet and detached but are good listeners. Part of their approach is to get as many different points of view as possible before making up their own minds. They like to think, analyse, deliberate, question, consider, reflect and plan. They like to do a learning review and to keep a learning journal to record and examine their experiences. They like to have objective data before arriving at conclusions and thus do not like to be rushed into making decisions. They hate to be drawn into situations which require action without planning. The Lord gave us two ends – one to sit on and the other to think with. Success depends on which one we use the most! Reflectors make good strategic planners.

In general, reflectors learn best from:

- reflective experiences

- observing a group

- listening to other people's points of view

- watching a video

- reviewing events

- exchanging ideas

- careful analysis of reports.

To develop a reflector style you should listen more attentively to others, become more thoughtful and methodical, and weigh the facts before arriving at conclusions.

See also **Activist**; **Pragmatist**; **Theorist**.

References

Honey, Alan (1994) 'Styles of learning' in the *Handbook of Management Development*, edited by Alan Mumford, Aldershot, Gower.

Honey, Peter and Mumford, Alan (1986) *Using Your Learning Styles*. Berkshire, Peter Honey.

Mumford, Alan (1997) *Management Development, Strategies for Action*, 3rd edition. London, IPD.

Mumford, Alan (1995) 'Putting learning styles to work: an integrated approach', *Industrial and Commercial Training*, Volume 27, Number 8, pp28–35.

http,//www.infed.org/biblio/b-reflect.htm

Reframing   Reframing is looking at something from a different viewpoint, seeing it with new eyes in a new context. Shakespeare said that 'There is nothing either good or bad, but thinking makes it so.' A manager may adopt the viewpoint of a customer to help him or her understand the customer's perspective. Metaphors and jokes are examples of reframing.

There are three points of view:

- your point of view

- the other person's point of view

- a detached or observer's point of view.

Gandhi, Einstein and Disney were reputed to be very proficient in seeing things from another's point of view. All inventors make reframers. A good marketing professional needs to be able to identify and anticipate customer needs. In strategic planning, when looking at the environment you should consider political, economic, social and technological aspects. Each of these provides different perspectives on the economy.

Reframing is your own internal learning device. Good learners anticipate positive learning outcomes. Sometimes we are so caught up in a situation that we find it difficult to stand back and look at it objectively and from different viewpoints.

You can also reframe the context and content of the situation. You can increase the significance of something by seeing it close up and you can reduce its significance by seeing it small and far away. You can reframe the content by reinterpreting it in a humorous light.

To learn a new behaviour, the following procedure has proved to be effective with many people:

- Identify the behaviour you want to change.

- Describe it and visualise doing it in your mind's eye.

- Now perfect the behaviour by substituting the new behaviour for the old.

- Anchor it by associating it with an appropriate word or action.

- Run it through like a mental film.

- Rehearse it until it becomes very familiar to you.

References
Adler, Harry (1996) *NLP for Managers: How to achieve excellence at work*. London, Piatkus.
Huczynski, Andrzej (2001) *Encyclopedia of Management Development*. Aldershot, Gower.
O'Connor, Joseph and Seymour, John (1990). *Introducing NLP: Psychological skills for understanding and influencing people*. London, Aquarian/Thorsons.

Reg Revans' model of learning

Reg Revans formulated a simple model of action learning which states that $L = P + Q$, that is, that learning is equal to programmed knowledge plus questions. During their training, specialists acquire a whole codified system of knowledge related to their specialty. For example, trainee accountants learn accountancy by P learning and managers may attend night classes to learn management by P learning. 'P' can be thought of as techniques that can be learned to solve routine problems. This information is acquired from books, papers, studies, lectures, and training programmes. P learning is put together and written by people who are experts in their subject – but the trouble is, they don't know anything about the unique circumstances of the learner or the organisation.

On the other hand, 'Q' activities deal with unprogrammed problems calling for creativity, judgement, intuition, reflection and insight – the day-to-day problems that occur in the workplace. This latter process is called action learning. These are the types of abilities that are needed by successful managers and are developed through on-the-job experience rather than formal training.

Management is about dealing with unprogrammed problems. There are no ready-made off-the self solutions to such problems. Hence the risks involved in management decision-making. General managers need to be able to ask the right incisive questions to maximise specialist input and to manage effectively. Managers need to maintain an enquiring mind so that their functional experts or management consultants will not take them in. Otherwise, managers can be blinded by science and confused by jargon.

Mumford has suggested that Revans' original equation should be adapted. The most effective learning is driven by the need to resolve management problems Q1. This leads to the acquisition of relevant knowledge P which then triggers further management opportunities Q2. The revised equation is therefore Q1 + P + Q2 = L..

References
Mumford, Alan (1997) *Management Development, Strategies for Action*, 3rd edition. London, IPD.
Revans, Reg (1998) *An ABC of Action Learning: Empowering managers to act and to learn from action.* London, Lemos & Crane.
Zuber-Skerritt, Ortrun (2002) 'The concept of action learning', *The Learning Organisation*, Volume 9, Number 3, pp114–124.

Relaxation   You learn better when in a relaxed state of mind. Trainers should create and maintain an atmosphere of relaxed alertness, involving low threat and high challenge. Dr Lozanov, the Bulgarian advocate of Suggestology, found that Baroque music such as that of Bach, Handel, and Vivaldi induces a state of relaxation if played at low volume while learning. These composers used very formal harmonies and patterns that tend to synchronise our minds with our bodies. Playing baroque music is a way of engaging your right brain while concentrating on left-brain activities.

Stress inhibits learning and memory. One study revealed that people over 55 years of age showed improved concentration and were better at recalling faces and names after learning relaxation techniques, such as deep breathing and progressive relaxation. 'Take a music bath once or twice a week, for music is to the soul what water is to the body' – Oliver Wendell Holmes.

See also **Accelerated learning**.

References
DePorter, Bobbi and Hernacki, Mike (1993) *Quantum Learning: Unleash the genius within you.* London, Piatkus.

Reminiscence effect   For a short period some time after a learning event, the memory of the learning may become fresh again before fading away: this effect is known as the reminiscence effect. Ballard discovered it in 1913. Some children who had partly learned a poem were able to recall it better after a period of time than immediately after the learning session. One view is that inhibition builds up during a learning task. However, after the task, inhibition gradually disappears to facilitate better recall.

References
Malone, Samuel A. (1996) *Learning to Learn.* London, CIMA.
Wingfield, Arthur (1979) *Human Learning and Memory: An Introduction.* New York, Harper & Row.

Repertory grid technique   The repertory grid technique was developed by George Kelly, a US psychologist, and may be used to evaluate training. It is based on the theory of personal constructs. We all use words in particular ways to understand the world around us. We all have different mental maps. Our mental maps contain elements – the objects of thought such as people or words. They also contain constructs – the qualities used to describe these elements. For example, for one person mountains may be regarded as beautiful, and for another they may be perceived as dangerous.

The repertory grid can take the form of a structured interview or questionnaire. The objective is to explore the content and structure of a person's value judgement. Has a participant's attitude changed as a result of going through the course programme? 'Before' and 'after' studies must be done to find the answer. A manager might use the technique to find out what makes one person more effective than another in different aspects of the job. For example, one person might be very good at building rapport with customers in comparison to another. The reasons for this could then be explored further.

Operative training may be comparatively easy to evaluate whereas management training outcomes may be difficult to measure. This is especially so in areas like industrial relations, which is concerned with attitudes and perceptions. The repertory grid is particularly appropriate here.

Typical uses for the technique are:

- to identify what is important to employees before designing training programmes to meet their needs

- job analysis and counselling

- to assist in self-development, team-building or organisational development interventions

- to identify what the term 'quality' means to different people

- to identify the behaviours such as skills or attributes that are associated with success in a particular company

- to identify relevant issues before designing a questionnaire

- to find out what management mean when they refer to the 'culture' of the company.

See also **Attitude**.

References

Huczynski, Andrzej (2001) *Encyclopedia of Development Methods*. Aldershot, Gower.
Kelly, G. A. (1955) *The Psychology of Personal Constructs*. New York, WW Norton.
Prior, John (1991) A Handbook of Training and Development. Aldershot, Gower, published in association with the Institute of Training and Development.

Stewart, Andrew (1997) 'Diagnosing needs' in the *Handbook of Management Development*, edited by Alan Mumford, Aldershot, Gower.

Repetition   The more frequently you repeat something, the more likely you are to recall it. Each time you repeat something, try to see it from a different angle so that you are not just repeating the same thing. This approach will engage your creativity and lay down more connections in long-term memory.

Professional actors learn their parts in a play by rereading their lines many times over a short period. For example, they may read their part five to 10 times a day over four days. For non-actors the best way to commit a passage to memory may be by the 'progressive part method'. In this method, the learner adds a new line while continuing to rehearse the other lines. For example, you learn the first line. Having learned line 1, you then learn lines 1 and 2. When you have these memorised, you then tackle lines 1, 2 and 3, and so on. Such procedure ensures:

- that the short-term memory is not overloaded

- the practice and retention of earlier lines, otherwise forgotten through interference.

For best results, the 'progressive part method' should be combined with the 'holistic method'. In other words, get an overview of the material first before using the progressive part method. This is the concept behind the SQ3R system and learning maps. Build up a framework of the area to be studied and then develop this as your studies progress.

Overlearning ensures that the item goes from your short-term memory to long-term memory storage. Overlearn so that in examinations you won't have difficulty recalling information if under stress.

See also **Recall**; **Review**.

References
Hermann, Douglas L. (1995) *Super Memory: A quick-action programme for memory improvement.* London, Blandford.
Higbee, Kenneth L. (1990) *Your Memory: How it works and how to improve it.* London, Piatkus.

Repression   Freud believed we forget many things because we unconsciously wish to do so – we repress them. These may be unpleasant or painful experiences that we feel are best forgotten. This is also called motivated forgetting.

For example, people who like to gamble remember the few times they won rather than the many times they lost. People with a hangover soon forget and repeat the process.

References
Ratey, John (2001) *A User's Guide to the Brain.* London, Little, Brown.

Retention of learning   Retention is a factor of how effective the original learning was. Following a revision plan can facilitate the retention of learning. Most experts recommend that revision should take place shortly after the learning, again within 24 hours, again after one week, again after one month, again after three months, and occasionally thereafter to make sure the information is not forgotten. Information is retained better if participants see a meaning or purpose for the information.

See also **Review**.

References
Hermann, Douglas L. (1995) *Super Memory: A quick-action programme for memory improvement.* London, Blandford.
Malone, Samuel A. (2000) *Learning Skills for Managers.* Dublin, Oak Tree Press.

Retroactive inhibition   In retroactive inhibition, new learning interferes with the retention of old learning. When you learn a new piece of prose, for example, it may hinder the recall of a piece you previously learned. Similarly, if you memorise a string of words on list A and then memorise another string of words on list B, you may well find that the memorisation of the words on list B seriously interferes with the retention of the words on list A. Your memory for both lists will improve if you take a rest in between. This gives your mind a chance to consolidate the material and move at least some of it from short-term to long-term memory.

See also **Proactive inhibition**.

References
Baddeley, Alan (1991) *Human Memory: Theory and practice.* Hove, Lawrence Erlbaum Associates.

Retrospective learning   Retrospective learning involves reviewing and learning from past events. This type of learning is conscious and intentional.

The sequence has three stages:

1   Something happens.

2   It is reviewed.

3   Conclusions are reached and lessons drawn.

By reviewing, you acquire knowledge, skills and/or insights. The review may be carried out mentally, in conversation with others, or on paper. How can I learn from the past? Keeping a learning log is a great way of systematically reviewing the past and learning from it. Necessity and frustration is often the spur to learning and the mother of invention. Ermal Cleon Fraze (1913–1989) while on a picnic with his family had to resort to a car bumper to open a can. After reflecting on the problem for some time, he invented the ring-pull on drink cans.

See **Prospective learning**.

References
Mumford, Alan (1997) *Management Development, Strategies for Action*, 3rd edition. London, IPD.

Review   Review is an important way of getting information from short-term memory to long-term memory. Without review, information is quickly forgotten – hence the importance of drawing up a review plan when studying. A good way of reviewing information is from learning maps. Follow a review plan,

- review 10 minutes after learning

- review 24 hours later

- review one week later

- review one month later

- review frequently coming up towards exam time.

If you don't invest time in a review plan, you will spend more time relearning material all over again. Relearning something that has previously been learned but forgotten gets easier on each successive occasion, and this is why regular revision is a vital aspect of studying. Retrieval is facilitated when the original learning has been systematic, thorough and understood by the learner.

Review periods should be built in to course programmes. Reviewing helps create a favourable learning climate. It also establishes reflective learning as an important element in the course programme. Review helps participants to internalise the learning with their own experience and prior knowledge, and to see where the learning could be applied in the future to make them more effective in their jobs.

See also **Recall**; **Retention of learning**; **Spacing effect**.

References
DePorter, Bobbi and Hernacki, Mike (1993) *Quantum Learning: Unleash the genius within you*. London, Piatkus.
Malone, Samuel A. (1996) *Learning to Learn*. London, CIMA.
http,//braindance.com/bdimem2.htm

Rewards   Rewards can act as a reinforcement of learning and an incentive to go on learning. The stimulus, response, reinforcement cycle suggests that rewarded behaviour is repeated whereas non-rewarded behaviour tends not to be learned. The learner should know exactly why he or she is being rewarded. Reward systems should be clearly understood and consistent. Rewards can be praise, bonuses, salary increases, promotion, or any other type of recognition. Frequent rewards may be counterproductive because learners become immune. Rewards should be proportionate to the importance of the learning event.

See also **Positive reinforcement**.

References
DePorter, Bobbi and Hernacki, Mike (1993) *Quantum Learning: Unleash the genius within you.* London, Piatkus.
Malone, Samuel A. (1996) *Learning to Learn.* London, CIMA.

Right-brained   A 'right-brained' person makes more use of the right-hand cerebral hemisphere of the brain. This is the creative and artistic side of the brain. When you use your imagination as in creative writing you use this side of the brain.

Most of us have a bias towards left-brain thinking, particularly at work, as a result of education and conditioning. As schoolchildren we were encouraged to learn spelling and multiplication tables by rote, while at the same time we were discouraged from daydreaming or any other right-brain activity. In fact, many skills call on both sides of the brain. For example, systems analysis combines both logical and creative skills.

The right hemisphere controls the left side of the body. Damage to this side of the brain leads to poor results in non-verbal tests involving the manipulation of geometric figures, puzzles, completion of missing parts of patterns and figures, and other tasks involving form, distance and space.

See also **Left-brained**.

Reference
Adler, Harry (1994) 'The technology of creativity', *Management Decision*, Volume 32, Number 4, pp23–29.
Ratey, John (2001) *A User's Guide To The Brain.* London, Little, Brown.
http,//www.mtsu.edu/~devstud/advisor/hemis.html

Role model   See **Modelling**; **Observational learning**.

Role-play   Role-play is a type of simulation or acting within the context of a carefully initiated scenario. Acting out what you are trying to learn can make information more meaningful and memorable to you. Role-players may operate to a script or may act to general guidelines and ad lib. The aim is to give people a taste of the real-life situation. Managers learn by doing. In management training, role-play may be used to change attitudes and develop interpersonal skills such as empathy, negotiation, assertiveness and interviewing for use in customer relations, conflict resolution, and so on.

Role-playing is used to change attitudes particularly through 'role reversal' when roles are swapped to get different perspectives. In this respect, it is a type of reframing. For example, in a negotiation role-play, the manager may play the role of the employer and then play the role of the trade union official. It is a good way of learning empathy skills, because to do it effectively you must take on the persona of the role. As Shakespeare's famous passage in *As You Like It* says,

> **❝** All the world's a stage,
> And all the men and women merely players;
> They have their exits and their entrances;
> And one man in his time plays many parts. **❞**

Role-play is a way of experiencing various roles that one would not normally experience and seeing things from the unique perspective of that role. Some people find it uncomfortable to take part in role-play because they may be shy or consider the process artificial. Nevertheless, it is a powerful tool for experiential learning but requires careful preparation and sensitive facilitation. Role-play lends itself to discussion and therefore encourages active participation and feedback.

A logical extension of role-play is the use of drama in management development. Drama is short scripted plays that may help managers act out situations that they may be confronted with in real life. This can help managers see things from different perspectives. To ensure that the role-play runs smoothly, the trainer should arrange for all the learners to possess some predetermined baseline of knowledge, understanding and proficiency. Otherwise, the objectives of the role-play may not be achieved.

See also **De-roling**; **Empty-chair technique**; **Games**; **Role reversal**; **Simulations**.

References

Craig, Robert L. (1987) *Training and Development Handbook, 3rd edition. A Guide to Human Resource Development*. New York, McGraw-Hill.

Fee, Kenneth (2001) *A Guide To Management Development Techniques*. London, Kogan Page.

Feinstein, Andrew Hale, Mann, Stuart and Corsun, David L. (2002) 'Charting the experiential territory. Clarifying definitions and uses of computer simulation, games and role play', *The Journal of Management Development*, Volume 21, Number 10, pp732–744.

Reid, Charles W. and Kleiner, Brian H. (1996) 'Which training methods are effective?', *Management Development Review*, Volume 9, Number 2, pp24–29.

File,//C,\Program Files\Britannica\BCD\Cache_17_PreviewRil.htm

Role reversal   Role reversal is where people who are taking part in a simulation exercise or role-play swap roles. By swapping roles people can experience different behaviours, attitudes and perspectives. For example, in industrial relations training one person might alternately take on the role of industrial relations officer and trade union official. Such simulations provide a unique opportunity for members of each side to get inside the skin of members of the other and see how their minds work. Different behaviours can be tried out in a safe environment to find out what effect they have on the outcome. It can be used to resolve conflict, misunderstanding or mistrust between two employees. Role-plays can be recorded on videotape for review or discussion, and/or to maximise learning insights.

See also **Role-play**.

References
Fee, Kenneth (2001) *A Guide To Management Development Techniques*. London, Kogan Page.
Huczynski, Andrzej (2001) *Encyclopedia of Development Methods*. Aldershot, Gower.
Muney, B. F. and Deutsch, M. (1968) 'The effects of role reversal during discussion of opposing viewpoints',
Journal of Conflict Resolution, Volume 12, Number 3, pp34–56.

Room arrangements Certain room configurations encourage dialogue, collaborative learning and socialising, whereas others discourage social intercourse. There is no perfect configuration for all training needs. However, the way you lay out the room does make a difference. It determines to whom course participants talk, how they may feel about the trainer, and how well they can see each other and see the visuals. For example, the 'U', 'V', circle, and cabaret-style arrangements encourage dialogue and participation. These are learner-centred configurations. Classroom formation is a teacher-centred arrangement.

Rote learning Rote learning is learning by memory without thought or understanding of the material being learned. It is commonly known as learning by heart. Rote learning without understanding prevents the acquisition of further meaningful learning. Rote learning on its own does not equip learners to use what they have learned in meaningful, productive ways. However, rote learning does have its place in learning and business. Symbolic information such as the alphabet or multiplication tables are best learned by rote. In business, managers who can recall information quickly such as names, products, code numbers, financial facts and other details are often admired. Mnemonic devices can be used to help this process. Trying to recall material memorised by rote is more difficult than when the material is meaningful.

See also **Mnemonics**; **Surface learning**.

References
Huczynski, Andrzej (2001) *Encyclopedia of Development Methods*. Aldershot, Gower.
Kidd, J. R. (1977) *How Adults Learn*. New York, Association Press.
Malone, Samuel A. (2000) *Learning Skills for Managers*. Dublin, Oak Tree Press.

Routine   See **Habits**.

S

Sabbaticals   A sabbatical – unpaid time off in which to do something particular (even if only to take a much-needed rest) – is a feature of professional life for university teaching staff but is also available in many other organisations. Such career breaks are often used to give managers an opportunity to pursue an outside interest. For example, you might wish to take a year off to write the book that you always intended to write but never seemed to have the time for. You might also want to spend more time with your family. Others might wish to pursue an educational programme.

Sabbaticals enable managers to leave a job and subsequently return after an agreed period of absence. It is important that re-entry is guaranteed to be at the same level. Sometimes a rest is better than a change, and a sabbatical may revitalise a manager's interest in a career that has become stale and stagnant.

References
Forrest, Andrew (1995) *Fifty Ways To Personal Development*. London, Industrial Society.
Huczynski, Andrzej (2001) *Encyclopedia of Development Methods*. Aldershot, Gower.
Malone, Samuel A. (2000) *Learning Skills for Managers*. Dublin, Oak Tree Press.

Santayana review   A Santayana review is an investigation by an organisation into its past dealings – its successes and failures, its highs and its lows – in order to learn from them. Such a review is named after the US philosopher George Santayana, who in 1905 coined the famous expression, 'Those who cannot remember the past are condemned to repeat it.'

Companies should learn from past experience. They must review their actions and inactions, assess them systematically, and record the lessons for all employees to see and learn. The knowledge gained can be used to enhance new developments. Boeing used lessons from earlier development to help produce the 767, the most successful, error-free aircraft launch in history. Unfortunately, too many managers today are indifferent, even hostile, to the past, and by failing to reflect on it they let valuable knowledge escape, and risk repeating mistakes.

See also **Learning from mistakes**.

References
Malone, Samuel A. (2000) *Learning Skills for Managers*. Dublin, Oak Tree Press.

Schema   A schema, or mindset, is a mental model – a person's idea of how things are or what another individual is like. It may thus focus on a person, an object or an event, or be quite general about a situation or a preference. Mindsets help people to act in situations even when they do not have full information.

We all come to learning situations with different prior knowledge and experience. This means that we also learn very different things from the same event. Essentially, a schema is an organised body of information or beliefs, which may or may not be entirely accurate, about some subject or concept.

Schematic learning that builds systematically on previously acquired knowledge is more efficient than rote learning. Trainers should therefore proceed from the familiar to the unfamiliar, from the simple to the complex, and from the known to the unknown.

See also **Mental maps**; **Mental set**.

References
Baddeley, Alan (1991) *Human Memory: Theory and practice*. Hove, Lawrence Erlbaum Associates.
http,//www.web-us.com/memory/generic_ltm_memory.htm

Secondment   A manager may be seconded (sent) to another organisation to gain training, new perspectives, experience and further development. Secondment should be used as part of a planned management development programme. Learning objectives should therefore be set, consideration should be given to how these objectives are to be met and, on the manager's return to his or her own organisation, an evaluation should take place. This may take the form of a report.

A civil servant may be seconded to a commercial organisation to learn how a business operates in a competitive environment. On the other hand, a manager in the commercial sector may be seconded to a civil service department to find out how government departments operate. A manager working in a multinational may be posted overseas.

Secondment provides a unique opportunity for managers to operate in a new environment, experience a different company culture, and learn new perspectives, systems and procedures. They learn how to make decisions based on their own judgement and experience. They also extend their networks of business contacts. A manager moving from a large to a small company often learns to become more self-reliant, because the back-up and support facilities of a larger organisation are not available.

When a person on secondment comes back, he or she should be debriefed by his or her own manager on what has been learned and how he or she proposes to apply this learning to the organisation.

See also **Job rotation**.

References
Fee, Kenneth (2001) *A Guide To Management Development Techniques*. London, Kogan Page.
Forrest, Andrew (1995) *Fifty Ways To Personal Development*. London, Industrial Society.
Huczynski, Andrzej (2001) *Encyclopedia of Development Methods*. Aldershot, Gower.
Mumford, Alan (1997) *Management Development, Strategies for Action*. London, IPD.

Self-assessment   Self-assessment requires making a sort of mental checklist of one's own skills, strengths, achievements, weaknesses and development needs. (An actual inventory drawn up to contain this information is known as a self-audit.)

Self-assessment may also be carried out as part of performance appraisal. The employee fills out a self-assessment form which may be compared subsequently with a manager's assessment.

A skills self-assessment concentrates on the skills one has in relation to the skills one needs to do one's job more effectively or progress in one's career. Examples of such skills include those required for information and communications technology, and presentation, negotiation and assertiveness skills.

Checklists and psychometric tests are commercially available that can help with self-assessment. For example, doing the Learning Styles Questionnaire will make you more aware of your particular learning style. Getting feedback from your colleagues is another good method of self-assessment.

See also **ASPIRE model**; **Self development**.

References
Ukens, Lorraine L. (2001) *What Smart Trainers Know*. San Francisco, Jossey-Bass Pfeiffer.

Self-development   Self-development is not only increasing one's own knowledge and skills but taking the responsibility for doing so, and continuing to make the effort. Self-development is the overall process of training and developing oneself for personal and career progress.

Criteria for success include:

- the use of self-development affirmations such as 'I can make a difference at work,' 'I am capable of achieving more than I am at present,' 'I can improve my interpersonal relationships by getting and acting on feedback from others'

- the reframing of situations to see them from different points of view – As well as seeing things from your own point of view, learn to see things from others' points of view and from a detached point of view.

- designing your own self-development programmes – Use the principles of action learning. You develop yourself by working on real-life issues that confront you or your organisation.

■ focusing on using your 15 per cent of influence to change your organisation – W. Edwards Demming, the quality guru, estimated that the power of individuals to influence change in their organisation amounted to a maximum of 15 per cent – 85 per cent of the power was constrained by the structure, systems and procedures of the organisation.

See also **Self-assessment**.

References
Forrest, Andrew (1995) *Fifty Ways To Personal Development*. London, Industrial Society.
Burgoyne, John (1999) *Developing Yourself, Your Career and Your Organisation*. London, Lemos & Crane.
Megginson, David and Whitaker, Vivien (1996) *Cultivating Self-Development*. London, IPD.
Pedler, Mike and Boydell, Tom (1999) *Managing Yourself*. London, Lemos & Crane.

Self-directed learners Self-directed learners – also known as self-managed learners – are adults who take responsibility for their own learning. The goal of general education should be to produce lifelong self-directed learners. It should enable people to identify their own learning needs, set their own learning objectives, plan, carry out and evaluate their own learning. Self-directed learning can take place at work, in one's personal life or more formally when pursuing academic programmes. Because of the short lifespan of knowledge in the business world, self-directed learning is particularly suited to the workplace.

In training and development, self-directed learners no longer operate as passive receivers of information but have an input into their own growth. In this new paradigm, the trainer becomes a facilitator and ultimately a resource to be tapped by the learner.

Lorraine Cavaliere (1992) studied how the Wright brothers learned to design an aircraft that could fly. She identified five stages in their learning:

1 enquiring – involving perceiving a need to solve a problem

2 modelling or observing similar phenomena and developing a prototype model

3 experimenting and practising, involving continuous refinement and adjustment of the model

4 theorising and perfecting their skills and the product

5 actualising or receiving recognition for the outcome of their learning efforts.

Much the same process is facilitated by personal development plans.
Key characteristics of self-directed learners include:

■ They are able to identify their own learning needs.

- They can identify the human, material, equipment and financial resources they require to help them achieve their learning goals.

- They have a high level of self-belief, self-confidence and self-esteem in respect of their capabilities as learners.

- They foster social networks and peer support groups for emotional sustenance and educational guidance.

- They have initiative, independence, curiosity, persistence and self-discipline, and see problems as learning opportunities rather than as obstacles.

- They have learned how to learn, or are in the process of learning.

- They are able to draw up their own learning objectives.

- They are able to design a learning programme and learning strategies to meet their learning objectives.

- They have identified their own learning style.

- They know their strengths and weaknesses as learners. They are able to reflect on the learning process and on their experiences as learners.

- They are able to motivate and discipline themselves to the learning task.

- They can evaluate their own learning. They know when to change direction and take corrective action as appropriate. Evaluation is an important aspect of self-directed learning since it is a skill needed in professional life and for lifelong learning.

- They may like to negotiate a learning contract with their manager. The learning contract can be used as a vehicle for setting personal learning goals.

Adults need to know the reason for the learning, have experiences which they need to share, like to solve problems, and see learning as a way of making themselves more effective in their personal and work lives. The trainer should help learners identify their specific learning needs, locate learning resources, and choose learning and evaluation strategies.

Organisations should encourage their staff to take responsibility for their own learning. They must create a culture of learning and an organisational context that the learner perceives as democratic, flexible, challenging and non-threatening. People should be encouraged to learn from their mistakes.

Some organisations have educational support schemes that refund fees on successful completion of certificate, diploma and degree programmes. In many cases these programmes need not necessarily be job-related because general intellectual skills such as concentration, perseverance, writing, summarising, etc, developed on these programmes are highly valued. Jobs can no longer be guaranteed for life and employees should be helped to make themselves as marketable and as employable as possible. The traditional model of work as a permanent and pensionable job is gone, and various configurations are now available instead, such as part-time work, flexible working hours, sub-contracting and teleworking. Employees must be trained for these options.

Employees who have been away from study for a long time can benefit from learning-to-learn skills such as study and exam techniques, time management, note-taking, memory techniques and learning maps. Such skills help learners to become 'learning self-aware', which means they have an appreciation and understanding of how they learn, their own learning capabilities, and the outcomes they wish to achieve. Learning-to-learn skills equip learners to go on learning for the rest of their lives.

A learning styles questionnaire may be used to help staff determine their own particular learning style. Knowing the learning styles of individuals helps trainers in the design and delivery of training programmes. The two most widely used inventories of learning styles are Kolb's Learning Style Inventory and Honey and Mumford's Learning Style Questionnaire. Psychometric tests may be provided to help staff decide on career paths to suit their unique talents. Large organisations may set up corporate learning centres to help their staff develop a whole range of skills using modern technology, including computer-based training. Self-directed learning has its place but should not take away from the appropriateness of co-operative learning in certain circumstances.

See also **Co-operative learning**.

References

Cavaliere, Lorraine A. (1992) 'The Wright brothers' Odyssey, their flight of learning', *Learning for Personal Development. New Directions for Adult and Continuing Education* Number 53. San Francisco, Jossey-Bass.
Fee, Kenneth (2001) *A Guide To Management Development Techniques.* London, Kogan Page.
http,//www.ni.edu/ace/Resources/Documents/AdultLearning.html
http,//www.infed.org/biblio/b-selfdr.htm
http,//fohweb.macarthur.uws.edu.au/ot/egsdlp.htm
http,//fohweb.macarthur.uws.edu.au/ot/infosdl.htm
http,//www.wlv.ac.uk/~bu1821/files/self-dir.htm
http,//www.mapnp.org/library/trng_dev/methods/slf_drct.htm

Self-efficacy   Bandura (1977) defines self-efficacy as the conviction that one can successfully execute the required behaviour to produce the desired outcome. Bandura suggests that self-efficacy operates in three different ways:

- through choice of behaviour

- through persistence at a task

- through one's thoughts and emotional reactions.

To have high self-efficacy means you believe that you have everything you need to succeed at a particular task.

See also **Competencies**.

References
Bandura, A. (1977) *Social Learning Theory.* New Jersey, Prentice Hall.
Waters, Michael (1996) *The Element Dictionary of Personal Development.* Shaftesbury, Element Books.

Self-esteem   Self-esteem is the regard we have for ourselves. Low self-esteem results in low performance. High self-esteem is crucial to our well-being and our self-development. To be successful learners we must see ourselves as capable and effective learners. A trainer should be aware of the importance of supporting or even enhancing a learner's self-esteem. Confidence-building measures should be part of the trainer's repertoire. People with high self-esteem see threats as opportunities and mistakes as learning opportunities. They engage in positive self-talk, and the possibility of failure is never entertained. Psychologists believe that there is a strong correlation between self-esteem, your sense of well-being, and your capacity for self-development and true success in life.

Managers with low self-esteem lack confidence and do not believe in lifelong learning, and thus never reach their true potential. Unfortunately, they often stifle the development of their staff as well. High self-esteem means a willingness to take risks, to respond to challenges and seek opportunities for learning and self-development. Research shows that fluctuation in the neurotransmitter serotonin within the brain is correlated with high and low levels of self-esteem.

See also **Positive thinking**.

References
Cheetham, Graham and Chivers, Geoff (2001) 'How professionals learn in practice: an investigation of informal learning among people working in professions', *Journal of European Industrial Training*, Volume 25, Number 5, pp247–292.
Knasel, Eddy, Meed, John and Rossetti, Anna (2000) *Learn For Your Life.* London, Prentice Hall.
Malone, Samuel A. (2000) *Learning Skills for Managers.* Dublin, Oak Tree Press.

Self-fulfilling prophecy   A self-fulfilling prophecy is a prediction made by one person to and/or about others, which the others thereafter consciously or unconsciously make come true. In a learning context, and with the prediction less explicit (in the form of expectation), an example is the Pygmalion effect, where a teacher's evident high expectations for his or her students are borne out by results that might have been lower had the teacher's expectations also been lower. Self-fulfilling prophecies are also possible in relation to oneself. In fact, positive thinking that leads to positive results is another variant on self-fulfilling prophecies.

People move in the direction of their dominant thoughts. You become what you expect to become and you achieve what you expect to achieve. Expectation is a powerful form of suggestion. If you think you can, you will. If you think you can't, you won't. You see and achieve what you believe.

People's perception of reality is not reality itself. The map is not the territory. We tend to find what we look for in people or situations, good or evil, problems or solutions, opportunities or threats. If we have low expectations for ourselves, we shall never achieve much. Unconscious beliefs such as 'I am no good at mathematics' become self-fulfilling prophecies.

What the mind can conceive and believe, it may achieve. You are limited to a large extent by your own expectations, beliefs and fears. Expect the best and the best is more likely to happen. Convert problems to opportunities and see the positive side to life's trials and tribulations. Everybody has problems. Nobody escapes the normal ups and downs of life. Don't expect to be happy all the time. You must be able to live with the bad days as well as the good. Become solution-centred rather than problem-centred. See the best in people rather than the worst.

See also **Pygmalion effect**.

References
Davies, Ivor K. (1971) *The Management of Learning*. McGraw-Hill.
Malone, Samuel A. (1996) *Learning to Learn*. London, CIMA.

Semantic memory   See **WISE model of memory types**.

Seminar   A seminar has been defined as a short course making extensive use of participating methods and devoted to the exclusive study of one subject with the aim of furthering knowledge in that area. An expert may facilitate it. Like conferences and workshops, seminars provide a great opportunity to exchange views, learn from other people's diverse experience and set up networks with others. The success of a seminar depends on the skill of the trainer or facilitator. The trainer must weld the individuals into a group and make the sessions emotionally satisfying as well as productive.

See also **Conference**; **Workshop**.

References
Fee, Kenneth (2001) *A Guide To Management Development Techniques*. London, Kogan Page.
Huczynski, Andrzej (2001) *Encyclopedia of Development Methods*. Aldershot, Gower.
Malone, Samuel A. (2000) *Learning Skills for Managers*. Dublin, Oak Tree Press.

Senses   For effective learning engage all your senses – visual, auditory and tactile. Visual for pages, diagrams and pictures; auditory for paraphrasing, recitation and reading aloud; the sense of touch for taking notes, drawing diagrams and keeping cue cards for revision. Forming mental images or drawing diagrams, flowcharts and learning maps will help you understand information and remember it better. Drawing or note-taking uses the left side of the brain while visualisation draws on the right side of the brain. Your ability to recall the information is thus more than doubled.

It may help you to remember the acronym SHE, which stands for See, Hear, and Experience.

- See yourself achieving your goal.

- Hear the approving comments of your peers.

- Experience the feelings and sense of pride in knowing that you have accomplished your targets.

See also **VAK model of learning**.

References
Malone, Samuel A. (2000) *Learning Skills for Managers.* Dublin, Oak Tree Press.
Meir, Dave (2000) *The Accelerated Learning Handbook.* New York, McGraw-Hill.

Sensitivity training (T-group)   Sensitivity training in T-groups is a type of behaviour modification training developed by Kurt Lewin aimed at making people more sensitive to their own motives and behaviours and to the behaviours of others. T-groups consist of between ten to twelve members. They meet on a part-time or full-time basis over a period ranging from three days to two weeks. The objective is to explore personal and group dynamics with the help of a facilitator. They focus on issues of interpersonal awareness, leadership, authority, and the dynamics of change in organisations. Participants learn to give and receive feedback and to empathise with others. The facilitator does not structure or lead the group but may intervene if necessary to resolve interpersonal conflict. The group itself is the source of the learning. The facilitator is there to help participants to explore their interpersonal relationships.

In T-groups there are four key elements:

- feedback – Feedback is most effective when it is generated from here-and-now observations and is given as close to the event as possible. The receiver of the feedback should be able to check it out with other group members to verify its validity.

- 'unfreezing' – People must be motivated to change if change is to occur. The group helps members question deeply-held assumptions about themselves and how they relate to others. Trainers seek to create an environment in which values, beliefs and attitudes can be brought out into the open, challenged and re-evaluated.

- participant observation – Members involve themselves emotionally in the group and try to observe themselves and the group objectively. This is a difficult process but is essential if people want to learn and develop.

- cognitive aids – Such aids may include the Johari Window, lectures, video, reading assignments and theory sessions. The task of the T-group is to facilitate the learning of members.

T- groups have to be handled with great sensitivity because they cause anxiety in those who are insecure. The benefits of T-groups for participants include:

- the development of a better understanding of themselves and of others

- a greater openness, receptivity and tolerance of differences

- the acquisition of interpersonal relationship skills

- greater capacity for co-operation.

References
Craig, Robert L. (1987) *Training and Development Handbook, 3rd edition. A Guide to Human Resource Development*. New York, McGraw-Hill.
Huczynski, Andrzej (2001) *Encyclopedia of Development Methods*. Aldershot, Gower.

Shadowing   Shadowing is learning by observing someone else doing a specific activity over a specific period of time. The idea behind this approach is that you can learn best from observing a person who is experienced. Shadowing gives you the opportunity to observe the job of (for example) a senior manager at first hand. You observe the manager while negotiating, handling complaints, compiling budgets, delegating tasks, answering correspondence, answering the phone, attending meetings, interviewing staff and drafting reports. You should pick up new insights, tips and techniques on how to be more efficient and effective in your job. You will learn that different managers do things differently and have different types of leadership and communication styles. You will doubtless also learn that there are some things that you can do better than your manager!

The approach has some pitfalls in that the learner may be treated as little more than a runner of errands and that the method may be subject to bias.

References
Fee, Kenneth (2001) *A Guide To Management Development Techniques*. London, Kogan Page.
Huczynski, Andrzej (2001) *Encyclopedia of Development Methods*. Aldershot, Gower.
Malone, Samuel A. (2000) *Learning Skills for Managers*. Dublin, Oak Tree Press.

Short-term memory   Short-term memory is the capacity of the brain to store information for immediate or near-immediate retrieval and re-presentation (without rehearsal or practising). Information within the short-term memory decays rapidly without rehearsal and continued attention. In fact, it is generally forgotten within 6 to 30 seconds if it is not rehearsed. As with long-term memory, interference seems to be the prime cause of forgetting in short-term memory.

The capacity of short-term memory is held to be between five and nine items of information. However, its capacity can be extended if the material is grouped. For example, a memory span of seven letters can be increased to 35 if the letters form seven five-letter words. So chunk your learning points into related groups of between five and nine items. In this way isolated words such as acronyms can be easily memorised if you are astute enough to organise them into a meaningful sentence or a little story. Whole areas of a topic can thus be recalled quite easily.

Remembering a telephone number is more difficult if the number is given to you orally. You will have to repeat it to yourself over and over again; and, if interrupted, you will probably forget it. Similarly, if you are dialling a new telephone number and are interrupted, you will probably have to look it up again.

There are three theories about why we forget information in short-term memory:

- displacement – Existing information is replaced by new information when short-term memory capacity is full.

- decay – Information is forgotten over time.

- interference – Previously stored memories distort new information.

The regions of the brain that are important for memory are being mapped. Research shows that short-term memory is more dependent on the frontal lobes. On the other hand, long-term memory is more dependent on a portion of the temporal lobe called the hippocampus. Researchers have found that short-term memory deteriorates noticeably for most people in their forties, but don't know why.

See also **Long-term memory**.

References
Baddeley, Alan (1991) *Human Memory: Theory and practice.* Hove, Lawrence Erlbaum Associates.
http,//www.web-us.com/memory/memory_encoding.htm
http,//www.ntu.ac.uk/soc/bscpsych/memory/goodhead.htm
http,//www.ntu.ac.uk/soc/bscpsych/memory/horsley.htm

SIMILAR model of intelligences   The SIMILAR model is an acronymic guide to styles of intelligence based on Howard Gardner's theory of multiple intelligences. SIMILAR stands for,

- Spatial
- Interpersonal
- Musical
- Intrapersonal
- Linguistic

- Analytical (mathematical)
- Reflex or kinesthetic.

In 1996 Gardner added an eighth intelligence he called natural intelligence. Other authors have suggested spiritual and practical intelligences. Gardner claims that we are all born with potential in all of these areas. Many individuals show talents in more than one area. Musicians, for example, need not only an understanding of music but also need kinesthetic intelligence to manipulate the keys on a saxophone or draw the bow across the strings of a violin. Conventional education concentrates on the linguistic and analytical (mathematical) intelligences. In a training situation, trainers need to draw on as many of the intelligences as possible.

See **Analytical intelligence**; **Emotional intelligence**; **Interpersonal intelligence**; **Intrapersonal intelligence**; **Kinesthetic intelligence**; **Linguistic intelligence**; **Musical intelligence**; **Natural intelligence**; **Practical intelligence**; **Spatial intelligence**; **Spiritual intelligence**.

References

Armstrong, Thomas (1993) *Seven Kinds of Smart: Identifying and developing your many intelligences.* London, Plume.

Gardner, Howard (1993) *Frames of Mind: The theory of multiple intelligences.* London, Fontana.

Vincent, Annette and Ross, Dianne (2001) 'Personalise training: determine learning styles, personality types and multiple intelligences online', *The Learning Organisation*, Volume 8, Number 1, pp36–43.

http,//www.cio.com/archive/031596_qa_content.html

http,//www.mathmatters.net/mupintel.htm

http,//www.metronet.com/~bhorizon/teach.htm

http,//www.newhorizons.org/trm_lwilson1.html

Simulations   Simulations are learning activities designed to replicate real-world situations. They are artificial representations of real problems. Simulations provide opportunities for trial-and-error solutions, and any mistakes that arise are a great source for learning.

Simulations as a way of learning are not new. Simulations involving games such as chess were developed thousands of years ago. The Prussians developed war-game simulations in the early 1800s. The war games became very popular and were adopted for military training throughout the world. A well-designed simulation can provide safer and more efficient and effective training than the use of the actual equipment while avoiding unacceptable risk. Best-known examples include business games, flight-simulators, driving simulators and power-station operation simulators.

Police officers learn 'seek and search' techniques in simulated streets and houses. Soldiers learn how to fire missiles in simulated conditions. Bank officials learn cashier techniques at simulated counters. Paramedics learn how to deal with accidents in simulated accident conditions. Accountants use what-if analysis with spreadsheets to simulate financial situations. Barristers perfect their skills in mock trials.

Multimedia courseware enables employees to explore safely the operation of expensive and potentially dangerous equipment in a risk-free environment. Modern computer technology now enables the creation of virtual reality so technically perfect as to simulate surgery and is creating further extraordinary opportunities for the use of simulation.

The Open University has a virtual science laboratory. Here students can carry out experiments safely. Expert systems are computer programs that mimic expertise in a particular area of knowledge such as medicine or taxation. As with any model, however, a simulation is only as good as its underlying assumptions. If these assumptions are incorrect, the model will not reflect real-life conditions.

Dangers of using simulations include:

- Course participants may reject them as unrealistic or irrelevant.

- They may go on for too long, leaving participants with the feeling that the value of the exercise is not proportionate to the time spent.

See also **Games**; **Role-play**; **Virtual reality**.

References
Cheetham, Graham and Chivers, Geoff (2001) 'How professionals learn in practice: an investigation of informal learning amongst people working in professions', *Journal of European Industrial Training*, Volume 25, Number 5, pp247–292.
Craig, Robert L. (1987) *A Training and Development Handbook, 3rd edition. A Guide to Human Resource Development.* New York, McGraw-Hill.
Reid, Charles W. and Kleiner, Brian H. (1996) 'Which training methods are effective?', *Management Development Review*, Volume 9, Number 2, pp24–29.

Single-loop learning   Single-loop learning – also known as adaptive learning – is learning that does not rely on or lead to progress. Skills may be improved and errors corrected, but there is no leap of understanding to initiate a new phase at a new level. It corresponds to learning by rote – the emphasis is more on memorisation than on comprehension.

In an organisational context, single-loop learning takes place when an organisation improves its ability to achieve known objectives. It is concerned with correcting errors in the current operating environment. It is associated with procedures, routines and behavioural learning. The emphasis is on techniques and making techniques more efficient. Single-loop learning is like the thermostat in your home that controls the central heating system by turning it on and off in response to changes in room temperature. In single-loop learning, an organisation learns without making any significant change to its basic assumptions. It is associated with incremental change. In a business context, the budgetary control system is a good example of single-loop-learning. Here actual costs are compared with budgets, variances analysed and corrective action taken to put the actual cost back on target again.

See also **Deep learning**; **Double-loop learning**; **Surface learning**.

References

Matlay, Harry (2000) 'Organisational learning in small learning organisations', Education and Training', Volume 42, Number 2/5, pp202–211.

Moingeon, Bertrand and Edmondson, Amy (1996) *Organisational Learning and Competitive Advantage*. London, Sage.

Mumford, Alan (1997) *Management Development, Strategies for Action*, 3rd edition. London, IPD.

http,//www.infed.org/thinkers-schon.htm

http,//www.infed.org/thinkers-argyris.htm

Sitting by Nellie

'Sitting by Nellie' is a somewhat unsystematic approach to training that represents a means of inducting a newcomer or learner into the intricacies of a job by seating him or her next to an expert doing it. It is a method that is still used in many organisations. If 'Nellie' is a proficient worker, a good tutor and coach, and has a sound understanding of learning principles, the approach may work well enough. However, this is an unlikely scenario, and 'Nellie', even if proficient, is unlikely to possess the requisite training, tutoring and coaching skills. It is unlikely too that 'Nellie' has any knowledge of how adults learn and about learning theory in general. In addition, 'Nellie' may not have the time or interpersonal relationship skills to deal with trainees and may in any case be unwilling to pass on the 'secrets of the trade'. In practice the good as well as the bad work habits of 'Nellie' are passed on to the trainee.

Nonetheless, this model is still prevalent in small companies or where managers do not believe in the value of formal training.

See also **Modelling**.

References

Mumford, Alan (1997) *Management Development, Strategies for Action*. London, IPD.

Skills

A skill has been defined as expertise developed in the course of training and development. Skills include trade or craft skills, professional skills, social skills and sporting skills. On a more basic level, motor skills involve motor co-ordination and timing. Skills become better with practice and training – practice makes perfect and practice makes permanent.

Four important points are:

- Continuous improvement will take place only with feedback and knowledge of results. The more precise the feedback, the better the results.

- Strategies and information acquired in training for one task may transfer to others. This means that learning the second task is speeded up considerably.

- The benefits of the learning curve are acquired through the passage of time. People get more proficient at their jobs with experience. Improvement with practice is typically rapid at first and then more gradual but lasting for a long time. For example, the speed of some repetitive work in factories improves with time on the job over several years.

■ Once high levels of skill have been attained, they last for several years. There is a loss of skill without continual practice, but it can usually be regained relatively quickly.

See also **Attitude**; **Knowledge**; **Learning stages**.

References
Boydell, Tom and Pedler, Mike (1999) *Managing Yourself*. London, Lemos & Crane.
Buckley, Roger and Caple, Jim (1992) *The Theory and Practice of Training*. London, Kogan Page.
Malone, Samuel A. (2000) *Learning Skills for Managers*. Dublin, Oak Tree Press

Skills analysis   A skills analysis corresponds to a detailed and systematic study of the skills needed to perform a particular task. This analysis is then used to draw up a training programme.

References
Thorne, Kaye and Mackey, David (2001) *Everything You Ever Needed To Know About Training*. London, Kogan Page.

Skimming   Skimming is a technique used in speed-reading, and intended to get a superficial overview – just the gist – of a book or text. It is not conventional reading as we understand it. Skimming involves studying the table of contents to get a general sense of the book's structure, checking the index for the range of subjects covered, reading chapter headings, section headings, subheadings, topic sentences and chapter summaries.

Make one-word summaries of each paragraph, combine these in the form of a learning map for each chapter, and condense them into a learning map for the whole book. You now have a permanent and quick overview of the book, which you can review as the need arises.

See also **Speed-reading**.

References
Malone, Samuel A. (1996) *Learning to Learn*. London, CIMA.
Wainwright, Gordon (2001) *Read Faster, Recall More*. Oxford, How To Books.
http,//www.ucc.vt.edu/stdysk/readbook.html

Sleep   Getting adequate sleep is vital to your success as a learner. While you are sleeping your brain disconnects from the senses and revises and stores memories. Shakespeare called sleep the 'balm of hurt minds' and 'chief nourisher in life's feast'. Lack of sleep affects all activities adversely, but it seems to affect memory more than physical tasks. So before an exam get a good night's sleep.

Staying up all night studying before an exam is certainly not a good idea. Research shows little improvement in performance, and no amount of sleep the following two nights can make up for the detrimental effects of not sleeping the first night. Lack of sleep impairs your ability to concentrate and lay down new memories. Lack of sleep, *per se*, does not interfere with memory. However, tiredness greatly affects your motivation to learn new things, accept new challenges and exercise your memories. It also adversely affects your ability to concentrate.

Sleep learning does not work. Sleep learning machines which were popular in the 1960s have now disappeared. Studies proved that no learning took place. However, learning important facts and concepts just before you go to sleep consolidates the learning. It seems that unconscious processing during sleep consolidates learning. It is further strengthened if you review on waking up.

Rapid-eye-movement (REM) sleep occurs while we are dreaming. Adults spend about one fifth of sleep time in REM sleep. It begins about 90 to 100 minutes after a person falls asleep. The first REM period lasts about 10 minutes but each REM period gets progressively longer after that with periods of up to one hour. Some researchers believe that learning is consolidated during this type of sleep. Some studies show that when REM sleep is interrupted, people have much poorer recall of the previous day's events. Most people at some stage have gone to sleep with a problem and woken up with the solution. This shows how the brain can work out difficulties during sleep.

To get a good night's sleep experts suggest:

- Stick to a regular bedtime schedule.

- Reserve the bedroom for sleep and keep it cool, dark and quiet.

- Don't take tea or coffee before bedtime because these are stimulants which keep you awake.

- Alcohol interferes with sleep, so don't drink before bedtime.

- Don't take heavy meals and cut back on fluids close to bedtime.

- Go to bed when you feel tired and sleepy. A hot bath or playing soft music will relax your body for sleep.

References

Hermann, Douglas J. (1995) Super Memory: A quick-action programme for memory improvement. London, Blandford.

Higbee, Kenneth L. (1990) *Your Memory: How it works and how to improve it.* London, Piatkus

http,//www.brain.com/about/article.cfm?id=20606&cat_id=300

http,//www.findarticles.com/cf_0/m1355/2_99/68648289/print.jhtml

SMART objectives   SMART is a well-known acronym used by trainers in various contexts but with particular reference to behavioural (including learning)

objectives. The acronym stands for Specific, Measurable, Attainable, Relevant, and Timely.

- *specific* – Learning objectives should be specific rather than general. The outcomes should be described in behavioural terms.

- *measurable* – What can't be measured is rarely done. If you can't measure it, you can't manage it effectively. Behavioural objectives can be measured. Actual results should be compared with targets so that corrective action can be taken, if necessary.

- *attainable* – Objectives should be capable of achievement. Unrealistic goals and goals that are too difficult to achieve become demotivational.

- *relevant* – Objectives should be relevant and pertinent to the course programme.

- *timely* – Objectives should be time-bound. That which can be done at any time is rarely ever done. Time constraints concentrate the mind.

References
Fee, Kenneth (2001) *A Guide to Management Development Techniques.* London, Kogan Page.
Malone, Samuel A. (1999) *Success Skills for Managers.* Dublin, Oak Tree Press.

Social theory of learning
The social learning theory centres on the fact that people learn from observing and modelling themselves on others and that, by definition, such observations take place in a social setting. But the social learning theory also includes the concept of self-regulation, which suggests that people can regulate their own behaviour by visualising the consequences of it. Some models of behaviour are more likely to be imitated than others, notably people who are regarded as attractive, competent, powerful or famous. Your self-efficacy – that is, the competence you know you have and the confidence you have in knowing it – will determine your effectiveness or otherwise in dealing with others and with the environment. There is a reciprocal aspect, in that people influence their environment which in turn influences the way they behave.

In management, Mary Parker Follett came up with the principle of reciprocal influencing or circular behaviour. If a manager approaches an employee in a negative manner, it can elicit a negative response. This negative response in turn affects the manager's attitude and subsequent response. Whereas if the manager had approached the employee in a positive constructive way, the employee would probably have responded in a similar way, which once again would have affected the manager's response. In other words, initial behaviour comes back around to affect subsequent behaviour.

The concept of the locus of control is also part of social learning theory, and has particular bearing on the individual's expectation that a particular outcome is achievable and that the reward is worth the effort expended. Social learning theory has been applied also to role theory, group learning and mentoring.

The social theory of learning has three important connotations for trainers:

- Learning centres on the relationships between people. Dialogue is an important aspect of collaborative learning.

- A key role for trainers is to help people become more socially effective in the workplace.

- Learning is an active process. Learning is part of daily living. Problem-solving and learning from experience is a central part of the process.

See also **Behaviourist theory of learning; Cognitivist theory of learning; Constructivist theory of learning; Humanist theory of learning.**

References
Merriam, Sharon B. and Caffarella, Rosemary B. (1999) *Learning in Adulthood: A comprehensive guide.* San Francisco, Jossey-Bass.
http,//www.infed.org/biblio/learning-social.htm

Spacing effect   The existence of an interval between a learning event and a repetition of the learning event (or something very like it) improves the memory of the learning. It is an effect that is related to the lag effect, in which the recall of items given spaced repetition improves as the interval between repetitions increases. Both effects result from the way that memory fixes relevant information in the brain. An event may by itself be temporarily transferred to long-term memory and forgotten about in a matter of days. However, if you encounter the event again, your memory assumes an increased probability of the event's occurring yet again in the future, and this increases the duration of memory retention.

If you want to retain information you must operate a revision plan.

See also **Review.**

References
Hermann, Douglas L. (1995) *Super Memory: A quick-action programme for memory improvement.* London, Blandford.
http,//www.supermemo.com/articles/kowal.htm

Spatial intelligence   Spatial intelligence is one of the seven intelligences discerned by Howard Gardner in his book *Frames of Mind.* People with spatial intelligence like objects and shapes, charts, designs, diagrams, pictures and maps. They like to draw, design and create things. Well-known outstanding examples of people with this intelligence would include Pablo Picasso, Rembrandt, Leonardo da Vinci and Michelangelo. People with this ability are excellent at visualisation and think and remember things in the form of pictures. Graphic artists, architects, decorators, surveyors, guides and navigators have this ability. We all have this ability to a lesser or greater extent.

To enhance this ability read maps and charts, use learning maps, pictures, diagrams, graphs, flowcharts, colours, and your powers of visualisation.

See also **SIMILAR model of intelligences**.

References

Armstrong, Thomas (1993) *Seven Kinds of Smart: Identifying and developing your many intelligences.* London, Plume.
Gardner, Howard (1993). *Frames of Mind: The theory of multiple intelligences.* London, Fontana.
Vincent, Annette and Ross, Dianne (2001) 'Personalise training: determining learning styles, personality types and multiple intelligences online', *The Learning Organisation,* Volume 8, Number 1, pp36–43.
http,//www.famu.edu/sjmga/ggrow/7ln/Spatial.html

Speed-reading   It has now been established that with training most people can without any loss of comprehension read considerably faster than they do. A reader's ability to increase speed significantly depends on many variables. These include intelligence, knowledge, vocabulary, motivation, diligence and previous reading experience. The average reader reads at a speed of 240 words per minute. This can be improved, with a little training, to a speed of 360 words per minute. With sustained effort and plenty of practice 600 words per minute can be achieved when reading easy material. For more difficult material, and in order to maintain comprehension levels, you should be satisfied with a reading speed of 400 words per minute.

On the other hand, according to research studies, there appears to be a minimum reading speed of 200 words per minute below which the reader may fail to process the meaning of the text effectively. Reading below 200 words per minute apparently reflects inefficient, word-by-word reading that is not conducive to integrating and comprehending text in a meaningful way. Research has also shown that when the term 'reading' is interpreted in the sense of comprehending most of the words on a page, it is impossible to read faster than 800 to 1,000 words per minute and that comprehension suffers significantly above a speed of 400 words per minute. The capacity of the working memory is also a constraint.

Of course, higher speeds can be achieved when approaches such as skimming, scanning and skipping are employed, but these should be distinguished from genuine reading.

Tips that may speed up your reading include:

- Read for ideas rather than reading each individual word. Broaden your reading span to include two to three words at a time. Read in phrases or thought units. The brain takes information in more easily if it is grouped in meaningful chunks.

- Use a guide such as a pencil when reading and create a smooth movement when going from one line to the next. Using a guide will prevent your eyes from losing your place on the page.

- Vary the speed ,in line with your purpose and the difficulty of the text. Speed up for simple material and familiar ideas. Slow down for technical material and unfamiliar concepts. Skim over examples, explanations and illustrations you are already familiar with. Try to read only material essential to your purpose. In general, speed up the time it takes you to read each group of words.

- Use your peripheral vision to read the edges of each line by focusing your main vision a word or two in from the left and from the right all the way down the page.

- Don't subvocalise structure words such as 'and', 'the', etc. The average reader does not subvocalise full stops and commas, so get out of the habit of subvocalising structure words too.

- Don't go back over words you have already read.

- Don't vocalise or say words to yourself.

- Skip information that you already know.

- Get 80 per cent of the information in 20 per cent of the time. Achieve this by concentrating on titles, subtitles, first and last paragraphs, and chapter summaries.

- Increase your vocabulary so that puzzling over unknown words will not slow you down.

See also **Skimming**; **SQ3R model of reading**.

References
Buzan, Tony (1997) *The Speed-Reading Book*. London, BBC Books.
Konstant, Tina (2000) *Speed-Reading*. London, Hodder & Stoughton.
Malone, Samuel A. (1996) *Learning to Learn*. London, CIMA.
Wainwright, Gordon (2001) *Read Faster, Recall More*. Oxford, How To Books.
http,//www.selfgrowth.com/articles.Scheele2.html
http,//happychild.org.uk/acc/tpr/mem/0101.sprd.htm
http,//selfgrowth.com/articles/Allen9.html
http,//www.mindtools.com/speedrd.html
http,//www.coun.uvic.ca/learn/program/hndouts/rdgspeed.html
http,//www.utexas.edu/student/lsc/handouts/512.html
http,//www.ucc.vt.edu/stdysk/suggest.html
http,//www.utexas.edu/student/lsc/handouts/529.html
http,//www.coun.uvic.ca/learn/program/hndouts/psq5r.html
http,//www.adm.uwaterloo.ca/infocs/Study/reading.html
http,//www.coun.uvic.ca/learn/program/hndouts/readtxt.html
http,//www.coun.uvic.ca/learn/program/hndouts/readbk.html

Spiritual intelligence   Spiritual intelligence is a type of intelligence posited by some authorities as an addition to the intelligences discerned by Howard Gardner in his book *Frames of Mind* (1984). People with spiritual intelligence – also known as existential intelligence – like to ponder over the reason for their existence, the nature of God, their place in the universe, the ultimate purpose of life, and other philosophical questions. The search for God has led to some of the greatest works of art, literature, music and architecture.

A person with spiritual intelligence has values, beliefs, principles and high ethical standards. Moral issues have become increasingly important in modern society and in organisations. Business ethics is now a university degree subject. Issues such as equality, racism, ecology, pollution, animal welfare, social responsibility, genetics and reproduction, and conservation have become the mainstream concerns of modern society. People with spiritual intelligence are not necessarily religious but believe in truth, justice, honesty, integrity, and a high standard of business ethics. They are ready to stand up for their beliefs. Spiritual intelligence gives them a sense of purpose and a reason for living.

Every civilisation in the world has channelled its spiritual intelligence into one brand of religion or another.

See also **SIMILAR model of intelligences**.

References

http,//www.newhorizons.org/report_confprice.html

SQ3R model of reading   The SQ3R model is a technique for effective reading invented by Professor R. P. Robinson, and is rather different from speed-reading. SQ3R stands for Survey, Question, Read, Recall, and Review.

- *survey* or overview – Study the preface, contents list, index, layout, diagrams and pictures, chapter summaries if provided, and so on. Note who the author is, and the date of publication. Pay special attention to the first and last chapters because they are often introductory and summary chapters. This scanning may achieve your purpose and you may not need to go any further.

- *question* – Pose questions to yourself that you want answered. Generating questions is at least as good as answering questions. Turn headings into questions. Such questions may be prompted by studying the review questions, if any, provided at the end of each chapter.

- *read* – Read with a purpose, actively in search of ideas and answers to your questions. Textbook material will have to be read twice. The first reading can be fast to get a taste for the material. The second reading can be slow and deliberate to identify the key learning points. Reflect while you read. Think of practical applications. Relate it to what you know.

- *recall* – Try to recall and record the key learning points during the second reading, preferably at the end of each section. Compare this with the text to identify gaps in your recall. Prepare notes as you go along in the form of learning maps.

- *review* – Use your learning maps to systematically review and revise what you have learned. Review the major learning points and the answers to your questions. Make rehearsal a part of your reading approach. Research indicates that comprehension and retention are improved when you 'elaborate' new information. This means that you reflect on your reading, compare and contrast, connect it to your knowledge and experience, and rearrange the material to suit your purpose.

See also **Speed-reading**.

References

Malone, Samuel A. (1996) *Learning to Learn*. London, CIMA.
http,//www.ucc.vt.edu/stdysk/sq3r.html

State-dependent memory

State-dependent memory   Memory is often linked to a particular context – what is learned in one place is best recalled in the same place. Hence the advantage of taking examinations in the room in which you studied. The state-dependent phenomenon in memory is well known to the police, who often recreate the scene of a crime on television in order to prompt people's memories of events. Witnesses are sometimes brought to the scene of a crime to help them remember details. Some studies suggest that mood exerts state-dependent effects. The mood becomes part of the memory and the memories are recalled better if you are in a similar mood to when the memories were laid down.

In an experiment, divers who memorised words under water had better recall of the words under water than they did on dry land. A person who learns something after a few drinks can recall that information better while drunk than when sober. Similarly, a person who learns while sober may then have difficulty recalling it when drunk.

References

Baddeley, Alan (1991) *Human Memory: Theory and practice*. Hove, Lawrence Erlbaum Associates.

Story-telling technique

Story-telling technique   In a learning context, the story-telling technique is a well-known but comparatively unusual method of teaching. Story-telling is one of the oldest forms of communicating information. Every culture in the history of the world has relied on stories and song to teach its history, traditions, culture, values and life skills. Jesus used parables to get across complex religious points. Trainers can do exactly the same thing. Stories are powerful ways of helping the mind to make meaningful, intelligent connections. Learning points can often be put across more effectively if wrapped up in the form of a story. Stories may add interest to an otherwise dry and technical topic. A well-constructed story can evoke emotional responses from learning thereby improving learning and retention. Consider the success of the bestselling management book *The One-Minute Manager*, which presents its ideas wrapped up in a story. Analogies and metaphors are very effective in this context. Narrative chaining is a type of mnemonic strategy in which items for recall are incorporated into a story.

According to brain research, we organise information in a non-linear or story-form way. Stories allow us to bypass the linear left-brain and access both the right brain and left brain in whole-brain learning. Hence the advantage of using learning maps.

See also **Learning map**; **Whole-brain learning**.

References
Huczynski, Andrzej (2001) *Encyclopedia of Development Methods*. Aldershot, Gower.
Meir, Dave (2000) *The Accelerated Learning Handbook*. New York, McGraw-Hill.
http,//www.newhorizons.org/ph_reneefuller.html
http,//www.newhorizons.org/arts_carroll.html
http,//www.newhorizons.org/story_gabriel1.html

Stress and learning   A certain amount of stress can be helpful to you in your goal as a learner. A healthy level of stress is protective and is known as 'eustress'. Too much stress, however, is a barrier to learning. People learn best under low to moderate stress. Social support, as provided in learning sets, may act as an antidote to stress. Relaxation training, such as progressive relaxation or meditation or closing your eyes to imagine a calm place, will help you control stress levels. Biofeedback may help you become aware of internal processes and thereby facilitate control over the physiological manifestations of stress.

There is some evidence that high levels of stress may impair memory retrieval for a period of time. Chronic stress over a long period of time can produce large amounts in the body of the hormone cortisol (hydrocortisone), which may have seriously deleterious effects on brain cells. Elsewhere in the brain, the hippocampus is part of the limbic system and has some responsibility for learning and memory. Magnetic resonance imaging has shown a decrease in the overall volume of the hippocampus of people who have suffered severe stress. However, imaging also shows that this damage to the hippocampus can be reversed, provided the stress does not continue for too long.

See also **Biofeedback**.

References
Cotton, Julie (1995) *The Theory of Learners*. London, Kogan Page.
Malone, Samuel A. (2000) *Learning Skills for Managers*. Dublin, Oak Tree Press.
File,//C,\Program Files\Britannica\BCD\Cache_22_PreviewRil.htm
http,//home.clara.net/figurehead/mensa.htm

Study buddies   A 'study buddy' is a co-learner who may, in some ways and at some times, turn out to be something of a teacher as well. People have different learning styles and draw different lessons from the same learning material. To capture these different learning perspectives, you could explore your subject and exchange learning with a study buddy. A study buddy can inform you when you are missing important concepts or misunderstanding an idea. Take turns in being the presenter and the listener. Co-operative learning is not only useful for formal learning but is also an important aspect of action learning.

See also **Co-operative learning**; **Study circles**.

Study circles   Study circles are groups of from six to 20 people who come together to study a particular topic. Such groups are popular in the USA and Sweden. Members of community groups, churches, business groups, and unions have used study circles to generate understanding and agreement when faced with difficult problems or hard choices. The interest in study circles stems from a belief that there is wisdom in groups, that education and understanding go together, and that learning is available for all. In study circles people learn to listen to each other and accept different viewpoints and perspectives. Participants are given an opportunity, with the help of a facilitator, to develop their communication, interpersonal and logical skills. In a study circle there is equality, empathy, trust, and respect for others. A study circle has been described as 'education for life'.

In a business, study circles may be used to develop a positive learning climate by involving managers, employees and trainers in a partnership to learn about a topic, develop learning-to-learn skills and encourage lifelong learning. Study circles focus on self-actualisation of participants while bringing about change in business and in society.

The Study Circles Resource Center in the USA offers the following advice to those running study circles:

- Maintain an open mind. Explore possibilities and different viewpoints.

- Strive to understand others who disagree with you. Try to see things from their point of view.

- Value your own experience and opinions. You have unique knowledge and experience. Make sure that you share it with others.

See also **Co-operative learning**; **Study buddies**.

References
Huczynski, Andrzej (2001) *Encyclopedia of Development Methods*. Aldershot, Gower.
http,//www.context.org/ICLIB/IC33/Andrews.htm

Subconscious learning   We were always told that to learn something we must focus our attention on it – now research shows that people can also learn something even when they are not consciously trying. Perceptual learning – such as taking in cues from the environment – can take place even without attention, awareness or task relevance. This is part of our evolutionary heritage . . . but may contribute to information overload today.

References
Meir, Dave (2000) *The Accelerated Learning Handbook.* New York, McGraw-Hill.

Succession planning   Succession planning refers to the process and actions that aim at identifying and developing a pool of potential successors for senior management or key specialist jobs in the future. Succession planning arises because of retirements, redundancies or reorganisations. Succession charts may be drawn up explicitly to plan the process. Unlike replacement planning, succession planning is more strategic, proactive, long-term-oriented and development-focused. It ensures the continual supply of qualified executive talent to lead and support business growth.

The performance appraisal process may be used to identify people with the talent for future managerial positions. A systematic management development programme is one of the ways to plan for management succession.

References
Moorby, Ed (1994) 'Making it happen', in the *Handbook of Management Development*, edited by Alan Mumford, Aldershot, Gower.
Mumford, Alan (1993) *How Managers Can Develop Managers.* Aldershot, Gower

Suggestology   Suggestology – also known as 'learning by suggestion' – is a teaching theory based on the notion that suggestions can and do affect the outcome of learning. People learn through both the conscious and subconscious mind. Everything makes a suggestion. A learner may be consciously listening to a trainer but at the same time his subconscious mind is aware of the learning environment, the trainer's mood, body language and tone of voice, and the general ambience of the room. Everything is constantly being mentally processed including atmosphere, symbols, rituals and associations. Trainers can influence learners by the words they use, the attitudes they display and the body language they employ. They should make a conscious effort to make the learning environment as enticing and non-threatening as possible. Dr Georgi Lozanov was the founder of Suggestology. His methods included using music as students enter the classroom, leave the classroom and during break times, to help create a positive learning atmosphere.

See also **Accelerated learning**; **Lozanov**.

References

DePorter, Bobbi and Hernacki, Mike (1993) *Quantum Learning: Unleash the genius within you.* London, Piatkus

Huczynski, Andrzej (2001) *Encyclopedia of Development Methods.* Aldershot, Gower.

Ostrander, Sheila and Schroeder, Lynn (1999) *Super-Learning 2000.* London, Souvenir Press.

http,//www.newhorizons.org/trm_deporter.htm

Surface learning

Surface learning is learning by concentrating on the memorisation by rote of facts, formulas, and concepts without any real reflection and understanding in order to pass exams. Students passively accept ideas and information and fail to recognise fundamental concepts, principles and patterns. The motivation is extrinsic in the form of a qualification, and fear of failure is very much in mind.

One researcher has found that anxiety and low self-esteem is associated with surface approaches to learning.

See also **Deep learning**; **Single-loop learning**.

References

Hassall, Trevor and Joyce, John (2001) 'Approaches to learning of management accounting students', *Education and Training*, Volume 43, Number 3, pp145–153.

Knasel, Eddy, Meed, John and Rossetti, Anna (2000) *Learn For Your Life: A blueprint for continuous learning.* London, Prentice Hall.

http,//www.newhorizons.org/lrnbus_marchese.html

Surveys

Surveys are used in many different business contexts, but particularly to identify training and learning needs. The most common method of obtaining data in a survey is by asking people to respond to a questionnaire.

See also **Questionnaires**.

SWOT

SWOT is a well-known acronym particularly used in the analysis of skills and competencies. SWOT stands for Strengths, Weaknesses, Opportunities, and Threats.

- *Strengths* are things that you are good at. Strengths might include your positive attitude, experience, prior knowledge, qualifications, and good IQ.

- *Weaknesses* are things that you find difficult to handle. Weaknesses might include a lack of certain skills, your tendency to harbour negative thoughts, be reactive and to procrastinate.

- *Opportunities* are external changes that can affect you positively. For example, an opportunity might be an offer of promotion. Changes in technology and markets may also present opportunities for you.

- *Threats* are external factors that may affect you adversely. For example, a threat might be the possibility of company closure and redundancy. What obstacles do you face in life? Is changing technology or competition threatening your job at work? Carry out a strengths and weaknesses analysis of your capabilities.

Try to turn weaknesses into strengths and threats into opportunities. Redundancy has often been turned into an opportunity by which people have become successfully self-employed, releasing talents they never knew they possessed. Do a skills assessment. This concentrates on the skills you have in relation to the skills you need to do your job more effectively or progress in your career. Examples include information technology, presentation, negotiation, and assertiveness skills.

Ready-made checklists are available that can help with your self-assessment. Those for technical skills tend to be specific while those for mental and behavioural skills tend to be more general. You can focus on the gap between your current level of expertise and your desired level. Consider what you need to do to fill that gap. It might include further experience, training and educational qualifications. Write down your long-term and short-term targets.

References

Malone, Samuel A. (2000) *Learning Skills for Managers*. Dublin, Oak Tree Press.
http,//www.mindtools.com/swot.html

Symposium   In a training context a symposium is a series of lectures delivered by three to five qualified people. They speak on different aspects of the same subject. The objective is to present a range of viewpoints on the one subject. Symposiums are particularly useful for a new subject or to create food for thought. The length of each speech is generally between three and 20 minutes. A chairman is in charge, and there is no participation by the audience.

References

Craig, Robert (1987) *A Training and Development Handbook. 3rd edition. A Guide to Human Resource Development*. New York, McGraw-Hill.
Huczynski, Andrzej (2001) *Encyclopedia of Development Methods*. Aldershot, Gower.

Synaesthesia   Synaesthesia is condition in which information from different sensory modes becomes confused so that stimulation of one sense triggers a reaction in another. As a result, sounds may be perceived as tastes and touch as sound. Synaesthetic imagery appears to be a fairly common form of memory encoding. Low-pitched tones are experienced as soft whereas high-pitched tones may be experienced as sharp. Similarly, blue feels cold whereas red feels warm. A person experiencing synaesthesia might for example see colours when another speaks.

A famous case of synaesthesia, known as 'S' was studied by the Russian psychologist A. R. Luria from 1920 to 1950. When asked to recall a word, S would not only hear the word but would also taste it and see it in a unique colour. All of these sensations helped S to have a phenomenal memory. When tested by Luria, S was able to remember items perfectly 15 to 20 years later.

The more you involve your senses – vision, hearing, smell, taste and touch – the greater your ability to recall the information that you have learned.

References
Cytowic, Richard E. (1993) *The Man Who Tasted Shapes*. London, Abacus.
http,//www.happychild.org.uk/acc/tpr/gtm/1098slvs.htm

Synchronous learning
Synchronous learning occurs when several technologies connect online learners with the trainer in real time in a virtual classroom. Other examples of e-learning include real-time chat-rooms and video or audio conferencing.

See also **Asynchronous learning**.

References
Sloman, Martyn (2001) *The E-learning Revolution: From propositions to action*. London, CIPD.

Syndicates
Syndicates, in a training context, are groups of course participants set up to discuss a particular topic. They may be allocated to syndicate rooms, if available. A group chairman should be elected by each group to report back, but the trainer may also ask other group members to elaborate or clarify issues as appropriate. A time limit should be set for discussion and arriving at conclusions, but this may be flexible depending on time constraints and on the needs of the group.

The trainer should monitor and facilitate the needs of each group, making sure that everything is running smoothly.

Syndicates can energise course programmes and introduce a little bit of friendly inter-group competition. Apart from learning about the topics under discussion, group members get some experience in public speaking and putting a case across.

References
Fee, Kenneth (2001) *A Guide To Management Development Techniques*. London, Kogan Page.

Synergy in learning
Synergy happens naturally in learning in that the more you know about a topic, the easier it is to learn more about the same topic. Your original knowledge forms a framework in which the new knowledge can be placed.

Synergy may also be considered in the context of combining left-brain and right-brain activities such as logic and creativity. It is not widely known that Einstein was an accomplished violinist and when stuck with a problem often relaxed by playing the violin, which put him in a relaxed and reflective state of mind.

Organisations are stocks of knowledge. Every organisation contains knowledge and expertise accumulated through experience. The notion of synergy suggests that teams as well as individuals create knowledge.

See also **Group learning**.

Systematic training model   A systematic model for training includes:

- the identification of training needs

- agreeing a training and development solution to meet those needs

- drawing up an outline design of a training programme

- drawing up a detailed design of a training programme

- training facilitators to deliver the programme

- the delivery of the programme

- the application of the learning by participants to the on-the-job situation

- a measurable improvement in business results

- the evaluation of the programme.

References
Garavan, Thomas N., Costine, Pat and Heraty, Noreen (1997) *Training and Development in Ireland.* Dublin, Oak Tree Press.

Tacit knowledge   Tacit knowledge is knowledge that is understood but not expressed in writing. Tacit knowledge is automatic, oral and intuitive. Tacit knowledge is intangible and difficult to separate from the person or context in which it was created. Tacit knowledge is often taken for granted and can be shared only when people volunteer information about their beliefs and perceptions, or describe and demonstrate their skills and experience. Tacit knowledge is at the unconscious level, in somebody's head, and not formalised.

A craft apprentice learns by watching the master craftsman. Learning is through demonstration, observation, imitation and practice. The apprentice is socialised into the craft. However, socialisation is a rather limited form of knowledge creation. The knowledge is transferred to the apprentice without either the apprentice or master gaining any systematic insights into their craft knowledge. The knowledge does not become explicit or captured in any tangible form, and as a result the company to which both belong is unable to use that knowledge elsewhere. Made explicit, the knowledge becomes intellectual property, which could be used to train other apprentices or generate revenue for the company in the form of consultancy fees or royalties.

When employees leave an organisation, they take with them tacit knowledge about customers, products, processes, organisation, competitors and personal relationships. The company realises its full commercial potential only when the knowledge is replicated and becomes organisational knowledge. This knowledge may be more valuable than such fixed assets as land, buildings and machinery.

See also **Explicit knowledge**.

References
Nonaka, Ikujiro and Takeuchi, Hirotaka (1995) *The Knowledge Creating Company: How Japanese companies create the dynamics of innovation.* Oxford, Oxford University Press.

Task force   In business a task force is often set up to solve a particular problem.
See **Projects**.

Team learning   Senge (1990) identified three essential elements of team learning:

- a common purpose
- a shared vision
- an understanding of how to complement each other's efforts.

In other words, teams should have a common objective and be committed to its realisation. They should learn from each other by constant dialogue and sharing experiences. They should see work and mistakes as learning opportunities. They should believe in lifelong learning and continuous improvement. Management should support the learning process by providing proper supports and incentives. Learning organisations are formed by teams that create, share and act on knowledge and experience.

See also **Group learning**.

References
Senge, Peter (1993) *The Fifth Discipline: The art and practice of the learning organisation.* London, Century Business.

Thalamus   The thalamus is a part of the brain that surrounds the top of the brainstem. It sorts and directs information from sensory organs to specific sensory and motor regions in the top of the brain. It plays a part in the control of sleep and wakefulness. The thalamus is active during memory and is involved in many cases of memory disorder. It is the part of the brain that automatically responds to extremes in temperature and pain.

References
Turkington, Carol (1996). *The Brain Encyclopedia.* New York, Checkmark Books.

Theorist   In the learning context, 'theorist' is one of the four learning styles: activist, reflector, theorist and pragmatist. Theorists are rational and logical and keen on basic assumptions, principles, concepts, theorems, models and systems. They like to be intellectually stretched. They feel uncomfortable with ambiguous experiences, creative and lateral thinking. They like to organise different facts into coherent theories. They are good people to have around because of their objectivity. In a group situation they may come up with interesting factually based alternatives and challenge the conventional wisdom. Theorists make good system analysts.

In general, theorists learn best from:

- systems, models and theory
- intellectual challenge

- structured situations

- concepts and ideas

- complex situations.

To develop your theorist style you should ask probing questions, look for flaws in other people's arguments and study conceptual models.

See also **Activist**; **Pragmatist**; **Reflector**.

References
Honey, Peter (1994) 'Styles of Learning' in the *Handbook of Management Development*, edited by Alan Mumford, Aldershot, Gower.
Honey, Peter and Mumford, Alan (1986). *Using Your Learning Styles*. Berkshire, Peter Honey.
Mumford, Alan (1995) 'Putting learning styles to work: an integrated approach', *Industrial and Commercial Training*, Volume 27, Number 8, pp28–35.
Mumford, Alan (1997) *Management Development Strategies for Action*. London, IPD.

Thinking Thinking skills include creative thinking, problem-solving, decision-making, the capacity to reason things through logically, and knowing how to learn. Thinking skills are extremely important in the modern economy.

There are two main kinds of thinking:

- *creative thinking*, also called divergent thinking – Creativity is the ability to make something that wasn't there before, and to see novel relationships between things, ideas and people. Apart from making something new, creativity can refer to changing or combining existing things in new or novel ways. For example, all musical compositions are formed from different arrangements of the same notes. Edward De Bono, one of the world's leading experts in thinking skills has coined the term 'lateral thinking', which is a type of divergent thinking. Highly intelligent people are not necessarily so practical with their intelligence. Some studies show that divergent thinking abilities decline with age.

- *Analytical thinking*, also called convergent thinking – Analytical thinking is a systematic step-by-step approach to problem-solving and decision-making. It often involves testing statements or evidence against objective criteria or eliminating bias from thinking. This type of thinking can be measured by intelligence tests.

Some experts have also classified thinking as reproductive or productive. Reproductive thinkers when confronted with a problem examine how they solved similar problems successfully before. Productive thinkers when confronted with a problem ask 'In how many different ways can I solve it?'

Learners naturally adopt any of four different styles of thinking:

- *Reflective thinkers* relate new information to past experiences: they examine their feelings about what they are learning.

- *Creative thinkers* like to play with new information: they create their own solutions.

- *Practical thinkers* prefer concise factual information: they seek the simplest, most efficient way to do their work; they are not happy until they apply their newly-acquired skills to their jobs.

- *Conceptual thinkers* like to see the big picture first before learning the detail: they like to know how things work, to know how different concepts relate to each other.

See also **Creativity**; **Learning styles**.

References
DePorter, Bobbi and Hernacki, Mike (1993) *Quantum Learning: Unleash the genius within you.* London, Piatkus.
Nelson-Jones, Richard (1989) Effective Thinking Skills. London, Cassell Educational.
File://C:\Program Files\Britannica\BCD\Cache_22_PreviewRil.htm

Time management   Time management, the detailed scheduling of working time, is a very important aspect of any study programme and a critical skill in management. Prioritising and drawing up a timetable is a good way of planning exactly what time you need to achieve your learning objectives and how you are going to spend that time.

References
Godefroy, Christian H. and Clark, John (1996) *The Complete Time Management System.* London, Piatkus.
Malone, Samuel A. (1996) *Learning to Learn.* London, CIMA.

Tip of the tongue   By tradition, this is where you claim almost to have a piece of information that you are actually unable to recall although you know you should. It is a failure of retrieval. Sometimes you can even recall related facts but not the specific information required. One way of trying to get at the information is to run through the letters of the alphabet. If that doesn't work, just relax and forget about it – and the item may just pop into your head.

See also **Law of reversed effort**.

References
Higbee, Kenneth L (1990) *Your Memory: How it works and how to improve it.* London, Piatkus.

Trainer competencies   Research has highlighted the following competencies in excellent trainers:

- Sets overall objectives for training.

- Develops training programme objectives and session objectives.

- Develops course programme plans and session plans.

- Keeps up to date in the area of expertise.

- Identifies training needs as appropriate.

- Provides course participants with advice.

- Designs training sessions that are easily understood.

- Provides positive reinforcement.

- Uses different training techniques as appropriate.

- Uses open-ended questions to involve participants.

- Facilitates group learning experiences.

- Clearly explains concepts.

- Presents training in a logical sequence.

- Accommodates different learning styles.

- Makes complex ideas understandable.

- Evaluates training outcomes.

The following behaviours are associated with excellent trainers. They can be recalled by means of the acronym FOREST, standing for Flexibility, Occasional humour, Responsiveness, Enthusiasm, Sincerity and Tolerance.

- *flexibility* – Trainers are able to adjust their style and content in line with the needs and expectations of participants. It might include diverging from prescribed material and using questions as appropriate to generate pertinent discussion.

- *occasional humour* – They can incorporate humour with real-life stories and examples during the training to relax trainees and create an open, participative and friendly environment. Having a sense of humour is an important trainer characteristic. Good trainers do not take themselves too seriously. At the end of the day learning should be enjoyable for both the trainer and the learners.

- *responsiveness* – They are able to accommodate the unique needs and learning style of participants. They are relaxed and empathise with participants. They know when to explore issues and when to end discussion. They know how to generate discussion, listen and provide feedback. They work the room and every learner in it. They are the conductors and the learners are the orchestra. All learners play different instruments and at different levels of performance.

- *enthusiasm* – They display a contagious passion for their subject. They keep up to date and are very enthusiastic about their subject. They are evident experts in their subject. They believe that planning and preparation are the key to successful training. They are prospective and retrospective learners. They mentally rehearse the training process in advance and reflect back on their actual performance to learn from their experience. They believe in continuous incremental improvement.

- *sincerity* – They do not pretend to know everything when they haven't the answer to a particular question but will always offer to find out. They take a sincere interest in participants and provide honest feedback on performance. They do everything possible to reduce participant anxiety.

- *tolerance* – They have a good emotional IQ. They do not react to personal criticism. They retain a cool composure. They handle conflict resolution in a positive and professional manner. They are willing and able to accommodate different learning styles. They are able to tolerate and diplomatically manage interruptions during training. Their main concern is to nurture and develop minds and talents.

See also **Competencies**.

References
Garavan, Thomas N., Costine, Pat and Heraty, Noreen (1997) *Training and Development in Ireland*. Dublin, Oak Tree Press.

Training objectives   Objectives of training should be expressed in behavioural terms that can be observed, described and measured. Some trainers break the overall training objective into learning objectives for each training session. This is easier to do in technical training but very difficult to do in management training where outcomes cannot be as clearly defined. The term 'criterion behaviour' (Mager, 1984) defines what the learner is expected to do at the end of the training. It specifies the tasks, procedures and techniques to be carried out, the circumstances in which the work will be done, and the standards achieved. The tasks, procedures and techniques must be demonstrated. Mere understanding is not sufficient. The circumstances in which the work will be done must closely resemble the workplace. The standards should relate to adequate job performance.

Generally, objectives should be SMART – Specific, Measurable, Achievable, Relevant and Timely. They should be derived directly from a training needs analysis. Trainers should evaluate training outcomes against objectives.

Training objectives should be tied to company business objectives and reflect employee needs. Training success should be linked to the attainment of learning outcomes and not to the amount of time spent training or the number of employees put through the training programme. Outcomes should be expressed from the trainee's point of view and should identify what the trainee will be able to do at the end of the training. Kirkpatrick's model of evaluation suggests that training objectives should be expressed at four levels – reaction, learning, behaviour and results:

- reaction – what trainees thought about the programme

- learning – what concepts, principles, facts, skills and attitudes trainees learned

- behaviour – what changes in behaviour occurred on the job as a result of the training

- results – what difference the training made to the organisation in terms of profitability, performance or productivity.

Another approach is to apply the CAP model – ie break down the objectives into cognitive, affective, and psychomotor components. In other words, what behaviours, knowledge, attitudes and skills will the learner acquire as a result of the training? Remember: no change in behaviour, attitudes and skills is likely after listening to a lecture.

See also **CAP model of learning types**; **Kirkpatrick's model of evaluation**.

References

Abrahams, Michael (1994) 'Choosing resources' in the *Handbook of Management Development*, edited by Alan Mumford, Aldershot, Gower.

Bramley, Peter (1996) *Evaluating Training*. London, IPD.

Mager, R. (1984) *Preparing Instructional Objectives*. California, Fearon.

Reid, Margaret Anne, Barrington, Harry and Kenney, John (1992) *Training Interventions: Managing employee development*. London, IPM.

Training plans

Plans for training follow the identification of training needs in a training needs survey. Decisions have to be made on who will do the training, on where the training will be held, on the required resources, on the number of people to be trained, and on the design of the training programme. Training may be organised in-company or outside the organisation, or could be a combination of both.

References

Garavan, Thomas N., Costine, Pat and Heraty, Noreen (1997) *Training and Development in Ireland*. Dublin, Oak Tree Press.

Training process

The key elements of the training process are:

- *preparation* – The training need should be identified and course objectives clearly stated in writing.

- *design and presentation* – Design the course to achieve the training objectives.

- *presenter* – In addition to being an expert on the course content, the presenter should be trained in presentation and instructional techniques.

■ *personality and attitude* – The presenter should have a personality compatible with a wide range of tastes and must be capable of being at ease in a broad range of social situations.

■ *learning process* – The presenter should know how people learn and present the material in a way that optimises the learning process.

References
Garavan, Thomas N., Costine, Pat and Heraty, Noreen (1997). *Training and Development in Ireland*. Dublin, Oak Tree Press.

Training strategy
Training strategy involves the identification, planning, direction, integration, implementation and evaluation of training to assist in meeting the current and future business objectives of the organisation. Training strategies include off-the-job and on-the-job training, e-learning, coaching, mentoring, secondments, project work, and distance learning.

References
Reid, Margaret Anne, Barrington, Harry and Kenney, John (1992) *Training Interventions*. London, IPM.

Training survey
The purpose of a training survey is to establish a training strategy for the organisation. Such surveys are normally in-house studies to find out what employees feel their training needs are in general or in relation to specific aspects of their work. Needs should be related to company objectives. Most surveys are conducted by questionnaire unless small numbers are involved, when interviews and group discussion can be used instead.

The questions a training survey is intended to answer are:

■ Who needs the training? For what categories of employees should planned training programmes be developed, and in what order?

■ What type of training is needed?

■ How many need to be trained in each category each year?

■ To what standards of performance should they be trained?

See also **Questionnaires**.

References
Garavan, Thomas N., Costine, Pat and Heraty, Noreen (1997). *Training and Development in Ireland*. Dublin, Oak Tree Press.

Transactional analysis (TA)
Transactional analysis classifies interpersonal behaviour patterns into Adult, Child and Parent. This was an approach to psychotherapy originally developed by Dr Eric Berne.

The adult is the self-activating, mature part of our personality that logically considers situations. The child is the immature part of our personality that desires instant gratification. The parent has entrenched beliefs, attitudes and values passed on to us by our parents which we automatically accept.

TA is used in business training as a method of improving social and communication skills. Once identified, behaviours can be analysed and changed.

References
Berne, Eric (1976) *Games People Play: The psychology of human relationships.* Harmondsworth, Penguin Books.
Harris, Thomas A. (1970) *I'm OK – You're OK.* London, Pan Books.

Transfer of learning
It is essential that the learning gained in a training course or programme is actually used in the workplace afterwards, whether or not the learning is assessed at the end of the training. Learning is not much use without application. Transfer of learning is not automatic and must be facilitated. Management encouragement, coaching and mentoring, and other kinds of follow-up support are needed to help learners transfer their new knowledge and skills to on-the-job situations.

Just as with reinforcement, there are two types of transfer:

- *positive transfer* – Like positive reinforcement, this occurs when the participants use the knowledge, skills and attitudes learned on the course.

- *negative transfer* – Like negative reinforcement, this occurs when the participants do not practise the appropriate behaviours.

Transfer of learning is most likely to occur:

- *by association* – Learners can associate the new information with something that they know already.

- *when it is immediately relevant* – The knowledge, skills and attitudes are extremely beneficial and can be transferred easily to the work situation.

- *in a supporting environment* – The work environment supports the new learning.

See also **Positive transfer**; **Retroactive inhibition**.

References
Malone, Samuel A. (2000) *Learning Skills for Managers.* Dublin, Oak Tree Press.
Reid, Margaret Anne, Barrington, Harry and Kenney, John (1992) *Training Interventions.* London, IPM.
File://C:\Program Files\Britannica\BCD\Cache_14_PreviewRil.htm

Transformational learning
Transformational learning, also called triple-loop or deutero learning, occurs when you solve a problem by understanding the

relationships of various parts of the problem. It may occur suddenly, as when you look at a specific problem for some time and then suddenly grasp its solution, or it may come at the end of long consideration. Part of transformational learning involves reflecting on what you have learned and how you have learned it, and improving the learning process.

It is possibly the most important type of learning, because it changes your whole perspective, system of beliefs, values and attitudes and relationship with the world. In creative thinking, it is the 'Aha!' experience when you suddenly see things in a different light.

In an organisation transformational learning occurs when the basic purpose of an organisation is questioned and changed, new missions, visions, goals, corporate objectives and policies are formulated, and corporate plans, strategies, structures and practices are implemented to achieve them. In the process, underlying paradigms, norms, values, attitudes, beliefs and culture may come under scrutiny and be altered forever. The learning is revolutionary rather than evolutionary and incremental.

On an individual basis transformational learners look for underlying meanings and try to see the relationships between different pieces of information, whereas 'surface learners' tend to try to learn by rote or adopted routine.

Mezirow (1991) says the transformational learning process involves specific stages:

- disorienting dilemma – a particular life event such as being made redundant or the death of a loved one may start the process in motion; conventional problem-solving strategies do not work in such situations

- self-examination – often accompanied by feelings of depression, anger, guilt and anxiety

- critical assessment of assumptions – possibly including a questioning of the true purpose and meaning of one's life

- recognition that others have gone through a similar situation

- exploration of options for forming new roles, relationships and actions

- formulation of a plan of action that has four steps: acquiring knowledge and skills, trying out new roles, renegotiating existing and new relationships, and building competence and self-confidence

- reintegration – the final step of the process, where a new and transformed perspective is adopted.

Major discoveries and inventions have often been made when people have had 'Aha!' experiences in the most unexpected times and places. Transformational learning can bring change, renewal, restructuring and problem reformulation, and is therefore occasionally known as innovative or breakthrough learning. This kind of learning drastically changes the sense of self and the feeling of competence, and may bring forth new talents and capacities not apparent before. It is a dramatic, fundamental change in the way an individual sees the world and himself or herself. For example, you may suddenly regard your job as a source of great satisfaction rather than a mere means of earning money.

In modern times, business process engineering is a radical redesign of business processes to achieve dramatic improvements in productivity and efficiency. It is planned transformational learning.

See also **Deep learning**; **Double-loop learning**; **Incremental learning**.

References
Garratt, Bob (2001) *The Learning Organisation: Developing democracy at work.* London, HarperCollins Business.
Mezirow, Jack (1991) *Transformative Dimensions of Adult Learning.* San Francisco, Jossey-Bass.

Transmission model　　The transmission model is a model of teaching based on associationism and behaviourism – schools of psychology associated with Edward Thorndike and B. F. Skinner. It focuses on the way a teacher transmits information to a student, regarding the process as one in which the student plays an essentially passive role and is the object of stimulus-response strategies, such as being rewarded for correct answers.

See also **Jug-and-mug approach**; **Operant conditioning**.

Triple-loop learning　　See **Transformational learning**.

Triune brain　　The composite nature of the human brain as a result of three stages of evolutionary development. This model of the brain and its functioning derives as a theory put forward by Dr Paul MacLean. The three parts are:

- *the brain stem (or reptilian brain)* – This is the part of our brain at the base of the skull, emerging from the spinal column. We share this brain with lower life-forms such as lizards, snakes, crocodiles and birds. This part of the brain controls breathing, heart rate, and instincts such as the fight-or-flight response. The territorial imperative also comes from here. This part of the brain is responsible for stimulus/response learning.

- *the limbic system (or mammalian brain)* – This is the part of the brain that we share with all other mammals. The main parts of the limbic system are the hypothalamus and the amygdala. It controls the secretion of hormones, thirst, hunger, sexuality, emotions, pleasure centres, metabolism and the immune system. The hypothalamus is an important contributor to long-term memory. The limbic system as a whole is responsible for social and emotional intelligence. Things that involve emotion, controlled by the limbic system, are very well remembered. That is why learning maps which involve creativity, colour and art are so effective as learning devices.

- *the neocortex (or thinking brain)* – This acts as a covering around the brain. It is about 3 millimetres (an eight of an inch) thick and if spread out flat would be about the size of a broadsheet newspaper page. This is the part of the brain that we think with, solve problems with and plan for the future with – it is the seat of intelligence. The neocortex is subdivided into parts for speech, hearing, vision and touch. It is also divided into two hemispheres. This part of the brain is responsible for creative and innovative thinking.

See also **Brain hemispheres**.

References
Ostrander, Sheila, Schroeder, Lynn and Ostrander, Nancy (1999) *Super Learning 2000*. London, Souvenir Press.
Greenfield, Susan (2000) *Brain Story*. London, BBC Books.

Tutor   A tutor is a person who gives knowledge and guidance to an individual or small group of students in a classroom or lecture-hall, or to trainee employees in an off-the-job informal training situation.

See also **Coaching**; **Mentoring**.

U

Understanding   Understanding implies more than mere knowledge: it implies knowledge plus the ability to use the knowledge and to relate it to other knowledge in a useful way. Understanding thus comprises the capacity to explain, provide supporting evidence, give examples, generalise, compare, contrast, and apply the knowledge in different situations. Conversely, if knowledge and skills are not understood, a learner will find it impossible to apply them in a meaningful way.

Understanding is facilitated if trainers:

- provide performance standards, immediate ongoing feedback, and opportunities for reflection

- use conceptual models, practical examples, stories, metaphors, and analogies to help understanding

- relate new knowledge to the learner's past knowledge and experience, and suggest ways in which the knowledge can be applied when the learner returns to work: this provides purpose and meaning

- give an overview so that the learner can integrate the topic within the broader concepts of the discipline

- get learners to draw up their own representations of what they've learned, perhaps in the form of learning maps or block diagrams: this will provide learners with a vehicle for reflection on and integration of the new knowledge

- create a learning environment which approximates to the one the learners will return to – experience is the best teacher.

See also **Comprehension**; **MUD model of learning**.

References
Malone, Samuel A. (1996) *Learning to Learn*. London, CIMA.
http://www.21learn.org/arch/articles/perkins.html

Unlearning   Unlearning means letting go of what we have already learned or have become used to mentally leaning on. It is often harder to unlearn than to learn. These days, many old ways of doing work have to be unlearned and replaced by new ways. Inefficient practices and processes are replaced by newer and better approaches. We must free up our minds to take the new challenges and explore new ideas. The old learning habits die hard and may interfere with our new learning. When exchanging an old car for a new model, we often have to unlearn old habits and learn new ones to operate improved controls and layouts. With PCs, new and updated programs come out all the time. Often, previously learned commands for old machines, which have gone into our long-term unconscious memory, give new and unexpected results and new commands must be learned to get the results we want.

Most of us are reluctant to unlearn what we know. In unlearning, we must drop existing knowledge, an existing pattern of behaviour which is now redundant to make room for something new. Psychologists use desensitisation and behavioural therapy programmes to help people unlearn destructive habits and substitute more appropriate behaviour.

To learn something new you often have to let go of assumptions about yourself. Old instincts, habits, attitudes, old ideas and models get in the way of the new learning and must be discarded if you want to learn effectively.

See also **New learning**.

References

Malone, Samuel A. (2000) *Learning Skills for Managers*. Dublin, Oak Tree Press.
O'Connor, Joseph and Seymour, John (1995) *Neuro-Linguistic Programming*. London, Thorsons.
http://www.mithya.com/learning/whatunlearn.html

Using your brain   Keeping mentally fit is just as important as keeping physically fit. Anything that stimulates the mind is helpful, such as reading, attending lectures or training programmes, doing crosswords, learning new words and keeping a learning log. Remember to keep both sides of your brain active – the creative as well as the analytical.

An interesting study on the effects of ageing is taking place in a convent in Manikota, Minnesota, USA. It has been found that nuns who earned college degrees live longer and are mentally sharper than nuns who did not. The reason for this seems to be that the more educated nuns continue to learn, read, write and intellectually challenge themselves. On the other hand, the less educated nuns do most of the physical work around the convent, such as cooking and cleaning. Post-mortem analysis of the brains of nuns who died showed significant structural differences. The nuns with higher education had a thicker cortex, more densely-packed brain cells, and more synapses and dendrites. Dendrites are known to facilitate communication and interconnections between brain cells.

See also **Age**; **Plasticity of the brain**.

References
Greenfield, Susan (2000) *Brain Story*. London, BBC Books.
http://www.brain.com/about/article.cfm?id=21005&cat_id=16
http://www.findarticles.com.../article.jhtml?term=%2Bshort-term+%2Bmemory+%2BResearc

V

VAK model of learning   The VAK model is an acronymic guide to the three basic styles of learning. The acronym VAK, developed by practitioners of neuro-linguistic programming (NLP), stands for Visual, Auditory and Kinesthetic.

We learn mostly through these senses – seeing, hearing and touching – but in a learning context many people have a preference for one particular style. The other senses, such as taste and smell, do not seem so important, although smell can often invoke strong memories of linked past events. Experts estimate that we learn 60 per cent through our visual senses, 30 per cent through our auditory senses, and 10 per cent through our kinesthetic senses (via the sensation of touching, which includes moving).

In a learning context, then, VAK stands for:

- *visual learning* – The visual cortex in the human brain is five times larger than the auditory cortex. Not surprisingly, therefore, many people have a preference for visual learning. Visual learners have vivid imaginations, learn by seeing things, and may find verbal instructions difficult. Visual learning might be by means of videos, DVDs, CD-ROMs, learning maps, graphs and diagrams. Visual learners relate most effectively to written information, notes, graphs, diagrams, learning maps and pictures. If you have trouble remembering spoken instructions but can follow written instructions, you obviously have a preference for visual learning. Visual learners can remember what they see and reproduce it visually. They like to see the big picture and purpose. They prefer a time line to remember historical events. At presentations they like to take detailed notes, even when notes are provided. Visual learners tend to be best at written communication. They tend to use the sentences 'I see what you mean,' 'I get the picture,' and 'The future looks bright.' Visual learners should make learning as visually appealing as possible.

- *auditory learning* – Good auditory learners learn through reading aloud, asking questions and listening to audiotapes. Unlike visual learners they generally do not create images in their minds. Auditory learners relate best to the spoken combined with the written word. They tend to listen to a lecture, and then take notes afterwards, or rely on handouts. They learn best if they write summaries or outlines of course material in their own words. Often written information will have little meaning to them until it has been heard. For more effective learning it helps auditory learners to read out loud. They like to talk through a concept they find difficult to understand. Auditory learners may be very good public speakers and they tend to favour professions like law or politics. They like to be involved in group discussion. They have a good ear for accents and can mimic people quite easily. They use sentences like 'Sounds good to me,' 'Explain it to me,' and 'I hear you loud and clear.' Auditory learners should make as many auditory cues as possible.

- *kinesthetic learning* – Kinesthetic or tactile learners learn through physical and emotional experience. They find it difficult to remain still for extended periods of time. Learning may be by means of Post-it notes, cue cards, exercising while listening to audiotapes, the hands-on approach, role-play and/or mental rehearsal. They like actively researching and completing a project or assignment. Kinesthetic learners learn effectively through touch and movement, and take up skills by imitation and practice. The cerebellum – a part of the brain that stores skill or muscle memory – regulates physical movement, and this kind of memory is particularly long-lasting. People who learn how to swim never forget. As Aristotle said: 'Anything that we have to learn to do we learn by the actual doing of it... We become just by doing just acts, temperate by doing temperate ones, brave by doing brave ones.' Infants have a preference for kinesthetic learning. An infant may pick up a toy, look at it, touch it, shake it, move it around, taste it and sometimes break it. The infant combines all these actions to understand the object. Passive observation is insufficient. As the old Chinese proverb says: 'Tell me and I forget. Show me and I remember. Let me do and I understand.' Kinesthetic learners can appear slow on the uptake if the information is not presented in a style that suits their learning preference. They remember feelings, emotions and movements and get an overall impression of a subject. They use such sentences as 'I like to get a feel for the situation,' 'Let's try it out and see what happens,' 'It feels right,' 'I feel we're moving in the right direction,' 'I'd like to get a better handle on this information,' and 'I must get to grips with the problem.' Kinesthetic learners should imagine performing actions when learning. Trainers should encourage them to take notes, draw learning maps, take stand-up-and-stretch breaks, generally learn by doing.

See also **Diagnostic instruments**; **Learning styles**.

References

DePorter, Bobbi and Hernacki, Mike (1993) *Quantum Learning: Unleash the genius within you*. London, Piatkus

Malone, Samuel A. (2000) *Learning Skills for Managers*. Dublin, Oak Tree Press.

Meir, Dave (2000) *The Accelerated Learning Handbook*. New York, McGraw-Hill.

O'Connor, Joseph and Seymour, John (1995) *Neuro-Linguistic Programming*. London, Thorsons.

Rose, Colin and Nicholl, Malcolm J. (1997) *Accelerated Learning for the 21st Century*. London, Piatkus.

Vincent, Annette and Ross, Dianne (2001) 'Personalise training: determine learning styles, personality types and multiple intelligences online', *The Learning Organisation*, Volume 8, Number 1, pp36–43.

http://mindtools.com/mnemlsty.html

http://www.gracehome.org/traits.html

http://snow.utoronto.ca/Learn2/mod3/tchprocess.html

Values   Values are guiding principles and what the ideals and goals involved in them mean to you. Values are 'caught' rather than taught. If you value education highly, you are more likely to become an effective and lifelong learner. If you want to progress in a company, it is important that your values are congruent with those of the company.

See also **Attitude**; **Beliefs**.

References

O'Connor, Joseph and Seymour, John (1995) *Neuro-Linguistic Programming*. London, Thorsons.

Verbalise   To verbalise is to express something in words aloud. Reading out loud to yourself is a good way of learning. It is also a good way of reviewing key learning points when preparing for making a presentation or for exams.

Vicious learning cycle   A vicious learning cycle begins when learning is not perceived as relevant and is therefore not put into effect. In an extreme situation, this might mean that all new learning is perceived as irrelevant and not worth the effort, and that as you grow older, your short-term memory capacity may decline and learning may thus become more difficult unless you stimulate your mind with new challenges. The combination of these two factors becomes a vicious circle. You are less inclined to exercise your mind with new learning challenges. But your failure to exercise and develop your brain means that you become more resistant to new learning, making it still harder to learn – and further demotivating yourself.

See also **Virtuous learning cycle**.

References

Mumford, Alan (1997) Management Development Strategies for Action, 3rd edition. London, IPD.

Video conferencing   Video conferencing is real-time two-way transmission of video images between two or more locations. It can be used to conduct meetings and training sessions between two or more remote locations, thereby avoiding the time and costs of travel. Video conferencing is frequently used in television news reporting. It is sometimes alternatively known as teleconferencing.

Virtual learning centre   A virtual learning centre is a learning centre that is on the Internet and thus does not rely on its participants' assembling at a physical location. It can be accessed from work, from home or when travelling. Businessmen away from base can access a vast array of knowledge and learning materials via their mobile phones or laptop computers. Access may be available on a 24-hour basis. Virtual learning groups can be facilitated in a company with a regional organisation. Many multinationals now operate virtual corporate universities.

See also **Just-in-time learning (JITL)**.

References

Fee, Kenneth (2001) *A Guide to Management Development Techniques*. London, Kogan Page.

McFadzean, Elspeth and McKenzie, Jane (2001) 'Facilitating virtual learning groups', *The Journal of Management Development*, Volume 20, Number 6, pp470–494.

Virtual reality (VR)   The illusion of a real-time real-dimensional environment as produced by a high-quality computer program. The program permits a user to navigate through this world at will. Typically, the user wears a head-mounted dual-focused screen over the eyes that produces stereoscopic images. Gloves containing electronic sensors allow the user to 'touch' and manipulate objects in the virtual environment. Larger and less personal (but no less complex) examples of virtual reality include those produced by flight simulators for airline pilots and launch simulators for astronauts, both of which also rely on computer-controlled cabin movement. In a different form of virtual reality, architects can simulate and manipulate the dimensions of proposed buildings and interior designers can visit each room and experiment with decor. Virtual reality can be used to train surgeons and even mechanical technicians and engineers.

Augmented reality (AR) is a new form of virtual reality. This technology digitises the real-life view through a pair of electronic goggles in such a way that virtual objects – such as prehistoric dinosaurs – can be electronically superimposed on it: the dinosaurs then appear to roam in the real world.

See also **Simulations**.

References

Fee, Kenneth (2001) *A Guide to Management Development Techniques*. London, Kogan Page.

Sloman, Martyn (2001) *The E-learning Revolution*. London, CIPD.

http://www.newhorizons.org/tech_winn.htm

http://www.newhorizons.org/blab_dickinson.htm

Virtual teams   Virtual teams are teams organised as such through the Internet or an intranet. They are generally made up of people working in a multinational organisation or people working in a large company with branches located throughout the country. Meetings can be organised over the Internet or intranet at times to suit participants. Contact can be maintained through e-mail. Teams learn from each other by exchanging views and experiences.

References
McFadzean, Elspeth and McKenzie, Jane (2001) 'Facilitating virtual learning groups', *The Journal of Management Development*, Volume 20, Number 6, pp470–494.

Virtuous learning cycle   A virtuous learning cycle begins when learning is seen as relevant, when it is successfully transferred to an on-the-job situation and when the outcome is rewarded by recognition of some sort. These comprise all the elements of the stimulus, reward and reinforcement sequence. Motivational theory states that rewarded behaviour is likely to be repeated.

See also **Vicious learning cycle**.

References
Mumford, Alan (1997) *Management Development Strategies for Action*. London, IPD.

Visits to other organisations   A visit to an appropriate organisation can often enhance the study of management and bring it to life. Such visits provide an opportunity to learn by seeing things at first hand, observing people in their working environments and discussing practical problems they have experienced. For example, in a tour around a factory, manufacturing processes and procedures can be observed and best manufacturing practice studied for use in benchmarking. Ideas for improvement may be duplicated in your own organisation.

References
Mumford, Alan (1997) *Management Development Strategies for Action*. London, IPD

Visualisation   Most of us are better able to remember what we see than what we hear. One way of remembering personal names is to visualise the name written in large capital letters across the person's forehead. Visual associations use images or pictures. An example of visual association in action is the use of the shape of a riding-boot to remind you of Italy. Use visualisation to make information more memorable. Visual associations are most effective if they interact and if they are vivid.

Visualisation is an accepted tool for enhancing performance in sport. Using all the appropriate senses – visual, auditory, and kinesthetic – can help an athlete to create more vivid images of sporting excellence. Like physical skill, the psychological skill of imagining must be practised to be effective.

Try to create an image of yourself as a person with a good memory. See yourself remembering the dates, numbers, names and facts necessary for your personal and business success. As a learner, visualise yourself achieving your learning goals. As a trainer, help your learners visualise themselves as successful learners. Get them into a state of relaxed alertness by asking them to visualise a peaceful scene. Before making a presentation, visualise yourself speaking successfully and receiving positive emanations from your audience. Visualisation works because it programmes the mind to work as programmed. The mind cannot perceive the difference between an actual event and one that is imagined. We tend to move towards those goals that are clearly visualised.

It has been found that people who can spell well visualise the image of the word and get the 'feel' that it is right. They evidently combine visual and kinesthetic learning to maximise results. The assumption behind such techniques as creative visualisation is that it is possible to realise desires through mental imagery and focus. Visualisation has been used in sales training and some remarkable improvements in selling performance have been claimed.

A common technique of creative people when confronted with a problem or a new subject is to block out all verbal thoughts and concentrate instead on visual images. For example, Friedrich Kekulé von Stradonitz's discovery that the molecular structure of benzene and other organic molecules corresponds to closed chains or rings came as a result of a dream in which he saw snakes swallowing their tails.

See also **Imaging and imagination**; **VAK model of learning**.

References
Alder, Harry (1994) 'The technology of creativity', *Management Decision*, Volume 32, Number 4, pp23–29.
Fletcher, Sarah (2000) 'A role for imagery in mentoring', *Career Development International*, Volume 5, Number 4/5, pp235–243.
McFadzean, Elspeth (2000) 'Techniques to enhance creative thinking', *Team Performance Management: An internationl journal*, Volume 6, Number 3/4, pp62–72.
O'Connor, Joseph and Seymour, John (1995) *Neuro-Linguistic Programming*. London, Thorsons.
Pattison, Sherry A. (2001) 'Staff meetings: an opportunity for accelerated training of employees', *Journal of Workplace Learning*, Volume 13, Number 4, pp172–179.
Rose, Colin and Nicholl, Malcolm J. (1997) *Accelerated Learning for the 21st Century*. London, Piatkus.

Vitamins and learning Proper amounts of protein, carbohydrates, the lipid (fat) lecithin, and vitamin B1 (thiamine), are in particular considered essential to the chemical processes in the brain when we register, retain, and remember. Some research suggests that vitamins C and E have a role in keeping the memory sharp. Vitamin E's most important function is as an antioxidant. Among the best food sources of vitamin E are polyunsaturated vegetable oils, nuts, seeds and wheat germ. Research shows that eating blueberries, strawberries and spinach improves short-term memory. High levels of antioxidants in the form of vitamins A, B and E are found in these foods. Antioxidants protect cells in the brain from damage by excess free radicals, which are the harmful by-products of radiation, pollution and even normal metabolism. Some free radical activity is essential for health. However, an excess of free radical activity damages cells, which leads to ageing, degeneration diseases and memory deterioration. A diet rich in fresh fruit and vegetables will protect the brain from the ravages of free radicals.

Other research shows that vitamin A affects brain cell activity in an area of the brain associated with learning and memory. If you are preparing for an exam, you might do worse than have an extra helping of sweet potatoes or other foods high in vitamin A. Some vitamins such as B1 (thiamine), folic acid, and B12 are essential for the proper working of memory.

Vitamin D helps the assimilation of minerals such as calcium, magnesium, and iodine, which in turn increase alertness. Most vitamins can be got from eating bread and cereals, fresh fruit and vegetables. At least some of the vegetables should be eaten raw, because cooking can destroy natural nutrients. If you feel your diet is deficient in any way, a multivitamin tablet a day will do you no harm and may do you a lot of good.

See also **Nutrition**.

References

Carper, Jean (2000) *Your Miracle Brain*. London, Thorsons.
http://www.retiredlifefun.com/rlfllc.htm
http://retiredlifefun.com/rlflb.htm
http://onhealth.com/ch1/briefs/item,35952.asp
http://www.findarticles.com/cf_0/m0FKA/5_62/62702348/print.jhtml
http://www.findarticles.com/cf_0/m1264/11_29/54050913/print.jhtml

Voluntary organisations   Voluntary organisations such as clubs can provide marvellous opportunities for social networking and gaining experience in roles that you would not normally fulfil at work. Opportunities for learning include acting as president, secretary, treasurer, public relations officer, education officer or membership officer. Some of these jobs may have a high profile, so that you may get experience dealing with the media, liaising with other organisations, organising conferences and chairing meetings. They will give you an opportunity to develop your interpersonal relationship skills in formal and social situations. Even ordinary membership may increase your self-confidence, enhance your self-belief, and give you an opportunity to make friends, learn and change in the context of the organisation and with others. Experience in a voluntary organisation may act as a springboard for taking on other responsibilities at work and in your personal life.

References

Malone, Samuel A. (2000) *Learning Skills for Managers*. Dublin, Oak Tree Press.
Mumford, Alan (1997) *Management Development Strategies for Action*. London, IPD.

Von Restorff effect   The Von Restorff effect (named after the psychologist Hedwig von Restorff) is the apparently easier recall to memory of things that are novel, unique or in some way outstanding. It is for this reason you tend to remember only the funny or strange incidents of your holiday. The rest is over-familiar and merges in with many other similar and routine experiences of our lives. In a list of words, it is the unusual word that stands out and can be recalled. Pop stars often dress in an outrageous fashion or do outrageous things to attract attention and make them unique and outstanding – and of course memorable. Items can be made to stand out on learning maps through the use of cartoons, colour, two-dimensional figures and symbols. Key learning points are thus easier to remember.

References

Malone, Samuel A. (1996) *Learning to Learn*. London, CIMA.
Wingfield, Arthur (1979) *Human Learning and Memory: An introduction*. New York, Harper & Row.

W

Whole-brain learning Whole-brain learning is engaging the left- and right-hand side of the brain in learning. It means consciously engaging both analytical and creative functions. The whole brain would seem to be engaged in learning anyway, whether we try consciously to engage both parts or not. For example, memory relies on many parts of the brain.

Memory has been compared to a hologram in which the whole exists in all the parts combined. The brain processes parts and whole simultaneously. Our culture has a tradition of focusing on parts, rather than on the whole. This approach is called reductionism. In training we break course programmes down into modules, and modules into training sessions, and sessions down into key points. At the heart of any intelligence is the ability to deal with parts and wholes simultaneously. Creativity is an example. Schutz (1979) is one of the many writers who have promoted a holistic approach to learning.

See also **Brain hemispheres**; **Whole method**.

References
DePorter, Bobbi and Hernacki, Mike (1993) *Quantum Learning: Unleash the genius within you.* London, Piatkus.
Schutz, W. (1979) *Profound Simplicity.* London, Thurstone.
http://newhorizons.org/blab-caine.html

Whole method The whole method of learning involves focused concentration on learning or practising an operation or system until proficiency is reached. This is in contrast to the 'part method' in which the operation to be learned is broken down into parts and practised or operated separately, so that when a certain level of skill has been achieved in each part, the parts may be gradually brought together in appropriate combinations until the whole operation has been mastered. Part learning by small steps may be inappropriate where the knowledge or skill relies on sequence in some way. For example, theories, concepts and principles should be learned in their entirety or the relationship between the parts may be lost.

'Wholists' are learners who like to scan information, getting overviews rather than detailed impressions. They tend to be intuitive and impulsive, and are better at seeing similarities rather than differences. They have no difficulty in 'seeing the wood for the trees', but may have difficulty in 'seeing the trees for the wood'. Wholists may benefit from information in advance of learning which provides an overview and shows the structure of a topic. Learning maps may be useful in this context. Wholists may be contrasted with 'analytics' who prefer detailed step-by-step sequential learning.

Research shows that the whole-to-part method – by which an overview of the topic is presented first – is at least 50 per cent more effective than the part-to-whole method, which involves learning general concepts before getting to grips with specific details.

A useful analogy might be a tailor who teaches apprentices to put together a garment from precut pieces before they learn to cut the pieces themselves first. This allows the apprentices to build a conceptual map before getting to grip with the details.

Such an approach achieves two purposes:

■ Each apprentice has an overall conceptual model that helps him or her make sense of the parts that he or she is working with.

■ The conceptual model acts as a benchmark, pattern, control mechanism, and feedback device because the apprentice knows what the final result should look like.

The SQ3R method of effective reading is based on this principle. The method focuses on a reader's getting a general framework, or overview, before filling in the details.

See also **Gestalt**; **Whole-brain learning**.

References

Malone, Samuel A. (2000) *Learning Skills for Managers*. Dublin, Oak Tree Press.
Sadler-Smith, Eugene (1996) 'Learning styles: a holistic approach', *Journal of European Industrial Training*, Volume 20, Number 7, pp29–36.
Wingfield, Arthur (1979) *Human Learning and Memory: An introduction*. New York, Harper & Row.

WIIFM   An almost unpronounceable acronym that stands for 'What's in it for me?' A successful learner always sees a personal, positive purpose for the learning.

To learn effectively you must:

■ take responsibility for your own learning

■ realise that to earn more you've got to learn more

■ develop learning-to-learn skills

■ clearly define your learning objectives

- have self-belief in your ability to learn
- see the relevance of the learning and how it will help you achieve your personal and career goals.

References
DePorter, Bobbi and Hernacki, Mike (1993) *Quantum Learning: Unleash the genius within you.* London, Piatkus.
Malone, Samuel A. (2000) *Learning Skills for Managers.* Dublin, Oak Tree Press.

Wisdom
Wisdom is the ability to understand situations, anticipate consequences and make sound decisions. Wisdom entails extensive learning and broad experience. Wisdom is soundness of judgement, having insight and common sense. Knowledge is not wisdom – reflection and common sense must temper knowledge before it becomes wisdom.

Wisdom is having the right priorities in life, being flexible and being open-minded. Wisdom is the highest form of learning. Wisdom means being able to learn from the experiences of others, to learn from others' mistakes as well as from one's own. Wisdom means being able to listen to others, weigh advice and deal with a wide variety of people. Wisdom means being able to anticipate potential problems and formulate strategies to avoid them. Wisdom is having the ability to see the humour in life's contradictions.

By tradition, wisdom is linked with age, although age and wisdom do not necessarily go together. As US columnist Abigail Van Buren put it, 'Wisdom doesn't come with old age. Nothing does – except wrinkles. It's true, some wines improve with age. But only if the grapes were good in the first place.' Our parents, grandparents and past generations can nevertheless be a great source of wisdom because they may already have dealt with many of the problems that currently confront us. This source of wisdom is often ignored in modern Western society.

Wisdom has nothing to do with IQ. People with a high IQ may yet be emotionally immature. Wisdom has nothing to do with education. There are many highly-educated failures in the world.

Business ethics is a manifestation of moral wisdom for the guidance of behaviour in organisations. In business the practice of poor ethics and values has seen the demise of many a company – notably Enron and WorldCom.

See also **Knowledge**.

References
Clarke, Thomas and Rollo, Christine (2001) 'Corporate initiatives in knowledge management', *Education and Training*, Volume 43, Number 4/5, pp206–214.
Fenchuk, Gary W. (1995) *Timeless Wisdom: Thoughts on life . . . the way it should be*, Richmond, Va., Cake Eaters Inc.
Malone, Samuel A. (1999). *Success Skills for Managers.* Dublin, Oak Tree Press.
http://www.horizons.org/lrn_botkin.htm

http://www.newhorizons.org/lrnbus_fuller1.html
http://www.newhorizons.org/blab_wisdom.htm

WISE model of memory types   The WISE model is an acronymic guide to types of memory: the acronym stands for Working memory, Implicit memory, Semantic memory and Episodic memory. These types of memory are located in different parts of the brain.

- *working memory* – This is our short-term memory. It enables us to link ideas with existing experience or stores of knowledge and generate completely novel ideas. The new information lasts for only a few seconds unless reinforced in some way. Miller's law of short-term memory states that our memory span is only seven plus or minus two items. So if you are dialling a new telephone number and are interrupted in the process, it is very likely that you will have to look up the number again. If you dial the same number frequently over a period of time, it is likely that it will go into your long-term memory so that you won't need to look it up when you want to use it again. Some people refer to it as the 'blackboard of the mind'. Others compare it to random access memory (RAM), which is the working memory in a personal computer.

- *implicit memory* – This is a kind of kinesthetic or motor memory, and corresponds to our memory for automatic responses such as walking, driving, cycling, swimming, typing, playing the piano and tying our shoelaces. Grammar is a particularly good example of implicit memory. With grammar, people have acquired and obey abstract rules but are very often unable to articulate explicitly what guides their speech and writing. Implicit memory is hard to articulate or express in words. Barring some major physical or psychological disability, until we die we shall remember how to walk, pick up our glasses and drink, or sign our name. Even after a lapse of many years, implicit memory will come back with a little practice.

- *semantic memory* – This is our memory for language, information, rules, facts, concepts and knowledge. Semantic memory is acquired by observation and learning. Most people have a vocabulary of anything from 20,000 to 50,000 words which is stored in semantic memory. Semantic memory allows us to define, order and operate within the world. It helps us to remember the countries of the world and their capital cities. This is the memory that helps us do our jobs, solve crossword puzzles and answer TV quiz shows. It helps us to categorise things as plants or animals and to distinguish the meaning of the red and green signals on traffic lights. Provided we keep our minds active, this memory will improve throughout our lives as we acquire more knowledge and experience.

- *episodic memory* – This is the memory for autobiographical details and specific events such as what you had for lunch yesterday and the place you are going to for the meeting tomorrow. When we reminisce, we are using episodic memory. This is the memory evoked by photos from the family album about past events in our lives. Personal recollections of your first day at work, your wedding day and the birth of your first child are calling upon episodic memory. Episodic memory can be recalled quite quickly.

See also **Long-term memory**; **short-term memory**.

References
Malone, Samuel A. (2000) *Learning Skills for Managers*. Dublin, Oak Tree Press.
Parkin, Alan J. (1993) *Memory Phenomena, Experiment and Theory*. Oxford, Blackwell.
Wingfield, Arthur (1979) *Human Learning and Memory: An introduction*. New York, Harper & Row.

Workshop　　A workshop is an organised group of people with a common interest or problem who meet to improve their proficiency or understanding of a subject by study, research and discussion, or practical experiment. The great thing about workshops is the degree of help given to those who attend, either by fellow participants or by a supervising facilitator, in an atmosphere of cordial flexibility. Learning situations tend to be based on interests and needs identified by the participants themselves rather than by experts. Workshops provide an excellent opportunity to learn from others with different backgrounds.

References
Fee, Kenneth (2001) *A Guide To Management Development Techniques*. London, Kogan Page.
Malone, Samuel A. (2000) *Learning Skills for Managers*. Dublin, Oak Tree Press.

Workplace learning　　Workplace learning corresponds to both the informal and the formal learning that takes place within an organisation. Informal learning situations might include business meetings, making and hearing presentations, writing and reading reports, learning to use new computer software, teamworking, going on outside visits to benchmark best practice and informal discussions during the tea-break. More formal learning includes training courses run inside the company, learning centre courses, coaching and mentoring. The Internet provides a vast resource of knowledge and learning materials. There are virtual universities on the Internet and many multinational companies have their own corporate universitities.

See also **Virtual learning centre**.

References
Malone, Samuel A. (2000) *Learning Skills for Managers*. Dublin, Oak Tree Press.
Mumford, Alan (1997) *Management Development Strategies for Action*. London, IPD.

Write it down　　One of the best ways to remember something is simply to write it down. It also clarifies your thinking. Being forced to articulate your experiences in writing is a great source of learning. Being asked to prepare a paper for a conference or training programme is a very good learning experience. Managers who take on a mentoring, coaching or training role usually find it a very good developmental experience. External memory aids such as pocket diaries, address books, learning logs, and desk diaries are best.

Writer's block   Writer's block is the desperate feeling of simply being unable to think of anything to write. A learning map is a good way of breaking writer's block. It can be used for individual brainstorming.

Y

Youth Younger people generally learn quicker than older people do. Memory peaks in our twenties, then declines gradually over the rest of our lives. Some research suggests that younger people are more creative than older people and that creativity declines as we grow older. Studies show that people over 60 tend to have good long-term memory, but they do have difficulty with short-term recall and processing new information. Considerable evidence indicates that the learning ability of young adults is superior to that of older adults, and that the faster the pace of the task, the more difference age makes. However, one experiment showed that older people performed almost as well as younger adults on memory and cognitive tests when given ample time and comfortable conditions. Yet when the older folk were put under pressure, their performance dropped much more sharply than those of the younger adults did. It seems that the minds of elderly people work quite well provided they are not put under pressure. It is true that reaction time slows down as we age. Our senses also deteriorate, particularly eyesight and hearing.

See also **Age**.

References
Higbee, Kenneth L. (1990) *Your Memory: How it works and how to improve it.* London, Piatkus.
Parkin, Alan J. (1993) *Memory Phenomena, Experiment and Theory.* Oxford, Blackwell.
File://C\Program Files\Britannica\BCD\Cache_5_PreviewRil.htm
http://www.findarticles.com/cf_0/m1264/11_29/54050913/print.jhtml

Z

Zeigarnik effect   The Zeigarnik effect is an apparent increase in the ability to recall material under concentrated study if the study is interrupted. It is a principle – named after its discoverer, the Russian psychologist Bluma Zeigarnik – which supports the idea that to improve your recall you should take breaks from study at appropriate intervals rather than studying straight through.

References
Malone, Samuel A. (1996) *Learning to Learn*. London, CIMA.

INDEX